INCOMING!

Secrets of a Contract Warrior
in Afghanistan

A Memoir

by
Thomas Josef

INCOMING!
Secrets of a Contract Warrior in Afghanistan

Copyright © 2018 by THOMAS JOSEF

ISBN - 10: 0-692-11646-X

ISBN - 13: 978-0-692-11646-3

Acronyms

BAF	Bagram Airfield
B-hut	Barracks Hut
CAC	Common Access Card
CBT	Computer-Based Training
CDC	Central Distribution Center
CLEP	College-Level Examination Program
CJTF	Combined Joint Task Force
CSO	Country Support Offices
DADT	Don't Ask, Don't Tell
DCMA	Defense Contract Management Agency
DFAC	Dining Facility
DoD	Department of Defense
DPW	Department of Public Works
DUI	Driving Under the Influence
EAP	Employee Assistance Program
ECP	Entry Control Point
EOD	Explosive Ordnance Disposal
FOB	Forward Operating Base
GMO	Genetically Modified Organism
HIPAA	Health Insurance Portability and Accountability Act
HR	Human Resources
HRC	Human Rights Campaign
IED	Improvised Explosive Device
ISAF	International Security Assistance Force

ITT	International Telephone and Telegraph
JAG	Judge Advocate General
JIB	Joint Industry Board
JOC	Joint Operations Center
RBK	Rednecks, Bubbas, and Kinfolk
LGBT	Lesbian, Gay, Bisexual, Transgender
LLC	Limited Liability Corporation
LOGCAP	Logistics Civil Augmentation Program
MWR	Morale, Welfare, and Recreation
NATO	North Atlantic Treaty Organization
OCN	Other Country National
PLO	Palestine Liberation Organization
PPE	Personal Protective Equipment
PT	Physical Training
PX	Post Exchange
R&R	Rest and Relaxation
RDQ	Recommended for Delayed Qualification
RSOI	Reception, Staging, Onward Movement, and Integration
SAARC	South Asian Association for Regional Cooperation
TOA	Transfer of Authority
TSA	Transportation Security Administration
UAE	United Arab Emirates
UK	United Kingdom
UN	United Nations
USO	United Service Organization

Military Phonetic Alphabet

Letter Spoken

A	Alpha		N	November
B	Bravo		O	Oscar
C	Charlie		P	Papa
D	Delta		Q	Quebec
E	Echo		R	Romeo
F	Foxtrot		S	Sierra
G	Golf		T	Tango
H	Hotel		U	Uniform
I	India		V	Victor
J	Juliet		W	Whiskey
K	Kilo		X	X-ray
L	Lima		Y	Yankee
M	Mike		Z	Zulu

Maps of Afghanistan

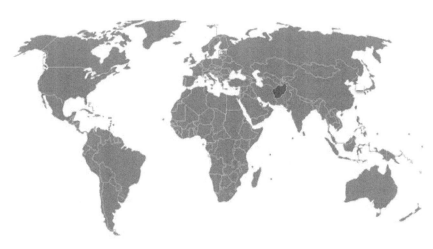

*A portion of the proceeds of this book will benefit
the Wounded Warrior Project.*

*To the men and women who are serving or have served in
the Armed Forces, thank you for your service.*

Everyone has a story.

This is mine.

October 2009 to February 2010: The First 90 Days

Destination: Hell's Kitchen

"It don't matter where y'all sit. We's all goin' to the same place . . . Hell's Kitchen!" cackles a husky black fella with a Fred Sanford strut. I can tell he's a LOGCAP (Logistics Civil Augmentation Program) veteran and likely worked in Iraq for years before this stint in Afghanistan. This guy feels at home in a war zone. Other passengers are taking note of his frustrations and getting the hell out of his way. There are 180 seats on this plane and none of them are assigned. It's first come, first served; and it looks like it may be a full flight.

We're scheduled to depart Dubai International Airport around 8:00 a.m. for the three-hour flight to Bagram Airfield (BAF) in Afghanistan, about 40 miles (62 kilometers) west of the capital of Kabul. This aircraft looks like it's been through some rough and turbulent times. I think it's an old cargo plane refurbished as a civilian plane. Hell, the armrests still have ashtrays in them and the FFA banned smoking on flights in 1988. The seats are stacked on top of one another with no legroom. I'm a medium-sized guy and I feel crunched in here. I don't think I have so much as 10 inches of room to the back of the seat in front of me. At least it's endlessly entertaining to watch some of the bigger guys trying to squeeze their fat asses into a window seat by straddling the aisle.

I can just imagine hearing the company CEO of the plane saying to his top executives, *"Less cost and more profit if we can pack 'em in like sardines! It's all about the bottom line! Who cares about their comfort? They're going for a free ride to a war zone!"* Well it's not exactly free, I guess. The company pays the aircraft provider, who is then later reimbursed by the U.S. Army.

I feel like I'm on the *Con Air Jailbird* flight. Some of these passengers look pretty rough, like they've been around the block a few times. Some of them look like they could have done some time in the clink. I guess I could pass as Cyrus the Virus with my shaved head and salt-and-pepper goatee, but these guys . . . they look weathered, wrinkled, and fatigued. Some of them are exposing neck tattoos, and one guy has a tear tattoo in the corner of his eye. I wonder what the hell he felt when he had that permanently inked to his face. Pain? Sadness? It's certainly not a tear of joy. Another guy has a tattoo that looks like a fine, thin-lined beard or ribbon from each of his ears and down to this chin. Surely he was drunk when he had it done.

I've heard and seen many military tattoo stories. I know a guy who had the Bud Man tattooed on his stomach—and it definitely wasn't small. He got it while on leave from the military in an Asian country and doesn't even remember having it done. Knowing some of the military personalities and their pranks, I wouldn't be surprised if the guy passed out and his buddies carried him to a tattoo parlor to have it done as a bad practical joke. Either way, I think he resents it and feels embarrassed about it. I wonder how the guy with the tear tattoo will feel someday.

While most of these guys look pretty hardcore, the majority are honored vets. They've done their time: Persian Gulf War, Iraq, Afghanistan, Vietnam, Somalia, Panama, Bay of Pigs—pick a tour. I'm sure someone on this plane has been there and done that. They've seen, smelled, and endured death that I can't imagine. Just the thought fucks with my mind. I've never served in the military or even held a gun, unless you count a squirt gun, or the BB gun my brother got for his birthday when we were young. I'm more altruistic: I served as a Peace Corps Volunteer in Tunisia and now I'm headed to a damn war zone. What am I thinking?

I'm one of the 25 newly hired Barron Industries employees on the flight. Barron is one of the main Department of Defense (DoD) military contractors to build, service, and maintain the military bases in Afghanistan to support U.S. national strategic objectives. I'm college educated and I bring a wealth of experience in the field of training and development. The DoD contract is the Logistics Civil Augmentation Program, or as we call it in the field, LOGCAP.

Like 99.9 percent of the civilian workforce in a war zone, the only reason I took this job is the money. For me, it's a short-term sacrifice for a long-term financial gain. There's a lot of risks to consider, like possibly being shot, injured, or killed by missile and rocket attacks. However, I have faith in our military's superiority and feel safe working on a military base. As far as I'm concerned, it's probably safer than walking the streets of Detroit or Chicago. I tell myself, *"I'll be just fine."* I've never feared death. If it's my time to go, it's my time to go.

Wheels Up

October 25, 2009

Fred Sanford and the rest of the *Con Air* passengers are ready for takeoff. Now that everyone is situated and seated, the people on the plane are resting and quiet. In fact, nobody is talking. Most of them have the window covers pulled to block out the morning sunlight as they rest their heads on the headrest with their eyes closed. Some have earbuds in their ears to drown out any intercom announcements or other noise. I notice only one woman on the flight. I find that rather interesting. Why just one woman? I wonder what her job is.

We taxi on the runway for about 30 minutes. We wait another 15 minutes in queue for takeoff. Finally, we are cleared and it's "wheels up" to Afghanistan.

As we start our descent into BAF, the passengers start to wake up and move about in slow motion. Chairs are in the upright position, seat belts buckled, and window covers are up, allowing more daylight into the cabin. I look out the window to note that the region is a beige, dry, and dismal land.

The houses appear to be made of mud and blend into the wheat-colored earth. There's little, if any, greenery. There are no obvious signs of water—no streams, no rivers. I don't even see a well. There are no paved roads, just tire tracks in the sand. The topography is carved out from rain and years of erosion, and the dry riverbeds create an endless, free-flowing movement through the earth. Except for the snow-capped Hindu Kush Mountains that surround the air base, the area around BAF appears to be a very undesirable place. I wonder what the rest of Afghanistan is like.

As the plane taxis to its apron on the large paved area near the makeshift terminal, I see military aircraft perfectly aligned and parked in stalls with cement barriers on either side of them. Some of the smaller aircraft are parked on a tie-down. Trucks, Gators, and forklifts are moving in and around the paved area like well-oiled machinery. The buildings and tents that line the runway are colors of muted tan, orange, and yellow to blend in with the desert landscape.

Boots on the Ground

Boots on the ground. It's a phrase commonly used by the military that means soldiers are physically present or troops are in place. For me, it's time for boots on the ground. After the plane makes a complete stop, the passengers move like molasses to get up and out of their seats, an apparent expression of their excitement about arriving in Hell's Kitchen. I take a deep breath as the airplane door opens.

A tall and confident woman with short, spiked hair boards the plane. Her body language indicates she's a fierce devil and not interested in taking any shit. She's a Barron representative named Trixxie who's here to escort those of us making the pilgrimage to this hellhole. She instructs the passengers to form single lines on the tarmac according to whether we're American or non-American and if we are assigned to BAF or one of the other 75 bases in Northern Afghanistan. She trumpets her directions with precision: *"I will escort you to a badging facility where the military will collect your passports and common access cards (CAC) for verification."* Her directions are loud and clear. Maybe she was a drill sergeant in a previous life. I like her already.

We are directed into an Alaskan tent where the U.S. military has set up a passport control area to monitor and verify who comes and goes on base. Afterward, Trixxie leads us outside behind the passport control tent to a sandpit. Yes, a sandpit—how welcoming. We're definitely in Afghanistan. I think someone needs to pinch me to verify this is real. We wait in the sandpit a while for our bags to be delivered and claimed. It's high noon and the sun feels pretty intense, especially at 7,500-feet elevation. The air stands still.

Several forklifts come barreling through a chain-link fence gate with our luggage hanging on pallets. The pallets are dropped into the sandpit and kick up the cindery dust. It blows into my eyes and down my throat. People sift and tumble through duffel bags, suitcases, backpacks, and footlockers to find their belongings. One by one we toss our luggage into a small cargo truck.

After we load our luggage, Trixxie instructs us to board an old Blue Bird school bus. It's painted an unappealing, ghastly color of green, and it looks like it hasn't been washed in years. Faded and dusty cloth curtains hang from the windows. The floor has a thick layer of mud that has dried into dirt. Most of the seats are covered in brown vinyl, torn with metal springs poking out. I grab a seat next to one of the other new hires who made the 8,000-mile journey across the ocean to this infernal region.

As Trixxie takes a final roll call, I look out the bus window. I see ol' Fred Sanford with another guy walking away from the sandpit, dragging their luggage behind them. They know where they're headed.

Tour of Bagram

Leaving the sandpit and driving away from the airfield, we turn onto a street named Disney Drive. It's an eight-mile loop that encompasses BAF. Cyrus the Virus had been right when he said, *"We're going to Disneyland!"* Initially, I think someone has a twisted sense of humor for naming the main drag on an Army base after the Walt Disney World Resort. When we reach the end of Disney Drive, I see the memorial remembering and honoring the first fallen soldier of BAF, Jason Disney. It's a sobering and somber sight.

Driving south on Disney Drive, Trixxie points out landmarks and areas that she refers to as rally points. Rally points? I'm not sure what she's talking about. It must be a military phrase. I just left state government, where a rally point is a place of protest. Is it like a high school pep rally to cheer on your teammates? I snap out of it. It's a military rally to gather and organize. Got it.

I notice all the side streets are named after states: Florida, California, Oklahoma, Nevada, Kentucky, and of course, Texas. One of the Air Force housing areas is named Texas Hall. I remember seeing it while waiting in the sandpit for my luggage. Texas is bigger than Afghanistan, but the U.S. has more Muslims than this country. I wonder how many Americans know that. Bagram currently houses more than 30,000 personnel and is expected to grow to 40,000 during the peak of the surge over the next year or so. It also employs 4,000 Afghan locals.

We drive past a few of the ally compounds with their own field hospitals that face the main drag: Korean, Egyptian, and Polish. In the midst of the ally compounds is a blue-roofed mosque. Trixxie points out the Post Exchange (PX). It's also one of the rally points. In the PX area are motorcycle and auto satellite shops offering military discounts, a couple of Afghan jewelry and rug shops, electronics shops, sunglass huts, a barber shop, and more. Hell, there are even American fast-food places and a coffee shop called Green Beans. Of course, they charge—capitalism at its best even in a war zone—but it is a comfort from home for which many will gladly pay. Pizza Hut even delivers! They have mopeds equipped with a red insulated compartment on the back.

At the south end of Disney is Entry Control Point 1 (ECP-1). There are several small huts that the military uses for badging and biotechnology. A row of metal detectors stand side by side. It's here where the Afghan locals process through each morning, a process I hear can take two or three hours. Like the rest of the perimeter, ECP-1 has a 10-foot chain-link fence with reels of electrical, barbed wire on top, alongside strategically placed 10-foot cement T-walls. Because of the bevy of electrical barbed wire, anything outside this area is referred to as "outside the wire." It all looks like a prison. It's not pretty, but it's here to keep the people on base safe.

We make a left turn at ECP-1 and start heading east to the other side of the base. On the corner next to ECP-1, a local bazaar of Afghan goods and crafts holds sway every Friday. Vendors sell their handicrafts and goods—things like silk-cashmere scarves, wood-carved bowls, marble tableware, jewelry, blankets, rugs, and antique artifacts of the region. There's even a variety of black-marketed, fake big-name brands of everything from underwear to purses to sunglasses. So I guess I've got my pizza needs covered and access to faux-Calvin Klein tighty-whities, if I feel the need to wear them. I prefer to go commando.

Eventually the road turns from a blacktop surface to gravel. The airfield runway ends on our left. I can see outside the wire from here and get a glimpse of what daily life looks like for the locals. Civilians are not allowed outside the wire, but it's interesting to see how the locals live.

We finally make it to the materials yard, where we are sized and issued personal protective equipment (PPE). It consists of a ballistic vest that protects the chest, stomach, and back, and a bulletproof combat Kevlar helmet. The PPE helps absorb impact, provides protection from shrapnel and projectiles from explosions, and can prevent bullet penetration. This is the final reality check, being sized and fitted with all of this garb. We are definitely in a war zone. Welcome to Afghanistan!

After we are issued our PPE, we are brought to our billet. I soon learn that a *billet* is another fancy word for an assigned lodging, bed, or bunk. Mine is a huge circus-like tent set up on a parking lot of large gravel a mere few hundred feet from the runway in a camp called Warrior. Inside the tent are four rows of 50 green Army cots to house 200 of us. The cots are only about eight inches apart from each other, so we're packed in here like a can of sardines. There are splatters of black stains and spots on every cot, many of which look like disgusting sweat stains that have permanently discolored the fabric. I'd like to think they're only sweat stains and not blood stains that have turned black. Who knows where these cots have been?

There's a tent dining facility (DFAC). A permanent DFAC is being built, but it looks like it will be a long time before it's completed. Alone in a gravel parking lot about 100 yards from our tent are the bathrooms and showers located in a gold-like concrete building with white trim. It reminds me of the humdrum buildings and landscape of El Paso, Texas—a city of gravel landscapes. There's a breezeway in the center of the building that basically splits it into quadrants with half male and half female facilities. The interior of the bathrooms look clean and new. The walls are painted white, with white porcelain sinks, toilets, and showers with cheap chrome fixtures. I'm sure our government buys them from the cheapest bidder. What a waste of taxpayer dollars to buy this cheap shit just to replace it over and over again. A greater concern of mine at the moment is getting up in the middle of the night to relieve myself. I'm dreading having to put on my boots and make the lengthy walk across the large chunks of sharp gravel.

I remember reading the job description before I came here. It addressed the austere living conditions and tents. It even mentioned those long walks to the bathrooms. I have prepared for this mentally. I'll be sharing this *wonderful* experience with 200-plus roommates. Some of them are prior military and will endure the hardship without any issues. Others worked in Iraq previously and had their own private hooch and a shared bathroom. Knowing us Americans, we're going to bitch and whine regardless. We can be put up at the Taj Mahal and we'll still find something to bitch about. I wonder if other nationalities act the same way.

Four of us stick close together and claim cots next to one another to watch after our belongings. I have a backpack and a duffel bag that take up most of the space under my cot. Some of the guys have their belongings spread out in the narrow aisle. Many of them simply packed a lot of stuff and don't know where to put it. There's nothing like getting by with less, so I packed light. I'll wear the same set of clothes for a few days. This is a war zone; I'm not out to impress anyone.

It's late in the afternoon as we settle in. We're all jet-lagged from our transatlantic journey from Greenville to Atlanta, the 15-hour flight from Atlanta to Dubai, and then the 10-hour time difference. We arrived in Dubai around 8:00 p.m. and were up at 4:00 a.m. to get to the airport for our flight to Bagram.

Shortly after the sun sets, a busload of about 50 more guys arrives at our tent. This group comes from the Balkan countries of Bosnia, Kosovo, Macedonia, and maybe Serbia and Albania. In their cultures, they stay up half the night and go to work around 10:00 a.m. Many of these guys have been through the LOGCAP drill before. They set up their cots, unpack their coffee makers, and gather outside until 1:00 a.m.

The Balkan guys tend to talk and laugh loudly, brew a lot of coffee, and come and go from the tent at all hours. Compared to the air movement and close proximity to the runways, however, the ruckus that the guys make sounds like a mere shimmer of noise. Planes and helicopters come and go all night long. Nighttime is the best time to fly because planes are not easily seen or targeted and lower temperatures during the wee hours are advantageous for takeoff. The F-15s always take off in pairs with thunderous accelerations. Some of the air movement is mission; some of it is operational exercise. All of it sounds like it's a stone's throw from my tent.

There's also the hot gunnery range. I can hear the firing practice, and even if I didn't, there's The Big Voice to remind us. It announces across the base, *"The aerial gunnery range is now hot."* If the exercise is an hour, it feels like 10. When all the hot commotion ends in the middle of the night and things start to settle down, The Big Voice announces, *"The aerial gunnery range is now cold."* I hope I can get some shut-eye.

Over the course of a few weeks, I check my watch to monitor the start, finish, length, and pattern of the air movements, but there isn't any established pattern. It's all the time. It's a damn chaotic mess.

Like the austere living conditions and sleeping in tents, the noise was addressed in the job description and they advised bringing earplugs. I brought some along, so I try them. After a few tosses and turns on my cot to shift to a comfortable position—if that's possible on a cot—the earplugs eventually fall out. Shit.

As a teenager, I listened to Janis Joplin. On one of her live albums she renders to the audience, *"Why sleep, man? I might miss a party!"* This is quite the party.

New-Hire Orientation

"Oh my God, my head is bobbing and I can't stay awake," I keep saying to myself throughout the day of new-hire orientation. *"This is torture! Death by PowerPoint!"* It doesn't help that most of the presenters are inexperienced and don't know what they're doing. Most have their asses facing the audience and read directly from the screen. The whole day becomes a blur.

I'm only really fascinated by two of the topics covered: blood-borne pathogens and the security brief.

The blood-borne pathogen presentation isn't riveting by any means, but just the topic of blood and guts gets the attention of most people— as do the pictures. The topic is very important in a war zone, as is knowing what to do if you come into contact with blood or someone who has been injured. Better safe than sorry.

The second presentation covers security. The presenter is actually the best I've heard all day. I can tell he's a polished speaker and military trained to present briefs. His build, looks, and demeanor are very professional and direct. He's loud and clear, and he skips the fluff: *"The enemy is upon us. They're on base."*

I can understand his point of view. With Bagram's 4,000 locals on base, I'm sure there are a few who may be working with al-Qaeda or under their threat. Al-Qaeda robs workers who are seen leaving the base, kidnap family members, and do some pretty cruel things to get people to carry out an action. The military works with these people to reduce or eliminate the threat. It's a serious issue, but the security presenter words it in a way that seems like he views every Afghan as the enemy. This strikes a nerve with me. People are already so judgmental and have preconceived notions when dealing with our local labor force. Why perpetuate the issue?

After the long day of orientation, my new boss, Rupert, comes to meet me. He's a medium-height British gentleman with silver hair and a few wrinkles across his pale face, probably pushing 60 or so. He has a big smile and reaches out to shake my hand. After a brief introduction, he walks me to our makeshift office in an Army tent where I will report for duty starting in the morning.

For the next 90 days I will be working 12 hours a day every day of the week. On the ninety-first day, I will be eligible to take my first R&R. The countdown begins.

My Routine

It's 4:30 a.m. I lightly shake the cot next to me, aligned head-to-head with mine. My coworker, Brian, occupies it and I nudge his cot to wake him up. We agree to start our day with a morning workout at the gym. I met Brian while we were going through our training back at the company headquarters in Greenville. I was there for almost a month, and each night after work I would go to the gym down the road. Brian had an identical routine. He had a car, so we eventually started riding to the gym together.

Brian is a former Army captain, young and slim, and quite the philosopher. Though Brian and I are at the gym every morning, we do our own workout programs. I am more into body maintenance like toning and cardio. Brian is more focused on power lifting and stays on a diet to bulk up. I'm almost 50 and that's not my cup of tea. More power to Brian. After my workout, I hit the shower, get ready for work, and grab breakfast at the nearby mess hall. This is going to be my daily routine for the next 90 days.

The chow hall reminds me of old army television shows. Backpacks, purses, laptops, or bags of any kind are not allowed in the chow hall for safety and security reasons. Breakfast is always pretty hot, but it's the cheapest-quality shit that money can buy and served on a cardboard tray. Again, that's the way the government works. They tend to award contracts to the lowest bidder and I'm sure the food is in that category. Luckily the DFAC is always clean—and it has to be. It's checked constantly by the Defense Contract Management Agency (DCMA) on specific standards set by the military to ensure there is no possibility of any kind of foodborne illness. I'm glad about that at least.

After a quick breakfast and a cup of coffee, I grab a second cup to go for the walk to the bus stop to make the commute from east side to west side. Walking along the side of the road is like walking through moon dust. A very fine, brown talcum powder covers everything, everywhere. The air traffic kicks up the dust and we breathe in that shit. I'm learning to wear a scarf to cover my mouth and face like the locals.

The bus is scheduled to pick up on the hour and then again 30 minutes later. Some mornings it's right on time; other mornings it runs a little late or doesn't show up at all. The commute is about four miles from my tent to my office. It takes about half an hour on the bus. During the drive along the perimeter fence, I can see outside the wire and watch children tending herds of goats amidst the minefields created during the Russian occupation. I've heard stories about children or goats stepping on mines. They're rushed to the Egyptian children's hospital on base for emergency care of their life-threatening wounds

It's an interesting time for Barron. We are transitioning 12,000 workers from the incumbent contractor, RBK. RBK initially won the no-bid, noncompetitive, single-award LOGCAP III contract in Iraq, thanks to a former vice president who was CEO of the mother company. The LOGCAP IV contract was split up and awarded to three primary contractors: RBK, DimeCorp, and Barron. Barron received the contract to service and maintain the bases in Northern Afghanistan that were run previously by RBK. We have an arduous task ahead of us. The current military personnel in Afghanistan is roughly at 65,000 with a troop surge increasing the population to 100,000 over the course of the next year. The surge will drastically increase and change our scope of work.

I work for the country management office. I'm hired as a training coordinator to test incoming employees and help identify any gaps or training needs that are unique to this environment. Currently our offices are in two tents that are side by side, with 24 people crammed into each. Rupert occupies the first desk. He's the manager of the Department of Public Works (DPW). They cover many craft positions like electrical, plumbing, and HVAC. Next to Rupert sits Kathleen, a gorgeous redhead. I take an open desk next to hers.

I soon befriend Kathleen. She's an American with a residence in South Africa with her fiancé, Ethan, a native of South Africa. They met on a project in Iraq, and although I don't know Ethan, I hear a lot about him from Kathleen. I can tell she's madly in love with him. I love listening to him talk when they're on the phone together. His South African accent is charming. I've always loved to hear different dialects and accents. Some of them make me feel warm and fuzzy, but Ethan's accent makes me melt. I bet the accent has the same effect on Kathleen.

Kathleen is intelligent and has worked on the LOGCAP project in Iraq. I am so green behind the ears when it comes to working LOGCAP, so she explains all the ins and outs of the project to help me along. She knows a lot of people who worked in Iraq and are here now, so she has a whole network of folks to draw from for their expertise. She introduces me to numerous people. In addition to the good folks, she knows the dirt on plenty of shady characters, their poor work ethics, and shit they pulled with RBK. Some of it ranges from unethical behavior, like sexual harassment and selling corporate information, all the way to issues with alcohol and drugs and possession of pornography. It all happened in Iraq and I'm sure it's happening here in Afghanistan right now. This project is a *Peyton Place* or a *Melrose Place* meets *Hogan's Heroes*. Life is very interesting.

I'm getting to know Kathleen pretty well because we spend so much time together: morning coffee, breakfast, lunch, and sometimes dinner. She knows DFAC food pretty well and tells me what is good and what to avoid. We walk around base and snap pictures, check out the bazaar, pick up a few supplies from the PX, go to aerobics class or the gym, check out the guys, and go through the pirated movie selection at the local Afghan shop. In the evenings, we both sit at our desks and laptops with our earplugs in and watch a movie. She's a great coworker and we have a lot of fun together. I don't know if I would make it through my first 90 days without her.

Kathleen has big round eyes, a few freckles across her nose, a dazzling white smile, and a shapely figure. Naturally, she gets a lot of looks from both the contractors and the soldiers wherever we go. When she stands up in the DFAC, I can see a lot of eyes zoom in on her with jaws dropping. Everyone is enamored with her. I can see it on their faces and in their eyes. I can read their filthy minds. Their sexual desires and fantasies are unleashed with her near them.

Kathleen introduces me to a website called *I Love Bagram*. People share their stories, experiences, rants, and raves on this website. I think it took the place of writing on bathroom walls. You don't see much of that around here. Entry number 236 just might be Kathleen. The post reads, "*Yes, I am a female. Yes, I look good. Yes, I have red hair. Yes, the friggin' curtains match the bedspread, and no you can't see for yourself, you stupid mouth-breathing, knuckle-dragging, trailer-trash, swamp-ass, flea-infested idiot.*"

That's kind of Kathleen's attitude toward most of the men around here because she's hit on and gawked at so much. I've seen these sex-crazed, male chauvinist pigs slobbering when they see a good-looking woman walk down the sidewalk—honking their horns, whistling, or shouting things out the truck window to get their attention. It's like they're from Bumfuck, Georgia, and have never seen a woman before. It can really suck being a beautiful lady on this base.

People always see the two of us together and probably think we're a couple. But what most people don't know about me yet is that I am happily partnered with another man. He's not here with me, but he's holding down the fort back home in Texas. My sexuality is a nonthreatening situation for Kathleen and other women. They don't worry about sexual advances or passes. Instead we love to talk about all the good-looking men serving in uniform and the hot guys in the gym. And there are plenty of them.

GI Jane and GI GU

I hit the DFAC a little later than usual and realize half the base is on that schedule. The dining facility is packed. As I make my way through the chow line, I scan the dining hall for a place to sit. I spot an open seat at a table across from a female soldier. I put my plate of food down and grab the seat. As the soldier across from me finishes a bite of food, she looks up at me and says in her firm voice, *"How are you this morning?"* I make a friendly reply as I look into her round coffee-colored eyes that complement her smooth, brown complexion and black hair.

As we casually talk for a bit and as she leaves the table, I examine her broad shoulders attached to her small waist, perfectly round butt, and ample legs. She has a beautiful V-shape and a determined walk. This girl is one tough cookie with her gun strapped across her back. I picture her doing pull-ups and flexing her upper torso and arms with every move. She's the epitome of Demi Moore in *G.I. Jane*. I think she may have been sitting alone because she intimidates her young male troops. She actually looks pretty hot from a gay man's perspective. People know physically beautiful people when they see them.

Later in the week, I meet GU (pronounced "Goo") during my normal morning workout. I name him this because I don't know if he reminds me of Gomer Pyle or Urkel, so I combine the first letter of each and come up with "GU." I notice his tall, lanky body waltzing into the gym like Gomer Pyle—swaying shoulders, with a goofy grin on his face. He takes the bench next to me as I'm doing chest presses.

Between sets, I putz around with my iPod, trying to find the right song and beat to get me in the groove. When I start my next set of reps, my left arm flings upward with all the weight on my right side. I maneuver the bar to catch the weight from falling. I then realize that GU took the weights off the left side of my bar and put them on his. He notices and gives me that Urkel look: *"Did I do that?"* We smile at each other and laugh. GU puts a ten-pound and a five-pound plate on each side of his bar. During my set, I hear GU's plates sliding off the bar and crashing onto the padded floor. I quickly set my bar of weights down and jump up. GU looks at me again with the Urkel look: *"Did I do that?"* This time he's a little embarrassed and quickly picks the weights off the floor and puts them back on his bar. Yeah, he's a bit more Urkel.

Now, given these two personality types of GI Jane and GU, I can't help but imagine the two of them out on the battlefield as a team: GU running across the battlefield, tripping on a rock, and falling to the ground as his helmet flies into the air. He's caught in a crossfire when GI Jane sees that he's in great danger and yells, *"I got ya covered, GU!"* She flies to his rescue by launching a few grenades into the enemy line of fire. She mows them down with rounds and rounds of machine gun fire. She scoops GU off the ground, throws him over her shoulder, and runs to a nearby tank for cover. They find shelter in the tank, where GI Jane yanks the driver out of his seat, gets behind the wheel, and floors the tank directly into the line of fire. She's amazing! I've watched too many action-packed war flicks, but that's the GI Jane and GU of my imagination.

Spiders, Scorpions, and Snakes ... OH MY!

LaWanda is all dolled-up today. She's wearing a dazzling red dress and her cherry-colored wig. She looks like she's going on a date with no place to go. It seems odd to me that she would be wearing a dress on a construction site in the middle of a war zone. I can just picture us getting an incoming alert and having to run to a bunker with LaWanda stumbling around and messing up her wig.

That's all I really have to think about as we're sitting here in the dark tent around high noon. The power is out, so there are no lights, no computer usage ... nothing. It's amazing how much we depend upon electricity, especially with today's technology, even in a war zone. Gas generators produce the electrical power, so there must be a major issue or scheduled maintenance with the generator. It wouldn't surprise me if nobody was notified and the electric or power generation department just decided to pull the plug.

Two managers leave to see if they can find out when we'll have power again. The rest of the staff disappears shortly after their departure. I'm not sure where they're all going, but it's around lunchtime, so maybe some of them are going to the DFAC, PX, or Green Beans. I guess it's better than sitting in this tent, doing absolutely nothing. We're paid by the hour and not the job, so I'll stay put just to justify that I bill my time correctly and accordingly.

We have the doors open on each end of the tent to allow the midafternoon daylight to shine through our darkened space. It's the end of October and the nights are pretty chilly. LaWanda and I are talking about the mice that come in droves across the camp, looking for a warm place to spend the night. A couple of them have taken up residency in our tent and I make LaWanda aware of this. I've seen a few people jump or scream when a mouse appears out of nowhere to pay us a visit or run across someone's feet or lap. Of course, if you see one mouse, there are probably ten more hiding. I tell her that I've seen one of the guys feeding a mouse. LaWanda replies, *"I won't be feeding no damn mouse!"*

A few days ago one of the guys had a mousetrap below his desk. It was a dirty desk, so I decided to clean it up one night. I discovered a mouse nest amidst his stack of papers. Where there are mice, there are other critters—like snakes. There are some pictures floating around of a cobra caught on a sticky mat inside a B-hut. It happened here at Bagram just a day or two ago. Wouldn't that be lovely to wake up to?

Some time passes and a few guys from vector control happen to stop by to chat with LaWanda. They arrive at the time LaWanda and I are talking about the cobra found in the B-hut. They pipe in about the incident and act as though it's a common occurrence on the job for them. One of them tells LaWanda that they had to pull a rat snake out from the floorboards of a B-hut. The snake was so fat that they couldn't coax it to slither its way out, so they had to remove the floorboards to get to it.

While the story is being told, LaWanda squirms like a fish out of water. Her russet-colored eyes are as big as chestnuts, her jaw hanging in disbelief at the sheer thought of snakes. She jumps up and starts pacing the floor, her head motioning side to side, her hands fluttering with one hand in the air and a finger pointing upward and shouting, *"I don't like me any snakes! You need to kill 'em all."* The three of us laugh at her reaction to the topic. She quickly turns to the left, then to the right. She moves like a supermodel and all I can think of is RuPaul saying, *"Work the runway, sweetie! Work it, girl! . . . sachey, chantey, chantey, chantey, chantey."* LaWanda sits back down. The two vector guys must get the thrill of the day by fabricating and exaggerating stories of what they see and catch sometimes.

The conversation switches to scorpions, and LaWanda pipes up with another story about scorpions she has seen on *60 Minutes*. While serving in Iraq, a scorpion stung a soldier and LaWanda was there at the same time. LaWanda jumps up again and exclaims, *That girl had to be medevac'd back to the U.S.!* When the soldier felt the sting, she woke up, caught the scorpion, and brought it to a medic on base. Tough gal! She had to seek immediate medical attention since it was one of the deadliest scorpions in the world. LaWanda continues with the story of how the medics had to give that soldier epinephrine shots to keep her alive and prevent her from going into anaphylactic shock. Not just one epinephrine shot, but four of them! No, thanks.

After the conversations wind down, the vector guys inform us that they're here to set up a trap. There's a feral cat living under the office tent. I've heard it meow a few times at night when leaving the office. It's very scraggly and skinny, and I think it may have mange. I've seen DCMA officials across the street leave it food and milk. We're not supposed to be feeding or keeping animals because rabies is rampant in Afghanistan. Besides, it's a violation of General Order 1. A general order is a published directive originated by a commander and is binding upon all personnel under his command. A general order has the force of law. I guess their motto is, *"Do as I say, not as I do."*

We never did find out why we lost electricity, but LaWanda made up for it all.

Bagram's Tuckerman Ravine

The fresh snow on the rugged Hindu Kush glistens stunningly against the blue skies. I enjoy studying the terrain. The slopes are steep and rigid. It reminds me of Tuckerman Ravine that snuggles Mt. Washington of the White Mountains of New Hampshire. I worked in the White Mountains for the Appalachian Mountain Club for three seasons in the mid-1980s after hiking the Appalachian Trail from Georgia to Maine. During the winter season, I worked as a snowshoe and cross-country ski guide. It was one of the coolest jobs that I've ever had, even if it didn't pay much. As part of my job and training, I learned mountain search and rescue, avalanche forecasting and safety, and how to build snow shelters.

Tuckerman Ravine is nature's challenge and the gateway into the White Mountains from Gorham Notch. It's famous for its spectacular scenery, deep snow, and challenging terrain. It also has some of the worst weather recorded in the United States. It's pure wilderness. There is no chairlift or rope tow. It's a challenging hike in the snow to experience the hair-raising thrill of setting your own path down the ravine through the iced drop-offs that will last a whopping 10 to 15 minutes. The ravine is a mysterious drop of boulders and drops covered by ice and snow.

In the winter, a group of us made the six-mile round-trip trek from our base camp at Pinkham Notch to the base camp at Tuckerman Ravine. Wrapped in layers of warm winter active wear with crampons attached to our hiking boots, we set off for our journey for the day. Each of us carried downhill skis tucked into the side pockets of our climbing packs—a balancing act as we made our ascent to the base camp. I wiped out about every 25 feet during my first trek down. I couldn't see or tell what was ahead of me, but it was worth the experience.

I dream someday that Afghanistan will be free and that the borders open to other people and investors around the world. They need to see the rustic charm and majestic beauty of this country. I envision active ski resorts in the winter and mountain biking, rock climbing, four-wheeling, and hiking in the warmer seasons. I've seen gorgeous pictures of the Hindu Kush landscapes and I can imagine hiking trails with a series of huts and teahouses connecting remote villages like in the Alps and the Himalayas.

The land is rich in so many ways. There's so much opportunity, but this country needs to come to grips with peace before anything like this can unveil.

The Move

Today we move into B-hut offices down the road in Dragon Village. The *B* in B-hut stands for "barracks" made of shoddy, thin plywood floors and walls with a tin roof. We have a small row of six B-hut offices to house about 120 or so employees and a large tent for new-hire orientations and meetings. It's definitely a step up from the current work tents, especially with our growing workforce.

However, the sleeping tent situation in Warrior is getting worse. One night we have rockets and missiles launch from outside the base to the inside. When they are detected, The Big Voice announces over the base, *"Incoming, incoming, incoming!"* It's time to run for cover into a bunker. We have only about 10 to 15 seconds before the first rocket will hit. For the veterans working in a war zone, they couldn't care less. It's like a game of Russian roulette to them. Many stay put on their cots, rolled up in their sleeping bag or buried in blankets. Some of them are pretty hard sleepers and sleep through the commotion altogether. As for some others and me, the missiles sound a little too close for comfort.

We fumble around to put on our PPE and go head to coverage. Following the pack, we are led to open space only to discover there are no bunkers near our sleeping quarters to accommodate and protect the 100-plus employees currently assigned to our tent. As part of our situational awareness training, everyone should know where the nearest bunker is at all times. We've all failed. There are no protective walls to stop shrapnel from penetrating through the tent. If a rocket or missile hits us here, we're dead. Some guys are pretty upset and others shrug it off. I'm livid that a major safety factor has been overlooked and the space was approved to house hundreds of us without any kind of protection. Hell, the enemy can see us through the chain-link fence. We're an open target. We're sheep amidst a pack of wolves.

In the few short seconds of standing in the open gravel pit, I count three incoming missiles. One after another the missiles are launched over the fence and hit the ground close by. I'm guessing the impact is less than a half-mile away. Finally the missiles stop and the military respond. Soldiers are in place, helicopters and planes flying overhead and ground tanks in motion. The whole event unfolds in less than five minutes. Regardless, I'm sure our security department and upper management will hear about this in the morning.

The fixtures in the bathroom are breaking. A sink has already separated from the wall. There isn't proper water pressure—when we're lucky enough to have water—and the toilets do not flush adequately. I don't know where these toilets were designed or where they came from, but they don't flush everything down. The porta potties may be a better alternative, but the shit in the porta potties has hit seat level. It won't be long before guys are shitting on the floor.

If the water is shut off for a day or more, we take showers using bottled water. This past week we had no water four out of seven days, and the people keep coming—the inevitable surge. Tents are going up at such a rapid rate to accommodate the influx of military personnel and contractors that the command can't keep up with the demand of services. RBK is on their way out, Barron on their way in, and everything else is a total state of chaos.

There's no accountability whatsoever for the maintenance services that are to be performed or for the people after an incoming attack. After our incoming incident, nobody came to check on us. I'm sure the management was sleeping peacefully in their hooches on the other side of base. They should have a manager or two assigned to every tent, account for their people, and live like the rest of us. Where the fuck is the DCMA?

Some of the guys are pissed. I overheard one of them grumble, *"I'm going to contact my congressman and send pictures of this hellhole!"*

That's not a bad idea. His bark got a few others to join in on the conversation. I hope it's not just talk and each one of them takes action. How else will our American leaders know?

Sometimes we all make sacrifices. Sometimes these sacrifices include welcoming about 100 new roommates into already very constricting quarters. Last night some eight dozen Indian and Filipino subcontractors moved into our space. Today the tent smells like soured, seasoned meat. I thought I was going to puke when I walked through the door. With every influx of people who transfer from wherever they came from to Bagram, they are carrying days of sweaty and dirty laundry. Many of them have not showered during this time either. Dirty laundry bags hang on bedposts, under the beds, and on the floor. Air fresheners could do wonders in here, but they're sold out at the Post Exchange (PX).

I have concerns about theft and sharing accommodations with other country nationals (OCNs). Some of the OCNs are sent here with nothing. They see Americans with all their belongings—electronics, warm sleeping bags, coats, shoes, and boots, much of what we take for granted—and they have nothing. Things start to disappear. There are even thieves among our own. I'm considering storing my belongings at my desk and sleeping in the office or in the bunker next to it. It's against the rules, but I'll take my chances if I have to.

I notice that Brian and three of the other guys I came here with are gone. Where did they go? Was this the final straw? Did they demobilize? I'll need to find out in the morning.

Leaving the project really isn't an option for me. I'm here and I need the money. If I leave now without another job lined up, it will put me in financial distress and test my relationship with Greg, my partner. I don't want to do that. I said I was going to do this and I need to stick it out.

I track down the four other guys in their offices. They've found some open cots a short distance down the street in a military RSOI (reception, staging, onward movement, and integration) tent in the village of Cherry-Beasley. They scoped it out a few days ago, and when the other country nationals moved into the Warrior tent, they decided to make the move and squat. I'm following suit. And fortunately for us, nobody is keeping close tabs on us at the moment. It's a free-for-all—every man for himself.

There are showers located next to the tent. Instead of cots, there are bunk beds. There are some open, so I claim one of them. I ask two of my coworkers how they got bottom bunks. They laugh and tell me, *"Money talks. We paid soldiers $20 each to give up their bottom bunks."* Very crafty! I'll do that too. The guys tell me to hold tight briefly because this is a transient tent and most of them are leaving the next day. Sure enough, the next day I stop by the tent around noon and it's cleared out. Bingo! I get my bottom bunk. I feel like I've won the lottery! It's the little things here.

I walk through the RSOI tent. There are more than just the three other guys and me squatting here. I can tell by the personal belongings stored under the bunks and the blankets wrapped around them for privacy. I set up my bunk like I'm going to be here for a while. I wrap sheets around my bed and make a tent to block out light and for privacy. I feel like a little kid building a fort. I can handle this for now.

Observations at BAF

- Egyptian women in uniform wearing a *shey·la* (scarf covering the face). Most people confuse the *shey·la* with a *burq·ka*. The words are used synonymously. The women are nurses at the Egyptian children's hospital on base.
- Men holding hands and talking in the gym as they go from one weight machine to the next. The men are Arab and from the United Arab Emirates. What's even more interesting is

to see a big ol' American bubba—his cheek packed with chew—holding hands with a local national where holding hands with the same sex is a common custom. I've seen this and it demonstrates his acceptance of the other culture.

- Just for Men hair coloring for sale at the PX. I didn't expect that.
- Pink gym towels? I think somebody mixed reds with whites.
- The potable water comes in plastic bottles that are double-sealed and manufactured by Coca-Cola.
- Traffic. The current command is ordering 2,000 vehicles to be removed from base.
- An SUV with Minnesota license plates.
- A Lexus SUV. The men I see driving it appear to be Arab. My guess is that they're from the U.A.E. They also smoke inside their vehicle with the windows rolled up.
- The majority of the vehicles on the road appear to be made by Toyota. I would say one in five is a Ford. I've seen only two Chevrolets.
- Churchgoers armed with weapons as they enter the church.
- Pizza Hut delivery drivers driving ATVs.
- Disney Drive is lined with some kind of fir or pine trees that are a haven for these little chickadee birds. I'm not sure what kind of bird they are, but they look like a finch and scurry on the ground like mice. At dawn and dusk, these little fellas are loud and obnoxious. They remind me of the grackles in downtown Austin. It reminds me of home.

Rednecks, Bubbas, and Kinfolk

Barron is holding nightly town meetings regarding the transitioning of RBK employees to Barron. Night after night I take part in the town hall meetings to meet with incumbent workers who are assisting in the transition. There are very few who are choosing not to transition to the company and have decided to end their careers with RBK and go home. They've put their time in. We meet in a large military tent that seats about 50 people. Making transition offers and hiring must occur after work hours in the evening in accordance with our contract. I pull groups of skilled craft workers from the crowd to schedule them for testing and verify their credentials.

As I address the crowd, I scan the room full of people. In my mind I play this guessing game of who fits the stereotype of electricians, HVAC, plumbers, and carpenters by the way they dress, talk, and wear their hair. It's a tough game to play because the entire crowd looks pretty rough, even night after night of new faces. Another employee asks me, *"Do you know what RBK stands for?"* Before I can spit out my answer, he looks at me with a big grin and tells me, *"Rednecks, Bubbas, and Kinfolk."*

The movie *Deliverance* comes to mind. I know it takes a special group of people to do this line of work, but I've never seen so many people with poor hygiene and grooming habits. There are a lot of folks with missing, decaying, or crooked teeth. Some probably have serious periodontal disease, gingivitis, or trench mouth. I wonder if any of these folks have ever been to a dentist. They're making more than $100,000 a year and some don't have front teeth! What's up with that? Where are their priorities? I guess it must be Thailand because many of the same creepy guys spend most of their holidays there, where almost anything goes: prostitution, drugs, and mail-order brides. That can do some damage.

A number of them also have horrible chewing-tobacco habits. Some of them have big balls of tobacco packed in their cheeks a good portion of the time. That's probably how some of them lost their teeth. That has to make an impression from both a corporate and military standpoint—and not a very good one. It's embarrassing for a corporate image.

One of the major differences between DoD contracts with RBK and Barron are the new medical and health requirements and background checks. Both requirements are stringent. Before I could deploy to Afghanistan, I had to pass a physical that included blood work, an HIV test, chest X-rays, an electrocardiogram, body mass index, vision, hearing, and dental. Plus we have to pass a criminal background check and a credit check of the past 10 years. It's obvious a lot of these folks got to Afghanistan without the medical. Hell, maybe without the criminal or credit background checks.

When RBK lost the contract, it gave the military time to put these new requirements into place. The criminal background check reveals a handful of felons among us. Most are confronted and caught when heading out on their scheduled R&Rs. When word on the street gets out about that, a few try to hold on until they're forced out. Their plan was to stay in country, keep working, and collect a paycheck as long as they could, but Barron security tracked them down at their sites and escorted them out of the country.

With a new military contract in place, times are a-changin'! Out with the old and in with the new!

Dober Dahn

"My name is Nedzad, but people call me Ned," says the new guy in our office. His desk is right across from mine. I ask Ned, *"Where are you from?"* He replies in his Baltic, slow tongue drawl, *"BOZ niah,"* with a slight diphthong on the second syllable. Bosnians are arriving by the planeload to Bagram to work for Barron. Of course, all of them are required to be fluent in English, and most of them can bounce back and forth from their native tongue to English with relative ease. I've always been envious of others who could do that. I've learned three foreign languages, but I've never mastered any of them.

As I get to know Ned, I grow curious about his native language. I ask him how to say *"good morning."* He says, *"Dober yutro."* I ask him to repeat it, but I guess the language is so foreign to my ears that it will not register. I must admit that I have difficulty fine-tuning and breaking down syllables. He knows I'm struggling with it, so he tells me it's easier to just say *"good day."* I can use it for any salutation throughout the day. *"Good day"* is pronounced *"dober dahn."* Again, with no reference to the other languages that I've learned, I keep repeating it out loud and in my head. I start thinking of words that sound like the phrase in English. *Sober* is close enough to *dober. Dahn* is *Don. Sober Don.* Hmmm . . . I smile, thinking of my friend Don, who likes to drink a little. *"Sober?"* I chuckle to myself.

I play the rhyming word game: *Doberman* . . . *Sober man* . . . Sober *dahn* . . . Sober Don . . . Sober *dahn* . . . Doberman . . . *Dober dahn.* He spells it out for me and pronounces each letter and syllable. It's pronounced just like it's spelled: *"dobro dan."* I'm a visual learner, and now that I've seen this new Bosnian phrase spelled out, I will remember it. I think. I hope.

Another Balkan guy in the office asks me in a serious tone, *"What do you call people who speak three languages?"* I reply sincerely, *"Multilingual."* Then he asks me, *"What do you call people who speak two languages?"* Is he testing me? I think and then reply, *"Bilingual."* With a straight face, he asks me, *"What do you call people who speak one language?"* As I am thinking about it he blurts out with a laugh, *"Americans!"* It makes a big difference when foreigners—more so Americans—learn and acknowledge other nationalities in their native language. There are too many ugly Americans who won't even attempt to learn a word in another language, even if they're in the host country.

Each day, I meet a newly transitioned or newly hired group of employees at new-hire orientation. As I speak with other American workers, I catch how many of them bastardize the English language. I'm no linguist or English professor, but many of them do not speak

English properly. They can't even get the noun-verb conjugations correct. Many people who learn English as their second or third language are impassioned about how they speak English and sound to others. I realize—or the truth is—many of them speak English better than many of the Americans. What does that say about us?

The F-Word

I hate the F-word, but probably not the one most would assume. This F-word touches me personally and the word is *faggot*. I'm not one to overreact when I hear someone using it, but it will certainly get my attention. In my younger and closeted days, I was too shy and embarrassed to speak up. I would stand and listen to the racist slurs—*nigger, faggot, bitch*—as though we were all second-class citizens. I'd listen to the bigots degrade the human race because others were different than them. I was too naïve and scared to speak up.

Today a newly hired Bosnian comes into the office to talk to one of his buddies. I've seen this guy in our office a few times and he's always been fairly friendly. I'm in the center of the room, using an external cable line to check personal email on my laptop. He sees me corresponding on my laptop and starts making fun of its small size. He calls my laptop, which is actually a netbook, a "girlie" computer. To see if he can get a rise out of me, he says, *"Is Barron going to have a bunch of faggots working here on girlie computers?"* I reply, *"The more the merrier. If we have more faggots around here, I know the job will be done right!"*

Sadly the Bosnian continues the conversation using the word. As I listen to him, I listen to the sound of his tone and the use of the word. It's derogatory—hateful. Does he know whom he's talking to? I am proud of who I am and what I am. I am very proud of my partner, Greg, and what we've accomplished together in our compatible, sincere, and loving relationship. I am proud of our families for accepting us warmly for who we are. I am proud of Greg's customers, our neighbors, and the community that we live and work in for befriending us and knowing our relationship is no different than their own. I am proud to be working for a Fortune 500 company that embraces and includes diversity. I don't have to be subjected to this.

I've had enough and I stand up to exclaim, *"Hey, buddy. Look over at my computer monitor. Check out my screensaver."* I have a 30-inch work computer monitor at my desk that is easily seen from across the room. The screensaver is a picture of me with my arm wrapped around Greg at Millennium Park in Chicago. I also have a rather large corner desk and one of the largest spaces in the office. He appears to realize that I may be someone important.

The Bosnian looks over at my monitor and seems surprised. I tell him, *"That's my partner and me. I'm a faggot and I don't like how you're using the word. You need to watch what you're saying around here. You're working for an American company that embraces diversity and inclusion, which is why you're here too. If you have a problem with it, I can report this incident and have you on the next flight out of here—guaranteed."*

He knows he's stepped over the line as he stands at the center table with his head bowed. He thinks about it for a few minutes before quietly leaving the office. No apology. Nothing. He just leaves.

Unfortunately it doesn't stop there. Kathleen, too, has heard plenty of slurs around the office and base, especially toward women. As she's listening to the discussion become more heated between the Bosnian and me, she starts sending emails to the higher-ups. She is sharp and courageous.

The word gets back to U.S. headquarters within hours. The single-slide HR presentation that references diversity in the workplace will now be expanded into an entire program and a site-wide campaign covering diversity, dignity, and respect. I haven't seen the Bosnian since.

Thoughts During a Procession

We are reminded constantly of death while on base. Many camps, roads, and facilities are named after fallen soldiers. It's rather grim, but it's reality. It serves as another reminder that we're in a war zone.

Today I witness my first procession. I am walking down Disney Drive from an on-site project when I notice people ahead of me stopping and lining up along the sidewalk, facing the street. I turn around and see the same thing happening behind me. Down the road is a distinct military vehicle with soldiers and a flag waving in the air. Soldiers and civilians from all parts of the world are lining the walkway from one end of Disney to as far as I can see, so I stop what I'm doing and follow suit. People remove their hats and place their hands over their hearts or salute. Others bow their heads and clasp their hands in front of or behind them. We all take a moment of silence as the military vehicle that is carrying the fallen soldier drives by slowly.

This vividly reminds me of a small-town procession back home, where cars pull off the road, people get out of their vehicles, and they place their hands across their hearts as the procession passes by. Yes, they still do that in small Texas towns. I've seen it and taken part: Stop to pay respect to the dead.

As I stand silently during the unannounced ceremony, waiting for the vehicle to pass, thoughts of war run through my mind. Just in my relatively short lifetime it seems like the U.S. has always been involved in war and conflicts: Vietnam, the Cold War, Invasion of Grenada, Iran-Iraq War, Invasion of Panama, Gulf War, Somali Civil War, the collapse of Yugoslavia, Bosnian-Kosovo Wars, the bombing of Libya, and now the War on Terror, War on Drugs, War on Christmas—war, war, war. The American attitude. Will it ever stop?

I think of the thousands of lives—both soldiers and civilians—lost in battle. I imagine the hundreds of thousands of veterans who have been traumatized, wounded, maimed, or paralyzed, both physically and psychologically. I'm saddened by the eternal damage that has been done to them. I think of all the losses of men and women who were children, grandchildren, spouses, parents, siblings, aunts or uncles, friends, neighbors, and extended family of others. Oh, how the loss impacts their lives. As the vehicles near me, I think of the body or bodies in them being transported: bodies blown to pieces, torn or detached limbs, burned flesh, mangled and unrecognizable faces, blood and guts oozing from the body bag. My heart sinks with sadness and grief as the procession drives by me. I want to release a stream of tears building up inside, but I manage to hold back. An astatic wave of electrochemical neurons transmits through my body, creating goose bumps from head to toe. I am stoic and numb at the loss of life.

War definitely comes at a cost. The annual global military expenditure stands at more than $1.63 trillion dollars (in 2010). The U.S. with its massive spending budget is the principal determinant of the current world trend, and our military expenditure now accounts for just under half of the world total at 41 percent. Including the U.S., the 15 countries with the highest military spending account for over 81 percent of the total. The top five military budgets are the U.S. at 41 percent of the world total, distantly followed by China at 8.2 percent, Russia at 4.1 percent, and U.K. and France both at 3.6 percent.

The U.S. appears to be a magnet for war. The more U.S. dollars spent on war the more our country is drawn to these climates of turmoil. If the U.S. military budget were greatly reduced, how would that change the U.S. approach and involvement? I don't believe they want to think smarter because they have too much special-interest money filling their pockets and war is profitable for them. We don't listen. I remember President Eisenhower's warning in 1961: *"A vital element in keeping the peace is our military establishment . . . In the councils of government, we must guard against the acquisition of unwarranted influence, whether sought or unsought, by the military-industrial complex. The potential for the disastrous rise of misplaced power exists and will persist."*

Based on the 2009 U.S. federal budget, we spend 54 percent on defense, 6.2 percent on education, and 5.3 percent on health. As an altruistic society, defense, education, and health should have equal budgets. I dream of a day when defense, education, and health are equal priorities to our government. I imagine the U.S. as an educated and healthy society—a society that can prosper and defend itself more intelligently through discussions, communication, and technology without destruction and antagonism.

I think of the creation of the United Nations after World War II. The U.N. was set up to commit to preserving peace through international cooperation and collective security. While the U.N. is not perfect, it is revealing that the world can spend so much on their military while contributing so little to the goals of global security, international cooperation, and peace. I wonder what the intent was by the founders of the U.N. and if we're meeting that intent today. Our own U.S. Congress and Senate can't come to agreement on many issues, and it seems to me that the U.S. is standing farther apart in the U.N. as other countries rise to power, wealth, and diplomacy.

The overlooked costs, such as short-term and long-term obligations to wounded veterans and the Veterans Administration, are staggering. For many veterans who witness and endure trauma in the war zone, they're led to suicide upon their return home. I think of the active-duty soldiers who commit, on average, a suicide a day. I think of the veterans who drown or elude the reality and their fears in alcohol and drugs, not only upon their return home but also in the field as they carry out the next mission or repeated tours of duty. Is it really the true cost of freedom? Are the threats real or perceived? Is it based on fear and profit? If war is a last resort to international peace, does it signify a failure of leadership, intelligence, communication, negotiations, and diplomacy? I believe we can do better.

As the procession clears, I refocus on the people along the road and sidewalks as they pay their moment of silence and respect to the fallen soldier. Immediately after, they go about their business like ants on a kicked mound. I wonder what the last minutes or hours of that soldier's life were like. What did he or she endure? What about the other soldiers working with or attempting to save him or her? I wonder if the fallen soldier was prepared for the greatest sacrifice he or she could give: his or her life and the legacy each one leaves behind.

Finding Peace in the Midst of War

There are four stages of culture shock. The first stage is the euphoric stage where everything is unfamiliar and exhilarating. It usually takes place during the first few days or weeks of experiencing something new and different. I experienced this stage when I gave my notice to the state of Texas and took off for my stateside processing with Barron. It was all such an exciting, untrodden adventure. It came to a grinding halt shortly after my boots hit the ground here.

The second stage of culture shock is the negotiation or withdrawal stage. It's during this stage when one feels homesick, sad, negative, and anxious. I'm aware of the emotional roller coaster ride that comes with culture shock. I've been here about six weeks and I'm in the second stage. I'm feeling down. The other two stages will come in due time.

When I'm feeling the blues, I like to listen to the song "Yulunga" by Dead Can Dance, a prolific duo from Australia. The song title translates to "Spiritual Dance." What is evoked is an ambitious, emotive soundscape that is eclectic but utterly unique. They blend medieval learning with more exotic Eastern influence, often employing authentic antique instruments into their music. When I first heard this music, I thought it might have been Eastern Indian. I was surprised to find out they are Australian.

When I listen to "Yulunga," I close my eyes. I go to my secret place in my mind to escape the clusters of people, the dust, and the depression that I experience both visually around me and inside me. It puts me in a trance. As I listen to this enchanting song over and over, I create my own pieces of art and my own canvases and choreography, adding different and unique details and fine-tuning the timing and the steps.

I envision standing alone in a valley of tall, soft green grass and abundant wildflowers of every color. Rigid, snow-capped mountains surround me with a perpetual full moon hovering over one of the peaks against a canvas blue sky—the prettiest shade of blue I'll ever see. As I stand in the valley, soft winds penetrate through me and the wildflowers sway harmoniously with the breeze. The colors come to life and swirl around me, diffusing scents of gardenia, rose, desert willow, and lemon. They are some of my favorite garden fragrances at home.

My mind shifts to a different location. I'm standing in a doorway with Greg, facing the backyard of fresh fruit trees. The robust essence of orange and grapefruit stimulates my senses. The blossoms smell like a freshly cut rind of the fruit. The snowy mountains still surround me and the eternal moon is following me. I know where I am and have been here before. This magical bouquet of fruit stimulating our senses brings us to another place and time.

We're driving along a country road in Latin America. We drive miles and miles through the orange tree orchards with mountains and moon towering through the tree branches on either side of us. The drive through the orchards seems wonderfully endless. My olfactory senses are taken prisoner to the fresh bouquet of fruit that fills the air. My taste buds are drawn to the hypnotizing smell of it. We stop at a roadside station to get a cup of the freshly squeezed potion of fruit juice. My first sip penetrates the papillae and taste buds of my mouth. I tilt my head back to get the last drop of the nectar and the last sliver of pulp.

I'm back in the valley. The sun is leaving the earth and falling behind the white-topped mountains. The moon remains balanced on the peak, illuminating the dark, evening sky. Off in the distance echoes the ancestral sounds of Native American drums culminating blends of nature, rattle, and calls of the wild. It's enhanced by a richly textured chant. We're at Burgdorf. In the heart of the mountains of Idaho, miles and miles from civilization and the nearest road, our hearts follow the native beat of the drum. Our spirits embrace and take a symbolic walk through eternity.

Our spirits are joined, following a path through the valley on a stroll to a sandy beach. The sound of ocean thunder brings us back to life. The waves splash over our feet. We sink lightly into the wet sand as it massages the bottoms of our feet and oozes between our toes. We're walking hand in hand along the beach as the sun quickly sets behind the endless turquoise ocean, coloring the sky peach and pink with a hint of lavender. We're in Hawaii—one of our favorite travel destinations and where we celebrated our 10-year anniversary.

Everything goes black. I'm envisioning a theater full of people. The lights are dimmed. The theater is dark. There is complete silence.

A shiny, white piece of material glimmers from the spotlight above. It represents the secular spirit of life. Showing through the draping cloth of the spirit is a face painted white with its chin aimed down, hands crossed over the upper chest. The eyes are closed. The spirit is emotionless in a deep trance. It lies in the center of the stage, amidst a cloud of white fog. Forming a half circle around the spirit are dancers dressed in black, on their knees, faces down to the floor, arms stretched forward as if bowing to the spirit. But I can't see them, as they're covered in the fog and away from the light. The dancers represent elements or the energy of spirit.

As the hum of "Yulunga" comes through the sound system, the spirit begins to rise. It's slowly hoisted upward, frozen and inflexible. The legs are drawn closely and tightly together. The arms are resting firmly along each side of the body. The cloth drapes and hangs on the body loosely and freely.

Slowly the spirit awakes from the trance, raising the chin and face upward as though trying to capture a ray of sunlight on the face. The spotlight shines on it instead. The eyes open gradually. The arms expand gracefully, yet strong, from each side of the body and open like wings on a bird. The drape covering the spirit flutters with the motion. The spirit continues to rise until it's suspended high and above the stage, into the air.

At 02:09 of the song, the dancers dressed in black begin to rise calmly. They cherish the spirit and gently rise to their feet. They look upward toward the sky, toward the spirit, as it is their deity.

At 03:03, the first beat of the drum lights the stage with a lightning flash. The spirit and the elements come to life. The spirit erupts into a *grand jeté* formation suspended in the air, motions like a pendulum, and becomes a ballerina flying in the sky. The elements do a sequential tap-jump-thump and follow the percussion into a rhythmic tap dance. A ballet combo swirl onto the stage from the right and double twirl-waltz as they repeat the steps across the stage. A couple of modern dancers emerge barefoot onto the stage, one on each side of the stage, and perform a duet of personal expression and lyrical movement. The ballet combo exit stage left and repeat from the start. A gymnast appears, performing a series of jumps, dance elements, back handsprings, and acrobatic skills. The spirit flies across the stage in a pendulum rhythm. There's a silhouette of a drummer below the spirit, perhaps off to the side of the stage, tapping on an antique African drum as they follow the percussion beat of "Yulunga."

The fog on the stage turns into an array of pastel colors: lavender, pink, peach, and a streak of blue like a Texas sunset after a seasonal thunderstorm. The fog quickly lifts and I can clearly see all of the dancers' movements and ranges of spirit.

The next 03:30 or so, the spirit sways by the action of gravity and acquired momentum, stirring the elements and energy into a blended orchestrated epiphany of celebration, dance, and accordance. It keeps going and going and going. I don't want it to end, but at 06:55, the dance comes to a complete halt as the music finally ends.

The seven- or eight-minute piece feels like thirty. I feel good and my choreographed piece receives a standing ovation. I feel much better now.

Rebel Without a Cause

I've never been subjected to so many rules in my life. A general order is a published directive, originated by a commander, and binding upon all personnel under his command to enforce a policy or procedure unique to his unit's situation that is not otherwise addressed in applicable service regulations, military law, or public law. It's the force of law. Some of the directives in the general order address topics such as host country artifacts, weapons, alcohol, pornography, and cohabitation.

Under the general order, there may be base commands or base policies specific to the area addressing things like wearing a seat belt while driving, not using cell phones while driving, smoking in designated areas only, and not using iPods or earphones while running or walking. Those are just a few of the base command rules on BAF.

After the general order and base policies, there's usually a third layer of rules set by employers, such as having a dress code, establishing quiet hours and lights out in B-huts from 10:00 to 5:00 (both a.m. and p.m. due to night-shift workers sleeping during the day), and requiring a ground guide while driving a vehicle in Barron Village. Barron has its own set of corporate and project rules. Safety is the company's number-one priority, and if someone breaks a safety rule imposed by the military or the company, they'll be sent home.

There are so many rules that are only enforced when upper management or the military wants to enforce them. One rule is that there's no sleeveless shirts or tank tops allowed in the gym. Military personnel follow this rule because they have fitness attire they're given and must adhere to. Civilians, on the other hand, tend to break the rule and will wear their tank tops or sleeveless shirts. Another rule that is highly abused or overlooked is cohabitation. Men are not allowed in women's B-huts and women are not allowed in men's. So how does the military explain nearly a pregnancy a day among its personnel? I guess they'd have to catch them in the act.

As for me, the base policy that I don't like is not being allowed to listen to music with earbuds while walking or running outdoors. The base is pedestrian friendly since people walk everywhere. I'm sure there are folks who don't pay attention to their surroundings. I was told that someone was hit by a car while running and jamming out. They put the blame on the runner. So now nobody can listen to music while on the move. Just like the shoe bomber going through airport security: Now everybody who passes through airport security must take off his or her shoes. At least in America—this is not a global practice. One mistake or idiotic move and everybody else pays the consequence.

Music is my escape. Sometimes when walking after dark, I have my iPod in my front pocket and feed the earbud wires up through my shirt and behind my head and then wrap them around my ears. I hide them with my hooded sweatshirt, hoodie over my head, slightly bowed like a Jedi on a mission. I feel like a true outcast by cranking up the music and jamming to some Led Zeppelin, AC/DC, or Jet's "Are You Gonna Be My Girl?" I think that's the theme song on one of the Apple iPod commercials, where a silhouette of heads are bopping, dreadlocks flying, arms grooving, legs dancing and twisting. It makes me feel like bopping down the sidewalk or dancing in front of the military police. It makes me feel like I'm in a music video. It makes me feel like a rebel. It just makes me feel alive.

Cherry-Beasley

Bagram is divided up into camps, villages, or communities. I think of them as neighborhoods: Warrior, Dragon, Black Jack, Camp Cunningham, Camp Mad Dog, etc. Upon my arrival, I was assigned to my billet in Warrior on the east side of base. I worked on the west side of base in Dragon Village, about a four-mile commute from Warrior. Next to Dragon is Camp Mad Dog, where they train and keep all the military police dogs. At the very end of North Disney Drive is the village of Cherry-Beasley.

I moved to Cherry-Beasley about a month after my arrival to escape the squalor conditions—and so I wouldn't have to depend upon the shuttle to go to and from the office. But there's another reason I moved to Cherry-Beasley: the magnificently appointed gay district of the base that offers comfort and style in an international NATO setting within a gated community. We call it the *gayborhood*.

All NATO nations are represented in Cherry-Beasley; however, the U.S. doesn't have any military personnel living here because of the current "Don't Ask, Don't Tell" policy that's being enforced. I am hopeful and confident that will change soon. I hope under the current U.S. leadership that they will take the opportunity to educate, respect, honor, and embrace diversity to those serving regardless of sexual orientation, instead of dishonoring them and treating them as inferior. Fortunately, as a contractor and through some NATO connections, I am able to secure my housing here. The community is a mix of foreign military personnel and contractors.

Let me introduce you to this lovely community and give you a tour:

The entrance to Cherry-Beasley resembles a fortress. It has enormous, black, decorative wrought-iron gates of wisteria with two garrison-style military posts supporting each side of the gates. The top of each station has a crow's nest and also serves as a military guard post and lookout. Residents are identified by a retinal DNA scan. The scans are actually picked up by sensor several hundred feet away, put in a computer queue to retrieve each person's facial identity and personal information, and pop up on a computer screen for the guards as each person enters the gate. It's really high tech.

The guard stations look like the castle pieces of a chess game and are made of a gray Afghan slate with striations of blue and black. Beautiful stone, such as slate and marble, is plentiful in Afghanistan. There's a man-made pond lined with earthy tones of Afghan river rock. Inside the guard station stands a series of computer screens that fill a counter. They identify the retinal scans and identities of the people entering Cherry-Beasley. Above the counter of computer screens are wall-to-wall security monitors that pick up the activity inside and outside from "The Big Eye in the Sky."

After the guard station verifies each person's identity, he or she is signaled to pass through the pedestrian or vehicle gate to enter "The Village." The entrance to Cherry-Beasley has a smooth blacktopped drive lined with low-growing desert grass similar to Texas buffalo grass. A backdrop to the undulating, wavy grass takes the form of a scrupulous landscape of evergreen hedges of boxwoods, viburnum, yaupons, and creatively sculpted topiaries—all artistically landscaped to prevent erosion from the autumn rains.

After passing through the gates and the security guard station, there are several things that are obvious about Cherry-Beasley. The Village is immaculate and well maintained, and it's hard not to notice the huge, oval drive. It serves to shuttle residents inbound and outbound, but it's also a 44-meter running track. In the center of the track is a grand park-like atmosphere with a huge pond and fountain. On one end of the pond is a covered pavilion for special events and a gathering place to relax. There's a Starbucks inside the pavilion with outdoor seating.

There's Wi-Fi and a deck that extends out and over the pond, where live music performances occasionally take place and residents sit back, relax, and take in the atmosphere.

Then there's the Clamshell, a fitness center that opens on each end of the facility into an open-air gym resembling a clamshell, hence the name. The gym stretches in length about half the size of a football field and is open 24 hours a day. Its massive size fulfills the demand of its members and is filled with every type of gym equipment imaginable: free weights, nautilus, Pilates, and cardio. There are studios for yoga, aerobics, and boxing. There's a steam room with platforms for massages. The farther into the maze the heavier, thicker, and hotter the steam becomes. At the end of the maze is a small fountain of sizzling water—a perfect way to melt away all the aches and pains and mental fatigue of working in a war zone.

There's an Olympic-sized pool for lap swimming and a leisure pool for lounging in the water or playing water volleyball. Both pools are surrounded by sundecks lined with lounge chairs and tables. The Hindu Kush Mountains serve as a majestic backdrop view.

So it comes as no surprise that the men and women of Cherry-Beasley are incredibly fit. Some of the men are huge and bulging with muscles without an ounce of body fat. They look like real action figures. Those big, bulky, buffed boys and some of the girls make me look and feel petite standing next to or near them—and I'm not pint-sized, by any means. I wonder if I'll run into GI Jane here.

The Clamshell is the epicenter for staying healthy and socializing. On Friday and Saturday nights the fitness center turns into a dance club. The dance parties are very popular and draw just about every resident inside and outside The Village for the best in trance, club, and progressive house music. Colorful laser shows and themed parties accompany the thunderous music. Adding to the glimmer and sparkles, residents sport their fuchsia-colored reflective belts that are required to be worn on base from dusk to dawn. The volume is high, the bass thunderous, the beat penetrating, the temperatures rising, the lights flickering and glowing, the arms in the air, the hips swinging, and the bodies bumping, grinding, and glistening with sweat.

One wouldn't think with a war going on that there would be much to celebrate, but the month of December has a huge lineup of parties. We have the Red-n-Green party, Deck the Halls party, Naughty or Nice party, Merry Grinchmas party, the Silver-n-Gold party, the White party—I can't remember them all.

Serving of alcohol is prohibited at the parties. No alcohol is allowed on base or in the country in accordance with General Order 1. If you are caught with it, it's automatic termination for the contractor; military has other consequences such as demotions or latrine duty. The alcohol-free zone doesn't stop these men and a handful of women from dancing and having a good time.

Now that you got the beat, we'll groove on and continue the village tour. There are a number of satellite stores with limited merchandise. Amidst the shops are several village offices, such as the billeting office, a laundromat, a barbershop, and several small dining facilities. There's also a tailor shop that professionally designs and fits military-approved attire with a Lycra/cotton blend to fit the shape of every lean, defined, muscular physique. In the center of all the shops is the tallest building: a two-story movie theater called The Flamingo.

Branching off the shopping area are sidewalks to The Village residences. Around the parameter of The Village housing is a gorgeous hike-and-bike trail full of panoramic mountain views. It's interconnected with other villages on base and runs into the main part of Bagram. The sidewalks have the blue, crushed Afghan stone mixed in them and resemble banded, tumbled marble flooring. All the resident buildings and units look like miniature row houses made of galvanized-metal siding and roofs.

Inside each unit are floors made of stained concrete with 12-foot ceilings. A lighted fan is mounted in the center of the ceiling. On the back side of the room is a built-in bed with drawers underneath and storage space above. Each room is about 150 square feet. Married couples from other countries have special housing privileges and are issued larger rooms.

Since marble is very beautiful and inexpensive here, the bathrooms are made of marble floors and counters. The sinks are stainless with Italian brushed-nickel fixtures. The mirrors above the sink counters are framed in neatly lined, tiny marble tiles, with hand-blown Afghan light fixtures hanging on each side. The toilet stalls are stainless with white porcelain toilets and the showers are marble. Residents can choose their own showerheads. Most will either pick the Amazon rainforest or the detachable water-massage showerheads.

Some of the residents modify their units and use the storage space as a loft for their bed and use the allotted bed space as a built-in couch. Others purchase their own microwave and mini-refrigerators, reconfigure the bed area as a mini-kitchen with cabinets, and have a loft bed above. Afghanistan is known for its colorful silk fabrics, earthy hand-woven wools, and vibrant embroidered cloth murals. Some of the folks have matching drapes, bedspreads, and pillowcases made for their unit. Some install the marble flooring; others use the crushed-marble terrazzo flooring. But most tenants are satisfied with the stained concrete.

Each housing unit has a wrought-iron decorative street lamp with two miniature banners. The banner that points closest to the housing unit shows the country flag of those residents. The other is a rainbow banner representing all colors and cultures. It's fun to walk around The Village and see all the different country flags and representation.

The New Zealanders have the cutest banner of their national bird: the kiwi. They also have one of the best housing setups. They have a series of sundecks off the back of their housing that overlooks the stunning mountain ranges. They have an outdoor hot tub, televisions, and sound systems too. Next to the New Zealanders are the Germans, the Danish, the French, and the Polish. They, too, have a series of sundecks with the beautiful mountain views—the only difference being that their sundecks are clothing optional. That's the Europeans for ya!

Now forget everything I just said about Cherry-Beasley, because that version is a figment of my imagination. Maybe it could be this way if the military were run by gays. Gays would probably make it nice, pretty, and fun. The real village of Cherry-Beasley is a shantytown. A ghetto. District 9. It's a dump. It's a shithole. It has many, many names and references. None of them are good.

The real Cherry-Beasley is on the other side of a series of cement barricades on Disney Boulevard. Behind the barricades are three large tents. The tents were once white, but now they're so dust covered and baked with the sandy grit that they're earth colored. It makes for better camouflage, I suppose. There aren't doors, just flaps. The flap is easy to spot because it has never been washed and has a coating of black, oily resin from years of hundreds of men entering and leaving the tents with their dirty hands. Inside the tent are about 100 bunk beds to house contractors and transitioning military. I've seen homeless shelters that are cleaner and more accommodating than these tents. Again, I think of the many times I've heard *"the best for our military"* from politicians, yet many of our elected officials have cut veteran benefits in medical, health, and education. Their pay sucks. And they're sent to shitholes like this.

Our bunk beds are flimsy. I usually keep a sleeping bag on the top bunk to make it look like it's occupied. At night when I lie on my bed, I examine the welding of the bed frame above me. The welds are tack welds—a bead of metal holding the ends of the wire to the frame. Some of them are broken. I can just imagine a 225-pound man climbing onto the top bunk and all the welds popping off like buttons on a shirt, with the bed, mattress, and guy landing on top of me. I'd be left with the wire pattern imprinted on my face. I wonder if that's what happened to the bunk next to me. The mattress and wire platform are gone. I'm not sure if it was removed intentionally or if someone crashed through it. The beds obviously do not go through any kind of quality control check, and they certainly are not rated for the average-sized American man. These beds look like they're made for children, not grown adults.

There are leftover carryout containers with food in them lying on the floor amidst empty water bottles and energy-drink cans. The floor is a fucking garbage can for some of these soldiers, but not the contractors. I've been observing this small group of soldiers for several days. They're violating a base command, as trash attracts rodents. When I brought this issue up to a lieutenant in our tent, he replied, *"That code of conduct goes out the window in a war zone."* His troops are bringing in food and leaving it on the floor, and their possessions are scattered throughout their tiny assigned space. They live like pigs, but they don't have to. Their leader could be holding them responsible. Instead the rest of us have to be subjected to it.

If our tent had a man-made distillery like on *M*A*S*H*, maybe it would be more bearable. Of course, I'm sure some good brawls would erupt from the presence of hard liquor. Drunks and guns don't sound like a good combination. Add a third element to that—post-traumatic stress disorder (PTSD)—and it sounds like a recipe for disaster.

The driveway entry into Cherry-Beasley is a dirt road covered with huge, sharp gravel. The only resemblance of a pond is the huge sinkhole filled with stagnant, dirty water from days and days of rain. The sinkhole is so big that you could probably hide a tank in it and nobody would know. Maybe that's what happened to that missing Hummer.

During the dry season, the rain softens the ground and swallows the gravel, allowing the dirt and mud to surface. The hot sun bakes the moisture out of the dirt and what's left is a talcum-powder texture of dust. Add a little rain to the dirt and you get something that looks like dysentery. After sloshing around in the mud that is almost unavoidable, it turns into a dry paste that cakes onto your boots and eventually leaves a pathway of smeared dirt and mud in the offices, latrines, and rooms.

Sometimes I enjoy watching the mud-covered tanks, Hummers, and Ospreys plow into the driveway, hovering down into the large potholes and squashing the moguls of gravel like they're driving an obstacle course. The only clean spot on the armored vehicles is from the path of the windshield wipers trying to keep the window clear. Impossible task!

The perimeter of Cherry-Beasley has a 10-foot-tall chain-link fence with spirals of razor wire on the top like the perimeter of a prison. Some sections of the fence have a green worn-torn, weather-stripped cover that's been shredded by the wind and weather, now left dangling on the fence. The only thing holding the material onto the fence are small clumps of dried mud. The cover on the fence is supposed to serve as a privacy barrier from outsiders being able to look into the base. That's a lost cause.

The B-huts, laundry, and gym are constructed of cheap and thin plywood from Pakistan that's infested with a beetle that chews through the wood like a termite and leaves a trail of wood dust. If a door fell off the frame of a B-hut, it might be rehung with a piece of plywood and hinges—a quick fix in a place where material shortages are common—if rehung at all. I've seen some rooms with just a blanket over the entryway because the door fell off and hasn't been replaced. Most of the B-huts are designed to last about five to eight years. In Cherry-Beasley, most of them reached their life cycle but look twice that old, no thanks to the harsh, cold winters and the baking-hot summers.

I hit the gym almost every afternoon. It's closed from 11:00 to 12:30 for what they call "cleaning," but I highly doubt that the gym has seen a cleaning rag or supplies. The floors look like they are mopped with muddy water or swept by merely moving the dirt around. Some of the cardio equipment has weeks or months of sweat caked onto the equipment. I think the caked-on sweat is holding some of the equipment together. Maybe that's why the cleaning crews are afraid to wipe them down.

The gym is divided into two rooms. The cardio room has very low ceilings and the room reminds me of a cheap add-on to a house or cottage. There's a row of windows that look out back to a generator encompassed by a wooden fence and you can see the roofline of the B-huts. There are two side doors, so I open the doors to get a cross breeze and air out some of the stench. I'm not sure if the flooring is uneven or if the cardio machines are off balance, but when I run on the treadmill the whole room seems to shake. I watch the cycle in front of my treadmill jiggle for the duration of my run. Sometimes I think it's going to jiggle across the floor and right out the door.

Cherry-Beasley's gym is probably the rattiest gym on base and probably the only one without an attendant. Maybe it was abandoned at one time, probably like the rest of Cherry-Beasley. Some of the other gyms are top-notch, but I use this one because of convenience. It's close to my office and living quarters.

The local showers and bathrooms are prefabricated metal wet containers called connexes. Those, too, are built to last about five years, but a couple of them look like they've been around much longer than that. Recently someone told me they were only a year old. I wonder about the drainage system of these units. A couple of the older ones have standing water around them that smells like a mixture of Pine-Sol and raw sewage. I noticed the exterior pipes leaking with gray water from the upstairs shower units.

I make the extra journey to the large bathroom and shower facilities that are nicer and used by the long-term residents. Not only are these nicer restrooms/showers spacious and clean, but I am almost guaranteed hot water. Hot water is always a hit or miss in the morning and evening, so I time my showers right after my morning workouts. I'm fortunate to work next to the Air Force camp, Camp Cunningham. Again, the Air Force seems to have a higher standard on everything. Hell, they have the best gym on base. As a friend and former airman told me, *"It's not that the Air Force has the best of everything. We're just smarter."* Of course!

Cherry-Beasley is probably one of the oldest spots on base and needs to be bulldozed to the ground. There are many other villages that are nicer, but until those better accommodations are made available to me, I'll have to continue to settle into the numbness and routine of Cherry-Beasley. It's grown on me.

Facts:

- Some of the Bagram Airfield villages really are named Warrior, Dragon, and Camp Mad Dog.
- There is a village of Cherry-Beasley (named after two fallen soldiers).
- The U.S. is the only NATO nation that has a "Don't Ask, Don't Tell" policy.
- There are massive-sized tents called clamshells. One of the clamshells on Bagram is a gym. They do host live music, country line dancing, hip-hop night, and an occasional techno night (but a shirt is required).
- There is massage offered on base. Most of the massage therapists are from the former Soviet Union countries.

- There's no sauna, no steam room, and no swimming pools. I'm lucky to get a hot shower.
- There are men who really look like action figures and superheroes.
- Bagram has a circular drive that is an eight-mile loop and closed from 0500 to 0730 for runners and cyclists. It is not padded, and there are some pretty rough potholes and uneven spots.
- Reflective belts are required to be worn from dusk to dawn. It's a base policy. The reflective belts come in a variety of colors. Some guys buy the fuchsia belts, as they're less likely to be stolen by other men.
- No alcohol is allowed on base or in the country.
- We have two satellite stores: The North Face and Oakley.
- Army post offices are on base along with FedEx and DHL.
- There is Burger King, Popeyes Chicken, Pizza Hut, Subway, and DQ.
- We have several very small movie theaters in MWRs. None of them are called The Flamingo. One of the theaters is called The Vulture's Nest.

Candy Land

There are a lot of hot men and women on base—so much eye candy! From the physical standpoint, there are many fit and athletic men and women—ripped, buffed, and clean-cut. Eye candy is beauty to the eyes, windows to the soul. I see the beauty in the people on base. There are so many different nationalities, cultures, beliefs, colors, and sizes. This common demonic force called war brings us all together. I witness many acts of kindness to make someone laugh or make a person's life just a little bit more comfortable while we're all here. Considering the circumstances that we're in, one can't imagine how something taken for granted back home could mean so much here.

It brings a very unique dimension of unity. I refer to it as "unity in the community."

Meanwhile, Skullcandy is the name of the manufacturer of one of my pairs of earbuds. How brilliant! Skull + candy = music to the ears. I love those two phrases, and both are very important when it comes to mental motivation and the positive impact they have.

I try to stay in pretty good shape and have made exercise a part of my lifestyle. I always schedule some form of exercise or activity. BAF, I told myself, would be no exception. In fact, with all the military personnel and some of the contractors working out and staying fit, it is easy and more motivating for me to hit the gym and engage in some base runs.

I try to get Kathleen to go running with me, but that seems like a lost cause. But she always cheers me on when I go to the gym or for a run. She admires my dedication and schedule.

Thanksgiving

I survived my first month. Today is Thanksgiving, but it's just another normal 12-hour workday. Nobody gets a break. No contractors. No military. It's business as usual, as it should be in a war zone. Everyone is on alert.

Kathleen walks through the door, greeting everyone with a *"Happy Thanksgiving!"* She's dressed in a white winter down jacket with a bright-red Christmas scarf wrapped around her neck. Her crimson hair is full of bounce and curl. It's cold outside and in the tent. She has two piping-hot cups of chai latte that she picked up from Green Beans on her way to work. She hands me one of them. The steam lifts from the cup as we each take off the lid to this liquid delight. I smell some autumn festive flavors like cinnamon and nutmeg, maybe even a little pumpkin. I've never had a chai latte before. I thought it was a coffee, but it's a tea. I take a sip—it's heaven. The blend of flavors is very appropriate and satisfying for today's holiday.

After the lattes are long gone, Kathleen turns to me and tugs on my jacket. She orders me, in her soft, serious whisper, *"Come on, let's get out of here."* I ask no questions and follow her footsteps. She tells me some of the people in the office are driving her nuts and she just needs to get out of there for a while and take a breather.

We walk on the gravel passageway toward the PX. The passageway is wide like a road, but it's used more as a walkway. Military-issued ATVs or Gators are allowed to drive on them. One of the tan Gators is decked out as a well-proportioned turkey, all hand-drawn and colored on cardboard as tall as I am. A young soldier is standing nearby, so Kathleen asks him if we can get on the Gator and take a few photos. He gladly grants her permission. Kathleen and I get on and start snapping photos like we are on a professional photo shoot. I pretend she's a model. She could be; she's that beautiful. I tell her to do different poses as though she's being photographed for *Glamour* magazine. She's on the front of the Gator, then standing in the back and hanging onto the roll bar, and then in the driver's seat. She has her hand on her hip, in the air, a side pose, and a front pose. She flings her hair in different directions. Her white smile radiates. We have a lot of fun with it before we move along.

Kathleen and I decide to have our Thanksgiving lunch around 2:00 p.m. I think everybody has the same idea. The line to the DFAC is long and goes along the total length of the building. We get in line and it moves at a moderate pace. The people waiting seem to be in good spirits. Though none of us are home with family and friends, I am thankful to share this day with a close work friend.

The DFAC is decked out for the holiday. Streamers in autumn colors dangle from the ceiling. Life-sized, handmade statues of pilgrims and Indians made from reclaimed Styrofoam are part of a Thanksgiving Day display. There are pumpkins and gourds and colored leaves. It really adds to the mood and the celebration.

High-ranking military personnel are serving food as we walk along the buffet line and thank both the soldiers and contractors for their service. I think it's a great gesture. The food smells really good. Turkey, dressing, mashed potatoes, sweet potatoes, gravy, corn, and biscuits round out the offerings. We load up our plates and go through the next room to look for a table. There's more food. There's a shrimp cocktail station and a smorgasbord of desserts, mainly pumpkin pies, pecan pie, and some dessert breads. There are also colorful wrapped candies that fill the empty spaces among desserts. It looks very festive. The DFAC workers put on a good show.

The food tastes pretty good. I guess I've learned to lower my standards with the DFAC grub. I'm sure the military buys low-quality, bulk foods loaded with preservatives and who knows what else from the lowest bidder. The shrimp are rubbery and chewy. The turkey is just a turkey roll. It tastes enough like turkey, I guess, and smothering it in the brown gravy helps. I'm so hungry I try to forget about all of that and eat it anyway. Our stomachs are full of today's holiday offerings.

My First

Thanksgiving Day comes as fast as it goes. Really, I wouldn't have known it was Thanksgiving Day except for the dinner at the DFAC. Working the required 12-hour shift takes away from any holiday spirit. That's fine. I'm not big into holidays or crowds.

Over the weekend I get online on my personal computer, searching to see if there are other like-minded men on base. The internet provider on base tries to block most social and dating sites, porn sites, Skype, and most any other site that will take up bandwidth or stream video. I do, however, find a couple of pseudo-gay sites. It's there where I meet a young man in his mid-twenties who is very close to my office. After a bit of chatting, we agree to meet the next day for dinner.

Between the darkness of two B-huts a shadow appears into the light. As he gets closer to me under the generator-powered streetlight, I see he is tall with a medium build, a flat-top haircut, a manicured beard, and beautiful bistre-colored eyes. We greet each other officially. His name is Larry. He came to Afghanistan during his military tour and now again as a contractor. He's been here a while. He's confident and relaxed. I, on the other hand, am nervous. I don't know what to say and his presence shoots my hormones into outer space.

We walk a short distance to have dinner at the DFAC. I'm able to compose myself at dinner and carry on a halfway decent conversation with Larry. When I talk to him I can't help but consider his big, round eyes and notice how perfect his hair and beard are. He's very handsome. We really don't have much in common other than we're both here, we're both gay, and we're both runners.

I invite Larry to my office to show him where I work. Between the DFAC and my office is a large dormitory building for soldiers. I'm told most of the military hospital staff lives in the dorms since the hospital is on the other side of my office along the runway. The office door is locked and everyone has gone for the night. I get the hidden key, unlock the door, and flip on the lights. I gesture for Larry to go in front of me. He takes a quick glance around the office and eventually turns around to face me. We're so close to one another, I reach out and put a hand on each side of his waist. I pull him closer to me.

We gaze into each other's eyes intensely. I slightly tilt my head to move in slowly, just as he does to meet me. I brush my lips with his and then we kiss. I kiss the top of his lip and the corner of his mouth and back to the center. I sweep my tongue on his lips before I break a couple inches away. Our eyes meet again. The sight of him pleasantly overwhelms me. We smile. Both of us are relaxed and feeling intimate.

We close our eyes as he sweeps the tip of his tongue on my lower lip. We take turns exploring each other's mouths, deeper, passionately, and more intensely. We take a quick breather. I lock the door in anticipation of what may be coming next. I turn out the lights and the neon glow from all the different computer screens gives a warm, surreal sensation as though we've jumped years into the future.

We remove our shirts and caress our bare skin against one another and continue with deep passionate kisses. I run two of my fingers down his chest and take a moment to unbuckle his belt and jeans while we embrace one another. I run my hands down across his crotch and feel the firmness filling his jeans.

The only place to lie horizontally in the office is on the perpetually dirty, dusty floor. I take my steel-blue, mid-length canvas winter coat, open it up, and lay it flat on the floor, careful not to kick up any of the dust around us. Larry lies on his back with my jacket underneath him. He has a smooth, lustrous white body that glows in the surrealistic light, flawless—no moles, no tumors, no freckles, no scars. I slide my lips across his sensual, fleshy lips. I explore every erogenous zone, crack, crevice, and hump on Larry's body. I hit every spot and indulge in the sweet delicacies of the body.

Eventually I use my mouth to cover his cock as I work his shaft up and down with pressure from my hand. I eventually move my hand down to his scrotum and then to his ass. I stop and use my fingers to start tapping at his back door. He's receptive and totally uninhibited. I use saliva on my fingers and penetrate. I can see in his eyes the pleasure he is getting and awaiting. I lift his legs around my neck and shoulders, open his garage, and drive my Harley in. His engine is wrapped around mine. With every deep rev my chain drive transfers power between us. Pitching my power-drive unit with rugged power, I increase the torque and speed. His engine is idling high and purring in sheer ecstasy. My fuel injection system blasts fuel into his internal combustion engine in alignment with firing his ignition into ebullience. All our momentum is exhausted. We let our engines idle and then rest.

I'm shielding his naked body with warmth from the cool air that surrounds us. We lie still for a few minutes as I listen to his heartbeat slow down. We have one final kiss. As I consider his eyes, I run my right hand through his hair and trace his beard with my fingers. We get up, clean ourselves, get dressed, and call it a night, but the following week, Larry returns for a second tune-up.

We both have partners back home in the States. I don't know what kind of an arrangement Larry has with his partner, but my partner and I agreed to open our relationship, knowing the needs of our male anatomy and that celibacy and abstinence are unrealistic and unnatural. Both Larry and I work long hours every day. Neither of our sleeping arrangements can continue to accommodate sexual visits.

I run into Larry again and again, and sometimes we stop for coffee and talk. Our one common interest is running and we see each other at the sponsored weekend runs. I'm always there regardless of the weather or the time. If Larry doesn't show up, I give him a hard time by email or when we see each other in person. I might start out on a run with him but usually plow ahead, as my pace is a little faster than his. Though we had our two episodes of intimate sex and know it's not likely to happen again, I always enjoy seeing him. He emits good energy.

Me, Goran!

I head over to the flight line to meet the current round of our new hires from the Balkan countries of Bosnia, Kosovo, and Macedonia. There's a huge recruiting and hiring effort taking place in the Balkans because of their high unemployment rate (around 30 to 35 percent), skilled labor, and low wages. I believe this is a military directive to hire a ratio of 60 percent foreign labor and 40 percent American labor, or is it a corporate profit strategy or a combo of both to keep the military budget aligned? I'm not sure. They arrive at BAF by the dozens every day.

It's the same process that I went through upon my arrival. The new hires and incumbent workers return from R&R and go through the routine: take roll call, collect passports, scan into a database for tracking and accountability by the military, and return to the owner. Everyone is escorted to a tent for an orientation of expectations and base operations. Following the orientation, the new arrivals are brought through the windowless cinder-block airport terminal. We escort everyone through the terminal and outside to the sandpit to claim their luggage.

A bus waits for the new hires and incumbent workers to board. The old bluish-gray Blue Bird school bus with dust-covered seats, dirty windows, and no A/C is gone. These new hires got an upgrade! They're boarding an old Greyhound-style bus with rickety reclining cloth seats that are stained and soiled with lovely, dingy-brown curtains. The bus probably hasn't been cleaned in years and has a musty odor like it's just been pulled from a swamp. The old Blue Bird bus is our standby. Poor ol' bird—probably has seen better days. These buses remind me of some of my journeys through Central America. All we need are a few chickens or baby pigs squealing on the bus.

This is my official greeting to all the Barron personnel. I greet the Balkan crowd with "*dobro dahn*," meaning "good day." I didn't have time to look at the roster of names before heading over here because it was handed to me by the HR office mere moments beforehand. I'm not sure how meeting and greeting the new hires arriving at BAF fell under the responsibility of human resources. HR is already short-staffed, but I jump in to assist whenever and wherever I can.

I slaughter a bunch of names trying to pronounce them for the first time: *Ivitsa, Selajdin, Memetriza, Shpejtim*, and *Trajche*. And the last names—yikes! Why couldn't they have single-syllable names? I scan the list for a name that I hope I can come close to pronouncing correctly. I come across the name Goran. I call out his name, "*Goran.*"

Goran sits toward the front of the bus and close to me. He replies in his Serbian-Croatian accent, *"Me. Goran."* When he says it, I wait for him to pound on his chest with his clenched fists like Tarzan. He's solid, beefy, and tall. He looks like he could be an American football player or a rugby player.

I ask Goran, *"How good is your English?"* He replies confidently, *"I speak very good English."* I could tell by his rapid response that he does, in fact, speak very good English. I show him the roll call and explain what we must do. His English grammar and pronunciation are very good, but he doesn't pronounce "th" very well. His "th" sounds more like "ta." Instead of saying *"third,"* it sounds more like *"turd."* I love foreign accents.

I hand the list of names to Goran to take over the roll call and to account for everyone who's on the flight manifest. He immediately takes charge. He takes the roster, calls off the names, records their blood type (a requirement upon entry to the base), and checks off their names.

The bus makes the journey to the other side of base. As Trixxie did with my group, I am now pointing out the rally points, neighborhoods, the PX, the coffee shop, Barron country support offices (CSO), and the gym. We pull up to a shipping container in the materials yard to issue the new hires their personal protective equipment (PPE). My PPE is on the floor under my desk, collecting dust. I hope it stays there.

Then there's the billeting assignment. I thought my first billet was bad with 200 roommates. These newbies are assigned to a huge clamshell tent that sleeps 400 people, with the nearest bathroom about 100 yards (meters) away. The way some of them look when they see where they will sleep reminds me of the way people react when they witness a tragic auto accident. They can't believe their eyes. They stand there with their jaws open and eyes wide open. We'll lose about 10 percent of the new hires here. Regardless of what they read or are told of the living conditions at the time of application and hire, some of them refuse to believe it until they see it. After one night in the clamshell tent, some of them will be standing outside the HR door in the morning to return home. They'll never even make it to their job assignment. After an incoming attack, we'll lose some more. The turnover rate is probably about 30 percent.

We get the folks settled into their new sleeping arrangements. Goran strikes a homerun with me when he asks if there is anything else he can do to help. Since I work and live on the other side of base and Goran will be staying here, I ask him if he can make sure everyone makes it to the new-hire orientation tomorrow morning. He responds, *"Sure. No problem, man."*

The next morning, I meet with my boss, Rupert. Goran is hired as an HVAC mechanic for our department, but I explain to Rupert the benefit of having Goran working directly as an administrator and a coordinator. Every office seems to be overwhelmed, including DPW. There are so many new people that it takes a few weeks to bring them up to speed. When I arrived in October there were about 450 Barron employees. Today we have close to 5,000 employees countrywide due to the transitioning of contractor services and increased scope of work. Rupert agrees. Goran will be working with us in the office and is the newest member of our team.

A Christmas Carol

Night after night it rains. Kathleen and I usually stay in the office late and watch movies after everyone has left for the day. Kathleen loves to watch movies and she's a regular shopper at the DVD black market on base. Whatever's released in the theaters will soon be in stock on the black-market shelves here.

Kathleen comes back from the market with about 12 new movies. I think she watches just about anything she can get her hands on. I'm more selective. She pops each DVD into her computer to check out the quality. Sometimes there's nothing even on them. One of the movies is *A Christmas Carol.*

She uploads it onto her 30-inch computer monitor. I glance over to look at it and notice the credits are tilted at about a 45-degree angle and some of them are cut off from the screen. The person filming it in the theater must've had it on zoom and straddled on his knee. Of course, all I could think about was the *Seinfeld* episode where Kramer filmed a black-market movie for one of his friends. We're laughing at how bad it is and how the recorder must've been propped on the guy's knee. I can picture him fumbling with the camera during the movie—and whenever there's a jerk in the filming, the guy must've twisted his whole body to see if someone behind him was watching, just like Kramer. It's like that for the entire movie. Oh, do we laugh. It's a good thing he didn't film the 3-D version!

A Cold, Wet December

It's raining and cold again. It's that kind of bitter, damp air that chills me to the bone. Rupert is ready for R&R. He's heading home to Florida for the holidays soon. Some afternoons Kathleen and I catch him gazing at his computer monitor with a 3-D fireplace screensaver. He looks like a little kid bundled up in his winter jacket and staring at the screen like he's watching a real fire. There's no work on his screen, just the lovely, fervent fire crackling in a red brick fireplace in front of him. There are even stockings hanging from the fireplace. Kathleen and I look at each other and smile. He deserves his moments of imagination and warmheartedness in this cold and bleak place.

It's mid-December and the temperatures really drop at night. Each morning as I look out at the Hindu Kush, I see a fresh blanket of snow accumulating on the mountains. The snowlines are getting lower and lower as they reach closer to the valley floor. I wonder if we'll get snow in the valley. For most of us here, it's our first winter in Afghanistan. Nobody really knows what to expect.

For now, instead of snow, we are getting rain—lots of rain—in the valley. If there is any break in the rain, then it must sneak in when I'm sleeping and end when I'm coming to and going from work. The days have become dark and dreary. The ground is saturated and the rainwater collects on the surface. The moon dust and rain turn the landscape into what looks like a single, immense cesspool. Pallets are used to create temporary walkways across the water. Instead of dust, mud is tracked everywhere.

My leather boots are soft and soaked from walking in the rain. The leather is so soft that I can imagine slicing it from a sharp piece of gravel. The moisture has penetrated to the inside of the boot. The cool, damp evening air doesn't allow my boots to dry even if I remove the sole inserts. Wearing them 12 to 16 hours a day means that my feet are constantly moist as well. I have a foot fungus between my toes that is escalating into something more serious. I think it's the onset of foot rot. I'm not sure what foot rot is, but that's what I'll call it around here. There are no externally visible or physical signs on the feet showing that anything is wrong, but the arch of my foot is gnarling uncontrollably. It simply will not relax. I wash my feet every night, apply a foot powder to them, and allow them to air-dry during the night as I sleep, but that's not enough.

I'm sure this foot problem is a common issue among the military. I see them wearing their combat-ready, ankle-high boots that are probably waterproof and don't breathe. I ask one of the LOGCAP veterans about it: *"Sherman, my feet are really hurting. I have a little bit of athlete's foot between the toes, but the arch of my foot feels like it's going into a convulsion."* It all sounds quite familiar to Sherman, who instantly questions, *"Are you using an antibacterial soap?"* I thought all soaps were antibacterial, but apparently not. He continues, *"You have to use an antibacterial soap and spray them with an antifungal."*

I take his advice and go to the PX to start the treatment immediately. Within a few days my feet start to clear up and my arch is relaxed again. Problem solved!

Kathleen doesn't live too far from the office and I live a short distance down the street from her. I'm so glad that I'm working and living on the west side of base and don't need to make the commute back and forth. Some nights I walk Kathleen to her B-hut when we both stay late at the office. The buddy system is highly encouraged for safety reasons. Tonight, as we are walking to her B-hut, I look ahead and think I see this big furry animal in the middle of the walkway. Kathleen sees it too and says, *"Oh, a kitty. The cute little kitty is looking for a warm place to sleep."* Feral cats are somewhat common around here, so it could be a cat. As we walk closer she puts her arm in front of me and across my chest to gesture me to stop. She says, *"Wait a minute, Thomas. I don't think that's a cat. I think it's a rat."* We continue ahead with smaller strides, and when we can better focus in the dark, we realize that the cute little kitty is, in fact, a very large rat. I bet there are rats running around in the B-huts late at night while we are sleeping. Shit!

Rupert left for R&R a couple days ago. Kathleen is getting ready to go too. As she's getting ready to walk out the office door to head to Air Operations to catch her flight, she offers me some advice, *"Make sure you take all 21 days of R&R. You may not get paid for all those days, but take 'em. Burnout on a project like this will come quickly. Twelve hours a day, seven days a week . . . we deserve the full 21."* No project is worth the burnout. She speaks from her project experience in Iraq.

The days go by nice and slow. I'm lost without Kathleen here. I start counting the days toward her return because when she gets back, it's my turn to go. The money and R&Rs are what we live for over here!

Christmas

It's Christmas. I've received about a dozen Christmas cards from home and tacked them on the shelves around my desk. Two of my friends sent me homemade Christmas cookies. Andrea sent me her famous rum balls. This year she doused them with some extra spirits before sealing the box to be shipped to Afghanistan. She told me she sprinkled some extra rum on them because she wasn't sure how soon I would receive them and didn't want them to dry out. I bet she takes a little nip to get into the holiday spirit when she's making these cookies. I know I would. I think I caught a buzz just from the aroma when I opened the box.

I also get a box of gingerbread cookies from my ol' Peace Corps friend, Marg. We're still in contact 20 years after we completed our service. I only saw Marg once in those 20 years after she left the Peace Corps. Her box of gingerbread cookies is cushioned with about a dozen magazines and newspaper articles. She's a retired journalist and always sends interesting letters and articles. She makes sure to highlight the articles I must read and usually has a comment in red ink. She still prefers to handwrite a letter than email.

Marg's gingerbread reminds me of home and a good pumpkin or zucchini bread baking in the oven this time of year. I add my goodies from home to the large center table in the office where others put their goodies to share: chocolates, hard candy, peanut brittle, cookies, peppermint bark . . . I'm going to get a sugar high! One of the guys in the office indulges in the rum balls. I think he's trying to get drunk off them. I'm not even sure that's possible. They are pungent, but they're all gone by the end of the day.

Outside there are a few decorated B-huts on base, but you really wouldn't know it's Christmas. It doesn't feel like it. Just like Thanksgiving, it feels more like any other workday and nobody gets a break. We are once again expected and required to work our 12-hour shift. I started my day by running a base-sponsored Christmas Day 5K. I always like to participate in a run on the morning of a festive occasion, so I don't have to worry too much about what I consume the rest of the day. Besides, a run the first thing in the morning wakes me up and makes me feel good.

About a dozen of us from the office make plans to go to the DFAC for Christmas dinner. The DFAC is decorated nicely and tingles with holiday spirit. Again, military leaders are serving the buffet-style food to troops and civilians. They thank each one for their service. It's a very nice touch. There's a three-piece Army band playing live Christmas music. They sound pretty good. I'm impressed—and it takes a lot to achieve that.

The DFAC is packed with people, but our group manages to find a table big enough for all of us to fit. The Christmas buffet has symmetrical turkey-roll slices loaded with preservatives, cylinder-shaped cranberry gel that wobbles, and a pasty-textured dressing that sticks to the spoon. Just like at Thanksgiving, I try to think less of the content and texture of the food and try to enjoy the festivity of flavors and the reason for the season. I am grateful that this holiday brings us together. For the most part, the people at my table are strangers. I've known most of them about six weeks or less. It's just not quite the same as being home with family and friends. It's not my first Christmas away from home, nor will it be my last I'm sure.

I register to run in two more back-to-back, base-sponsored 5Ks. One is on New Year's Eve Day and the motto is "Finish Stronger." The other is on New Year's Day and the motto is "Start Strong." The runs take place around 6:00 a.m. I know I can run a 5K in under 30 minutes, shower, and still make it to work by 7:00 a.m.

At the end of each run, finishers are given a T-shirt. After the run, I flaunt my accomplishment by wearing the shirt to work. Quite a few people ask where I got the shirt and I tell them, *"You have to earn it!"*

They all want one, but most don't want to run for it—except for two older guys in my office. They're both experienced runners and willing to train for the MLK run in mid-January. In fact, Ted is a former triathlete. That's an inspiration! I haven't talked any of the young studs or studettes into it yet. Now I plan to continue to train and recruit for every running event on BAF, from 5Ks to full marathons. There are runs all the time. Rain, sleet, sun, or snow . . . we are running!

Thumper

It seems like no matter which gym I go to or which treadmill I get on, my heavy rhythmic pace echoes across the gym.

At Bagram Airfield, I work out regularly at the Cherry-Beasley gym. During the cold months, my routine generally starts at about 2:00 or 3:00 p.m., and every day I see many of the same faces—from all different branches—of young, clean-cut men and women in their military-issued physical fitness attire. Every other day I lift weights, and opposite days I run on the treadmill.

A lot of the guys work out in pairs or as part of a squadron. I know quite a few of them because I generally work out alone and feel comfortable asking any of them for an occasional spot. I also try to make small talk with a lot of them or at least acknowledge them if I don't interrupt their workout. Every one of them responds to me as "*sir.*" I feel so respected. They probably think of me as an old man since I'm old enough to be any of their dads. Or maybe they think of me as a retired lieutenant, master sergeant, or colonel. I'm old enough to fit into any of those ranks too.

I'm usually one of the first ones to show up at the gym in the afternoon. I fling my towel over the treadmill handrail, put my water bottle in the cup holder, and set my iPod in the indented compartment by the control panel. As I begin my jog, some of the usual faces filter in and take the other machines. Most of the other runners are slim—much slimmer than me anyway. Some look like marathon messengers. A couple of them look like teens or preadolescents. Of course, occasionally a pudgy guy tries on the treadmill, but mostly it's the athletic, fit guys who fit it in as part of their daily schedule around the same time, especially the Marines—there are three of them who show up together every day around the same time in their green shorts and T-shirts.

Across from the row of treadmills is a wooden bookshelf. On top of the bookshelf sits an old, black Panasonic television. It's big, clunky, and covered in dust. I don't know if it works since I've never seen it turned on. It was probably left from the Russian days years ago and no one ever disposed of it. On the shelf below the TV are cleaning supplies: cans of disinfectant spray, cleaning solutions, hand sanitizer, and cleaning rags. The bottom three shelves have stacks of small, clean gym towels—when they are replenished and supplied.

As I set foot on my run on the treadmill, my stout, sturdy body and galloping feet fall into a resonating pace. A profound pulse follows each stride. As I run, I watch the supplies on the wooden shelves in front of me. Everything on the shelf starts to jiggle and dance in unison with my pace. The harder or faster I run the more the stuff shakes. As they shake, they shimmy forward to the edge of the shelf and start to drop to the floor, one by one. First a can of disinfectant . . . and eventually the hand sanitizer follows it. Toward the end of my run, a stack of towels or two join the mess on the floor.

One day a couple of the runners enter the gym through the side door, as they normally do. They see me jogging on the treadmill and wave to me as they witness the first can of disinfectant drop to the floor. They put up their jackets and caps, and return to the cardio room to witness the second can follow suit. One of the soldiers claims his treadmill as the other goes to the bookshelf to grab a towel. A bottle of sanitizer drops to floor. Before the soldier grabs a towel, he quickly picks up the things that fell to the floor. He looks at me and then to his friend. With a big grin on his face, he looks at me and calls me *"Thumper."* I smile and his buddy laughs.

My new nickname is shared with a few other regulars in the gym. They all seem to get a charge out of the name. It sticks for a few days, maybe a week. It's cute while it lasts.

You Are So Beautiful!

The tears are welling up in my eyes as I listen to Joe Cocker sing "You Are So Beautiful." My lips are quivering, trying to hold back the tears. As I sit on the bus and listen to this song, I turn my head to look out the window so nobody can see my uncontrollable urge to cry. This is probably the rock-bottom point of the second stage of culture shock. I'm beyond fatigue and frustration. I'm beyond the unpleasant feelings and events of long, undefined workdays, constant noise, sleepless nights, moody people, poor quality of food, stark differences in hygiene, and homesickness.

Right now I just want to be home. I need a hug. I need that deep embrace. I need some sincere human touch. I just want a good meal, a clean bathroom, a toilet within 15 feet of my bed, and a warm and quiet place to sleep. I want to relax. I want to walk my dogs and pet and play with them. I want to hear them whimper with excitement and wag their tails when they see me. I want to hear my lover's voice. I want to feel his warm touch and hold his hand. I want to cuddle with him. I want to know that I'm loved.

Separation from your loved one(s) is the greatest challenge of this job. It may be a significant other, the family, the kids, or even a pet. Long-distance relationships are tough, but they can make us stronger. Music provokes emotion. I have many songs that help me reminisce about family, friends, and events that trigger fond memories and feelings. Distance does make the heart grow fonder.

Much of what I do on base, I do alone, especially after work hours. After being in an office all day with people, I welcome the break and I don't mind grabbing chow, working out at the gym, or watching a movie by myself. Occasionally I'll do something after work with coworkers, but it isn't very often.

There is a difference between being alone and being lonely. Loneliness is marked by a sense of isolation or emptiness. Being alone, on the other hand, is not having someone to be dependent upon. I also think of it as a time offering self-reflection, self-awareness, and self-interest. Being alone gives me peace and solitude. I have done some deep soul searching during my life, and I know who and what I am. I am very self-aware and happy in my own skin. I remember someone telling me many years ago that if I am in a room alone and do not like the company, there's a problem. I clearly don't have that issue.

Kicked to the Curb

It is mid-January and there's an eviction notice lying on my bed. I have been given the notice along with 30 other Barron employees who have been squatting in the same military RSOI tent. The military knows we've been occupying bed space that is reserved for soldiers. For accountability purposes, the military allowed us to temporarily stay in the tent for the past couple of months until they could work out a housing solution with Barron. Now the military wants to reclaim all of its billeting for transitioning soldiers. That's certainly understandable, and maybe it's an eye-opener to the military about just how bad the housing situation is on Bagram. When the military orders you to do something, you jump. Fortunately they're giving us two weeks to find other accommodations instead of their usual 24- or 48-hour notices.

It's been two weeks and I'm still going to be homeless unless the military or Barron management can tell us where we are going to be reassigned. I'm scheduled to leave for my first R&R tomorrow. I'm still not sure where I'm going to live when I return. I really don't care at this point, but I know one thing: I am not going to go into a clamshell tent housing 400 men. With the current surge taking place, that seems to be the short-term solution to address any of the housing issues at Bagram.

The situation on the Warrior side of base hasn't improved. In fact, I think it's gotten worse. Not only is the housing a huge issue and a mess, but so are the bathrooms and showers per capita, the lack of bunkers, and inefficient transportation services to get people from the east side of base to the west side, and vice versa. Some folks wait up to two hours to catch a shuttle. Rumor on the street is that the cleaning crews for the clamshell tents have been finding plastic bags of human feces left in the corner of the tent. People are also shitting in the showers and urinals. It's out of fucking control.

The military has set regulations on all aspects of housing, from the allotted square footage per person to the number of bathroom facilities per capita. I don't think they follow their own rules unless there's a whole separate list of rules applied to contractors and subcontractors. I'm surprised it hasn't made it to the eyes and ears of Congress. The message is clear from the contractors' perspective of how bad it is: They're losing people left and right, and many of the people state the reason for leaving is because of the sleeping and shower arrangements. The demobilization rate is almost double the expected rate. The billeting accommodations are the number-one reason people don't make it to their first R&R.

To top things off, my job satisfaction is at an all-time low. I've been testing non-American, DPW new hires in plumbing, electrical, HVAC, and carpentry. The testing is not a military requirement. It's a Barron requirement to show the military that the company goes above and beyond to meet expectations. I have a 100 percent failure rate among other country nationals (OCNs). Though OCNs are supposed to be fluent in English, this does not mean they understand the American measurement system. Every country in the world uses metric except the U.S., Liberia, and Myanmar (Burma). What does that tell us about the U.S. education system, especially in mathematics and science? Another frustrating issue with the testing are the technical terms in their respective professions. They may know the technical term in their native language, but they don't know it in English. The tests are not easy and the printing quality is poor. I understand they were originally created some 20 years ago, pulled off the shelf, and sent to Afghanistan for me to test individuals. The testing is supposed to help identify training needs, but it's failing miserably.

After the testing, I create a focus group with all the test-takers to provide input for improvement. I can see where some of these guys fail because of their English proficiency. I swear some of them don't understand a word of English. I watch one guy mark his answer sheet in about three minutes without reading one test question. Out of 50 questions, he gets four of them correct.

I document all the testing results and issues. I address them with senior management. Additionally, reviewing the contract, we are supposed to be hiring already qualified workers. So why are we testing? I get senior management to agree to suspend all testing, review the contract, and address the qualification requirements with the recruiters. So I'm not sure what kind of job I will have when I get back from R&R. I'm crafting a letter to the HR director about the current situation and asking to please be moved into a more critical, essential position. I'll see where that goes.

With the eviction notice in hand, the rumor is that everyone will be sent back to the east side of base to a clamshell. The rumors spread like wildfire around here. I dread the thought of living on the east side and commuting to the west side for work. I am not about to allow myself to be subjected to the nasty, crowded living conditions or that caliber of living. I must come up with my own plan. I hiked the Appalachian Trail and lived outdoors for six months in lean-to shelters and tents. I hitchhiked coast to coast several times and slept in cornfields, grassy meadows, abandoned buildings, barns, and roadside rest areas, and under overpasses. I stayed in churches, college dorms, and truck stops. I traveled the "gringo trail" through Mexico and Central America, and slung a Yucatan hammock between trees and under *palapas* over the course of six months. In other words, I am hardy. I figure if worse comes to worst when I return to Bagram, I will camp out in my office—which is against company policy—or in a bunker. I won't tell anyone. I'll just do it. Either of these options will be better than living on the other side of base in a clamshell. That's my plan. I'm going to stick with it and not worry about it.

It is the night before my departure and I hear by word of mouth— again, a rumor—that the 30 of us who are being evicted from the military RSOI tents are on a list to be assigned housing in the Barron/ RBK Village. Most of Bagram Airfield is still being operated and maintained by RBK, and we are in a transitioning phase to Barron. The military has a camp—or village—assigned for its Bagram prime contractor and is referred to by the expats as "The Village." But this rumor arrives too late to confirm and the billeting office is closed.

The next morning, I get up at 0600. A couple of colleagues help me load my belongings into a company van and bring it to a container for storage. I have to check in at the terminal by 0930 and have my luggage weighed and checked in. I am issued a boarding pass and told to return to the Dubai Flight Service (DFS) building at 12:30 p.m. to be escorted to the plane. After I leave the terminal, I swing by the office to lock up my work computer and a few other company and military-issued assets. Two of the guys who work in HR and are also my tent mates, Elijah and Justin, stop by on their way to the Barron billeting office to check the rumor. Are we or are we not on "the list"? I tell them I have a little time to spare and go with them.

Elijah, Justin, and I make the lengthy walk to the billeting office. Sure enough, we are on the list. We are reassigned to a tent with 30 men total, all Barron employees—about one-fourth the number of guys compared to the military tent where we've been bunking. The Barron tent is in The Village, centrally located and close to everything. It will be a farther walk to and from work, but that is not a problem. I am just relieved to get this space and not have to worry about it while I am home on break.

We sign a paper for our new billeting assignment with a numbered space and cot in the tent to which we are assigned. This is how everyone is accounted for: by assigned accommodations for both billeting and work. I get a corner spot in the tent—here, that's prime real estate. The three of us are happy and relieved. Then the billeting coordinator, Milena, asks if we can move our belongings into the tent today. I look at my watch and have 60 minutes until I must be at the DFS building. Elijah and Justin tell me not to worry about it, as they will move my stuff for me.

After the running around this morning, I make it to the DFS building by 12:30 p.m. as instructed. DFS is operating out of a shipping container near the PX in the center of Bagram. There are about 75 Barron employees waiting to board a bus to take us to the flight line. It's a sunny and warm afternoon. I am hot and sweaty, and wish I could shower before boarding the plane to Dubai. As most things go in Afghanistan, there are no certainties or guarantees. We wait nearly three hours for the buses to show up to take us to the plane, and as usual, they are not pretty. They're more old, beat-up commercial buses with sunbaked orange curtains hanging sloppily over the windows that are smeared with dirt and fingerprints. Most of the seats are ripped, some exposing cushion springs. But nobody cares because we're about to get the fuck out of this hellhole.

We board the plane with other contractors. Every seat on the plane is taken. They don't turn on the engines or the A/C until takeoff. The plane is muggy and hot. It's February and I can't imagine what it will be like in August. Everyone sits quietly—reading, listening to music through his or her earbuds, and dozing off. This plane is old, with cigarette ashtrays in the armrests and no TV monitors or entertainment.

Our flight finally takes off around 4:30 p.m.— about four hours later than scheduled. It stops at Kandahar Airfield (KAF), Southern Afghanistan. Flying into Kandahar is like landing somewhere in the middle of the Sahara Desert with mountains of sand drifts surrounding the huge military installation. When people hear or think about Afghanistan, this is what they see. It's also the Taliban stronghold region and the scene of major fighting.

After refueling in Kandahar and swapping passengers, we are back in the air, flying toward Dubai—about a two-and-a-half-hour flight from KAF. The best part of the flight is being served free Heinekens, but they can't be served until we clear Iranian airspace. When the cart of beer is trolleyed down the aisle, it sparks a little life into the passengers. The stewards can't hand out the beer fast enough. I manage to get one before they run out.

I know several folks on the plane. I can hear people talking about where they are headed: London, Thailand, Sydney, Jamaica, the Caribbean, and many destinations in the States. For the remainder of the flight, I sit back and relish in the thought of being back in the States. I'll be home very soon.

2010

Welcome to Dubai, United Arab Emirates

Our chartered plane from Bagram to Dubai must be assigned the last available parking space at the Dubai Airport. We taxi on the runway for about 30 minutes before the plane finally stops. We are parked far from the terminal, next to a vacant field where they pull off all the planes for scrap metal. I'm sure this plane is an eyesore compared to the Emirates' fleet.

This flight holds about 200 people and it is booked. There's at least one flight a day, if not more, that leaves Bagram with just as many people. That's a lot of contractors. I've been through plenty of international airports and customs, so I wing it alone and lead the pack with my fast pace. Arriving in Dubai is like Christmas: Everything is sparkling, clean, and new, and looks festive, especially after coming from dreary, dirty Afghanistan. It's a welcoming sight.

There are dozens of customs agents—all of them Arab, men and women, both in traditional attire. The women wear a very conservative, one-piece *abayah* (or *burka* to most Americans) that is black, fully draped from head to toe. The men wear a floor-length, long-sleeved, white robe called a *thawb or thobe*. Many of us refer to the men's white robe as a man-dress. There are many words that define the dress depending upon the region, but I prefer the word *dishdashah*.

It sounds more haberdashery. The men also wear a scarf-like head cover called a *gutra, schumagg,* or *keffiyeh.* Again, the name depends upon the region.

Another thing that I notice among the Arab men is how well manicured they are. Arab men, in general, are very hairy. Their beards are stylishly trimmed, short with precision, their eyebrows waxed, and their nose and ear hair gone. Their *dishdashah* is freshly pressed. It looks like most of them just came from a day spa. It even makes the ugliest one look somewhat pretty if he's clean, manicured, and well dressed.

When I go through customs I greet the passport control agent in Arabic: *"Saalem alaikum."* Peace to all. The men will generally look at me and smile, sometimes gazing deeply into my sky-blue eyes. I'm sure it's because they don't see blue eyes very often. Once in a while it's a disquieting stare, like they're trying to read my mind or send me a message. I think I know what they're trying to tell me. I blush pink. Heated arousal is galvanizing. It sends goose bumps through my soul.

I hear the response to my Arabic greeting: *"Walaikum Saalem."* Peace to you. Since a lot of folks going through customs know this common greeting in this part of the world, I expand my Arabic knowledge a little further and ask, *"Keef halik?"* How are you? Then they'll ask me how I am and I respond, *"Qwaise."* Fine. These are classic Arabic phrases. Sometimes I'll slip into the parochial Arabic that I learned in Tunisia: *"Shnoowa hawalik."* This phrase comes more naturally to me, as I lived in Tunisia for two years as a Peace Corps volunteer and learned the local dialect. The Emirates immediately know it's a phrase from a region of North Africa and will usually repeat it and smile bigger or ask where I learned it.

I notice if I greet an Arab woman, she may respond but rarely looks at me. She just looks at my passport, runs it through their high-tech system, and hands it back to me like a robot without so much as a glance. I'm sure this is all part of their religion and segregated upbringing. I'm also sure it's part of the misogynist attitude and treatment toward women in this part of the world. It's too bad because it makes them appear very arrogant and snobby toward foreigners.

After customs, I experience the monstrosity of this airport and the unique, modern architectural features. I feel and see the wealth. Dubai is the international hub of the Middle East and connection to all other destinations of the world, so there are people from across the globe here. The foreigners who live and work in the U.A.E. outnumber the local Emirates.

After claiming my baggage, I walk down the terminal corridor and exit the building. Masses of men—dark skinned with black hair, mostly Indian and Filipino—are waiting outside in the airport meeting area. Most of them are various company escorts waiting for employees. Some are guests holding up their signs: Barron, RBK, AIM, APS, PPI, and many, many hotel names. They, too, are always nicely dressed and professional. The contractors from Afghanistan stick out. We look like a bunch of poor, dirty slobs in our sun-faded, worn clothes. Most of the Barron escorts are Filipino and have no problem identifying us.

The guy who runs this end of the operation is an American named Sean. He works with another company subcontracted by Barron. Many of the Barron employees know him from their many years of doing contract work in this region, and everybody is glad to see him. He runs a flawless show. He has several staff to verify our arrival and porters to take our luggage to an awaiting bus just outside the arrival terminal.

Walking toward the company-chartered bus are other passengers being picked up in limos, Mercedes, BMWs, Bentleys. Not us. We board a big bus that holds about 50 passengers. It's sparkling clean and the A/C is cranked up high because Dubai is scorching most of the time. When the bus fills up and everyone is accounted for, we proceed to the company-paid hotel about 10 minutes away.

At the hotel, each person confirms their departure time, and Sean's staff will be there to pick us up about two to three hours before the scheduled flight departure. The process works beautifully and makes my welcome to Dubai very relaxing and enjoyable. It's great to be here!

Welcome to the United States

My flight departs Dubai at 10:30 p.m. and I arrive in Atlanta at 6:30 a.m. It's exciting to be back on U.S. soil! The passengers deplaning move quietly in one big mass toward U.S. Customs. Most of them are sleepy and dazed.

As the line draws closer to the luggage scanner, I can hear this TSA agent barking at people to remove jewelry, shoes, and computers from their carry-on bags. When I get closer to the man, I watch him slam down a gray tub and yell at a passenger to take his computer out of his bag. It appears no one can satisfy the TSA agent, as I hear his voice growling, snarling, and yapping at nearly every passenger. He's basically an asshole drill sergeant.

Another female TSA agent on the other side of the metal detector is hollering at this poor woman who obviously does not speak English. The agent repeats herself louder each time she tells this confused foreign woman to put her cell phone in a tray and run it through the metal detector. The foreign woman stands there frozen in front of the metal detector, trying to read the TSA agent's body language for a clue of instruction. I can't stand it and grab a small plastic dish from the stack next to the metal detector and hand it to the foreign woman. Then I point to her cell phone and the dish. She follows my instructions, smiles at me, and is signaled to walk through the metal detector. I look at the TSA agent and say, *"Was that really that hard? It's obvious she doesn't speak English."* Silence.

There seems to be a lot unnecessary stress and frustration among the TSA workers. I can feel the tension in the air. It's obvious they have little to no customer service or soft-skills training. Most of them look miserable. Maybe it's the older guy who's setting the example and tone for the rest of the workers. I know from experience what influence a boss can have on his or her staff. It sure isn't a warm welcome to the Land of the Free. Are Americans really that stressed out? Do they really hate their jobs that much?

Finally it's my turn at the conveyor belt. As much as I've been through airports, I don't wear a belt or jewelry. I wear slip-on shoes and put anything in my pockets into my backpack. I slip off my shoes and put them into one tub and put my laptop and backpack into another. The TSA agent yells at me because my tray is not straight as it enters the scanner on a slight slant. This hits a nerve.

I stare him down, take the tub with my shoes in it, slam it into the tub ahead of it, and push the tubs through the scanner, causing all the tubs ahead of mine to speed through the machine. Pissed off now, I look into his eyes and say loudly, *"Welcome to rude America!"* The guy behind me chimes in and says, *"Yeah, man, where's your compassion?"* I take a deep breath and say to the older guy, *"We just got off a 14-hour overseas flight. You're the first impression of America that we have and it's not very pretty."*

The guy behind me pipes up again, *"Who's the supervisor around here?"* The TSA workers fall silent. No supervisor steps forward. I think it may be the rude, older guy standing in front of me. The silence soothes things over as the crowd continues to move in a quiet, systematic pattern to get beyond this point.

After going through security, I make my way to the escalator to go to the terminal and catch my connecting flight to Austin. Ahead of me on the escalator are two fast-food workers heading to a smoke break. The girl has a cigarette and a lighter in her hand, ready to light up when she hits the exit door. The guy with her has an unlit cigarette hanging from his lips that bobs up and down while slang dances from his mouth like a bad rap song. He's wearing his jeans mid-rear with his boxer shorts sticking out and his baseball cap on sideways. Every word that comes out of his mouth is profanity as he's complaining about customers. He needs to see a reflection of himself in a mirror.

My mind shifts from the minimum-wage American worker to the 60-plus nationalities working on the U.S. bases in Afghanistan and all the jobs that have moved outside the U.S. It's no wonder U.S. corporations move overseas. They have large job pools of people who speak proper English, take pride in their appearance and their job, and probably offer better work skills. They're thankful for the jobs and work with smiles on their faces. Thirty years ago, while attending college, I remember my economics professor stating that the U.S. will become a service industry paying lower wages and creating a larger divide between lower and upper economic classes, shrinking the middle class, and becoming a third-world country. We certainly seem to be on a fast track in that direction.

I walk along the airport windows and look outside. It is a gray, damp, cloudy morning. I recall a story of culture shock from my sister when she returned to the States after a couple years of working and living in West Berlin. She said all the taxis in Germany are nice, clean Mercedes. Many of the drivers wear uniforms. When she got to JFK in NYC, she hailed a cab and a big, dirty cab with a dent in the door pulled up to the curb to pick her up. I can picture the dirty, yellow cab squealing around a corner as it pulls up to the curb, hubcaps missing, the trunk tied down, and the driver looking and smelly. The cabbie is a hard worker just trying to make a living. That image brings a smile to my face. That's the beauty of America. It comes in different forms and styles.

My mind shifts back to the Dubai Customs and how the image and operations present themselves as prim, proper, and homogenized. I think of the many trips that I have taken through airports. Some people loathe airports, but they excite me because I know I'm going somewhere. I enjoy being part of the chaos in airports and watching the people. I like the smell of jet fuel when I board the plane. I don't recall anyone being as rude as what I just experienced here today. That experience left a lasting, distasteful impression of not just the workers but the image of the U.S.A.

I get through that experience and focus on my connecting flight and my return to Home Sweet Home. I look forward to getting into my warm, soft bed. I look forward to having a bathroom just a few feet away with a clean shower and toilet. I look forward to many peaceful nights of long, uninterrupted sleep cuddled close to my partner—the love of my life and my soul mate. I look forward to lying on the floor with our two chocolate labs and giving them belly rubs, taking them for long walks, and feeding them treats. I'm spending a little over two weeks at home. I'm saving another two weeks of my leave to return for the Thanksgiving holiday. The time back home flies by quickly, as it always does when you're on vacation.

Sleep Deprived

The past three months have been brutal. Bagram is one of the busiest if not *the* busiest military air base in the world. I swear I have not slept in the past 90 days. I am so fatigued that I feel like a zombie. Air traffic is nonstop and so is the noise when you're sleeping in tents. The night is full of all sorts of bothersome sounds: snoring, coughing, sneezing, farting, talking, and whispering. There are the sounds of squeaky cots, the rubbing and sliding of synthetic bedding, and the sound of guys pissing in bottles because they don't want to get out of bed to use a urinal. The billeting management came out with a policy stating that urinating in bottles is not allowed. I don't think that has stopped any guys from doing it. The crafty Filipinos tell me that they add a red beverage mix to their urine bottle to make it look like a fruit-punch drink. As for me, I stop drinking water at 1800 because I hate having to get up in the middle of the night to go pee, especially when the bathroom is 100 yards away.

Troops show up at the RSOI tent at all hours, but there always seems to be a large group that comes in after midnight when most of us are trying to sleep. I'm not sure how some of the military guys function the way they do. They come into the tent late at night, utterly exhausted. They find the first available bunk and just plunk their tired bodies in full uniform onto the mattress, cot, or floor. A lot of them are gone on their next mission at the crack of dawn.

Sleep deprivation is common in a war zone. There are days my head bobs at my desk. Most days I walk around like a zombie. When I'm sleep deprived, I'm clumsy. My already bad memory is worse: I can't remember why I opened a certain computer file, or I'll forget what I was working on altogether. I think twice to recall the day of the week or sometimes even the month of the year. I draw complete blanks with people's names.

I go to see my doctor and he prescribes me a refillable prescription of a sleep aid to help me with my persistent sleep problem. I finally get some genuine rest for the first time in months.

Avenue Hotel

Before I know it, I'm back on a plane to Dubai. Barron employees are put up in a company-paid hotel the night before we fly back to Afghanistan. I'm informed that it is a requirement that we stay in the hotel for accountability purposes and for preflight registration the following morning, as sometimes the flight schedule changes. The military may ground commercial flight service into Afghanistan to fly combat missions, or there may be issues with the weather or the plane. There's no telling what may come up and one must always be flexible in regard to this.

Our company hotel is the Avenue located in the Deira city center of Dubai. The hotel is not in the "modern, high-end" part of the city that most people think of when one speaks of Dubai. Deira is the old town and this is probably a two-star hotel. Historically, it is the center of the city but has lost its importance with all the new developments of Jumeirah Beach, the Marina, The Palm, Dubai Creek, and many other new and flourishing areas in the past decade or so. Deira is home to more of the imported labor and working class of Dubai. There's a heavy Indian, Pakistani, and Filipino population in this part of the city.

At check-in, the front-desk staff informs me that rooms are based on double occupancy. I will be given a 3:30 a.m. wake-up call and must report to the lobby by 4:00 a.m. for checkout. They also give me a complementary drink ticket to their hotel lounge on the second floor. I find this interesting considering the U.A.E. is an Islamic country and drinking alcohol is forbidden.

I open the door to my room and it has a dingy smell. Perhaps it's from all the years it has been and still remains a smoking hotel. There's an ashtray on the table. Years of smoke has penetrated the wood, the sheetrock, the fabric of the furniture, the curtains, the mattresses, and the carpet. Nonsmoking rooms are almost nonexistent in the Arab world. I'm sure the Barron Balkan employees who are staying here don't mind the smoking room since most of them smoke. In fact, one of the guys I know really likes the hotel just for that reason: so he can smoke in his room.

I stop by my room to drop off my luggage. My roommate has his luggage next to one of the beds. He obviously showered too, as his towels are lying on the floor of the bathroom. The sink counter and mirror are splattered with water. I hate it when people don't clean up after themselves. He knows he's sharing this room. Absolutely no respect. And to top it off, I'm sharing a room with someone I don't know. Or at least I have my doubts that I know this person. I tell myself that this is for one night only and it's a step up from where I'll be sleeping the next 90 nights.

I decide to take advantage of the free drink ticket and check out the hotel lounge. In the elevator down to the lounge, there's a poster about the lounge and restaurant in the hotel. It has a Filipino theme. Outside the door is a bouncer. He acknowledges me with a nod of his head as I enter. The cloud of smoke hits me in the face as I walk into the bar. I'm not used to it; smoking in the bars is prohibited in Austin, Texas. There are only three other men at the bar and about 20 scantily dressed women standing at bar-height tables scattered around the small club. I grab a stool at the bar and order my complementary beer: a Heineken. I've been forewarned about the high price of drinks in Dubai. A draught beer will set one back about $10.

Within a few seconds of taking my first sip of beer, which tasted so good after the long flight from the States, a young Filipino woman in a short, glittery spaghetti-strapped dress (with heels to match) approaches me. She has long, straight, black hair, a smooth complexion, and a smile on her face that lights up the night. She's sweet and friendly. I think she wants me to buy her a drink, but within minutes she gets right to the point and asks me if I'm looking for some fun—more directly, sex. She's a prostitute! I smile at the girl's forwardness and tell her I'm not interested. She's persistent and lets me know that she can accommodate any of my needs. I chuckle. She continues on to say that if I'm not interested in her, maybe I'd like one of the other girls. I've never been propositioned like this before, so I don't know what to say or do.

The usual Barron security spiel about prostitution and public intoxication races through my head. It all fits now. Even though selling sex is *haram* (forbidden) under Islamic law and the U.A.E., the authorities rarely do anything about it. Of course, Dubai is also known as the Middle Eastern playground for Arabs in this region. Sex, liquor, fun . . . it's all here in Dubai.

I look over at the end of the bar, where two women are entertaining a guy a few years older than me. He looks like he's a punter and having the time of his life. The girls have their hands all over his body. One is kneading his shoulders. The other is running her hands through his hair as she unbuttons a couple of top buttons on his shirt and pets the hair on his chest. The three of them are laughing and seem to be enjoying every minute of it. I guess he didn't hear the little speech about prostitution on the bus. Then again, maybe he doesn't work for us. He's already bought both ladies of the night a drink, and the three of them look like they are going to be heading to his hotel room next. Good for him, I guess. Have fun, buddy!

Meanwhile, this provocative little lady keeps hanging on me. She's become very forward: *"You like blow job?" "You want nice hot fuck?" "You want two lady?" "What you like?"* I finally have enough of her, turn to her face to face, and tell her, *"I don't like girls. I like boys."* She giggles, *"You like boy?"* I say firmly, *"Yes, I do, darling."*

Then she asks me if I like sheboys. Oh no! I bet there are a few sheboys in her little clique. A type for every kind. Being afraid that may be a remote possibility, I become blunt with her, *"I like men. Real men. Arab men. Tall, dark, hairy, and masculine."* She thinks my response is funny and goes back to all the other girls to share it with them. I'm not sure what she's telling them, but she's pointing at me and giggling. At least she's off my back.

I'm in the bar about 15 minutes when I finish my beer. I've also had enough of the prostitutes, the smoke, and the loud music. I walk outside the hotel to look for a place to grab a bite to eat. The hotel is on Al Rigga Street, one of the main drags lined with a lot of other hotels, shops, and restaurants. It's a beautiful February evening and the street is hustling and bustling with people. I find a great Lebanese restaurant just a couple blocks away. They have an outdoor seating area, where I people-watch and enjoy my meal of hummus, *shawarma* (rotisserie chicken that is sliced into slivers of meat), freshly baked pita, and freshly squeezed mint lemonade.

Returning to the hotel, I spot another Filipino woman standing outside. She's eyeing me from head to toe. Her low-cut white top and miniskirt, high heels, and glittering jewelry give it away that she's working it. As I get closer to my hotel, I'm hoping she isn't going to approach me. I look away from her, but as I get to the hotel door, she springs into action and pops up alongside me, asking if I am looking for a good time. I try to ignore her and walk faster, but she's persistent. She keeps walking alongside me at a rapid pace. I finally tell her in a blunt voice to get the hell away from me and then walk into my hotel.

I get back to my room. Closing the door, I take a deep breath and wonder what just happened outside and if I handled that situation appropriately. I feel sorry for the prostitutes. Some of them come to Dubai hired as a nanny, but instead they're sexually and physically abused, their wages and passports are held, and they flee the situation with nothing. Their only means of making money is through prostitution. Some of them may be doing it to supplement their income too. I don't know.

There's no sign of my roommate. That's a good thing, I guess. I crawl under the blankets of my twin bed, turn on the TV to watch the news, and turn it off around 1:00 a.m. to sleep.

At 2:03 a.m. I'm abruptly reminded that I have a roommate when he makes a grand entrance and flips on the room lights. He's drunker than a skunk, with a cigarette in one hand and a bottle of booze in the other. He's swaying back and forth, bumping into the hallway walls. I take my pillow and cover my head. I am hoping this is just a bad dream, but it's not. I can smell the liquor from his breath and the cigarette smoke embedded in his clothes. He reeks like a dirty barroom floor.

Suddenly it's quiet. I lift my head from under my pillow and take a peek. I scan the room with my eyes. The lights are still on, but my roommate is passed out on his bed, fully dressed. I glance at the table and see the bottle of booze sitting there next to the ashtray where he stubbed his cigarette. I'm thankful that he didn't burn the place down. I hope he enjoyed his last big binge and party. I get up, turn off the lights, go back to bed, and hope I can catch the last hour of sleep before my 3:30 a.m. wake-up call.

"Hello, this is your wake-up call," says the voice on the phone. It's almost 3:45 a.m. Checkout starts at 4:00 a.m., but I don't think I've slept since I was awakened at 2:03 a.m. I've just been lying in bed.

Since I showered last night, I brush my teeth, wash my face, and pack a few loose things into my bag. I look over at my nameless roommate—not a sound or a move. I can smell the vodka vapor fumes from his breath. He's comatose. I could nudge him and tell him to wake up to catch our flight, but why should I? We're grown men, not 20-year-olds. Fuck this inconsiderate, drunk asshole. Face the consequences, motherfucker! I grab my bags and book it out the door to check out. I don't know what will happen to that guy and I really don't care. If his name is on the flight roster and he doesn't check out, I'm sure security will be knocking on the door and he'll be terminated. I'll let security and HR deal with it. I'm outta here.

Highway to Hell

While waiting in line to check out of the hotel, I see one of my colleagues, Josh. We went through our mobilization and deployment training together in Greenville in October, and he's just now heading over to Afghanistan. He's a young man from Tyler, Texas, and this is his first time overseas. He went through the police academy and was an officer for a couple of years. He thought about joining the military, but his family frowned upon the idea. Still, police work didn't suit him, so he decided to come work for Barron.

Josh is in his mid-twenties but looks more like a teenager with his baby face, buzzed blond hair, blue eyes, and nice build. I don't think he'd be able to grow facial hair if he tried. He's generally quiet and shy, and he always appears innocent. I can tell he's very observant, as I catch his eyes darting back and forth taking in all sorts of action and details.

As we sit in the hotel lobby, waiting for the bus to the airport, I download a bunch of movies and music from Josh's computer. He has some AC/DC. It's been years since I listened to them. Their raw energy and power-driven performance fits the band name very well.

At the airport, as we wait for our flight to Afghanistan, both of us have our headphones on, listening to music. I nudge Josh and ask him what he's listening to. He replies, *"Demented."* I laugh because I've never heard of them, but I like the name of the band. I tell him I am listening to "Highway to Hell" by AC/DC, as it only seems appropriate going into a war zone. He agrees and flips his iPod to the same song, bobbing to the beat and playing air guitar: *"Living easy, living free . . . season ticket on a one-way ride . . . going down, party time . . . I'm on the highway to hell."* We agree to make "Highway to Hell" our new theme song for the flight from Dubai into Afghanistan.

Change Is Inevitable

At Bagram, I learn quickly that change is inevitable and constant. It's an element of the job that keeps the atmosphere interesting and the work environment stimulating. People are not stagnant or working within their own little silo for too long. I see a slew of new people who arrived while I was on R&R. I also hear that a few quit while I was gone. I'm sad to hear of those who left and won't be coming back, but I can understand. This type of work and living environment isn't for everyone.

There's a new guy whose desk is by the front door. His name is Timmy Dwayne. He's a mammoth of a man. Not only is he tall, but he also weighs about 400 pounds. The poor guy is on a watermelon diet to drop weight quickly because he's afraid of failing his annual physical with the new BMI requirement. Another guy, Snacks, whom I have not met, isn't even trying to meet the new requirement. He's a truck driver and about as big as Timmy Dwayne, but he's just throwing in the towel. As for me, I'm all for the fit-for-duty requirement, especially here in a war zone. If we were under attack, those boys wouldn't be able to efficiently run to a bunker for cover. I think more professions should have a similar requirement. It would keep people in check with their health. There's nothing more discouraging than seeing an enormous health-care professional or an obese police officer.

Cliff, another new fella in the office, is easy to warm up to, and there's something about him that I really like. I'm not sure if it's his multicultural mix, his shape, his shaved head, his deviant laugh, or a combination of all those things. He just has an aura about him. Maybe it's his sexual energy. I've gone to lunch with Cliff a few times, and I figuratively have to wave my hands or lightly slap his face to snap him out of gawking and stalking the women in the DFAC. Sometimes I kiddingly hand him a napkin to wipe the drool off his face. When I tell him to snap out of it, he replies, *"Oh man, there's just something about a good-looking woman in uniform with a rifle strapped behind her back."* I know what he means because I feel the same way about the guys. Then he starts talking dirty. I like to listen to him talk dirty. He's so charged up that I figure he could go either way. I offer him a friendly proposition—on several occasions—but he laughs and kindly turns it down: *"I don't go that way, man."*

I'm informed that I will have a new chain of command. My current boss, Rupert, delivers the news himself. He's been here a year, fulfilled his contract and commitment, and Barron is sending him to another project. But word on the street is that he's a long-term Barron employee classified as a Tier 1, and they're paying him a shitload of money to be here. Stretching that rumor further, I hear that most of the 400-plus Tier 1 employees will be scaled down significantly, reassigned to another project, or sent back to the States. His departure is unexpected.

Rupert's boss is leaving too. He's the department manager and really didn't want to be here, so he's quitting. Kaput! They leave within a week of each other. Our country HR manager is leaving too. The transition HR manager, Huggy McPherson, whose role will end when the transition is complete, will replace him within a matter of weeks. I can't say that I'm sad to see them go. I believe their departure will generate new thinking systems and positive change. Change will also promote flexibility and a new driving force.

Another rumor on the street is that upper management is reengineering the organization with its transition and growth. Rupert is the Department of Public Works (DPW) manager. He also took the training department under his helm. The new plan is to split the departments and keep them separate. They're bringing in someone who is more cost-effective and experienced in training to take over that position. The training department will now fall under the HR umbrella run by Huggy. I will report to the new training manager when he arrives. Kathleen will be moving to a newly transitioned department that works with asset management. It's the IBM Maximo system that she learned and mastered in Iraq. She will be training new employees how to use the inventory tracking system. Goran will remain under DPW.

Kathleen informs me of a few other departures. One of them is the worker who ate all the rum balls at Christmas, trying to get a buzz off them—gone. Apparently he is a drunk and was caught intoxicated on base. Immediate termination for him.

Yet another departure and rumor is that three mid-level managers were hired by Barron to run the materials and supply warehouse division—and all three left the same day. She knew all three of them from Iraq. I ask her why they left, and she says she heard they left because the division was such a chaotic mess and because the sleeping arrangements were worse. Then I got another twist to that rumor: One of the managers who worked previously for RBK said they fired those three managers in Iraq for falsifying documents and shipping millions of dollars of goods purchased through the military to the Balkans for their own personal gain. If the military got word of that and could prove it, there'd be some serious consequences, including possible fines and jail time.

I can tell Rupert is a little unsettled and stressed about his departure. He's using the "B" word a lot: *This bloody computer is moving too bloody slow. My bloody computer is not programmed to the bloody printer. It's bloody cold outside. This bloody coffee tastes good! Bloody this and bloody that.* Kathleen and I hear his rants and raves, and we think it's rather charming and chime in from time to time.

Rupert hands me the resume of the new training manager and tells me that he's going to be my new boss. I glance over his resume. He's a retired Navy Seal named Trigger. Wow! I'm going to be working for a Navy Seal. Seals are hardcore—I wonder what his management style will be like. I can only picture someone like a drill sergeant slinging orders, and I probably won't be very receptive to that. All I can do is sigh for now. He will be here in three weeks, at which point Rupert will be leaving.

I have entered the third phase of culture shock: adjustment. I've grown accustomed to this culture and the routines. I know what to expect in most situations and working on BAF no longer feels new. It is what it is and goes hand in hand with knowing that rumors are our first source of information.

Goran and Mr. Deen

One of the new faces in the office is a man in his fifties from Sri Lanka. His name is Nilamdeen Sikkander Mohinudeen. Everyone in the office refers to him as "Mr. Deen." It's much easier. Greg thinks my family names like Unertl, Kuklinski, Weiderhoff, and Eggebrecht are tough names. Greg's family names are easy: West, Baker, Love, Hill, and

Smith. Most of them are a single syllable or no more than two. He'd have a heyday with names like Nilamdeen Sikkander Mohinudeen's.

Mr. Deen stands about 5'5" and looks like he's got the body and size of an American boy—a young boy, maybe 12 or 13 years old. He's dark skinned with espresso-colored eyes and pitch-black hair, and has a mustache with a touch of gray. He's fluent in six languages, including English, Hindi, and Arabic. Talk about a hodgepodge of languages. Those three languages are very different in their own ways: the way they are written, the sounds, the pronunciation, the grammar, and the sentence structure. Most Americans find learning one foreign language intimidating; I can't imagine learning three, four, six, or eight. I've never heard of the other three languages he speaks: Malayalam, Tamil, and Sinhala. When he tells me that he speaks *"Malayalam,"* I give him the "deer caught in the headlights" look and sigh, *"huh?"* He just giggles at my many attempts to pronounce it.

Mr. Deen worked for a U.S. Embassy in Sri Lanka and spent 25 years in Qatar. That explains where he learned his Arabic. He has only one son, who is studying in London. He's awfully proud of that, as he should be. He doesn't work for Barron directly but is instead a Barron subcontractor. He's waiting for his work orders to another base in Afghanistan, so as he waits for further instructions, he's making a temporary home in our office.

Since Kathleen is traveling quite a bit to other FOBs conducting training, Goran sits next to me and Mr. Deen takes the seat next to him. Watching and listening to the two is quite the comedy act. I guess I'm their anchor among the three of us. They tolerate each other more than anything because Goran can't understand a word Mr. Deen says and Mr. Deen can't understand most of what Goran says. So I interpret their English back and forth to one another. He said this; he said that.

I have a five-inch-diameter cosmetic mirror near my computer so I can see what's going on behind me. My back faces everyone. In front of me is a wooden wall and shelf. The mirror adds a little *feng shui* so I can see what's going on behind me without really having to turn around. Today I see Goran coming through the door a little later than Mr. Deen and me. Goran makes a quick dodge to my desk, picks up my mirror, straightens every hair on his head, and exams his good looks. I ask him, *"Do you need a toothbrush and comb with that mirror?"* He takes another look in the mirror and says, *"Mirror, mirror on the wall, who's the most handsome of us all? I am. I know."* I roll my eyeballs at him as he chuckles at himself. It must be his Macedonian pride.

Watching Mr. Deen is like watching a ricochet rabbit because he's constantly got to be doing something. He keeps his time occupied by sweeping the floor, emptying trash, wiping down counters or cleaning equipment, and stocking cases of water. He goes to the dining facility and brings back coffee, creamers, packets of sugar, honey, drink powders, hot chocolate, and tea. He brings back huge quantities as though he's hoarding them for a shortage. I have to laugh at him because we're supposed to take very limited quantities—two max, that's it. The military has a huge sign on the door as you exit the DFAC: Personnel are allowed only two items from the DFAC. Nobody says anything to Mr. Deen.

I picture Mr. Deen as a character on *Seinfeld*. I've seen him at the condiment counter in the DFAC, laying down his newspaper with his plastic shopping bag on top of it. He'll dump a container full of sugars or creamers into his shopping bag and fold his newspaper to hide the evidence. As he's doing it, he has that Newman look: mischievous yet so clever. When he returns to the office with the goods, he stacks the coffee creamers meticulously like he's building a tower from a deck of cards. All the creamer labels and water bottle labels face the same direction. Maybe he's a little OCD, but that's okay because I'm a little OCD myself and I love that.

For the weeks ahead, I take Mr. Deen under my wing. He follows me around like a lost puppy. He stays curious and intrigued to see what I'm up to and how I do certain things. He's always in the office before me. He keeps an eye on what time I come walking through the office door every morning between 6:30 and 7:00, and makes a mental note of it. One morning I oversleep and don't put in my contact lenses before leaving. Mr. Deen watches me closely as I do it at work. He says in his quick-fired tongue, *"IdidNotknowYOUwearContactLenses!"* After I pop in one lens, I look at him with all seriousness and respond in a low voice, *"These are not contacts. They're top-secret spy cameras. I really work for the CIA."* He bursts into a chuckle. I ask him, *"Why are you laughing? Haven't you heard of James Bond or 007? That's me."* He just sits back in his oversized chair, laughing.

Goran takes off to greet all the new hires at the flight line. The time of the flight arrival varies by the day. Sometimes he's out there early; other days it's late afternoon. The times of arrival for the planes are always tentative. Goran always comes back to the office to report to me about all the good-looking women who arrived. Since part of his job is to account for people and manifest people to other bases within the country, all the new hires come by our office. When he comes into the office with an entourage of new people, he rudely knocks the back of my chair to signal me to look at a hot woman. He should know I'm gay and that Greg is my partner. I have a picture of us on my screensaver. With the way he acts, one wouldn't be able to tell that he's married with two daughters back home.

Every morning I drag Goran outside to the back of the office to do push-ups. The flight is never here before 11:00 a.m., so I always make sure we get in three sets each before he takes off to the flight line. He gripes every morning, but he goes along with it. Mr. Deen stands, watches, and counts how many we do. Sometimes he'll call out Goran for not having his chest low enough to the ground or for not reaching the goal that I set for the day.

As I'm doing my set of push-ups one day, a very attractive young lady from Kosovo comes out of the office next to ours and watches us. She's wearing a tight-knit black sweater that shows off her defined figure. Her jeans are stylish and rest well on her hips with a thick, black leather belt wrapped around her waist. Her hair is long and fresh, and her makeup is light with bright-red lips. She is beautiful and athletic, and has a gorgeous figure. I know beauty when I see it.

I finish my set of push-ups, look at this admirable young woman, and ask her if she wants to do a set. I think maybe doing a few push-ups may puncture her femininity—her hair falling out of place or her sweater popping out of her jeans. But she says, *"Sure, I'll show you how a woman does it!"* She gets down on the ground and starts pumping out reps. Goran's eyes are growing larger as he watches her move up and down, her breasts almost touching the ground.

The woman pops up after her set and Mr. Deen shouts out, *"Twenty!"* She did a set of 20 reps. That may have put Goran over the top because he's only been doing sets of seven or eight, maybe a set of twelve. After she's done, she claps the dust off her hands and tucks in her sweater, and I ask her what her name is. She says her name is Hedia, but everyone calls her "Lucky." I introduce Goran, Mr. Deen, and myself. I tell her we're out here every morning if she wants to join us. After the brief introduction, she goes back to her office. I look over at Goran and query him, *"Am I going to have to pick up your tongue off the ground and pop your eyes back into their sockets?"* He acknowledges, *"Yeah, man. Now I do push-ups every day!"* Lucky never joined us again for push-ups.

One of the things that I love and will remember about Rupert is when I asked him if I could take a few hours off in the middle of the day to work out and shower. Most everyone else has a regimented schedule that they stick to like clockwork, but he had the most sincere and awesome reply: *"Thomas, it's hard enough being here. You do whatever you have to. Take care of yourself."* So every day I split the office and head out around 3:00 p.m. to work out and shower. Besides, there are fewer people in the gym, all the showers are open, and there's always plenty of hot water. I'm also in limbo with my job duties and responsibilities, and I focus on myself more just to keep my sanity.

Before I head to the gym, I take a workout supplement. I put a scoop of the powder in a cup and mix it with water. Mr. Deen—like a little kid—is watching what I'm doing. As I drink the supplement, he looks at me with curiosity and asks, *"WhatisDat youtake?"* I tell him it's my secret formula. Now every day when he sees me take it, he looks at me and smiles and says, *"yorSeecret fomUla, eh?"* and then he laughs. I must be a very interesting American spectacle for him to observe. He seems to laugh at a lot of things that I do.

The following day I get up from my desk to go to the gym around 2:30 p.m. Mr. Deen sees that I'm ready to leave the office and asks, *"WhereDoYouGoNow?"* I reply truthfully, *"To the gym."* He looks at his watch, gasps a little air, and says, *"not thwee o'clock yet."* I reply, *"So?"* He laughs as though I am tied to a strict schedule and breaking the rules. He thinks it's hilarious that I leave work for a couple hours in the middle of the day to work out.

Mr. Deen lives on the other side of base in one of those lovely clamshell tents with 399 of his closest friends. He shuttles back and forth every day. He tells me about the long wait for the shuttle on some mornings and how he's had to wait up to two hours. That sounds all too familiar. I'm surprised it hasn't improved by now, but with the influx of new people and military surge taking place, I guess it's to be expected. He continues to inform me that he wants to bring his laundry to the west side to drop it off because the laundry service on the east side is always closed before he leaves for work and after he returns. I tell him there's an easy solution: He needs to come to work late after he drops off his laundry and leave work early to pick it up. He thinks my solution is funny: coming in late and leaving early. He's so regimented.

I think of myself as a hybrid generation caught between the Baby Boomers and Generation X. I share common work ethics and values of both generations. Since the generational gaps are more of a Western ideology, Mr. Deen seems to do as he is instructed, which is traditional for him in his homeland. As my boss told me and I tell Mr. Deen, *"This place is hard enough. You need to take care of yourself over here. Nobody else is going to do that for you."*

Tex

Returning to Bagram, I bring a little slice of home with me: my Resistol Denison straw hat, a summer cowboy hat made from Shantung straw. Greg has a knack for spotting the perfect hat to fit my head. We walk into a store; he picks out a cowboy hat, plunks it on my head, and tells me that's the one. So now I have this summer straw hat with me in Afghanistan to protect my head from the sun. The brim shades my neck and the hat breathes. With the afternoons warming up and the blazing summer right around the corner, I know it will come in handy.

A few weeks after my return from R&R, I walk into the office wearing the hat. Scott, the first guy to greet me, says, *"Well hello, Tex."* I reply, *"Good morning."* Mr. Deen comments at 100 miles per hour, *"You look VeryVeryNice in DatHat."* Goran tells me I really stand out in the crowd wearing the hat. In his deep Macedonian jovial tone, he says, *"Now everybody knows that you're a big ol' redneck from Texas!"* I think, *"How rude,"* but reply, *"I beg your pardon?"* It's actually kind of funny hearing a big ol' guy from the Balkans say that in his Serbian accent. Then he adds that I would be a good target for a Taliban sniper. I tell him that's why I always ask him to walk with me—since he's tall. He's my bodyguard, an easier target, and can take the hit for me. We laugh.

I'm flattered by all the attention my hat gets when I walk through the door. That's their way of telling me how much they missed me.

Three days in a row, I pass an older military man in uniform—maybe a master sergeant, chief, or colonel. I just assume that the old-timers in the military have rank. Each day he spots me in passing on the sidewalk. The first day he says, *"I sure do like that hat!"* The second day he calls out, *"I really, really like that hat!"* The third day he exclaims, *"I just love that hat!"* I think maybe I should give it to him or tell him to order one online. I bet he doesn't know his hat size.

Some of the local Afghan men working on base stare at me when I'm wearing my cowboy hat, like they've never seen one before. It's like their eyes are saying, *"Wow . . . a cowboy!"* Ha, if they only knew I'm only an urban cowboy. Hey, maybe they're keeping an eye on me to see if I leave it somewhere so they can snatch it up.

I seem to be more approachable wearing my hat. Wherever I am, it seems like people draw up conversation with me easier. I've only seen a couple other guys wearing them around base, which kind of surprises me considering the number of Texans, bubbas, and good ol' boys working over here. Of course, they wouldn't look as good as me in this thing.

Mona Lee Cartwright

"Here comes trouble!" says Mr. Deen. Mona Lee Cartwright just walked through the back door of our office. She's an older Texas gal who transitioned over to Barron from RBK. She's been on this project for a while, and I can tell by the way she speaks and handles herself that she's been raised on a ranch around men. She always wears jeans, a collared buttoned-down shirt, and boots. While most Texans I know speak with a slow tongue, Mona Lee Cartwright is just the opposite. She's spunky, outspoken, witty, and sometimes naughty. She has a laugh like the Wicked Witch of the West. *"I'll get you, my pretty!"*

Mona Lee left quite an impression the day I met her. She was at the flight line to pick up a few new HR staff. I introduced her to one of her new coworkers, Shpetjtim. She asked him to repeat his name. She looked at him inquisitively as she studied his lips. She asked him to repeat his name a couple times and then to write it down. She looked at the spelling of his name and said, *"Honey, we're not going to call you that. We're going to give you an American name. Your name is Tim."* T-I-M are the last three letters of his real name. Tim didn't mind. In fact, he kind of liked his new American name. Mona Lee renamed a lot of the other foreign nationals with American names. That's just Mona Lee.

As Mona Lee walks through the door, she has a mischievous grin on her face. Although she's in our office frequently to scan paperwork from our copier, Mr. Deen and I can tell she has other intentions. She walks right by the copier and directly over to Keith's desk. She opens his email and types a quick memo, sends it, and closes the application.

Mr. Deen and I watch her suspiciously. If she's using someone else's computer, we know she's up to no good. After she logs off the computer, I look at her and ask, *"Mona Lee, what are you up to?"* She bursts out with her Wicked Witch of the West laugh that pleads her guilty of doing something wrong. She gladly reports to Mr. Deen and me, *"I wrote Charles a love letter from Keith's email."* Charles is a site manager, close friends with Keith, and sits across from him. In fact, both men are at lunch together. Mr. Deen and I burst with laughter because only Mona Lee could get away with that. It's against HR policy to be using someone else's computer login. She could get herself fired and Keith could get fired for leaving his computer unlocked and unattended.

As Mona Lee is walking toward the back door, she tells Mr. Deen and me to instant message her when Keith and Charles come back into the office. We do, and Mona Lee promptly returns so she can capture the expression on Charles's face when he reads the email. Sure enough, Charles's initial reaction is a nod of the head, a double take, and a squint of the eyes to see if he's reading the message correctly. Then he turns around and looks at Keith without saying a word and with a grimace on his face.

Mona Lee captures his expression and confronts him, *"What's going on, Charles? You look a little perplexed. Did someone send you an email?"* That's a dead giveaway to Charles. He knows Mona Lee and knows she probably had something to do with it. Charles looks back at the email to see what time it was sent and knows he and Keith were at lunch at that time. We all laugh, leaving Keith clueless to what just transpired.

The Interview

Craigslist doesn't exist for Afghanistan, but what I learned from a few of the military guys is that if you're looking for a hookup, they post under Iraq with the Afghanistan camp name for specific location. Very sly and tricky, and there are plenty of guys who have caught on to this for man-on-man casual sex. When I see a Bagram posting under Iraq Casual Encounters, I reply and meet Max.

Max's real name is Momchil. He's from Bulgaria. He goes by Max because people were starting to call him Mom for short and he didn't like that. When I think of Bulgarian men, I think Max fits the picture. He's tall, in his late twenties or early thirties, bearded, and muscular. He has a heavy accent too, and he doesn't use articles such as "the" or "a" or "an" when he speaks. It makes his English sound very choppy.

Both of us are in the same village, so we agree to meet in the showers one night, as neither one of us has a private room. Sure enough, late in the evening while most of the camp is in bed sleeping, the shower house is empty. We both take a separate shower across from each other, but Max comes over to mine for some man-on-man action and offers quite a bit more than just a back scrub.

Max is a lot of fun. He's young and horny all the time. Eventually he gets a temporary room during his last few weeks of closing up work ends and out-processing. He texts me to join him for casual sex since I'm close by. Very rarely do I pass up the opportunity, and sometimes when I show up there's another guy or soldier to join in on the fun.

He finds these guys from posting ads on Craigslist. I follow suit and post a few ads. When I meet up with another guy, they all seem to know Max. He gets around.

Max works for RBK. He's one of the last few stragglers still hanging on with RBK now that they're closing out their contract agreement. He informs me that after his contract is up, he would like to take a break from LOGCAP for a few months. He's been doing this for a few years but said he'd probably return because the money is good and it goes a long way back in his home country. I ask him if he has any hiring connections with Barron. He really doesn't, so I tell him I can introduce him to Sam.

Sam works in management and has some influence in hiring decisions. He's a few years younger than me, masculine with a nice firm chest and big biceps. I've seen him at the gym, where he's always working out with a Filipino bodybuilder. He's also Trixxie's boss. I have a pretty good hunch Trixxie's a lesbian, and when I ask a gay Air Force guy how to meet other gay guys on base, he says, *"Ask one of the lesbians. They seem to know a lot of the gay guys."* It's true and it works. I befriend Trixxie and when I ask about her boss, she gives me a lukewarm confirmation. She doesn't want to *out* him but gives me enough affirmation to believe that he is.

Eventually I befriend Sam and we hook up. I'm quite attracted to Sam. He's a good-looking man, but he's a smoker and I just can't get intimate with a smoker. No matter how hard they try to cover up their habit by brushing their teeth or rinsing with mouthwash, the nicotine surfaces back through their pores and skin. The heavier the smoker, the quicker and more pungent the smell or taste surfaces; and Sam smokes quite a bit. I'm not sure if it's his nervous energy, the anxiety of being in a war zone, or the pressure of his job.

Sam is a fun guy too—in and out of bed. He's always interesting and funny to listen to. Sam tells me he's been in Afghanistan for 16 months and I'm his first. Boy, have I opened a can of worms! And the more I listen to Sam and his connections within the company, I realize there's a very complex good ol' boy network that he's a part of. Not just the regular good ol' boys, but a few gay ones, or at least one major one who is high in the ranks. They used to date.

I tell Sam about Max. Of course, Sam wants all the details, so I share how we met and what I know about him. Aside from Max's job here, Sam tunes in more on the sexual encounters I share during our conversation. Sam says he is definitely interested in meeting and interviewing Max before he heads home and leaves base. Sam suggests we meet at his B-hut. But this meeting is not a work interview; it's just to get to know Max more on a personal level. Without clothes. In bed. Having sex.

I escort Max over to Sam's place. I tell Max that Sam wants to "interview" and get to know him before he leaves. To get better acquainted, Sam suggests we get naked and, of course, Max is very receptive to his request. Within minutes, none of us are wearing clothes and we have a wonderful ménage à trois. It's fun and quick, as all three of us need to get back to work. But what a fun midafternoon break.

When Max and I leave Sam's place, Max comments, *"That's the best interview I've ever had!"*

Barron's First Casualty

I hear whistling in the air that awakens me from a deep, sound sleep around 4:00 a.m. I hear the impact with a loud boom. A rocket hits inside the base and vibrates the tent. It's a little too close for comfort—it's damn close. The impact startles me. I freeze lying on my cot, waiting to hear the alarm over The Big Voice, and listen to hear if another incoming rocket follows. There's dead silence. Nobody is moving.

About 10 minutes later and 10 minutes too late, the sirens and The Big Voice go off alerting the people on base that we're under attack. *"Incoming! Incoming! Incoming!"* Again, most of the guys in the tent just roll over and try to go back to sleep, hoping that it's just a bad dream or that it will end very soon. I hear emergency sirens and vehicles drive by and stop within a stone's throw of the tent. There's a ton of commotion taking place outside.

It's Monday, March 15, 2010: The Taliban has launched a predawn rocket attack on Bagram Airfield. Generally the attacks are short and quick because the military can pinpoint the location of the attacker and make an immediate counterattack. Usually it's a rocket or two that will hit outside and rarely inside the base. Most of the time it's a nuisance more than anything else. Is that my complacency speaking? Regardless, the risk of danger is real. It's a game of hit or miss.

It's close to my wake-up time, so I get up to get ready for work and investigate. I walk to the shower room, and there's an ambulance and a few fire trucks in the alleyway between B-huts less than 100 yards from my tent. There's already enough commotion and spectators. I don't need to add to it, so I continue my morning business as usual.

In the office, I'm informed that there are casualties from this morning's attack. There's a fatality and several injured. The rocket hit a B-hut occupied by a Barron subcontractor and all the occupants are firefighters. We've lost one of our own and it marks the first fatality on Barron's watch.

I wait until things calm down and walk by the B-hut where the rocket hit. It's roped off with yellow barricade tape. I can see where the rocket went through the roof and into the guy's room. The person killed is identified as a Bosnian national, Almir. I don't know Almir personally, but I take a moment of silence on his behalf and for his family.

Two things are certain in life: your birth and your death. You can't turn back time. Almir was only 32 years old and had been working in Afghanistan for the past three years or so. His life was cut way too short. His death is a reality check to all of us working in a war zone. The military are not the only ones to put their lives in the path of danger. Almir's death brings the Barron and subcontractor community closer together, as we are all here for similar reasons.

Death in the field is not easy. It affects everyone. I'm not sure how military personnel in combat face it day in and day out. There's also a lot of red tape a Department of Defense (DoD) contractor goes through to get the body back to its point of origin: contacting the military and embassies, dispatching company representatives to notify the family, organizing a flight-line service, and arranging a flight through multiple countries. It's not an easy task.

A flight-line service is held in Almir's honor. A memorial announcement is sent to Barron employees and contractor staff. A few hundred people show up for the service and we line up along the side of the runway. It's dark, blustery, and cool. From the airport lights shining downward, it looks like it's snowing, but it's really the dust and dirt swirling in the air. We huddle closely and quietly next to one another as we watch a fire truck carrying the body of the honored to the awaiting plane that will take him to his final resting place.

As his colleagues lower the casket from the fire truck and carry it to the plane, the people stand in lines of formation. For many of us, including me, it's our first flight-line ceremony. We aren't sure what is expected of us other than our presence, thoughts, and prayers. Is there a right way or a wrong way I should feel? I'm not sure where or how I should stand. I look around and follow the stance of the career military men who have done this many times before: chin up, face forward, back and shoulders straight, legs spread slightly wide, and left hand over the abdomen with the right hand grasping the left wrist.

As we stand at attention on the sideline away from the plane, a smaller ceremony at the loading door of the plane is taking place. There's light shining from the plane's rear loading door onto the runway. I can see the pulpit and a small group gathered around it. There's complete silence while the chaplain speaks. I can't quite make out what he's saying but imagine the words of the prayer being shared. The coffin is loaded and strapped down in the plane and an American flag is draped over it.

As I stand in peace observing the service, tears well up in my eyes. I can hear sniffles among the crowd. The people are numb, trying to piece together and understand the meaning of death, questioning their own mortality and vulnerability. I don't know how to help others cope with the loss as I work through my own grief. For now I only offer and accept hugs.

Trigger

Trigger and Rupert are practically bumping into each other as one arrives and the other is leaving. Trigger has his boots on the ground as of today and Rupert will be gone tomorrow. There's no exchange of duties or any information. Trigger is starting from a clean slate.

Trigger is not what I expect. I'm expecting a lean, fit, muscular guy— someone who is regimented in his or her routine, highly disciplined with years of physical training. Trigger is stocky and stout but muscular. I don't picture abs of steel under his white-and-blue pinstripe shirt. As Goran says, *"Man, that guy looks like he ate the watermelon whole."* Where is my superhero, the man I envisioned wearing blue-and-red tights under his work clothes, with a bulging chest busting out at the seams? Where are the bulging biceps and small, lean waist? Like the superhero, the image and fantasy of my Navy Seal has been shattered.

Trigger's wife, Munera, is also here and is one of the first Barron employees I met several months ago. She obviously came on board months before her husband and is now spearheading the Afghan First program. The program is an initiative under Former U.S. Ambassador

Karl W. Eikenberry to hire local nationals to perform specific job functions and develop skills under American supervision on base. The program also encourages local procurement of Afghan products and improving the well-being of the Afghan people. The program employs approximately 10,000 local workers in Northern Afghanistan on the 70-plus bases that Barron maintains and services. Her program already has a lot of recognition by Barron and the military as well as other entities, such as the Korean Vocational Technical Institute, the Egyptian Hospital, and NATO.

I love talking with Munera. She speaks clearly and eloquently with a slight accent that I can't pinpoint. I really have no idea of her nationality. She always seems to use the precise word and technical lingo to explain her program, what it is, and where it is going. She speaks of the program with confidence, enthusiasm, and passion. So after meeting with Munera a couple times, I finally ask her, *"Munera, I love your accent. Where are you from originally?"* She smiles and replies, *"I'm from Algeria."* I respond, *"Oh really? I did my Peace Corps service in Tunisia and my assignment was close to the Algerian border."*

She adds that she and her husband got married in Tunis. Of course, that sparks more conversations between us and forms a common interest. Munera has been working in this region for many years. Arabic is her first language. French is her second. English is her third or fourth. I think she speaks about seven different languages.

I spend day after day with Trigger. I introduce him to the movers and the shakers of Barron LOGCAP. I can tell he is a thinker and an observer, taking it all in. I watch his special operations-trained eyes dart around the room, tracking, monitoring, and gathering information on all the activity. He becomes comfortable in his new leadership position very quickly. We bounce lots of ideas and experiences off one another, develop a plan for the training department, and start to act. Trigger has great leadership skills and preparation stressing an enduring commitment to individual initiative, personal responsibility, and mission accomplishment. He knows how to and will hold people accountable. He gets names and phone numbers, and sets a deadline. Unexpectedly, I find that I like working with him.

Trigger hires a third person to join our team. Her name is Cathy with a C. That's how I'll remember her. She earned her college degree from Penn State through a track scholarship—running and javelin—and is a former captain in the military. What's interesting about both Trigger and Cathy is that they gave up their lifestyles as power athletes. Kaput! Done. They hung it up after years and years of training and conditioning. Cathy vowed she would never participate in a track event after college. Trigger did about three hours a day of intense workout and training during his career with the Navy. He retired from the military a few years ago and hasn't set foot in a gym since. He tells me that he smoked and chewed tobacco up until the time he arrived in Greenville a few weeks ago for his in-processing and training, and then quit cold turkey.

Goran and I invite Trigger to do push-ups with us. Mr. Deen tags along to watch. It's great to have Trigger as part of our push-up team. Perhaps the invite will inspire him to get back in shape. With his background and plethora of physical training, he's instituting a Seal-inspired training program for us. I never knew there were so many kinds of push-ups: standard, wide-arm, military, diamond, incline, feet elevated, dive-bombers, Spiderman, clappers, one-arm, and handstand. I'm psyched to be doing all these different kinds of push-ups, but some of them are a bit extreme for me. I guess I'll never be a Navy Seal!

For a while Goran is really enjoying the pump and his new look. He grabs the mirror off my desk and flexes his muscle. When he knows I'm listening, he looks at me while admiring himself in the mirror and says, *"Why couldn't I have been born rich instead of handsome?"* Goran's heart is not into our daily push-up routine, so he makes up a lot of excuses not to join us.

As Trigger and I do our morning routine day after day on the back porch of our B-hut office, we get a few onlookers. One of the first questions they ask is, *"How old are you guys?"* We are flattered and laugh at that question. I am soon to be 49 and Trigger is 47, yet we're in much better shape than some of these 20- or 30-somethings. Trigger recently ordered a pair of "perfect push-ups" too, so now we each have our set with rotating handles.

Cathy with a *C* is scooped up by another department and leaves us almost as quickly as she joined us. I don't think any dust settled on her desk. She and the new country HR manager, Huggy McPherson, apparently don't care for one another, and rumor has it that he pushed her out of the department. My speculation is that Cathy is lesbian, outspoken, and assertive, and ol' "touchy-feely" Huggy doesn't like that about her. He has his own plan that includes bringing over his transition team favorites into HR.

Mr. Deen tells me that he saw Trigger in the gym last night lifting three 45-pound plates on each side of the bar. That's close to 300 pounds with the bar. He continues to tell me how the bar was gently curved in the center from all the weight on each side. I think, *"Is Mr. Deen stalking Trigger? What was Mr. Deen doing in the gym anyway?"* He just magically appears wherever.

I catch Mr. Deen smoking a cigarette outside. I didn't realize he smoked. He hides it well or at least he's a very light smoker. As I walk by the smoking area, I wag my finger at him in disapproval. I hear him snicker from a distance and see the smoke escaping from his mouth. I shout to him, *"I've got my eye on you, Mr. Deen!"*

Hunter

"Office?" pops up as a text message on my cell phone. *"Yes?"* I reply right back. *"I'm outside,"* the next text reads. It's late in the evening and Hunter knows I'm alone in the office after a certain hour. Hunter

is on the quiet side. He communicates with me mainly through text messaging or emails. When he does, the messages are extremely short—just a word or two. He's trained and conditioned that way to keep his communication very vague when replying.

Hunter is slightly taller than me, in his early to mid-forties, and has a beautiful and firm stature. He's a U.S. Army Mountain Ranger. A tag reveals his earned status as an elite infantry ranger, which he wears on his upper shoulder of his left sleeve of his uniform. He is trained to carry 65 to 100 pounds of weapons to fight with in enemy territory, usually in rough surroundings, and his great physical shape obviously shows it. As a Ranger he's sent on hazardous missions at the cutting edge of battle. His Ranger special training is mountaineering. Who only knows where he's been in these mountains of Afghanistan?

His concise but vague communication is another indication that he is well trained in situational awareness and operational security. The enemy is always near and listening. Hunter does not trust who may be within hearing distance. If he is sent on a mission, his reply to me is usually, *"Traveling."* There is no who, what, where, when, or why. I don't dare ask. I really don't want to know, as I would never want it to be heard or intercepted in satellite communications that give away his position. I notice his Velcro name tag has been removed. I'm not even sure if Hunter is his real name. My friendship with him is adventurous, spontaneous, and risky.

I go to my office door. Sure enough, he is standing outside my door in uniform with a full backpack on his back. It looks like he just returned from a mission, but in reality he just finished his laundry. He comes up the steps and into my office. It's not the first time he's come by for a late-night visit. He has something more on his mind. He locks the office door behind him and turns off the lights. The computer screens in the room illuminate dark, vibrant colors and shadows.

Hunter takes off his hat and unstraps his backpack to remove a blanket that he promptly sets on a worktable. We grin ear to ear at each other; we know what's coming next. He pulls me close to him and soon our tongues are twisting, tangling, and teasing each other. The uniform and clothes come off. The blanket is dropped and spread on the office floor. We lie down and explore each other's body from lips to toes. Our desires are stirring and stimulating. The feeling is sensual, lustful, and intense. His naked, buff body feels good next to mine. When we finish, we rest and lie next to each other for a while, just holding and cuddling each other. My intimate time with Hunter helps both of us escape momentarily from the hellhole that surrounds us. Granted, Hunter isn't the first or last guy to have sex with me in the office.

Hunter is endlessly impulsive and audacious. I never know when I will see him next or where we're going to meet. I'm glad to say that I get to see him quite often during his time on Bagram. Timing is everything. During the day, I break away from work to meet him at my tent, despite it being filthy. My bed space and wardrobe are blocked off with sheets to form a makeshift room and provide a very thin barrier of privacy. Everyone works days, so the risk of being heard or caught is minimal. We've even ended up in the showers together in the middle of the afternoon. Yup, the office, the showers, the bunkers—wherever we can find privacy. I've recently heard some guys talk about doing it in the porta john. I do have my limits.

During the six or eight weeks of knowing Hunter, our conversations remain minimal. What I know about the man is only skin deep. His stature and looks are beautiful. On our last night together, we invite Max to join us in the office. He gladly accepts and we leave Hunter with a bang to remember. After Max leaves, Hunter tells me that he is married with kids. He's heading back home to them and I will never hear from him again.

Baserunners

Momentum is building among my Barron colleagues to participate in running events. I have started a networking group of runners and keep them informed of upcoming events: 5Ks, 10Ks, 10-milers, half marathons, full marathons—there are enough running events to fit anyone's running ability or appetite. The events also provide a great opportunity to participate with our military personnel and meet some of the coordinators of the events.

I'm not a competitive runner. I just enjoy it to clear my head. It makes my body feel good and keeps me fit. It certainly helps improve my mood and emotional balance. It gives me peace. Running on base is more like trail running, which helps my coordination. Parts of the road are unpaved and combined with obstacles such as rocks (lots of rocks), sinkholes, fine dust, and mud. I learn quickly to maintain better control to prevent slips and falls.

It's also a great social networking opportunity. We're all striving for similar goals and results. My network of Barron runners has grown to about 50 runners. About a third of those folks are always on R&R in accordance to our rotation cycle, so we can have anywhere from 25 to 35 runners participating in an event. My coconspirator, Erin, helps to network and encourage people to participate. Clever Erin also came up with the name of our group: the Baserunners—runners who run around the base.

Organizing and notifying our group of the runs brings me great pleasure. It's wonderful to meet so many like-minded people and learn from the experienced runners. It's a bonus to help encourage and share knowledge with walkers and novice runners. I get to help them reach the goal of running a 5K and to maintain or further that goal. We have a great mix of people across all age groups, ethnicities, and sexes. It's a very positive and uplifting experience and a wonderful way to start the day. There are T-shirts for most of the runs, so now the competition is to see who can collect the most shirts. My goal for participating in all these runs is to collect as many as I can and have a quilt made from my collection.

Distance, occasion, and weather determine who and how many will show up for an event. Shorter distances, good weather, and a good-looking T-shirt will always draw the most runners. Fortunately, for major holiday running events like Fourth of July and September 11, the military has corporate sponsors that provide T-shirts and other running goodies for several thousand runners. I'm told those two events draw 4,000 to 5,000 runners each on a base of 35,000 people.

As we gather for the runs, I look for the Baserunners team. I try to greet each one by name with a handshake or hug, depending upon how well I know them. I introduce people to one another. We gather as a group, do a pre-run warm-up, and try to take a group photo if someone brings a camera.

Most of the runs have a 0500 show time and a 0530 sharp start time. The mornings in spring, summer, and fall are generally gorgeous. The birds are chirping loudly in the trees as the sun rises over the Hindu Kush and shines through the trees. The temperatures are perfect for running and draw a crowd of runners eager to start their day. Runners move from the staging area like a herd of cows.

Earbuds are generally prohibited or discouraged during a run. An announcement about the earbuds may be made at the beginning of a run, but it's not always enforced. I pop mine into my ears. I always have a playlist ready for a run to keep me motivated every step of the way. The run starts at the sound of a bullhorn, whistle, or someone with a megaphone broadcasting, *"On your mark . . . get set . . . go!"*

Most of us start off at a casual and comfortable pace. I start off with a few of the Baserunners, but some run ahead of me and others fall behind. I just go at my own pace, making sure I'm not breathing too heavily. I'm usually one of the top finishers in our group, so I try to stay at the finish line to cheer on runners and give each Baserunner a high five. I usually don't wait for the stragglers but make my way to the showers to be at work by 7:00 a.m.

At the office, the HR country manager I report to—and whom I encouraged to run with us—compliments me for bringing the group together. He tells me that he watched me interact with the Baserunners and is amazed that I know everyone and take the time to greet and introduce them. He adds that it's a great leadership quality. I tell him my leadership skills do not always come naturally, but they are learned and practiced. After all, I am in the learning and development profession. I take it as a compliment. I'm glad he noticed it and mentioned it, as I will make a concentrated effort to bring that quality to every run like I do in most work meetings.

I have a number of runners asking me when Barron is going to host a 5K. The timing couldn't be better. One of Barron's corporate values is safety. Every year and all over the world, company projects and office locations celebrate safety awareness by hosting a week of events in April. So I talk to the HR country manager about Barron hosting a 5K for its safety week. I present a short proposal and cost for T-shirts. He takes my proposal and presents the idea to our country management staff and safety committee. At first there are a few concerns on liability, and then a question of business ethics comes into play as it's presumed that sponsoring the event may influence business decisions. Good grief, it's a fun run, people! All sorts of businesses sponsor these kinds of events on base to promote health and community. Fortunately those concerns are not dragged out into deep technical and legal discussions, and without further ado, our vice president writes a check to cover the cost of T-shirts for the event.

There's a lot of logistics and organization that goes along with event planning. It's not like we can just get out there and run; it takes a lot of effort. I get the paperwork together to get approval from the base command. The military is always excellent, working with the sponsors and approving any physical activity or event that promotes health and fitness, as long as it doesn't impact personnel or a mission, or create a target of danger. I'm supported with a show of enthusiasm and motivation, so I gather and organize volunteers, get the command to provide energy drinks and fruit at the finish line, ask the Air Force to provide us with a sound system, organize water and aid stations, and have medics on standby during the event. It's a done deal!

Race morning is cool and rainy, but I'm not going to cancel this event because of a little rain. I tell everyone to proceed to his or her stations. I have our country manager of health, safety, and environment department provide a welcome, course details, and a safety topic. Of course, the safety topic is to be safe running on the wet, slick street. The construction country manager blows the whistle at the starting line, but the whistle fails. With his quick wit, he shouts out, *"On your mark . . . get set . . . go!"*

We have a good turnout and just enough T-shirts to give to each runner as they finish. All in all, it's a successful event bringing unity to the community.

HRC Cap

As a Human Rights Campaign (HRC) supporter, advocate, and activist for the lesbian, gay, bisexual, and transgender (LGBT) communities, I own a couple of clothing articles to show my support. One of the items I sport is an HRC cap that I brought with me to Afghanistan.

Most folks don't know HRC or what the logo signifies. The logo—a yellow equal sign in a navy-blue rectangle—is their symbol for equality. I figure that those who know what it means might trigger conversation or a smile. I get a few looks and smiles from wearing mine. It's my way to show my subtle opposition of the military's "Don't Ask, Don't Tell" policy. I've had a few people—women and men—smile and wink at me when I'm wearing it.

Kathleen and I go to lunch and I wear my cap. Of course, when entering the chow hall, everyone is required to remove his or her hat. I put mine on the table while we eat. After we finish lunch, Kathleen and I walk out the door and start walking back to the office when I realize I left it on the table. I walk back to the table where we sat, but the hat is gone. I ask the DFAC staff of Afghan workers if any of them picked it up or turned it in. Nobody claimed to have seen the hat. For several days I keep checking with the DFAC staff to see if someone turned it in. It never turns up. The hat was relatively new and I figure one of the Afghan workers thought it was a "cool *American* cap" and took it.

I smile because I know somewhere in Afghanistan is a guy wearing the cap without a clue what it stands for—or maybe he does?

Tickled

Mr. Deen appears tickled by something this morning. He can't stop laughing as he tries to tell me a story that happened last night during an incoming attack:

> Mr. Deen sleeps in a tent and the occupants are scrambling through it to get to a bunker during the incoming alert. As he makes his way to the exit, he sees this American guy sound asleep in the bottom bunk. As Mr. Deen tells it, *"da American was sleeping like baby."* Military security bursts into the tent and starts yelling orders to get to the bunkers. When the military tells you to do something, you do it!
>
> Mr. Deen continues with his story, *"Guy in the bottom rack still asleep, no budge."* The guy in the top bunk jumps onto the floor and shakes the entire bed, startling and waking the American in the bottom bunk. The American is dazed and starts shouting at the guy, *"What the fuck are you doing, man?"* The guy tells him, *"We're under attack! Get to the bunker!"* Mr. Deen observes all of this in a matter of seconds and is so humored by what

is taking place. I can just picture him standing there taking it all in. He keeps repeating the American's reaction: *"What the fuck you doin', man?"* and cackling like a hyena. Mr. Deen is easily amused.

One of the many hats that I wear for Barron is proctoring tests for skilled crafts. I administer testing in electrical, HVAC, plumbing, and carpentry to verify skill levels and identify training needs for the job functions in which they were hired. Or at least that's what I did during my first 90 days.

Though I do most of my work by computer, the testing I administer is done the old-fashioned way with test booklets, Scantron sheets, and number-two pencils. The testing is done this way because of the unstable internet connection in the field. We can't rely on it to stay up for the length of the exam and the speed is awful. Most days it takes about five minutes just to refresh or update a page. It might as well be dial-up.

I have an old turn-crank pencil sharpener mounted to my desk, which I use to keep the number-two test pencils sharp. One day a young guy from Bosnia is in the office and asks me what it is. I thought he was joking. Mr. Deen is within earshot of our discussion. I reply in a serious tone, *"It's a fingernail clipper. You put your finger in the hole and turn the lever and it trims your nails."* I hear Mr. Deen chuckling behind me. The kid from Bosnia is serious. He really doesn't know what a pencil sharpener is. I guess nowadays with electronics, one rarely uses a pencil. Mr. Deen gets a good laugh about it. After the young man leaves our office, Mr. Deen, laughing, stands alongside my desk and pretends he's going to trim his fingernails by putting his finger up to the pencil hole.

Mr. Deen has become my entertainment. I love having him around. I know my way around base fairly well and have a number of tasks I need to accomplish today. I feel sorry for Mr. Deen because he tries so hard to occupy himself and please others while he waits for his orders, so I invite him to go along with me. I drag him along to the DHL office along the airstrip to mail documents with wet signatures back to headquarters. He's never been in the PX, so I take him there. I tell him the PX is open to all, but he thinks I am wrong and he's not allowed in there. I can't convince him to go inside with me, so he waits patiently outside. I think he really just wanted to have a cigarette while I did my thing in the PX. When I come out of the store, he's sitting on a bench with his feet barely touching the ground, swinging his legs back and forth like a little kid.

We head over to the Army post office. Mr. Deen spots a shopping cart loaded with boxes. He says, *"I need shopping trolley to bring to DFAC,"* and we laugh. I like how he uses the word *trolley* instead of *cart*. I picture him hauling the shopping cart to the DFAC and loading up on all sorts of things like he's in a grocery store: the creamers, sugars, sodas, and snacks. Then I can see him wheeling the shopping cart across the gravel parking lot to our office. It's another *Seinfeld* snippet!

Before we head back to the office, we stop for lunch. He can't believe that the dining room serves leftover fresh fruit from the morning as a fruit salad in the afternoon. I ask him how he knows. He tells me that he just knows. As he's ranting about this unacceptable behavior, another snippet of *Seinfeld* travels through my mind. I picture him sneaking into the dining facility and peeking around a corner, watching the kitchen staff do this. I see his jaw dropping as he witnesses this and runs out of the dining facility to tell all his friends: Jerry, Elaine, George, and Kramer. They get into an uproar and all hell breaks loose.

Mr. Deen gets mad when he tells the server he wants one scoop of rice and he gives him two. He follows up with a rant about how the DFAC serves beef stew for lunch and changes the name to beef stroganoff for dinner and how they always have pasta for lunch and dinner. They did that yesterday. They can't fool Mr. Deen. He loves his fresh iceberg lettuce, cucumbers, and fruit. He puts raisins on a lot of things. He loves ice cream (with raisins), but only one scoop. I get two scoops and he nods his head back and forth in disapproval. I guess that's how he stays so skinny.

Mr. Deen tells me that he likes talking to me because he can understand me. He said I speak clearly and slowly, and enunciate my words. I put forth the effort, especially when speaking to non-native speakers. He said he can't understand some of the guys in the office: some mumble, some have unique accents, some run their words together or cut off the end of words, and others use a lot of slang. Most of them can't understand Mr. Deen simply because he speaks at supersonic speed. I usually end up interpreting for both parties, including his current direct report.

Mr. Deen is an observant man. He's fascinated by the American culture. During our conversation at lunch he asks me, *"DoyouknowhowAmericansgreetoneanother?"* How do Americans greet one another? I'm not sure what he's asking, so I reply, *"How?"* He says, *"They don't ask how you are or say good morning. They ask, what are you doing?"* I always thought this was a West Texas thing that only Greg's family does. This triggers another rampage by Mr. Deen on how ridiculous and improper it is. He says if someone asks him that he'll reply, *"I'm talking to you."* I ask Mr. Deen, *"You know what I would tell them?"* He responds, *"What would you say?"* I tell him, *"I'm dodging bullets!"*

Mr. Deen finally gets his orders to go to another base. I'm out of the office, and when I arrive at work the next morning he's already gone. I'm sad to see him go.

I wait a couple of days and call him on his cell phone. Instead of saying, *"Hello, how are you?"* I greet him with his pet peeve, *"What are you doing?"* He knows it's me right away, laughs, and says at warp speed, *"YouAmerican! I'mdodgingbulletshere, eh?"* It's a little more difficult for me to understand him on the phone.

Cell phone calls are often dropped in the field. I call Mr. Deen a few times to see how it's going. His site has been under a lot of attacks, and I know he does not like being there. I try to call him a few more times, but his phone will not receive calls. Eventually the phone calls stop. I'm sure if he left the project, he would have come through BAF to tell me or at least relay the message through a friend.

More time passes and I have not heard from him or seen him. I'll have to track him down in Sri Lanka one day.

The Simple Things

Gnarly, knotted trees line Disney Drive. They are frail and deformed from years of exposure to the desolate, harsh Hindu Kush winters and the dry, arid summers. It looks like there are only three varieties of trees. Two of the trees are deciduous and the other is a type of pine. I'm told the Russians planted all of them during their occupation of Afghanistan, December 1979 to February 1989.

The trees come to life in March. One variety sprouts clusters of little white flowers that look like jasmine—bunches of tiny white petals with yellow pistons. The bees are very much in love with this flower. The blooms last about a month and fall to the ground, and then the branches sprout bright-green, fern-like leaves that drape the low-hanging branches. I think it is an acacia tree or a close relative.

The other deciduous tree blossoms bouquets of raspberry-pink flowers. It reminds me of a Texas crepe myrtle, but I know it is not. From a distance they look like bunches of pink grapes in their triangular clusters. The leaves are small and round like an aspen.

The pine trees tower over everything. They have long, bare trunks with a thick, shingled bark. The little birds—maybe some kind of sparrow—love them. They flock to the trees by the hundreds and make all sorts of chatter at dusk and dawn.

One of the construction businesses has a rose garden in front of their entrance. The roses are colors of peach, red, yellow, and orange. After a nice rain shower, they always look so beautiful, but it isn't long before they are dust-blanketed with silt that makes them look dingy and droopy.

There are a few gardeners at Bagram. Some of them have excellent green thumbs, and it shows from their small gardens outside of their B-huts. I've identified hyacinth bean vines and plants of Mexican bush sage, pomegranate, salvias, thistle, spiderwort, and other inferno-loving plants that can handle the dry, nutrient-deprived soil. Some of the gardeners plant their gardens from seeds they brought back from the U.S. Others get their plants from the locals working on base. I've even seen wild poppies pop up in the fields around Bagram. The military cuts down all those dirty, nasty buggers. I laugh because the poppies self-seed. I can't wait to see what pops up next spring.

I relish these spring days: the flowering blooms, the Hindu Kush Mountains with frosted peaks, and the morning perfect weather. I brew a fresh cup of coffee, sit on the back porch of my office, and take in the morning sun. There's no scenery to take in on the back porch anymore. T-walls line the parameter of the base and block any view I once had. The sun peeks over the wall and my face captures its rays as I sit on a bench. I love the feel of the sun on my face and the light in my eyes. I realize I am now in the fourth stage of culture shock: acceptance. It doesn't mean that I understand this culture or the environment, but rather it signifies that understanding is not necessary to function and thrive here. I accept my surroundings for what they are.

Greg sent me pictures of our spring garden in full bloom at home. He took a wonderful picture of our thriving rose garden. I have that picture now as my screensaver. I pretend I'm looking out the kitchen window and fantasize of being home. I miss being home in my own bed, my own house, and my own backyard with my partner and our two dogs. Instead I make do with what's here and enjoy the simple pleasures of life.

Eavesdropping

"I love hearing your voice," he says into the telephone. Then comes the next line, *"What are you wearing now?"* He follows up to her reply with, *"I'm not wearing any underwear."* He continues talking in his low, sexy voice to his sweetheart who is somewhere back home in Idaho. *"I'd love to slip that off of you and kiss your neck,"* he says.

Little does David know that I'm eavesdropping on his conversation. There are only two telephones in our office with direct-line access to the U.S. One of the telephones is next to my desk. He has his back toward me with his ergonomic chair shifted into a low-rider position. He looks comfortable and right at home. When he made the call, he probably didn't think I'd hear him. I have my earbuds in my ears and was listening to some blaring music until a few minutes ago. It's my way to zone out everything around me. Little does he know that the music stopped recently and now I'm privy to this sex talk. I'm waiting for him to start breathing heavily, unbutton his shirt, rub his chest, pinch his nipple, grope himself, or just whip it out and start jerking his cock as his conversation gets more intense. But he doesn't. He's totally blocked out my presence.

There's an aura about David that I can feel. It's a sexual aura that goes beyond his wildest dreams with a woman. I can feel his sexual energy hidden under his redneck attire of his blue-gingham pressed shirt, his tight Wrangler jeans, and his brown leather boots. He has a nice pronounced bubble butt in those jeans. To add to his pseudo-machismo is his talk about guns and a pinch—no, a wad—of Copenhagen tucked into his cheek. There's a permanent embossing of the can in the back pocket of his jeans. He can't fool me. I have my suspicions he could go either way—with a woman or a man. Seismic tremors rumble on my intuitive gaydar.

I'm sure David knows that I'm gay. I don't advertise it around the office, but there are a few subtle hints. First, I talk to Greg every day on the phone. Second, my screensaver is of the two of us (when it's not our rose garden). A few people in the office ask about the other guy on my screensaver. Most think he's my brother. We do look quite a bit alike—muscular, shaved heads, same height. In fact, I probably have a closer resemblance to him than his four blood brothers. But I tell the truth to those who inquire. I tell them it's a picture of my partner and me. I don't know if people talk about it or not. I really don't care.

A couple of weeks pass after David's juicy one-sided conversation. He still doesn't know that it's freshly replaying in my mind. Today he sends me an instant message across the room through the company's online chat. It starts out casual with, *"Hey, how are you doing?"* We exchange a bit of office gossip, and then I tease him and tell him he's part of the office gossip. I provide the details of his nightly smutty phone calls back home with his girlfriend. I recite some of his lines. Our conversation becomes a flirt session. I can sense some of his laughter and sexual eagerness in our conversation. He logs off his computer and leaves the office.

David knows I'm always the last one to leave the office and lock it up at night. Tonight he returns to the office after he knows everyone has gone. He's wearing sweatpants and a T-shirt over his freshly showered body. As he's walking through the door, I can also tell that he's commando under those sweats. I see his stuff jingling side to side. I know he has something else on his mind besides talking on the phone or checking emails. In fact, he's not making any phone calls.

I see he's in the office and acknowledge his presence by walking over to him to start some casual conversation. We're talking and he has his back toward me as he sits in his office chair. We're talking in low, soothing voices about our earlier chat on Instant Messenger. I know David wants me to make a move on him. I can sense it. I can feel it.

There's something about this redneck that begs for a cock up his ass, and he acts so cool, nonchalant, and butch.

I begin to massage his shoulders. I work my hands and fingers with slow deliberate strokes that focus pressure on layers of muscles and tissue under his skin. I can sense and feel his body begin to melt and turn to butter. He turns his head to where his right ear is almost touching his shoulder. I move my face closer to his left cheek to see if he squirms or gets uncomfortable. There's no resistance to closeness, so I begin to kiss his cheek and massage his left ear with my lips.

I position my left hand under his chin and turn his face closer to me. We kiss. I can taste the fresh mint of his mouthwash. As our kisses become more amorous, his mouth begins to breath and sweats his deeply embedded Copenhagen habit. The hot air of his breath turns into a woodsy and earthy mist, and then quickly accelerates into a primordial soup of brown broth and decomposing matter. The kiss has gone from smelling like cool fresh mint to exuding what smells and tastes like shit. I'm grossed out and I pull away from his mouth. The intimacy is lost in the kiss. I'm not sure I can go any further with the kissing, so I pull down the sweat pants and bend him over the desk in front of his computer. Before long we are a solenoid. We are electromagnetic. We convert our energy into linear motion. We are equal and constant, and move along the same axis. I hold his head down on a bed of scattered papers on his desk and fuck him hard.

After it's all done, I grab a piece of gum from my desk to help get rid of the Copenhagen saliva swap. My conservative, corn-fed country boy tells me that he has had sex with men since high school. As he tells me in his own words, *"I was another guy's bitch in high school."* Hearing David tell the story of this relationship, it doesn't sound mutual, loving, or consensual. It sounds more like a forced and bullying relationship. To avoid plight and humiliation in rural America, David has kept this secret to himself. Even after his teenage experience, he still has an attraction to both sexes.

The morning after our escapade in the office, David is back on his computer, looking serious and all work. I instant message him and thank him for the evening. I remind him that I have an aftertaste of his Copenhagen in my mouth and that I'm not happy about it. I tell him he needs to quit that shit if we're ever going to hook up again.

The Gymnast, the Goddess, and the Marine

Almost every afternoon around 5:00, a tall Asian soldier arrives at the Clamshell gym in his Army PT (physical training) black shorts and gray T-shirt. Most days he claims his territory on the parallel bars and the pull-up bar just outside the gym near the pedestrian sidewalk on Disney Drive.

He lifts his body off the ground and onto the parallel bars, supported by his arms. He does about a dozen dips as a warm-up. Then he raises his legs to form a 90-degree angle with his body suspended from the bars. After he works his abs in that position for several minutes, he gracefully leans his head forward with his upper body below the bars and his elbows jutting out from the bar. He slowly raises his legs to his elbows, checks his balance, and raises them straight into the air to form a head-handstand. In the head-handstand position, he continues to do more dips—his chest pumping bigger, his shoulders and triceps bulging, and his upper body flexing with each movement up and down.

The people walking on the sidewalk turn their heads to watch him as he concentrates on his form and routine. Some freeze and stand in awe. The folks working out in the Clamshell gym take long glances at him between their sets. He's in his own little world. I'm not sure he's even aware so many people are watching him.

After he warms up on the parallel bars, he takes a little break and moves on to the pull-up bar. He jumps up to grab the bar and pulls himself up to do chin-ups. He pauses for a bit and allows his body to hang from the bar to stretch. He starts to swing his body like a pendulum. Sometimes he does a full 360-degree circle around the bar. Other times he'll raise his upper body above the bar and do forward somersaults around it. I've seen him hanging upside down like a bat from the bar as he does in-the-air sit-ups.

He twists his body like a pretzel with style and grace. I've never seen him lift weights. His body is naturally V-shaped and developed of lean, sculpted muscle from his gymnastic workout. Very impressive!

One evening I decide to check out the Infantry Village gym near the Polish Compound. The gym is separated into three different buildings. The weight room is a cinder-block building with a cement floor. Next to it is a B-hut lined with floor mats that serves as a calisthenics/yoga/aerobic room. Next to that is the cardio room. B-huts are plywood buildings with low ceilings that resemble a rundown cottage, about 20 by 40 feet. The cardio equipment is crammed into the facility like sardines: treadmills, StairMasters, and stationary cycles. The room holds only about 12 of the machines.

I go to this gym to get in a quick run. I am the only one on the treadmill. As I am running at a leisurely pace of about six miles an hour, a tall black woman comes into the room. She has a lean athletic body, very smooth complexion, short and black wiry hair, and long legs. She is wearing sapphire-blue shorts with a shiny white stripe and a white dry-fit top that fits elegantly against her dark skin. She looks like a Greek goddess.

She takes the treadmill next to me. As I am huffing and puffing at my 10-minute-an-hour pace, she cranks her machine to about a six-minute pace (10 miles an hour)—almost double my speed. She gets into a rhythmic pace, taking strides the length of the treadmill belt. As sweat pours from my skin, runs down my face, and spits all over my machine, she cranks her machine up a few more notches. Out of the corner of my eye, I look at her treadmill dashboard to see her readings. She is running like a panther at a ridiculous pace. She wears me out just watching her long legs gallop in strides the length of the treadmill belt.

We finish our runs about the same time. She probably ran about six or seven miles to my three. I am gushing with sweat that forms a puddle on the floor around my machine. My T-shirt and shorts are soaked. I didn't see a sweat bead on the goddess. I envy her!

Another day at the Clamshell gym, I take the treadmill next to a young, clean-cut kid. He has blond hair, cropped close to his scalp on the side and a bit longer on top to form a flat top. He's wearing fatigue-green sweat bottoms and a fatigue-green T-shirt with "Marines" scribed in black across the chest.

He's clipping along on his treadmill at a pretty good clip. I can hear the Metallica amplifying from his earbuds. I make my music selection on my iPod, get on the treadmill next to him, and get into the groove of my running pace.

A few minutes into my run, I see the Marine's arms flying at his side and above his head. At first I think he's trying to get my attention for something. I look over at him, and his arms are waving firmly up and down, from his left side to the right. He pretends to be playing the drums as he's running on the treadmill at a pretty good pace. I glance over at him quickly and then dart my eyes back to the treadmill dashboard and down at my feet to make sure I am still in line with the running belt. I do this several times—look at the Marine, dashboard, feet . . . Marine, dashboard, feet. I can see the expression on his face as he pretends to play the drums with such fierce emotion. I wonder who and what the hell he is listening to. All I can think of is him losing his balance during one of his drumrolls and flying off the treadmill. He makes me a nervous wreck. I'm glad when he stops and gets off the machine. His workout is complete and he's feeling mighty fine about himself. I can tell as he struts out of the gym, still jamming to his tunes.

A few days later I'm back at the gym on the treadmill. All the treadmills are taken except the one next to me. And who should walk in? The head-banging Marine. I catch a glimpse of him and think, *"Please don't run today. Please don't. Go lift weights or talk to one of your buddies. Please don't take the treadmill next to me. Please don't."* But he does. And I'd rather have the Marine next to me on the treadmill than some of the sweaty, stinky people who come through here.

The Happy Bus

I'm heading to Thailand for my next R&R in just a few more days. As I go through my checklist of things, I realize I don't have a flight confirmation from Dubai Flight Services that provides the air transportation from BAF to Dubai. I contact the Barron travel office. They confirm that they do not have me booked on the flight. Not only that, but the flight is booked full. Shit.

I quickly go through my emails and find my reservation request from two months prior and forward it to the travel office. They acknowledge it's partly their error because they did not book me, but they also try to put the blame on me because they currently do not book flights more than 30 days in advance. Well pity me . . . they put me on a flight to leave a day earlier.

Kathleen is laid up in her B-hut. After she landed back at Bagram a few days ago, something happened to her leg when she stood up on the plane. She's not sure if she twisted it or tore something. She's hobbling around on crutches for now. Everyone must be ambulatory on base. If her injury is serious or requires her to be off work for a while, chances are, she may be repatriated. The Barron HR department, travel office, and medics are arranging to have Kathleen go to Dubai for further examination. We're booked on the same flight.

I make a list of everything I need to do prior to departure. I have to collect a bunch of signatures: my supervisor's signature that indicates he's aware of my absence, a signature from preventative medicine (prev med) that shows I'm current with my vaccines, a signature from the government assets office that marks that I turned in any U.S. government-issued equipment like my laptop, another signature for Barron assets, a signature attesting that my PPE has been turned in, and finally, a signature for billeting that assigns a trustee to my belongings in the event I do not return to base. Gathering these signatures is like running in *The Amazing Race*. Each signature is in a different place on base with different hours. Sometimes there's a challenge like getting three more vaccine shots from prev med before they'll sign my document.

It's always tough to sleep the night before an R&R. I'm too anxious to get out of here and I'm always afraid I won't hear my alarm clock. I spend the night tossing and turning. My mind is moving a mile a minute as I review everything in my head to make sure I'm set to go: signatures, passport, my letter of authorization (LOA) by the military to be here, my airline ticket confirmations, hotel reservations . . .

When morning finally arrives, I strip my bed and put all my bedding in a couple of laundry bags. I carry my check-in bag to the luggage truck. I'd rather roll it, but that's an arduous task over gravel. I drop off my dirty laundry, throw on my gym clothes, and get in a quick workout before the base starts to buzz like bees.

My cell phone keeps ringing. Of course, the day that I'm leaving is the day the audio piece decides to quit working—damn shitty electronics, made in China. I arrange to meet Goran before I leave, as he is going to occupy my "room" in my tent while I am gone. It's close to the office, more private, and about a dozen guys live in it. Goran lives on the other side of base in a clamshell tent with about 399 other people. There's a lot of noise, tension, stench, long waits for the shuttle, and sometimes even a fistfight or two.

I swing by the office. My coworker, Tom, with his scraggly gray beard and wire-framed glasses, screeches with enthusiasm and excitement when he knows someone is leaving for R&R and gets to board the "Happy Bus." The Happy Bus is our last mode of transportation that takes us to the flight line to board the plane leaving Afghanistan.

Tom is one of my new running buddies. Tom and I still get along quite well. We're both runners and we both enjoy our coffee. We can joke around with each other and not be offended. Tom is around my age and has three teenagers back home. He sounds like Jim Cramer from *Mad Money* or Grover from *Sesame Street*. He speaks with an inflamed tone, with a higher pitch in the middle of each word or sentence. He's loud, with the inflection in his voice going up, then down, up, then down: *"THOMAS, yoU gEt to BOArd the HAPPY BUS toDAy?"* Tom is called "Grumpy" by another coworker, Mike. Tom calls Mike "Grumpier." When they get in heated discussions they sound like an old married couple. They're part of my entertainment in the office.

I'm supposed to turn in my personal protective equipment (PPE: bulletproof vest and helmet) and laptop, but I decide to leave them in the possession of my boss in a locked office cabinet. I am reluctant to turn in my PPE because I hear stories that people are missing the bulletproof plates from their vest when they return to base, or their laptops are reissued to someone else due to a shortage. I sign documents verifying what I am leaving, where, and with whom.

I was hoping to touch base with Goran about my room, but he's nowhere to be seen. I put my phone in my pocket. Of course—out of habit—I have it set on vibrate and I can't feel the weak vibration. I pull it out about an hour later and have 10 missed calls. I check my text messages and Goran has texted me to bring Kathleen something to eat. Kathleen has texted me to tell me she was starving and hasn't eaten since the day before. Goran can't bring her food because he doesn't know where she lives and he must meet the new hires at the flight line.

I'm hungry after my quick morning workout and all the running around. I grab a bite to eat at the DFAC. Civilians aren't supposed to take food to go from the DFAC, but if stopped and asked, I will tell them it's for Kathleen, who is on crutches. Here, coworkers really are your family. We watch out for each other. If someone is sick or stuck in his or her room due to illness or injury, a coworker brings them food and medicine, and checks on them. Kathleen's other coworkers are traveling intratheater to other bases, so it's up to me to help her out. I grab a to-go box, whip up a ham-and-cheese sandwich with all the fixins, and add chips, cookies, fruit, and drinks. I even put a couple of pickles and packets of mayo and mustard in her container. Her to-go box looks like a work of art by a culinary artist. I know she'll appreciate it.

I walk another mile in the opposite direction of the DFAC. I clip along at a pretty good pace. I know I am cutting my time very close. I get to Dragon Village, where Kathleen lives, but row after row of B-huts all look the same. As I text her to get her B-hut number, I also call out her name. While I'm doing that, Goran is texting me, wondering where I am. I tell him to meet me at the Dragon Village laundry—a common landmark in Dragon Village and not far from Kathleen's B-hut or the office.

Kathleen hobbles to the entrance of her B-hut and sticks her head out the door. She sees me and calls my name: *"Thomas, I'm over here!"* She lives in a women-only B-hut, so men aren't allowed, but I enter anyway. I've been in her room a few times when I've walked her home at night, usually carrying a package or two for her. Her room looks like a cyclone has gone through it. Her bed is not made and there are stacks of clothes everywhere. There's a ton of boxes from her internet shopping. (Amazon is a hit here.) It amazes me she can find anything. She's lost her military ID a few times in this mess and has had to tear the room apart consolidating heaps of clothes. It looks like she has never put it back together.

Kathleen is glad to see me. I haven't seen her since she got back on base. I give her a big hug and we start yacking away about what she's been through and what she's about to go through. She sits on her bed and opens the to-go box I brought her. She's impressed at how appetizing and neat her lunch looks! It was prepared by *moi*, so of course it looks wonderful. As she chows down her lunch, she manages to get a few words in between bites. I confirm she has transportation to the flight line, and we create a backup plan. One always needs a plan A and a plan B around here, sometimes a plan C. I tell her I have to cut our visit short because I'm on a tight timeline, I still have to meet Goran, and I'm scheduled to be picked up to go to the terminal within the hour. She understands the situation all too well from her LOGCAP experience in Iraq and now in Afghanistan. Out the door I go.

As I'm walking down the street to meet Goran, Cherlise—one of the women from the office next to me—goes by as a passenger in a little white pickup. She sees me and rolls down her window to blow kisses at me with both of her hands. She has a big, glowing smile on her face. She must know that I'm leaving base today for R&R.

I love Cherlise. She reminds me of Esther Rolle from the 1970s sitcom *Good Times*. Cherlise has a very round face, short black hair, a smile that lights up like the moon, and even a slight gap between her two front teeth like Esther. Every morning, Cherlise beams into my office wearing a different colorful hat. If there is someone she doesn't know, she introduces herself and strikes up a conversation. She is very personable and social with an eloquent vocabulary.

Goran is waiting for me by the laundry. We walk a mile up the road to my tent while he complains that I'm walking too fast. I have a flight to catch! I give him the combination to the cipher lock on the tent door. I show him my makeshift room, and where the closest community bathroom facilities are located, and give him my laundry receipts to pick up my clean laundry in a few days.

I grab my carry-on bag and out the door I go. Goran walks with me to the bus. I give the big ol' lug a hug farewell and board the bus heading to the terminal. I'm on the Happy Bus! Whenever I hear people talking about the Happy Bus, I think of Shirley Jones driving the geometrically colored Partridge Family bus, smiling, and singing like a jolly ol' mom with all the kids joining in. The Happy Bus is a newer bus than the last one I rode on. This beauty is clean and the air conditioning works. There are storage racks above the seat to set our carry-on baggage. We're living high on the hog now.

Our Happy Bus isn't quite like the Partridge Family's. As passengers board and occupy seats, it probably is the happiest group of folks on base at a single moment. Everyone is in a good mood and smiling because we're getting out of the sandbox. Some talk in low voices, but most sit back and rest their heads, gazing out the windows, staring into space, daydreaming, or listening to their iPods. I feel a great deal of relief and calmness in the air when I board the Happy Bus—no tension, no stress. I think most of the people are just tired and ready to get out of Afghanistan. Everyone's been working his or her butt off without a break for the past 90-plus days. We all deserve a break. We're ready for a cold alcoholic beverage, good food, and a clean bathroom a few steps away from a cozy bed. Most of all, we're excited to see our loved ones.

After I board the Happy Bus a young woman starts to sing, *"If you're happy and you know it, clap your hands. If you're happy and you know it, stomp your feet."* Her friend beside her joins in. They are having a good time. It reminds me of my kindergarten days, when the bus driver always started to sing a song and all the kids on the bus followed her lead. Sweet, innocent kids.

The Happy Bus is full. The two girls have a whole bunch of verses to that song that I never heard of: *"If you're happy and you know it, tap your head . . . pinch your ears . . . blink your eyes . . . squeeze your nose . . . raise your hands."* I think a few guys on the bus are ready to wring their necks, from the expression on their faces.

Off we go! The bus stops at the central distribution center (CDC) first to drop off people's personal protective equipment. It takes about 30 minutes. Of course, I left mine locked up in the office cabinet. Then we drive to the terminal. I can walk it faster, but the temperatures are heating up outside and I don't want to be all sweaty from carrying my luggage a half-mile from The Village to the terminal and then board the plane. There's a ton of people at the terminal and several other big buses and luggage trucks from other areas of the base. People are scrambling to find their luggage truck. We all must weigh and check in our luggage and get a boarding pass.

I see Kathleen. She's being assisted by a couple of HR folks and is sitting in the terminal. The line is long, so I find a nice shady spot under an awning and read a magazine until the line is down to just a few people. There's no sense in hurrying or standing in line unnecessarily. We're all going to the same place and the plane isn't going to leave without us. I check in my bags and get my boarding pass. Our estimated time of arrival in Dubai is 9:30 p.m. The way everything is going, I know this flight will not leave on time.

Kathleen sits in the small lobby space with another Barron employee who is assisting her. His name is Anthony. As I stand talking to Kathleen, I notice Anthony is staring at my crotch. I don't wear underwear, and depending upon the pants I wear, I may sport a pretty good package in there. I had a hunch he was gay, but this only confirms it.

Kathleen and I start to plot an action plan for when we arrive in Dubai. We include Anthony in the plan. We will stop at the Dubai Duty Free first, buy a bottle of wine or two, go to our hotel rooms, meet in her room, order room service, and toast the night away. For now, however, we sit in the crowded lobby and wait. Patience is a virtue around here.

From time to time, I catch Anthony checking me out. He's a nice-looking guy, close to my age, retired military still sporting a military haircut, a bit stocky . . . but he smokes. After David with the Copenhagen shit, he doesn't have a chance with me. I'm done with smokers and dippers.

Finally, three magazines later and a few chapters read in my book, we get the word that the plane has landed. It's three or four hours late. Everyone boards buses that will take us to the flight line. They are different buses than the pretty ones from earlier. These look like they were pulled from an abandoned field and just cranked up to be driven here . . . just like when I first arrived in Bagram.

We drive to the flight line. We sit on the parked bus as passengers unload from the arriving flight. One of the guys on my bus sees one of his friends getting off the plane. He gets off the bus to greet him. Then all his buddies—about 10 of them—get off to greet this guy. It reminds me of Mr. Deen. I swear he knows everyone from Sri Lanka who is working here. Goran too—I refer to him as the president of Macedonia. I'd bet he knows every Macedonian who works in Afghanistan and their spouses, brothers, sisters, and neighbors. I always find that interesting. Sometimes I wish I were that outgoing and social, but I am not. Plus I don't want to know everybody's business or have everybody knowing mine. I prefer to keep some things in my life private.

Finally we get word that we can board the plane. Kathleen is driven to the bottom of the stairs in a base vehicle, where Anthony and a couple of flight attendants help her up the stairs and onto the plane. She and Anthony get a seat in the front row. I'm assigned a window seat a few rows behind her.

Night has fallen. Finally it's wheels up! Given our late departure, it will put our arrival into Dubai around midnight. The plane is somewhat quiet as passengers relax during takeoff. We fly into the evening sky and up and over the Hindu Kush Mountains. In the dark night sky and the half-moon of light, I make out the snow-capped mountains. They are very high, rugged, and undisturbed. There's still snow on them and it's mid-May. Looking down from the moonlit sky at the texture of the mountains reminds me of a giant Bundt cake with icing or powdered sugar drizzled over the top.

After dinner is served on the plane, the Dubai Flight Service crew distributes complementary Heineken beers. Anthony is a beer drinker and scoops up two beers right away from the flight attendant. I think of Homer Simpson: *"Mmmmm . . . beer!"* This is where the crowd comes to life. I manage to get two beers myself. The first one tastes so good and goes down quickly. I can feel a buzz after I finish it. I think the guy next to me can too. He gets a third beer and hesitates to open it. He hands it to me, and I split the beer with the guy on the other side of him in the aisle seat.

After we arrive in Dubai, exit the plane, and go through customs, a mass of people flock to the Dubai Duty Free store. It's the first thing we see after leaving customs on our way to baggage claim. How convenient. I buy a bottle of wine to crack open for the night. Kathleen stocks up on several bottles since she doesn't know how long she is going to be in Dubai. Anthony buys a six-pack of beer. At the hotel, Kathleen and I are assigned rooms next to each other. I'm not sure where Anthony's room is. She orders a cheese-and-fruit platter from room service and we pop the corks on our bottles of wine. She drinks white. I drink red. Anthony cracks open his beer.

A few drinks later, Kathleen initiates talks about the current event: Don't Ask, Don't Tell. She knows that I'm a gay man. She knows that Anthony is too and probably figured it would be nice to bring the topic out into the open for the two of us to get to know one another. Anthony opens up about the discussion and confirms his sexuality. He's known of me and he knows that I am gay. He offers me this advice: *"Thomas, even if the government succeeds with the ban on 'Don't Ask,*

Don't Tell,' you will not want to be open about it. You shouldn't be open about it with the company either. You won't get promotions or raises. They won't include you as part of their network. They'll ostracize you." I can't believe what's coming out of his mouth. All I can think is "coward." He's a coward and will live behind a closet door. That may work for him and many others, but not for me. I whipped open that closet door years ago.

I speak up: *"Anthony, maybe that works for you and that's how it's worked during your military career. But I don't work for the military. I work for a multibillion-dollar Fortune 500 company. They have a diversity-and-inclusion program that includes and embraces people from all walks of life. I have a lot to offer the company with my background. I hope that I will be treated fairly and by my work performance. Besides, I am proud of who I am and proud to be with my partner. If it's an issue that I talk about my partner at work or have a picture of him on my screensaver, then it's not me who has the problem, but the beholder. I'm not going to work in fear. The more open I am about it, then the more I'm educating those around me. Diversity and inclusion. Enough said."*

The last time I looked at a clock, it was 3:00 a.m. We call it a night. I go to my room, fall asleep, and sleep in for the first time in a long, long time.

Ski Dubai

It's almost noon when I get out of bed. Since I have an extra day in Dubai, I decide to head to the Mall of the Emirates and spend a couple hours on its man-made ski slope. Ski Dubai is an indoor ski resort with 22,500 square meters of ski area. Mall of the Emirates is one of the largest shopping malls in the world. I hail a taxi and go to the mall. The thermostat in the cab reads 117 steamy degrees outside. It is freezing inside the Ski Dubai slope, of course. It must be to keep the snow from melting.

I purchase an all-inclusive lift ticket for $50. The all-inclusive includes two hours of skiing or snowboarding, a snow jacket and pants, ski boots, skis, poles, and a helmet (optional). The only two items I need to buy are a hat and a pair of gloves to keep my head and fingers from freezing.

The lift ticket is a computer chip card about the size of a credit card. I can put it anywhere on my body and the corral counter will sense it and scan it. I stick it into the top pocket of my bright-blue and red ski jacket. The pass is activated the first time I go through the corral to get on the chairlift. Each time after that, it tells me how much time I have remaining on my pass. Anyone can buy a lift ticket in segments of two hours and add more time to their card at the bottom of the ski run or in the lodge. Lessons are available for an additional charge, of course, and next time I would like to learn to snowboard. I have never snowboarded.

At Ski Dubai, I step outside the ticket-and-equipment area and hit the slopes. Just off the base of the hill is a small trail for kids to ride the "snowball." The "snowball" is a huge, clear, inflatable ball with a little hole to enter the center. An attendant rolls the ball onto the trail that tosses and turns the kids upside down and around as they roll down. It looks like so much fun. I want to get in one, but I don't think I would fit. There's a dad trying to talk his three-year-old daughter into riding it. She just stands there and cries because she's too scared to do it. Her older brother isn't. He's having a blast and she gets her thrill just watching him being tossed around like a rag doll as he rolls down the hill.

It's been ages since I skied, and I hope it's like riding a bike—something one remembers and never forgets. Skiing is the same. The first few runs break me in. By the third or fourth run, I'm zipping down the hill, parallel skiing, picking up speed, and stopping with a cloud of snow flying into the air. Ah, it feels so good. There are no lines for the chairlift, so I go nonstop, run after run.

Many of the younger kids are on snowboards. They're fun just to watch as they flip from side to side, jump up on the rail and ride it like a skateboard, plop back down onto the hill, and twirl by doing a few surface 360s. They're a group of little daredevils. A quick pause and they straighten up to pick up a little speed for a final descent, fly off one of the two snow jumps, and land near the bottom of the base, skidding on the snow and creating a wave of white dust in the air. Of course, most of the young kids I see look and sound American.

After an hour of skiing, I'm freezing. My nose, cheeks, and fingers all tingle from the cold. There's a small stone and wooden chalet in the middle of the hill that sells beverages and snacks. I stop there to get a cup of hot coffee, warm up, and check it out. There's another restaurant with a wall of windows overlooking the ski slopes that is accessible from within the mall. Facing the slope, the restaurant is designed like a Swiss chalet, complete with a fireplace. It seems like they think of everything in Dubai.

The Honeymoon

This is kind of weird: There are only eight people on my commercial flight from Dubai to Bangkok. Many people canceled their travel plans to Thailand because of the current political unrest between the pro-government "yellow shirt" and their "red-shirt" opponents. It's kind of nice because I can spread out across three seats and lie down during my flight.

Flying into Bangkok is somewhat eerie. It's an overcast tombstone morning. The highways leading to the airport are deserted. In the distance of the city, I see billowing black smoke fuming into the air from the arson attacks on civil and government buildings. The turmoil hasn't stopped us from coming, as we were informed that the protest and riots are in a confined area of the city.

After deplaning, I proceed to the airport hotel kiosk. The airport has a completely different vibe than the outside. It's vibrant and busy. A middle-aged Thai woman greets me with a big smile on her face, her palms pressed together in a prayer-like fashion, and a slight bow. It is the common Thai greeting "wai." She verifies my reservation, takes my luggage, and signals the driver to assist me to the hotel shuttle. I check into the beautiful Novotel Suvarnabhumi Airport Hotel. The hotel boasts the largest hotel lobby in the world, five stories in height with two buildings joined by a massive glass atrium.

I relax in my room for a few hours and then set out. Through the crowd of many black-haired, dark-skinned people appears a tanned, radiant shaved head. It's Greg. He looks handsome, as always. We greet each other with a hug and a kiss. Oh no! A public display of affection between two men hugging and kissing each other. What will people think? We don't care if anybody sees us or what his or her reaction or thoughts may be. We love each other and it's been a long time since we've seen each other. Really, I don't think anyone notices or cares, especially in Thailand.

I sweep Greg off to the nearby hotel, where we spend just one night. We talk, we swim, and we have a couple poolside cocktails. We catch up, we consider each other's eyes, we smile, we laugh, and we wine and dine. We hug, we touch, we massage, we kiss, and we make love. After a wonderful evening, the next morning we head farther south to Phuket for a few days and then on to Koh Samui to avoid the political crisis.

Landing at the airport in Koh Samui reminds me of the television program *Fantasy Island*. It's a single airstrip that is surrounded by manicured flowering gardens. The terminals resemble large, grassy, open-air pavilions. The land is exotic, lush, and welcoming. I instantly fall in love with Koh Samui.

A beautiful, young Thai woman who drives us to a gorgeous Balinese villa that we rented from Airbnb greets us. The homeowner is an

American filmmaker from L.A. The house is very private and secluded with a pool. It's top-notch in many ways: architecture, furnishings, lighting, landscaping, sculptures, and outdoor living. The meticulous house and outdoor lighting give the home an amber glow and a romantic feel. It's a heavenly retreat.

We don't leave the house for the first few days after we arrive. We enjoy our surroundings and ease into reacquainting ourselves after the last three months of being apart. It's a time for us to reflect and enjoy each other. It's a well-deserved break to share some private and intimate moments. We sip our morning coffee in the outdoor garden, skinny-dip in the pool, bathe together in the large outdoor rainforest shower surrounded by bamboo, savor the flavors of a bottle of red wine during sunsets, and cuddle next to one another in the soft, white cotton sheets with the doors wide open and the ceiling fans set on low.

From the time I saw Greg at the airport up until now, it's like a second honeymoon when things are at their sweetest. I don't want it to end. But as the aphorism goes, all good things must come to an end.

They Come and They Go

Kathleen is held over in Dubai for almost a week before she can schedule an MRI and get her results, but when she does, it reveals she tore her ACL. Her recovery will take more than 60 days and she will be repatriated. Her job in Afghanistan is over. That night of drinking wine and snacking on appetizers in her hotel room is the last time I will see her. She and Ethan are planning to get married, so maybe I'll see them at their wedding or in South Africa.

Josh, the young man who helped me dub the AC/DC song as our theme song from Dubai to Afghanistan, has also left the project. This wasn't his cup of tea. Maybe police work looks more appealing to him after his short adventure here. The grass isn't always greener on the other side.

Cherlise left too. I hadn't realized that morning she rolled by me blowing those wonderful kisses was the day she was leaving the project. I thought that was Cherlise being Cherlise. I will never see her again.

I will remember Cherlise by her "Contractor's Rules of Survival." Here are a couple of them that she shared with me:

1. You don't own a thing here except the clothes on your back, your integrity, your moral values, and your work ethics. Keep that in the forefront of your mind and stay committed to your goals.

2. Even if the job is great and everyone is super nice, always be looking for your next job. These big companies don't owe you a thing and won't think twice about cutting you if they must. Remember, we're contractors.

3. Set your monetary goals. Once you've accomplished your goal, go home and get a life. LOGCAP is not a way to live; it's just a job. It is not a career or a life.

4. Work like a whore and not a bitch. A whore will identify her needs, tell you her price, and only perform within her scope. Bitches work for free—working for 14 or 16 hours a day and claiming 12 on their timesheet, all the while thinking someone is going to notice his or her "hard work" and offer them a promotion. Remember, you are nothing more than a hired hand—nothing more and nothing less.

I guess she lives up to her words. She told me that she had been doing this type of work for five or six years. It was time to go. I didn't realize she'd leave so quickly.

My first love of Bagram, Larry, left. Though the attractive, Midwestern man and I hooked up only a couple of times, I saw him frequently: at the DFAC, the gym, and Green Beans; passing each other on the sidewalk; and at a few of the 5K runs. It was always nice to see his handsome face. His company transferred him to Iraq, and he is one less familiar face I will see around BAF.

I walk into my office and don't know a single person except Goran. I ask Goran, *"Are you the man in charge?"* He flaunts, *"I should be,"* follows that with his heavy laugh, and ends with, *"but I'm not."* He adds, *"Everybody moved."*

The RBK-to-Barron transition is finished. The life support area (LSA)—or living quarters—is no longer referred to as "RBK Village." Instead it is renamed "Barron Village" or just "The Village." Most of the Barron employees assigned to Bagram Airfield live here. The Barron LOGCAP headquarters is located here in the only two-story hard structure made of brick and mortar. It's painted a taupe earth tone to blend in with the color of the sand.

My department is assigned to a new, quaint little office with four makeshift cubicles on the first floor of the headquarters building. The others who shared the office B-hut with us were also assigned new respective spaces, some at other forward operating bases (FOBs). Goran is one of the last people awaiting his move, but he eventually makes it to the headquarters building with the rest of us. Though I had a pretty close working relationship with Goran at the B-hut, we are in separate offices in The Village, and our bond tapers off. I see him quite a bit, but our conversations are less and less.

The people are not the only things that move and change on base. While I was on R&R, all the fast-food places and shops have disappeared. General McChrystal, who is over the war efforts, ordered all of them out. As I hear of the fate of these businesses, McChrystal did a walk-through of the PX area, which is the main artery of Bagram, and made the comment, *"What are we running here, a damn country club? It's no wonder our people can't focus on the mission."* What a prick!

I don't think that's it at all. I think it's a show of power and control. Soldiers already make sacrifices with their families and loved ones back home. They take leaves of absence from their jobs. They are out in the field or tiny outposts for weeks and months at a time. Bagram is a little slice of home to renew friendships, reduce the stress, and relax a little bit—if that's even possible. I really don't think grabbing a burger or a slice of pizza is going to take away from the mission. Personally, I think McChrystal's decision is a morale buster.

Upon my return from my 21-day R&R, I notice significant progress of construction projects. There's a huge new hangar on the flight line, new 10-foot extra-wide pedestrian sidewalks that stretch from one end of Disney to the other, new sewage and drainage systems, and a few new housing complexes. The new wide sidewalks make me feel like I'm walking on a New York City sidewalk!

I see my Balkan friend, Arian. He welcomes me back to base with his big smile and a cup of coffee. He tells me that while I was gone, he had one of the worst days of his life. I ask him, *"What happened?"* He tells me the story of how they had incoming, and outsiders breached the wall and gained access inside the base. Military personnel were put in place: soldiers guarded buildings and activity; snipers were on rooftops and in the perimeter towers. During the incoming attack, The Big Voice instructed personnel to remain "shelter in place"—to take cover wherever they were. Arian was in his B-hut. Usually an incoming attack will be all clear in 10 to 20 minutes. But this one dragged on, and Arian could hear the intruders talking, running, and shooting just outside his building. He says when it quieted down, he asked the soldier guarding his B-hut what was going on. The soldier replied, *"If I were you, I'd be down on the ground wearing my PPE [personal protective equipment], and I'd stay there until the all clear."* Arian did just that and lay on his B-hut floor for about 12 hours. Listening to him tell the story made it sound scary. I'm glad I was not here.

Change and progress are two elements that I like about working over here. A lot of it is good. Sometimes you wonder why people come and go throughout your life. I think of it like characters in a book.

Some characters have great personalities and stories to tell and share. It's great to be in the moment with them. Others are not so great and I look forward to the end of their stories, the end of the chapter, and the closing of the book. Then it's time for a new book with new chapters and new characters. My life is a pile of great books with many entertaining chapters and some amazing characters in it. Those are the ones I remember and hold dear. The true connection between a friend and me are those cherished experiences that brought us together. We may go separate ways down another path, but I know I can pick up the phone or look them up on Facebook years down the road, and I know they'll open their arms to me as I would for them.

Though I will miss some of the people who have left impressions on me, there will always be new ones in my life.

Can't Let the Dust Settle

You can't let the dust settle too quickly in one spot around here. We're moving offices again to a hard-structure building that was formerly the RBK headquarters on BAF. It is now the Barron headquarters. It looks like a closet that was cleared out and made into an office for four people. Basically, one long desk with three dividers to make four stations. It looks a little cramped in here, and before long it looks like a library. I have volumes of training books that were sent over from headquarters—almost $10,000 worth. Most of them are still wrapped in their cellophane. I have them neatly stacked across the shelves that rest above our cubicles, but our space is still cramped.

On the upside, a new office location means a new push-up club. As Trigger and I continue our routine near our new space, we get four other guys to join us. Four of us are over 40 and the other two are 30-somethings. Trigger is the drill instructor, but he's more like a coach. He checks everyone's form and makes sure they're doing it right. He has the routine planned for us each day. I love that Trigger does this for us. Some days we do a fixed number of sets. Other days we do a continuous rotation until someone burns out. Any day that somebody passes by us, we encourage them to join in for a set or two: young or old, male or female, black or brown or white. Everyone is welcome.

Trigger is a mysterious man. Sometimes I want to pry into his brain to find out what he's thinking or unravel his life as a Navy Seal. During lunch I meddle into his head about his past life and experiences. He tells me about one night he was on a mission in a tropical, humid, mosquito-infested jungle. He and his team could not move or make a sound. While he sat there on the bush, he was covered with mosquitoes feasting on his face. He couldn't swat them away or slap them dead. Everyone had to stay still. I can't imagine. It makes me think about the smoking habit and how these guys keep their bodies from going into a coughing frenzy that would blow their cover. I guess that's why they take up chewing the nasty stuff.

I want to know more about his life and missions as a Navy Seal. I start to pry Trigger with questions about his sniper training background and how many kills he has under his belt. I want to know details about specific missions he was sent on. I don't get too far when he utters, *"Dude, I can't believe you're asking me that question."* I imagine he took a vow of silence or oath with the military. Or maybe that's just Trigger and it's better I don't know.

One morning I show up at the office bright and early, and there's a young, pretty blonde woman sitting in one of the cubicles. She stands up and introduces herself in her twangy Georgia accent, *"Hello, I'm Sissy."* She's one of Huggy's HR staff from transition and here to join our team.

Trigger arrives at the office and tells Sissy and me that he found some storage room in the basement. Sissy and I look at each other in unison. I can tell by the look on Sissy's face that she's thinking the same thing I am: *"Basement? There's a basement in this building?"* I bet Trigger discovered the basement during a special night mission. I have my suspicions he's here on another kind of business: a secret mission. I mean, why would we have a Navy Seal as our HR training manager? It's got to be a cover-up.

I've stopped by the office late at night to grab a cold sport drink out of our little refrigerator after a workout and caught Trigger with computer parts and system spread out all over the office, dissecting the machine. Why? There's got to be a better reason than simply building his own system. I picture Trigger scouting places to investigate and monitor activity in the middle of the night while most of the camp is quiet and sleeping. I see him dressed in all black to blend in with the dark midnight sky and crawling in confined spaces like the basement of the building. I can picture him scaling and rappelling the 10-foot T-walls that line the base. Yup, it's got to be a cover-up.

Another mysterious character is working among us. He's the country security manager, Will. His office is next to ours and he likes to hang out with Trigger and me. He likes his coffee and we keep his coffee cup filled. Will doesn't discuss his Special Forces military career, at least not with me. He and I have three traits in common: we were both born and raised in Wisconsin; we're both the same age; and we're joined here by LOGCAP. I have an instant crush on Will.

Will has an incredible body and the looks to go with it. He also has this constant smirk on his face that makes him look adorable at times. I think he's probably generating bad or comic thoughts of people with his wicked sense of humor. He doesn't talk much, but when he does, he has a very dry sense of humor and comes up with some good one-liners out of the blue. He has a few more wrinkles around the eyes than I do, so I joke with him that he must've had a more stressful life. He barks, *"Oh yeah, I'm paying for it now with my kid. He's 21 and a hell-raiser."*

Will is high up on the ladder in management and has a combined office and living quarters. It's much nicer than what most of us live in. Trigger and I tell him he lives in a suite. I ran into him at the laundry service and queried, *"Will, I thought you had a washer and dryer in your suite?"* Quick on the draw he retorted, *"No, I had to decide between the hot tub and the washer and dryer, but they wouldn't give me both."* I wish he did have a hot tub and I was invited to the party.

I have to read the minds of these men to figure out their training, background, and what they're thinking. They don't volunteer much about their lives as career military or the hardships they've endured. My imagination can run wild, and not necessarily about their past lives. I've already created an action-packed film, in my mind, of a Navy Seal and a Special Forces agent. Another movie of blood, guts, and murder? I'm thinking more of a hot romance!

Will and Trigger are well trained to remain calm in high-pressure situations and to make decisive decisions. I observe it in their thinking and actions. But behind the pacifying eyes, I wonder if they've killed and how many people. How was it done—by gun, knife, bullet between the eyes, snap of the neck? Where have they been? Iran? North Korea? China? Colombia? Under what conditions? To stop political provocation? Drug smuggling? Human trafficking? Covert action? It'll probably remain a mystery. I'll only see such action on the big screen.

Sissy

Sissy is young, smart, beautiful, energetic, and incredibly fit. She works at it and dresses the part, always looking good, wearing a snug shirt, and showing off her girlish curves. And I think that's okay. She's got it going on, so she may as well flaunt it. I can see why Huggy kept an open slot for her close to his office.

She joins Trigger and me in our daily push-up workouts. We expand our workouts to include some pull-ups. Not surprisingly, when Sissy does her push-ups or pull-ups, several other guys line up to the plate to join in, with an audience to follow. The men adore her. And while the guys are checking out Sissy, I'm checking out Danny doing his pull-ups. He's a Marine and a mighty fine specimen to look at.

Sissy always seems to have a trail of guys following her. Many of them stop by the office bearing gifts of candy, food from home, or coffee, or just to chat. She knows a lot of people from the other FOBs, as she helped transition many of them into their positions. Many of them make a point to pay her a visit whenever they come through Bagram.

Trigger and I observe how easily she can finesse most anything from a man, so we have a mission for Sissy. We send her off to the other department managers to get their current training materials, requirements, and agenda. Twenty or thirty minutes later she returns from her visit with exactly what we need to do our job to oversee all the training in the country. Then she's off to the second, third, and fourth department managers. She has been unleashed and she's running with it.

Though most men maintain a professional demeanor toward Sissy in our work and living environment, she has had a few run-ins with others. One guy struck up conversation with her in the self-serve laundromat. He only knew her name. By the time she returned to the office, the guy had found her on Facebook and sent her a friend invite. That's being excessively forward and she denied his friend request.

While transitioning employees at another FOB, Sissy went to the local barber to have her hair trimmed. The barber was a local Afghan man and she was the last customer of the day. Since she was not escorted by another person, as is expected of the local Afghan women, the barber thought it would be a good opportunity to take advantage of her. She had to forcibly push him off her, run out of the shop, and get Barron security. Security escorted him off base and he was prohibited from returning to work on base.

Sissy is always being asked to go to lunch by one guy or another. Some of them just seem creepy to me—snakes, with their slithering tongues, supple skin, and staring eyes. Most of them just want to get into her pants. Sissy plays it smart and cool, and invites me to tag along. I feel like her father or guardian being present during their date. I'm old enough to be her dad. In fact, I think her dad and I are around the same age. My presence is a safeguard. It filters unwanted or uncomfortable conversations and behaviors. And believe me, in an environment where men can outnumber women by about ten to one, women are prey. After tagging along for a few lunches, the guys usually get the hint that there's no interest there except a work relationship. Of course, she has nothing to worry about with me.

As cute and charming as she is, I never know what's going to come out of her mouth. When she was getting ready to leave for R&R, she said to me, *"The first cabana boy I see better watch out!"* I knew exactly what she meant and we laughed. This girl can talk some smut and keeps me laughing. Half the time, Trigger will be in the office with us and he'll be clueless to our conversations. He'll just turn and look at us through the top of his reading glasses and only imagine. Other times he'll just zone us out. Occasionally we'll be laughing so hard and so much that Huggy will hear us from down the hall and stick his nose into our office to see what all the commotion is about. All I have to do is point or look at Sissy and he knows.

Huggy wants a hug from every woman who walks by him. He's a pig. Mona Lee is pretty big chested and she's told me how he always asks her for a hug. She's also told me that he'll squeeze her bosom tightly and then let out a bellicose moan. She says she allows it simply because the tall, lanky old man is no threat to her. I can't believe nobody's reported him. He's the HR manager, for fuck's sake!

Sissy has her earbuds in, listening to music as she sits at her desk. She's fixated on whatever she has on her computer screen. Huggy walks into the office and sees Sissy totally focused at the computer. He motions to me with his index finger vertically across his lips signaling to me to keep quiet. He wants to surprise and scare her. I'm thinking he'll do it by jolting her body unexpectedly, but instead he softly puts his finger in the open gap between her shirt and jeans. His fingertip is at the tip of her tailbone. He lightly sweeps his finger downward to her crack like a bug is crawling down her skin. She screams and jumps out of her chair, nearly knocking over Huggy in the process. Huggy is the only one laughing. I give him an eye of disgust and tell him his behavior is totally inappropriate. He objects and claims it's out of fun and games.

After Huggy leaves the room, I ask Sissy if she thought his behavior was inappropriate. She sideswiped my question with the response, *"Oh, that's just Huggy."* I don't care if that's just Huggy or not; it's still inappropriate and unprofessional. I tell her she should call the company's ethics hotline and report the incident, but she won't. She likes and respects Huggy. Most of us do. He has a charming personality and he's a shaker and mover in management. He gets things done. He has a vision for the department and a plan to develop his team. But as much as HR preaches to other managers about professional behavior and integrity, he's out of line. I should make the call myself to report the incident, but I don't want to overstep the boundaries between Sissy and me, nor do I want to face the retaliation of our boss, who is easily in the position to make it harder on us.

Willllllll

Sissy and I are outside taking a short break. We're watching Will. He's always a hot topic with Sissy and me. Will is clueless that we're checking out his every move. His good looks, squinty blue eyes, the smirk on his face, determined walk, hard physique, and bulging biceps are plenty to keep our minds occupied.

I feel so adolescent, like a couple of high school girls in love. I spark the conversation by sharing a piece of my imagination of what's under

Will's shirt. A six-pack, I'm sure. Sissy and I take turns as we slowly strip the clothes on his body and share what we see underneath. He's a little goofy in a charming way, but he's such a hunk.

Sissy unwraps a Twinkie and starts to snack on it. One of her secret admirers ordered them online, had them shipped here, and brings her one almost every day while the supply lasts. I've never cared for Twinkies, but Sissy loves them. Since I've never cared for them, I ask her what she loves about them. She tells me how she loves to take a bite of the spongy exterior and suck out the cream filling that is so light and fluffy and sweet. As she tells me about this cheap elegant delicacy, Will zooms in on her enjoying each savory bite. He shouts over to Sissy, *"It looks like you're really enjoying that Twinkie!"* I respond softly, leaning into Sissy's ear, *"I would really enjoy Will's Twinkie, feasting on his soft spongy tube and sucking the sweet cream filling out of him."* She swings to hit me as she shrieks, *"Thomas Josef!"* as an order to behave myself. I couldn't resist. I'm sure she was having similar thoughts.

A few days later, poor Sissy is missing out. I'm having lunch with Will. Of course, I'm sure she could get her own date with him if she wanted to. Will's lunch choice today is a loaded hot dog—I thought he would make a healthier choice, as fit-conscious as he is. Will sits directly across from me. I watch him as he opens his mouth wide to take a bite of his loaded hot dog, gripping it with both of his hands, as it's a monster to fit into his mouth. He takes a bite and sets it down on his plate. Then he licks his lips and pats his mouth with his napkin. I watch him take each bite, imagining *my* hot dog in his mouth and him lusting over it. I never knew a hot dog lunch could be so seductive and erotic.

Bunkerhead

"BUNKERHEAD? WE'RE GETTING BUNKERHEAD!" shouts Sissy. I ask her, *"Who's Bunkerhead?"* She looks surprised. *"Oh my gosh, you don't know who Bunkerhead is?"* she inquires. *"It's Merissa!"* Merissa is

one of five HR people who will be ending their transition assignment and will be coming over to the training department.

Sissy shares the story of how Merissa got her nickname. She was seen going in and out of bunkers while they were on assignment with the transition team at various bases. Apparently Merissa has an attraction to men of the darker persuasion. When one of their coworkers saw her heading into a bunker with another guy, she peeked into the bunker to see what they were doing and caught Merissa giving head to the fella. Obviously this is where the name "Bunkerhead" comes from.

I have not yet met Merissa and I already have a story and image of her. I don't think I'll be able to look her in the eyes with a straight face when I do meet her. I'll be picturing her lips and mouth devouring a huge, black cock and working his shaft with her hands! This is about to get interesting. Really interesting.

Русский (The Russian)

As Sissy is preparing to leave the project to go back to work in the States, Valentina will be joining our team. Valentina prefers to be addressed by her American name, Tina. She's from the Greenville headquarters office and is being sent to join our team to do administrative tasks. She is of Russian descent, married to an American, and has an American passport and citizenship. I think the U.S. military prohibits Russians from working on base, but I'm not sure about that. She may be more American than Russian in most respects.

Tina is the first Russian I've ever worked with. She has a master's degree in English and has been living in the States for years while working for Barron. She's adjusted quite well to the American way of living and lifestyle, but she still has some deep-rooted Russian heritage in her.

One thing I love about most foreigners who speak English as a second language is that they are multilingual and learn to properly speak *and* write English. Most Americans who use English as their native tongue can't even speak the language properly, but Tina speaks and writes English far better than most Americans. I even ask her to proofread some of my reports and storyboards for training development. I know my English is not perfect, but I like it to be as accurate as it can be. People who speak English well come across as more intelligent. It drives both of us nuts to have to listen to managers who speak broken English and sound like complete idiots because they can't complete a sentence properly, don't use proper subject-verb agreement, or have no comprehension of parallel tense construction in their sentences.

It's a tough adjustment and takes years and years of learning, dedication, and loyalty to cross cultural lines. She has some of her Russian heritage and traits embedded in her. I hate to stereotype a culture, but I've always heard how Russians are stern, serious, stubborn, and inflexible. Tina shows these traits often. She doesn't have a warm and welcoming disposition. One must proceed with caution when approaching her. Sometimes I think she may be bipolar.

I've witnessed a very emotional side of Tina. I've seen her hang up on her husband and break down into tears. Tina's been the breadwinner in the family. Her husband tends to bounce around from job to job and goes periods without working. I've never met the guy, but from what I hear and see, and what Tina tells me, he's a big slug. Tina's independence and his dependence upon her create a lot of friction between them. I can't say they're a happily married couple. In fact, I think they're far from being happy. At least she isn't.

Tina shows me pictures of herself when she weighed more than 300 pounds, back before this job. I think her unhappy marriage made an emotional eater out of her. She heard there was a BMI (body mass index) requirement and was determined to get a job on the project and shed a lot of weight. That's the determination in her. I wonder if she really lost the weight to work on the project or to run away from her marriage.

Bagram Amazing Race

Yes, they call it the streak! There's a lot of commotion and conversation in and around the office this morning. A contractor decided to leave the project and did so with a bang. He got buck naked and streaked down Disney Drive during the busy breakfast hour this morning. He had a lot of spectators and the military police chasing his ass. Damn . . . and I missed it! I'm sure it was a sight to see. People were laughing about it all morning.

We're gearing up for another race but not in the raw. Bagram Airfield is host to an Amazing Race just like the television series. The competition will be one of the most memorable events of my entire experience in the Afghanistan War.

Participants form teams of four, so I put together a Barron team of four guys: my boss Trigger, the former Navy Seal, and two other guys who work in project controls, Jim and Crail. Jim is a mountain expedition hiker, and Crail is a basketball and soccer player. And me, I'm just the pretty one! But really, I guess I'm the runner and weight lifter. I run between 15 and 20 miles a week, plus an hour in the gym most days of the week. None of the other guys are runners or weight lifters, but all of them are in pretty good shape. The race is a test of mental *and* physical challenges.

Our combined experiences and backgrounds create a pretty solid, balanced team. Jim and I have been at Bagram the longest and know the base well. Trigger and Crail have each been here less than a month, so they're still fresh meat. Trigger contributes greatly with his military background and his leadership skills. Jim, Trigger, and I are also the oldest contestants among the 20- and 30-somethings. I'm the oldest of the three—a sprite 48, soon to be 49.

The race is very well planned and coordinated. I think of it more like a scavenger hunt. There are 36 teams. The coordinators break the teams into six "heats" (six groups to start at a time in 10-minute intervals). The race covers the western side of Bagram Airfield and will take about three hours to finish. It's also high noon and the peak temperature of the day, when the heat is at its best. We're starting at 1330, and I'm calculating we'll wrap it up around 1700. I can't figure out why they are starting this event in the middle of the day. Perhaps that's part of the physical challenge to see how well we pace ourselves and hold up.

The starting gun fires and the first heat opens their first clue. All the teams take off and head north. Ten minutes later the second heat takes off and heads south. Ten more minutes go by and the third heat is split. Half the groups head north, while the other half head south. I know why the organizers did this: to avoid congestion at the first challenge. They split us up and they'll keep the rest of the teams guessing where they need to go. So tricky, but smart.

My team is in heat five. Trigger reads our first clue out loud, *"Karaoke upstairs and Blockbuster downstairs."* At the bottom of the clue is a code: PA HAF 9800. All of us have blank looks on our faces. We have no idea which place to go, let alone which direction. Jim clamors, *"They do karaoke at the Eight Ball MWR."* We run a mile south to the Eight Ball recreation area. There are no Amazing Race signs or anything that looks like part of the game.

I take a second gander at the clue. I bluster, *"It has to be the two-story recreation facility in Camp Cunningham. It's right there by the starting line."* The only place I can think of is the Vulture's Nest. It has an upstairs theater with a room for other events such as karaoke, card games, and trivia. Downstairs is a video arcade, computer room, and library of books and movies—hence the clue *"Blockbuster."* The Vulture's Nest was right under our noses by the starting line! We hustle back to the starting line and over to it.

We pile into the building and everybody is going about his or her business as usual. It doesn't appear to be an Amazing Race stop either, but I know this must be it. I open the door to the library and see the Amazing Race sign taped to the front desk. We're now cognizant that the code PA HAF 9800 is the Dewey Decimal System. Each of us takes a row and starts scanning books and movies for the number. We end up huddling in a single spot, grab the movie, and bring it to the front desk. The clerk verifies the movie number with the code on our clue, keeps the clue, and hands us a new one.

The second clue is easier, and we know it's to go to the military College-Level Examination Program (CLEP) building. From the Vulture's Nest we jog about a mile up the road to the center. Since Crail and I arrive first with the clue, the CLEP administrator hands us a test. There are 30 questions and we must answer 15 correctly. As Crail and I scan through the questions, Jim and Trigger waltz into the room and take seats beside us. The questions are not easy. We answer some of the easier ones right off the bat:

- What year did WWI start? (1914)
- Who was the first African American Secretary of State? (Colin Powell)
- What year did WWII end? (1945)
- Author Khaled Hosseini wrote this book about growing up in Afghanistan in the 1970s to 1980s, and it became a best seller and a movie. What was the title? (*The Kite Runner*)
- What do you call something that eats both meat and plants? (Omnivore)
- Who said, "*And so, my fellow Americans, ask not what your country can do for you—ask what you can do for your country.*" (JFK)
- Who wrote the song, "Johnny B. Goode"? (Chuck Berry)

Some of the questions are more difficult:

- Who was the twentieth president? (Garfield)
- Who starred as James Bond in *On Her Majesty's Secret Service*? (George Lazenby—I've never heard of him or the film.)
- Who wrote the war novel *The Red Badge of Courage*? (Stephen Crane)
- In what year did Anne Frank die? (1945)

We're careful not to answer the questions too loudly since the room is full of other teams taking the same test. I look around the room of tables with groups of 20-somethings thinking, *"We'll whip 'em here."* Remember, this is before smartphones. Even if there were smartphones, I'm sure they wouldn't be allowed. There seems to be a whole lot of very hard questions. If I had to do this on my own, I would fail. I anticipate that most of these kids won't know the answers to these questions. I further discern this from my high school days that those who joined the military were not academic achievers. Maybe things have changed since my day. The gentleman proctoring the exam is older—definitely older than me. The other proctor isn't much younger. One of them even commented that we should have an easier time with the test than the rest.

We're able to answer only 11 of our 15 questions correctly. Before we can go back and take a second jab at the incorrect answers, each of us has to drop to the floor and do a push-up for each wrong answer. We make three more attempts before getting 15 correct. After the proctor gives us the thumbs-up, he hands us our next clue.

The third clue says, *"Take caution near the ER."* We run about a mile and a half to the Craig Hospital emergency room. I lead my team through a back way to the hospital rather than running down the congested Disney Drive. Near the ER entrance of the hospital is a caution sign and two game attendees directing us with hand signals to go to a volleyball court on the back side of the hospital. The volleyball court is boarded up in the front, so we can't see in to the court. We're instructed to elect a leader, so we elect Trigger. Crail, Jim, and I are blindfolded. We're instructed to interlock our arms as Trigger calls out commands. Trigger assigns Jim as the leader of the "Three Blind Mice." In other words, Jim will be walking forward, and Crail and I will be walking backward or sideways in unison. Trigger has done similar exercises in the past and is brilliant at this. We waste no time, and after we complete the course on the volleyball court, we march across the driveway to pick up and carry a gurney with three cases of water on it. Again, Trigger pipes up into his military mode, commands us to pick up on three, walk forward, *"Hup! Two, three, four!"* and down on three. We perform flawlessly. Next clue.

"You will find your faith in the shadow of the rock." All of us know "The Rock" is the Air Force gym, and we'll figure out the other part of the clue regarding faith when we get over there. I know there isn't a church near there, so I'm not sure what that could mean. Again, I lead the group through a back way and a shortcut. We run about a mile to The Rock, and directly across from the fitness center is a chaplain's office. I can't believe it. I walk by here nearly every day and never noticed the chaplain's office! I guess that tells you a little about my religious spirit and beliefs.

Crail waits by the office. I backtrack to direct Jim and Trigger to the building. Our challenge is to braid a keychain about four inches long using a certain kind of knot. I know nothing about knots, but Trigger pulls through again with his military knowledge and experience of them. He's a Navy man, so of course he knows knots!

Jim is lugging a small backpack holding our clues, energy powders to add to bottled water, and snacks. He relays the pack off to me since I have the greater stamina. I am now the pack mule for the team too.

The next clue says something about a cardinal's deck. We're clueless. Our only option is to use our one and only "lifeline" by phoning the coordinator. He tells us to go to the USO. The USO is a United Service Organization that provides morale, welfare, and recreation (MWR) services to uniformed military personnel. We don't know where it is or where to go. We ask people passing by and start running in whatever direction they point. It's about a half-mile up the road and along the flight line.

At the USO is a beanbag toss. Each team player has to toss a beanbag about 25 to 30 feet into a center hole of a board game. You can toss one bag at a time or as many bean bags as you can grab at once. As three of us toss beanbags, one stands behind the target and tosses them back to us. We complete the task in a few minutes.

The next clue brings us back to The Rock fitness center. We have to do a total of 10,000 pounds in weight repetitions of leg presses. Jim quickly calculates 200 pounds times 50 reps. I thought I could do that myself, but all team members have to do at least one rep. Crail and I slide a 100-pound plate onto each side of the machine. As we do that, Trigger takes the driver's seat to start off the reps. The strong ox that he is, he does 47 of the reps, leaving the other three of us with only one rep each. B-I-N-G-O. We are done with that task in a matter of minutes.

The next clue says something about some mad puppies. That has to be my old stomping grounds next to Cherry-Beasley: Camp Mad Dog! We jog about another mile north down the road to Camp Mad Dog. There are four teams ahead of us waiting to complete the task when we arrive, so I have Crail wait in line as I direct our anchors, Jim and Trigger, into the secured attack-dog area escorted by a soldier.

As we walk through the compound, we are immediately instructed not to open any doors or wander around the facility. The soldier instructs us that many of the dogs are housed with their trainers and may attack if a stranger enters their territory. I think, *"Cool, this is the job I would want if I was in the military."* I love animals. And yes,

I could imagine a number of people sticking their big ol' noses into someone's sleeping quarters and getting their face bitten off. These dogs are trained to attack, maim, and maybe kill.

As we are waiting our turn in line, we stand in a shaded resting area surrounded by a covered fence, shielding people from looking in. At this point in the game, we need to refuel. We hydrate ourselves and eat an energy bar. On the other side of the fence, we can hear the trainer from the obstacle course call out commands to the dog. At one point, we hear a girl screaming. A couple of guys prop themselves up onto some railings to look over the eight-foot fence to see what is happening on the other side. That's when we discover that somebody will have to wear the protective padded suit and run out into the obstacle course, and the trainer will release his dog to take him or her down. It appears there is a different attack dog for each team completing the challenge. Each dog has a look of excitement, and they're all wagging their tails like it's a game as the contestants put on the protective suit.

Jim is selected to do this round. We help him into the burdensome suit and cheer him on. He gets about halfway down the course and the dog nails him to the ground. The dog stays right by his head—his jugular—barking until the trainer calls him off.

We complete our dog-attack task and one of the soldiers announces that they do this every day after lunch if anyone wants to return to give it another round. That's nice and thoughtful. I guess they are looking for some good bait for the dogs to practice.

We are given another clue that we don't understand yet. One of the game volunteers feels sorry for us since we are the only civilian group. She asks if we know where the Polish Compound is located. I tell her I do. She further directs us that next to it is Camp Black Jack and the military radio station is located there. That's where we have to run to next. It's about two miles up the street.

I'm reminded that none of my team members are really runners. Crail has run alongside me up to this leg of the race. He starts to drag behind. Jim and Trigger are really lagging—especially Trigger, after doing all the leg presses.

I run to Camp Black Jack and locate our next challenge at Freedom Radio Station. I direct Crail to the station and wait by the road to point Jim and Trigger in the right direction. We can't start the challenge until all the team members are present. This challenge is creative like all the others, but easy. Two of us, Crail and I, are given a script to read and record for the military radio station. Crail's part turns into a comedy act because he has to pronounce all these Afghanistan villages and provinces, and talk about the various projects that the military implements in the various regions. I remember one of the projects as a greenhouse project because that's what I did in the Peace Corps in Tunisia. We complete the task by stating each of our names and hometowns, adding an affiliation or a motto, and then saying, *"I am Freedom Radio."* Of course, the mic is shoved in front of my face first, so I have to say, *"This is Thomas Josef of Austin, Texas. Hook 'em Horns. I am Freedom Radio."*

When the radio producer hands us our final clue, he has a stack of over a dozen envelopes, so I think we're doing pretty well with our time. Our final clue is something about 47 steps and Russian-built. The air control tower! The four of us dart to the control tower next to the Camp Cunningham town hall where we started the race.

When I train to run, I always train to pick up the speed for the last leg. So I dodge ahead of my exhausted team, taking shortcuts and back dirt roads about a mile to the control tower. I bolt up the 47 stairs like a ram, which feels more like 200 stairs, to the top of the tower, where there's a 360-degree view of the Hindu Kush mountain range surrounding Bagram Airfield. I'm gushing with sweat as I hand in the final envelopes of clues, grab a bottle of water, and down it quickly to quench my thirst. I look out the windows to watch my team come trailing behind. When they've all finally made it to the top of the tower, we snap a few photos. I review the photos and ask, *"What's wrong with this picture?"* They look at me and ask, *"What?"* I say, *"I'm the only one sweating."* They all laugh.

The first-place winners finish in one hour and 50 minutes. The second-place team finishes in two hours and 20 minutes. My team finishes in three hours and 10 minutes. There are six teams who drop out during the race, and a handful or two arrive behind us.

So my team got our workout in for the day. We had a lot of fun. We learned a lot more about the base and met some awesome folks today. It really was an Amazing Race!

Freedom Watch

Working as a military contractor with no prior military background, it's been refreshing to see how our military operates and have the mission more clearly defined. In the U.S. media, all you hear about is the fighting and the killing. A higher-ranking serviceman told me that less than 20 percent of the task force sees combat. When I participated in the Bagram Amazing Race, one of our challenges was to read some of the successes and the progression made between the Combined Joint Task Force (CJTF) and their Afghan partners. It was an educational experience to realize how much good we are doing for the Afghan people versus the propaganda of the news media focusing on the stories that sell: fighting, death, and destruction.

The mission has been to conduct full operations to disrupt insurgent forces, develop host national security, and support and develop the growth of the government and workforce to build a more stable and economic environment with sustainable and self-sufficient institutions. The workforce development and expansion includes securing the future through education by increasing educational opportunities through building schools, increasing attendance, and employing more teachers; training an Afghan National Army and Police Force responsible for the security of Afghanistan; encouraging the advancement of women, particularly in the fields of health, education, environment, and government; and many other projects, including agriculture and road construction.

In the June 2010 special edition of *Freedom Watch*, a monthly publication of the CJTF, they published the following statistics—most of what we do not see or hear through our own media.

The Regional Command (RC) East Key Fact (Northern Afghanistan):

- It is one of five regional command posts under the International Security Assistance Force (ISAF).
- It is the only U.S.-led region in Afghanistan and where the majority of U.S. forces are located.
- ISAF partners include Australia, Czech Republic, Egypt, France, New Zealand, Poland, and Turkey.
- The RC-East consists of 14 Afghanistan provinces.
- Afghanistan's capital, Kabul, is located in the RC-East.
- Local population is 9.9 million people.
- The RC-East area's size is 48,137 square miles—about the size of Mississippi.
- 450 miles of the RC-East is bordered with Pakistan.

JOC Jock

Jeff works for the JAG (judge advocate general), providing legal services and advice in all legal matters involving the Navy or the Command. His office is in the JOC (joint operations center), which is guarded 24/7. You need a special badge for access. Jeff's life seems to evolve in the JOC. At least while he's here. I guess everything he needs is provided: office, housing, food, and gym.

Jeff works long, hard hours for a general. Sometimes he's working 16 or 18 hours a day. It seems like he has very limited free time and is always at the beck and call of his boss. He may catch a workout or two during the day within his compound. He's lean and fit. Perhaps that's why the Navy makes it easy and convenient for him to be close—so he's always available at a moment's notice. Trying to get him to leave the JOC to meet for a cup of coffee at Green Beans, which is relatively close, always seems like a difficult task. I manage to meet up with him for a midmorning cup of joe and conversation a few times. We both love our coffee and the largest cup available is always an order. It's nice to share a coffee with a professional, like-minded man in uniform.

The JOC is located close to Barron Village. In fact, it's practically right across the street. If Jeff manages to finish the day early, usually before 10:00 p.m., and still has some life in him, he'll call me to come over and spend the night. Jeff meets me at the JOC gate, usually in his Navy PT attire: shorts, T-shirt, and running shoes. The guards at the gate are in their full battle rattle. Jeff signs me in with the security officer and they issue me a temporary badge. He escorts me onto the premises. I ask him if security has any concerns about me signing in at 2200 and leaving at 0600. It seems like I'm always the only person in the compound not in uniform. He doesn't seem concerned and tells me there are meetings in the JOC at all hours of the night. It's no big deal.

Jeff always seems so calm, cool, and composed while escorting me to his room. He acknowledges comrades and never seems concerned about anyone asking who I am. Jeff has his own digs. He lives in a 40-foot container with his own little living area, microwave, fridge, office area, and a queen-sized bed. All of this is a complete luxury over here. His place is probably one of the best living quarters that I have ever seen on BAF. I'm not sure what Jeff's rank or actual profession is, but I figure he must be high up or important to have a place like this. There's some kind of arousal to being with a high-ranking officer who works for a general with secured housing in the JOC.

After spending the night together, we each head our own direction. Jeff heads to the shower and I stop by the closest restroom, which also serves as a shower room. There's a ton of guys in here getting ready for work. When I walk in, I stand out like a sore thumb because I'm the only one in civilian clothes. Plus most of the guys are comparatively young. I'm not sure what their affiliation to the JOC is. I do my job and proceed to the gate unescorted, where I check myself out.

As I return to my tent, I wonder if any of the guys notice that I've been gone all night. I wonder what would happen if we had incoming in the middle of the night. How would anyone locate me? I usually don't tell anyone that I'm headed over to the JOC. I guess if there was incoming, I'd just wait for the "all clear" and show up in person for accountability since I'm close by.

I'm not sure how fraternization is defined by the military. While not policy that I know of, I *have* seen fraternization *defined* in two ways: 1) to associate in a fraternal or friendly way; or 2) to associate cordially or intimately with natives of a conquered country, enemy, or troop. It's one of those words left up to the interpretation of the person, kind of like pornography. If you ask 100 people to define or give an example of pornography, you'll get 100 different answers. If there was a fraternization policy, I wonder if it would be a strike against me if I'm sleeping with someone from the military. I may not know his full name or even *real* name. All I know is that we want mutual, casual sex. Is that fraternization?

Barron's current take on cohabitation is to stay out of the employee's bedroom, which I think is a good stance. Thankfully we have a corporate retired Air Force lawyer here on base, who said they would not police employees' sex lives. Good for her! I've also heard a rumor that she defends that policy because she also has a "green suitor" who spends the night with her. Besides, I'd rather shack up with a soldier and share his nice bed, cuddle, fall asleep with my arm wrapped across his chest, and feel his warm body next to mine to help fill the void of being away from my partner. It's better than being in a tent with 40 other guys snoring, coughing, sneezing, farting, and coming and going all hours of the night as I lie on my cot, trying to fall asleep.

I have been with Jeff on and off for a few months. As most people come and go on this base, it's his time to go. He's heading to a new assignment back in the States.

232 Days

I am finally issued my own private room in a B-hut—232 days after my arrival at Bagram Airfield. It's hard to believe that I've been in Afghanistan for eight months already. I've moved living quarters eight times since I've been here. I've moved physical office locations four times. The training department has moved from under the Department of Public Works to human resources. The military and Barron keep you moving!

My B-hut is an eight-room barracks made of plywood. Even the doors are plywood. I often wonder why B-huts are built in a place like Afghanistan. The wood is shipped in and must cost a fortune. Local buildings are made of concrete created on-site. There's even a cement processing plant on base. I guess it would take too long to cure a cement building instead of putting up a plywood one. But in the long run, the cement houses would stand up to the elements and critters far better than the plywood buildings and would provide better protection.

Entering the B-hut, I notice it has a very nice clean scent. Someone installed an automatic deodorizer that sprays a nice mist about every 30 minutes. It's nice and cool. I got the first room on the left, closest to the exit and the air conditioner. The rooms are tiny, maybe eight by eight. I think my walk-in closet back home is bigger than this room. It's barely big enough to fit a twin-sized bed and a shelving unit to hang and stack clothes. Anything else goes under the bed. I'm not complaining though because it's a step up from the tent.

Of course, the billeting office clears out the B-huts of any possessions left behind from previous tenants, but they don't clean them—or at least not to my standards. The previous tenant stapled woven mats to the floor. I pull those up and discover that this floor has probably never seen a broom or dustpan. I sweep five big dustpans of dirt off the floor and wash it. My bucket of clear, sudsy water quickly turns to a thick, murky liquid. I wash the floor three times before I feel confident that it's semi-clean. I set up my fan and turn it on to dry the floor so I can move in.

As the floor is drying, I return to my old tent to start packing and loading my belongings. Fortunately my move is just a few hundred feet away and I really don't have a whole lot of stuff, so I manage to carry everything over to the new place in just three short trips with no help.

Living in a tent has been very interesting. It may not sound all that glamorous, but I have been fortunate to always be a step ahead of the influx of people arriving and staying at BAF. All the tents have plywood floors and beam posts, so they're well secured and protected from the weather. I always had a bottom bunk and rarely had someone sleeping above me. Most of the time, I also had a corner spot, so I had only one neighbor to deal with, who was normally a good coworker of mine. After I claimed my spot, I would put up partitions to create my own room and run clothesline to create a curtain wall. Sometimes I'd find pieces of plywood and poles to create something sturdier. I'd go to the construction areas and pick up nails. I'd use a rock as a hammer. Nowadays I know a few carpenters and can borrow tools.

Up for grabs are all the belongings people leave behind. When people leave Afghanistan for good, they barely take the clothes off their backs with them. They either give it away or leave it all behind for the next person. I never really rummage through the garbage, but I do take a look. I'm always amazed at all the stuff that ends up neatly stacked outside a tent or B-hut. I once found a Carhartt jacket that was in great shape. I had it laundered and now it's good as new. I also found a jean jacket and some nice button-down shirts, but I gave those away. Brooms, dustpans, mirrors, drawers, blankets, rugs, clothes, DVDs, TVs, irons and ironing boards, etc. You can find it gently used in or next to a trash can eventually. If you're patient, you won't have to buy anything to furnish your room.

You can find some pretty good pickins around Bagram. In fact, the poor Egyptian military seems not to have much of a protocol on their uniforms. I think the men are only issued the jacket and pants. The name badges on their jackets look like they sign their own names with a black magic marker. I think it's really the Arabic script and the font they choose for their uniforms, but it looks handwritten. There doesn't seem to be a consistent shoe or boot that they are issued either. Some wear worn and dirty tennis shoes, and others wear scuffed boots. I think most of them got their footwear from the trash that the Americans left behind. I've seen a few of the Egyptians rummaging through the garbage at night. They can't afford shoes, but they can afford cigarettes. The U.S. military has a no-smoking policy on base except in designated areas. The other NATO troops are not familiar with this or disregard it.

There is a donation box where people can donate their goods to the local Afghan population, but I think either people don't want to deal with it, because they'd have to haul it to the single location that accepts the donations, or they don't know about it.

But oh, my lovely room. I clean it, move into it, and organize it. After all is said and done, I pretend it's my own little rustic mountain cabin. It's woodsy and quaint. I sleep soundly the first night without hearing any chatter, bunks squeaking or rattling, or alarm clocks. I think I'll like my new little place until I move again to another step above this B-hut.

A Cookie, a Pork Chop, and a Prune

My buddy Sam tells me he has a new nickname for one of the managers, Victoria. Victoria is a big girl. Most folks believe the only reason she's here is because she's upper management and has connections. She should've been disqualified to work in Afghanistan, given her body mass index (BMI).

Sam also tells me that she was given the job under the condition that she join the Army weight-loss program. I'm sure she finagled her way out of that. The Army weight-loss program is a dietary counseling program. It can also be brutal, not to mention humiliating if you're a soldier. Overweight soldiers are made to wear their personal protective equipment (PPE), which adds 25 to 30 pounds, and run up and down Disney Boulevard with their platoon. I've seen some drill sergeants or troop leaders running alongside the overweight ones and yelling in their faces, *"Can't you run any faster than that, soldier?"* I don't see where that builds confidence, character, or motivation in the person. It reminds me of episodes of *Gomer Pyle* when Sergeant Carter would be barking in Gomer's face and Gomer never seemed to be bothered by it. I've seen some of the Army women on Disney act like that too, as though the sergeant wasn't there. He's invisible. *"Is he yelling at me? What's his problem? I'm just going to give him a little push of my hip and bounce him off the road and out of my face."*

Sam's new nickname for Victoria is "Cookie." I ask him why he chose that name. He says that woman is always ordering junk food and has it shipped here for the whole office. He asks me if I saw their Easter spread. I remember it quite well. It was a colorful mosaic of candy and treats loaded on a table about 12 feet long, taking up every inch of space. He says Victoria ordered all of that. Sam says she reminded him of a big ol' cookie. Victoria is not the first fat lady to be called Cookie.

At the office, Trigger, Sissy, and I start talking about other nicknames people are given. Trigger adds that he met a plumber at another base. He says the guy was big and wore his britches like a lot of other plumbers: with his crack showing. When Trigger asked him what his name was, the plumber replied in a raspy voice, *"My friends call me Pork Chop."* Trigger's vivid description makes me feel like I've met this guy before.

The other day, Trigger and I sent Sissy on a mission. Again, the men just love it when Sissy comes around and they all soften up like butter. She's kind of like our collections agent. So Trigger and I gave her a list of names that were slacking on sending us data or follow-ups. On the list was Ted. I asked Sissy if she knew Ted. She didn't. I warned her that he has the driest, flakiest, toughest skin of anyone I know. I told her shaking his hand is like holding a cat's tongue. I suggested she give her hands an extra pump of lotion and rub it on Ted's hands when she shakes his hand.

Sissy returns from Ted's office and immediately darts to the bottle of lotion. She covers her hands with the gel. She says, *"That man's skin is like a prune! His body sucked the lotion right off my hands like they were begging for it."* She keeps referring to Ted as "The Prune." She states that Ted will be stopping by our office with the data we requested. I tell Sissy, *"When he comes to the office tomorrow, you should nonchalantly grab the bottle of lotion, squirt some into your hands, and then offer some to him."*

The next day, Sissy puts the plan into action. The Prune arrives, and Sissy grabs the lotion bottle, puts some in her hands, looks at Ted, and offers him some. Trigger and I look at each and smile. She just did it so effortlessly and naturally! Ted says, *"No, thank you."* Sissy, being quick-witted replies, *"Here, Ted, take some anyway. I put too much on my hands."* She doesn't let him think twice about it and starts to lotion his hands from hers. Then Ted says, *"Well maybe I will take a little more."* Sissy grabs the pump bottle and gives him a double squirt. I'm sure she's biting her tongue a few times, remembering to call him Ted instead of Prune.

Ted leaves and we start talking about the successful plan of action. Sissy says, *"Did you see his hands absorb that lotion? His hands started singing,"* as she trills like an opera singer, *"Haaaa-lleeee-lujah!"* During her hallelujah harmony, she comes up with this brilliant idea to create a gift basket of bath salts and lotions to put on his desk and leave it when he's not there. I'm sure he could use the bath salts to exfoliate the skin.

That's the story of a cookie, a pork chop, and a prune.

The Team

One thing on this project is that change is constant and inevitable. Sissy leaves the project and takes another position with Barron. The poor thing has been assigned to work on a project in Paris. How will she ever adjust? I'm so happy for her. "Good-Lookin' Body" Will also leaves shortly after Sissy. From what I hear, Will does not leave voluntarily. He screwed up. Or, as he tells me, he was set up. Apparently some confidential information got into the wrong hands. I believe Will. Gosh, I'm going to miss those two.

As Murphy's Law would have it, the remaining six on the transition team are assigned to the training department just as Huggy McPherson wanted it. So now our team includes Trigger, Tina, me, and the six new folks: Janet Atkinson, Mary Jane, Sharon, Claire, Howie, and Merissa ("Bunkerhead").

I finally get to meet Bunkerhead. She's nothing like I pictured her to be. After meeting Sissy and Janet from the transition team—both being fit, smart, driven women—I thought maybe Merissa would have some of the same characteristics, especially since she has the reputation of luring men into the bunkers for sexual favors. But Merissa has a flabby, rubbery, white body like that of the Pillsbury Doughboy. Her hair is red and cut short. She wears black horn-rimmed glasses that make her eyes look like an owl's. She comes across like she knows what she's talking about, but she really doesn't.

Neither Trigger nor I was involved in the hiring selection of our team. We were just told by Huggy that we were getting the final six. Janet and Mary Jane at least have a training background; however, Mary Jane adamantly voiced her dislike of being involved in training. The other four are primarily HR. HR and training are two very different skill sets, so I'm not sure if or how they will fit into the training vision, mission, and goals.

Trigger and I have a huge challenge ahead of us. Before we can move forward with our training objectives and priorities, we need to provide internal departmental training. In our first couple of meetings, I can tell my new staff is not enthusiastic about being in training. How will I ever be able to persuade or motivate them? To make matters worse, our office spaces are divided. Two of them are with Trigger in one office; I'm over here in an office tent with the others.

I am able, however, to task Mary Jane and Janet with assignments with very little supervision. The others need some mentoring. In addition, they need to learn or enhance their skill sets with writing, presentation development, and the use of software. This is not good. I feel like we are being set up for failure. Because they have boots on the ground, we've been saddled with this staff.

Time will prove to be of the essence.

One Year

Not long after we acquire our given team, Trigger says to me, *"Thomas, I've never worked with a woman in my life. I can't deal with all of their emotions and office gossip. You're going to have to deal with it."* As second in charge, I do exactly that.

"How's it going, Thomas?" asks Trigger. I know he's really asking how the team is holding up. I unravel my discontent and give him the lowdown. Neither one of us is satisfied with the current group dynamics of our team. I speculate that Trigger already knows how it's going with the team and just needs to hear it come out of my mouth. I'm frustrated—we're both frustrated—and I unleash the difficulties and challenges I'm facing with them. They're all great people, but they just don't have the skills and qualifications of people we need to run a training department. Trigger takes note of everything I tell him.

I also have a suspicion that Janet Atkinson has been feeding Trigger some information about the team since she had worked with all of them over the past year. The two of them have been sharing the same office for the past several weeks, and there's no telling what they've been discussing. She's an older athletic woman, smart, and has been with the company for a long time. She has a huge network of colleagues here in the field as well as back home at the corporate office. She knows a lot about HR, training and development, and many of the various departments that we interact with, which is just about all of them. She tends to have her nose in everyone's business and doesn't think twice about going directly to the project manager with her observations and input.

Huggy McPherson made a comment to me one day about how while they were on the transition team, Janet took it upon herself to keep a log of what time people came to work, when they went on break, and when they checked out for the day. She's that kind of person. Most people dislike her. Most people don't want her on their team. Some people think she's a mole for the company.

Off to Venice!

It's R&R number three! I'm meeting Greg in Venice with a couple friends of ours from Austin. We're going to embark on a week-long

Mediterranean cruise, with a few days in Venice on the front end of the trip and a week on Mykonos on the back end.

What's not to love about Venice? The old architecture, gas street lamps, cobblestone streets, foot bridges that cross the canals, gondola taxis, exquisite foods, lavish Italian clothing styles, the sweet melody of the language, and fine and colorful art. There are open piazzas to sip a morning espresso or an afternoon glass of wine and watch the hustle and bustle of the community life and marketplace. I can see why Venice is dubbed one of the most romantic cities in the world. It's full of warmth and charm and grandeur. I'm glad my lover and I are here to experience it.

After three days in Venice, we hop on the cruise ship and set sail into the turquoise-blue waters of the Mediterranean, with stops in Croatia, Turkey, and Greece. We disembark the cruise in Athens and jump on a ferry to spend a final week on Mykonos, where we meander on the flagstone walkways through a maze of white clay buildings with bright-blue trim. We frolic and hold hands with no guilt or shame. We spend our days at the beach, staring out at the many shades of water, from crystal clear to cyan to midnight blue. The water is so peaceful as we watch the sensational sunset behind it leaving a rippling glow. Our palates are overcome with many Mediterranean delights and our taste buds dance with splendor.

Again, all good things must come to an end. When Greg and I depart, we both have a few extra days before we return to our daily grinds. He heads back to the States to meet a fuck buddy of his in Colorado. Rather than spend my final couple days in Dubai, I decide to head to Bahrain, where I'm meeting someone.

Clean House

I'm returning from R&R and currently held up in Dubai for the night before heading back to Bagram. I run into a colleague heading out on

R&R who tells me that Trigger cleaned house. Sure enough, I get back to base and Mary Jane has been reassigned to provide HR support in Iraq. Claire has moved to another base to perform an HR support role where her qualifications are better suited. Howie left Barron to work for another contractor. Sharon decided she was totally out of her comfort zone as a trained nurse and decided to go home and return to the health-care field.

The team count is back down to five: Trigger, Tina, Bunkerhead, Janet Atkinson, and me. I'm not dismayed about the changes. I'm glad that the others found new and better opportunities, and are moving forward.

Christmas 2010

It's Christmas at Bagram again and I'm receiving lots of holiday cards. I enjoy receiving them and hang them up around the office to make it look a little more festive. I'm trying to get into the holiday spirit. I also receive my annual Christmas box of cookies and reading materials from Marg and Andrea's famous rum balls. Yum!

Trying to get out of Bagram around Christmas is hell. People book their flights from Bagram to Dubai months in advance. This includes people from the other forward operating bases that must come to the hub of Bagram to leave the country. Not only are the flights booked, but they're also unpredictable due to the weather in Northern Afghanistan and the surrounding Hindu Kush Mountains. We get snow and freezing rain, and the fog can be heavy too. Then the flights from Dubai back home to the U.S. are high-dollar and people must deal with connecting flights. I gladly let any coworker who wants the time off to take it. I prefer to go during a less-traveled time and when flights and airports are not as hectic or costly. So here on base it's pretty much just business as usual, as it was last Christmas and any other holiday. We're expected to keep the base running 24/7/365, so as usual, our 12-hour workday is the standard.

As I did last year, I go to the DFAC to enjoy our Christmas Day lunch with a group of coworkers. It's a completely different group this year, but a group I feel closer to as I've gotten to know each of them over the past year. The DFACs compete for the best decorated DFAC and create a beautiful spread of food with prime rib, roast, turkey, and all the fixins—this includes lots and lots of desserts.

We head over to the DFAC entrance, where there's a big inflated Santa Claus sitting on a chair. Of course we want to get pictures, so Clearance goes up to the Santa and props his butt on Santa's leg. We get his picture, and I follow and get mine. It's Tom's turn, and when he goes to sit on the inflated Santa's lap, he falls to the ground and the Santa floats on top of him. Classic act, Tom! Poor guy. He lies there on the cold concrete, laughing at himself. While we're all standing there laughing at him, a good soldier walks over to give him a helping hand. Tom tells us that we propped ourselves on Santa's lap so nicely that he thought it was supported from underneath or that the bench was real. So when he went to do it . . . Bam! Down on the ground he went.

Interestingly and obviously, a lot of people from other countries do not celebrate Christmas—nearly two-thirds of the world's population. I don't celebrate Christmas from a Christianity viewpoint, but it's been embedded more from family tradition. The meaning of Christmas fades deeper and deeper in me with each year that passes . . .

"12 Days of LOGCAP"

by Thomas Josef

On the first day of LOGCAP,
My contractor sent to me
A one-way ticket to a war zone.

On the second day of LOGCAP,
My contractor sent to me
Two hundred roommates,
And a one-way ticket to a war
zone.

On the third day of LOGCAP,
My contractor sent to me
Three-minute showers,
Two hundred roommates,
And a one-way ticket to a war
zone.

On the fourth day of LOGCAP
My contractor sent to me
Four kinds of rice,
Three-minute showers,
Two hundred roommates,
And a one-way ticket to a war
zone.

On the fifth day of LOGCAP,
My contractor sent to me
Five controlled dets,
Four kinds of rice,
Three-minute showers,
Two hundred roommates,

And a one-way ticket to a war
zone.

On the sixth day of LOGCAP,
My contractor sent to me
Six-digit salary,
Five controlled dets,
Four kinds of rice,
Three-minute showers,
Two hundred roommates,
And a one-way ticket to a war
zone.

On the seventh day of LOGCAP,
My contractor sent to me
Seven days a-working,
Six-digit salary,
Five controlled dets,
Four kinds of rice,
Three-minute showers,
Two hundred roommates,
And a one-way ticket to a war
zone.

On the eighth day of LOGCAP,
My contractor sent to me
Eight hours' bunker time,
Seven days a-working,
Six-digit salary,
Five controlled dets,
Four kinds of rice,

Three-minute showers,
Two hundred roommates,
And a one-way ticket to a war
zone.

On the ninth day of LOGCAP,
My contractor sent to me
Nine more vaccines,
Eight hours' bunker time,
Seven days a-working,
Six-digit salary,
Five controlled dets,
Four kinds of rice,
Three-minute showers,
Two hundred roommates,
And a one-way ticket to a war
zone.

On the tenth day of LOGCAP,
My contractor sent to me
Ten weeks a-waiting,
Nine more vaccines,
Eight hours' bunker time,
Seven days a-working,
Six-digit salary,
Five controlled dets,
Four kinds of rice,
Three-minute showers,
Two hundred roommates,
And a one-way ticket to a war
zone.

On the eleventh day of LOGCAP,
My contractor sent to me
Eleven people demobing,
Ten weeks a-waiting,
Nine more vaccines,
Eight hours' bunker time,
Seven days a-working,
Six-digit salary,
Five controlled dets,
Four kinds of rice,
Three-minute showers,
Two hundred roommates,
And a one-way ticket to a war
zone.

On the twelfth day of LOGCAP,
My contractor sent to me
Twelve-hour workdays,
Eleven people demobing,
Ten weeks a-waiting,
Nine more vaccines,
Eight hours' bunker time,
Seven days a-working,
Six-digit salary,
Five controlled dets,
Four kinds of rice,
Three-minute showers,
Two hundred roommates,
And a one-way ticket to a war
zone.

2011

Bagram Trailer Park

The Village is beginning to look and feel more like a trailer park. Our community looks like an economically depressed area comprised of the poor, the redneck, and the scoundrel. There are no hard- surfaced roads made of cement or blacktop here. Our roadways are gravel—big chunks of white and gray sharp rock that add to the dull and dreary landscape. The only greenery that I see in this thirsty land are a few sparse weeds that pop up here and there, and can survive the baking-hot sun. Trash barrels are about every 10 feet and give The Village an added touch. In the morning, the trash is stacked in big piles for pickup.

The metal shipping containers that make up our living quarters look like stacked trailer houses. The B-huts with the thin plywood walls have paint peeling. Cables are bundled haphazardly and awry, and are supported on anything that will hold them. A big bundle is supported along the soffit of the headquarter building and then divides off to the metal and plywood buildings. Some of the cables are tucked in between boards and doorframes, and behind and across light fixtures to a hole in the wall to run cable TV to somebody's room. Some of them are sagging and broken. It truly gives the camp that third-world touch. Windows are covered with aluminum foil or cardboard to block out light and the radiant heat. Our location in the Hindu Kush doesn't attract tornadoes, thankfully. We get enough devastation from the incoming missiles and rockets, not to mention the occasional earth tremor. Some windows are taped up to prevent shattering in the event of incoming, the vibration, or projectiles.

One morning I observe a big black woman in her pink robe, pink shower cap, and pink fuzzy slippers walking outdoors toward the restroom. She must have recognized this Indian guy who works for the cable company. She starts to harshly lay into the poor guy at the top of her lungs. I listen closely to hear what all the commotion is about. Her cable TV has not been working for a few days and she is taking the blame out on the poor little Indian guy.

I don't like the way she's treating the poor fella, so I put on my John Wayne hat and walk over to them and say in my softest voice possible, *"What seems to be the problem here?"* The woman lowers her voice about 10 decibels and tells me her issue with her cable TV. I think she's just glad that I'm listening, and I tell her I understand her frustration, which I don't because I couldn't care less about cable TV. I ask the little Indian guy if he'd check into it and take care of the problem. I ask him what his name is. He replies, *"My name is Chiranjeevi."* Not that I'll be able to repeat his name, but I tell him, *"My name is Thomas and this is . . ."* as I look at the woman with the issue. She mutters, *"Nita."* Chiranjeevi says he will take care of it, and I believe him because I think that lady scared the living Vishnu out of him. We shake hands and all is well. We go our separate ways.

People are starting to shuffle about in the predawn hours of the morning, going in and out of the bathrooms and to and from their B-huts or tents, and women are wearing housecoats with their hair wrapped up in towels, carrying big bags or totes of cosmetics, shampoo, conditioner, perfumes, blow dryer, etc. Some carry their stuff in baskets; others use plastic buckets. The men walk about in the morning in their robes, sweats, or shorts, or some in pajamas. I've even seen a few men walk to the restroom in their boxers like they'd pass as shorts, or maybe they didn't give a damn. Hell, I've seen one or two with just a towel wrapped around their bodies at the waist. Some tote just a towel and a bottle of body wash, others have a shaving bag, and some have backpacks. Those who are thriftier—or from lower-income countries, who arrived here with nothing—may just use a plastic bag they got from the PX to haul their necessities. People have to make do. It basically is a trailer park.

Most of the women walking to work have their hair washed and styled, or pulled and tied back. You can smell the clean fragrance from their freshly washed hair. Some wear perfume and you can smell that too. Many of the women dress in jeans and a shirt but still look nice and professional—it's obvious that they take pride in and take care of themselves. Of course, most of them work in an office setting or perform administrative work.

The men, on the other hand, are more trade and construction workers. Jeans, T-shirts, and boots, and they are ready to go. They're probably hurrying to get to breakfast more than they are getting ready for work. We also have a few sporting high-end, quality designer clothing and accessories with their mid-rear, oversized, baggy jeans and their boxers sticking out. They've got a $2,000 gold necklace around their neck while they work a marginal job in the DFAC or as a laborer. I guess we just can't dodge the thug look or priorities. Fortunately we're not exposed to that kind of trashiness too often because there is a company dress code addressing professionalism that gets down to the detail of even how to wear a baseball cap. I'm glad we have it. It shows a little more professionalism as well as courtesy to our uniformed personnel, who must adhere to strict uniform codes and proper grooming and hygiene. The only time we see the trashiness come out is usually when they're off work or leaving for R&R, but even then they're supposed to be adhering to the dress code policy.

I've had to tell a few of the new hires to pull up their pants or to fix their caps straight.

I have about a three-minute commute by foot from my B-hut to my office door. I can sleep in until 5:55 a.m. and be at work by 6:00 a.m. I slip on my clothes and out the door I go. There are plenty of bathrooms along the way to work. Bathrooms are generally in two-story container units with toilets, urinals, and sinks on the bottom floor, and showers, sinks, and a changing area on the top floor.

The two-story metal housing units in The Village look like mobile homes stacked on top of each other. The B-huts look like houses pulled from District 9 post-Katrina and reassembled here on top of a huge gravel parking lot. There's no grass or greenery. The roads are more like alleyways made with more gravel and no curbs. There's no drainage system. Our water is hauled in and hauled out. It's a 24/7 operation for all water: bottled water, non-potable water, gray water, and black water.

As I walk closer to the headquarters building, there's a black-water (sewage) truck pumping out the sludge from the septic tank. It reminds me of the dump stations at a trailer park. There are dump stations all over The Village and base—wherever there's a shower or a toilet, there's a dump station and water tanks. We call the black-water trucks "poo-poo trucks." The pungent odor and gases escape into the air we breathe. Some days in the afternoon, the nasty smell permeates the loosely sealed windows of the headquarters building and we evacuate for a while until the air clears.

The drivers and laborers are obviously used to the smell of the job. The other day I saw a laborer eating a sandwich while he was pumping the poop out of the septic tank and into the truck. I thought I was going to puke from the smell as I was watching him eat his sandwich. I was glad to see that where he grasped his sandwich, it was still wrapped in plastic wrap. I guess some things just don't phase people around here.

After I get past the shit truck, I'm in the back of the two-story headquarters building where my new little office is located on the first floor. As I walk toward the back entrance, a few of the senior managers and personnel are on the upstairs porch having a morning coffee, smoke, and chat.

I look over to my right and see Timmy Dwayne Fontenot come out of his office with his coffee pot. I haven't seen much of him since his watermelon-diet days. He obviously reached his goal and passed his physical. He walks to the end of his wooden walkway and flings yesterday's coffee onto the gravel. The gravel is stained black from days and days of tossing his leftover coffee onto it to bake in the hot Afghanistan sun. Timmy Dwayne looks up at me and says in his nicest Cajun voice, *"Good morning, young man!"* Timmy Dwayne's size, shaved head, big bushy eyebrows, and succulent ears remind me of Shrek. He's a big, big man, about 6'5" and 350 pounds, and wears wire-rimmed glasses. As he'll tell you, he's deaf in one ear and can't hear out of the other. He wears archaic hearing aids that protrude out of each of his ears like Shrek's antenna ears. He has an underbite and talks like he's gargling with gravel. I'm not sure whether it's part of his heritage or if years of heavy smoking has caused him to have a raspy, almost-inaudible voice. A woman told me that if he had a bolt on each side of his neck, he could be Frankenstein. He also walks with a limp from arthritis in his knees.

Everything Timmy Dwayne lacks in good looks he makes up in character, humor, and manners. He's a gentleman and funny to listen to. You never know what words will come out of his mouth. It's not that he has a bad mouth on him, but he uses the reddest of redneck Southern phrases that most of us have never heard. When Timmy Dwayne rattles off one of those phrases, we laugh and call them "Timmisms."

I wave and shout good morning to Timmy Dwayne and ask how he's doing. He replies with one of his Timmisms, *"I've been busy as an outhouse latch.*" I'm glad his work is keeping him busy. If Timmy Dwayne knew what transpired with Nita and Chiranjeevi, he probably would've said something like, *"She was meaner than a crocodile in a dry creek,"* or, *"She was all over him like a bad rash on a big ass."* I mean, I've heard him use both of those lines before.

Transition Complete

One of the major accomplishments in the past year is the successful transition—or as the military calls it, transfer of authority (TOA)—conducted between the LOGCAP III incumbent contractor RBK and the LOGCAP IV incoming performing contractor Barron. The transition of logistic contract support included 59 forward operating bases (FOBs) with a combined supported population of more than 70,000 military service members, coalition forces, and Department of Defense civilians and contractors, all geographically dispersed over an area slightly smaller than California. The transition involved more than 12,000 combined prime contractor and subcontractor employees of RBK and Barron, and it was completed in less than nine months. I was one of the first couple hundred employees who arrived with Barron. I am now one of thousands of Barron employees with more than 60 countries represented on base and more than 50 different languages—English being the common denominator.

To appreciate the significance of this transition, one must first understand the considerable impact LOGCAP has on operations in Northern and Central Afghanistan. In the northern half of Afghanistan, where I am stationed, LOGCAP provides operations and maintenance to more than 1,500 non-tactical vehicles, 1,800 generators, 7,500 facilities, and more than 40 dining facilities providing 4 million meals per month. Additionally, LOGCAP provides monthly 42 million gallons of water and 19 million gallons of fuel, and processes 150,000 bags of laundry. Afghanistan's austere infrastructure and hostile environment complicate this already challenging mission.

My workload, purpose, and vision in the past year have changed a few times. It's now been fine-tuned. All civilian personnel work 12 hours a day. Sometimes I find myself so entrenched in my work that I'm still in the office an hour or two after my shift is finished. There's plenty to do and my department only consists of a team of three for a while. We are tasked to incorporate training requirements as directed by the military, as well as at the corporate, project, and department levels of the project. It's a major undertaking and rewarding in many ways. I have no regrets leaving the Texas State government for the position that I'm currently in. I tell people it was an easy decision to go to work in a war zone rather than to continue working for the son-of-a-bitch boss I had working at the State. I'm blazing the path forward.

Lights Out

I've adjusted to my eight-by-eight living quarters. There's a lights-out policy from 10:00 p.m. to 5:00 a.m. It's a good policy for those of us who want to sleep. Most of the guys in my B-hut abide by it. There are a couple guys who consistently wake me though. One guy gets up in the middle of the night—almost every night—to relieve himself. He stomps so heavily when he walks that he sounds like an elephant going down the hall. Another guy generally gets up in the middle of the night to have a smoke to stop his smoker's cough. I first hear his incessant cough and then hear the door open. Sometimes he leaves the door ajar and I can smell the smoke. Occasionally one of the guys has his girlfriend over and I hear the bed squeaking in its rhythmic pattern, starting slow and picking up tempo.

The B-hut is infested with wood-eating beetles from Pakistan. It's like a termite. Every day when I return from work, they've left their evidence of sawdust scattered over my bed. In addition to the sawdust is the crud that's emitted from the A/C unit above the main door and next to my room. Between the sawdust and the A/C crud, I wonder how much I've inhaled during the night. I'll probably be diagnosed with pulmonary disease down the road from inhaling that shit.

Considering I came over here with my standards lowered to zero after the first 90 days, things are starting to improve. I've got a private room. We have higher water pressure in the bathrooms and showers. The office facilities are on a daily cleaning schedule; showers and bathrooms are cleaned twice a day. We're starting to get supplies we need to do our jobs better. We got rid of a lot of the riffraff we inherited from RBK. Some of them got new front teeth. And best of all, the management appears to be providing better direction with a vision, mission, policies, and procedures.

Annual Physical

Cole is a fellow Austinite I met here on base. He works for our electrical department. The word on the street is that he went out for his annual physical and R&R. He disclosed that one of the prescriptions he is taking is a sleeping pill and was put on a 60-day delayed qualification to ensure it's out of his system, as the military prohibits any kind of sleeping aid. I'm in the same boat!

In accordance with the military contract, every employee must have a physical every 12 to 15 months to ensure we are fit for duty. The physical is conducted in Dubai for Barron employees. It is stringent and bound to conditions of a war environment. Tests are taken for blood, urine, chest, heart, hearing, vision, and dental, and take up a good portion of the day.

Prior to leaving Bagram, everyone must go through a lengthy out-process and 30-minute departure orientation that goes over policies and procedures. LaWanda leads the instructional orientation. She stands in front of the room speaking loudly with her poor English, waving her long index finger and flinging her long-haired wig like a drag queen, of the dos and don'ts of the leave policy.

It's painful for me to sit through this session, listening to her in a supervisory role, when most of the foreigners in this room read, write, and speak far better English than LaWanda and most of the Americans on this base. It deflates me to know that she has supervisory authority and is a representative of this company. To top it off, she's a total bitch to the foreigners who nudge their buddies, asking for clarification because they can't figure out what the hell she's saying in her slaughtered English. She looks at it as being disrespected and walks right up to them and yells, *"You got a problem? Why you talkin' while I talkin'?"* It's an embarrassment. Maybe Barron should require Americans to take an English test before promoting them into positions of authority. I know there are far better qualified people who can do her job. Why is she in this position? I don't like the bitch, but she must be screwing someone at the top or have something on someone.

The first part of the exam is completing a detailed medical history disclosing what may be genetic, what surgeries you've had in the past, what medications or supplements you're currently taking, etc. The staff of doctors will examine each employee for certain physical and mental health conditions. The medical staff also looks for communicable diseases such as tuberculosis, HIV, hepatitis, and other sexually transmitted diseases. Blood and urine are taken to examine for anything that may have been revealed in your medical history, including drug and alcohol blood levels.

It's the morning of my physical in Dubai. We meet at 7:00 a.m. for a short briefing and then are transported to the medical facility about 20 minutes away from the hotel. Fortunately our group is small—about a dozen people—so I am hoping the process will be relatively fast so that I'll have a good portion of the day to enjoy Dubai. At the medical facility, we go through another briefing and complete more paperwork.

It's Friday. This is not good because Fridays in the Islam world are like Sundays in the Christian world, meaning that many businesses in the U.A.E. and the Muslim world are closed or have reduced hours.

We sit in the waiting room for what feels like ages. I'm not sure if the medical staff will show up. All of us here for the physical exam are fasting, as is required. All I can think about is my morning cup of coffee and a pastry that I eyed at the bakery we walked by as we entered the building this morning.

Finally, around 11:00 a.m., some of the medical staff show up to start the physical exam process. Each employee is sent to various stations for testing. I manage to get the blood test out of the way first, so I sneak downstairs to get a cup of coffee and something to eat. I return upstairs for the rest of the process.

I'm the last one to finish the exam. The final step is a consultation with the doctor to go over any findings, concerns, or questionable standards. All my test results are clean, but he questions me on the sleeping pills I'm taking. I disclosed this on my medical papers because tests nowadays can reveal just about anything and everything that's in a person's system. Maybe I was just paranoid. Fortunately I mentioned it to the medic escorting us this morning and he told me it's grounds for disqualification unless it's taken for jet lag only. Bingo! And that's what I tell the doctor. I get to use my "get out of jail free" card and off I go. I'm good for another 12 to 15 months.

Following the exam, I spend 17 days at home so I can return later in the year and still maintain my tax-credit status. As always, the time goes by quickly. It's great to be welcomed home to my partner's loving arms, the dogs nudging at my side, cooking on the outdoor grill, sharing a glass of wine, walking through the gardens that I created, and enjoying the rest of the comforts of home.

While at home, I have a lot of different discussions with Greg: family, events, travel, the gym, and our affairs. Not business affairs, but love affairs. I tell Greg about the lust and flings that I've had on base. Really, it's just sex. I don't have time to create an emotional tie with any of my sex partners there. As humans, we have sex for self-gratification and a release. I believe we are wired that way.

Greg reveals to me that after our last visit, he met another guy: a young, good-looking Iranian-American named Kamal. They've been seeing each other now for a couple of months. Everything that Greg shares with me about Kamal sounds favorable. Kamal really isn't a threat to our relationship anyway because he's a closeted gay and would not want his secret lifestyle disclosed among his Muslim community or family. He knows Greg and I are in a relationship and would not come between us. Shortly after I first got home, Kamal stopped by the house and left a bottle of wine at the door as a "welcome home" gift. He seems like a great guy and a great catch.

I finally get to meet him. He's pleasant on the eyes. Tall, coal-black hair, chestnut-colored eyes, very fair skin, and a toned body. He's also one of the most well-endowed men I've ever met. That pecker is huge! No wonder Greg fell in love with him.

During my time at home, the three of us fix dinners, go to the gym, walk the dogs, watch movies, hang out naked by the pool, talk, laugh, and sleep together. For many relationships, having an affair or bringing in a third may be a marriage breaker; for us, it's a marriage enhancer. Kamal adds a breath of fresh air and excitement into our relationship.

I have one more affair and story to share with Greg. The story is about meeting Rafik, and I'm heading to Lebanon to meet him after I leave here.

Lebanon

"My flight is canceled. I don't think I'm coming. It's just too difficult dealing with the airline, and if I can get on a flight tomorrow, that gives me just one night with you," I told Rafik on the telephone when I was destined for Bahrain a few months ago. *"No. No. No. You come! Give*

me your airline information and I'll deal with them. I want you here," he insisted. I did and he changed my flight to the next day.

When I arrived six months ago, I maneuvered my way through the Manama airport like any other. I told Rafik, when I exit the airport doors into the passenger arrival area, look for a guy in a Texas straw cowboy hat. I'd never met Rafik until then. We'd corresponded on and off for a couple of years through a website on the internet. When he told me he was working in Bahrain and the flights were so cheap from Dubai, I thought, *"Why the hell not?"* Prior to my arrival, we discussed different scenarios. We knew we were compatible and had many of the same interests, through our internet conversations. The main uncertainty was whether one of us might not be attracted to the other. But as Rafik assured me, *"We're both grown adults and we'll work it out."* In the worst-case scenario, I'd get my own hotel room. Money was not the issue.

The Manama airport was small and the arrival area thick with black-haired, dark-skinned men. I scanned the faces and bodies of the men and tried to match one with the picture that Rafik sent of himself. Coming into view from the crowd strolled a tall, handsome man with a gleaming smile. He reached out his hand to greet me with a handshake. We both stared deeply into each other's eyes with smiles on our faces. He led me to the parking lot, where a silver BMW was parked, and then grabbed my bag and plopped it into the trunk. We drove to his apartment, and within 10 minutes of closing the apartment door, the clothes came off and we didn't leave the bedroom until the next morning. That was how I met Rafik.

Now, six months later, I am heading to Rafik's native land of Lebanon. My Lebanese coworkers and friends I made back in Austin always spoke highly of Lebanon before the war. I remember them describing Beirut as the "Paris of the Middle East." It's been on my list of places to travel and now is the perfect opportunity to go.

I called Rafik a few weeks ago, informing him of plans to go to Lebanon. He said, *"Yes, come to Lebanon. I am here now. I will pick you up at the airport."* That made my decision very easy. I booked the flight and I'm heading to Beirut now.

On my flight from Dubai to Beirut, I'm flying Middle East Airlines. My seat assignment is next to a very beautiful, friendly woman. She's not shy at all about striking up conversation and offering me gum and snacks. I love the random acts of kindness from complete strangers. It seems to be prominent in Arab cultures. No matter how little they may have, they always offer you something. I look around the plane of black-hair heads and assume I am the only white person on the plane. I relish that I'm one of a kind, and it's not my first time when I'm the only white person around. Announcements are made in Arabic, then French, and then English—the order of languages in Lebanon.

I left Austin at 4:00 p.m. on Thursday and we're getting ready to touch down in Beirut at midnight on Friday. As I exit the plane, there is another mix of dark-skinned, black-haired Arab, Indian, and Asian people in the passenger arrival area. I told Rafik that if it got too late I would catch a taxi to my hotel. I wasn't sure if I'd see him here in the lobby, but then I notice him emerge from the crowd as he did in Bahrain, with a big grin on his face.

When we get into his Jeep, the first thing we do is kiss—a deep, elongated, passionate kiss. Then I buckle up and Rafik says to me, *"You don't have to buckle up. It's not a law here like it is in America. And we're not going too far."* I thought with a little hesitation, *"Oh, okay."*

Rafik has a "get 'er done" type of personality. If he sets out to do something, he'll do it and he'll do it methodically and the best he can. I guess he's wired that way genetically, to also become a master architect and Olympic skier. Plus, if he needs an answer right away, which he usually does, he gets on the phone and wants to know the who, what, where, when, why, and how.

Our conversation starts with the weather forecast and a rundown for the next 24 hours, as he already has the day planned. *"It's supposed to be a gorgeous day tomorrow, then turn bad tomorrow night, so we have to go skiing tomorrow."* Our original plan was to go skiing during a weekday to avoid crowds. Rafik continues the conversation as though he's giving me a command, *"You need to be up at 7:30. Breakfast and coffee at 8:00. On the road by 9:00. The ski mountain by 10:00."* Sir, yes, sir!

We arrive at the hotel, I check in, and Rafik and I stay up, catching up and talking. The last time I look at the clock, it's 3:00 a.m. I'm thinking I'll tucker out on the mountain by midafternoon at this rate.

We did not get up at 7:30. We did not have coffee or breakfast at 8:00 a.m. But we *are* on the road at 9:00! It's a beautiful, sunny morning in Beirut. It's warm. I can't imagine snow on the mountain. I insist that we stop for coffee. I need it to jump-start my day, especially after the hours of travel and staying up late. I watch as we pass a Costa Coffee and a Caribou Coffee shop, and Rafik ignores my request.

Rafik is racing through the traffic in his four-wheel-drive Jeep. He has one foot on the brake, the other on the gas, one hand on the steering wheel, and the other on the stick shift. We are weaving in and out of traffic, and I swear we are turning corners on two wheels. The windows are down and the wind is blowing through the car. Rafik is a thrill-seeker. He's a professional speed skier and competed in the Winter Olympics in Salt Lake City. He's also into race cars, racing snowmobiles, and anything fast.

Rafik realizes he just passed a Starbucks. Finally my plea for coffee registers with him, so he stops in the middle of the road, slams the car into reverse, and squeals sideways into a parking spot across from Starbucks. Perhaps that's a little dramatic and exaggerated, but it sure seems that way. He gets out of his car, calm and relaxed as though nothing out of the ordinary has occurred. Perhaps it is nothing out of the ordinary for him. That's just the way he drives—and so does everyone else in Lebanon.

I'm wide awake and laughing after that 10-minute roller coaster ride through the city. We have about another 45-minute journey to the ski slope. I order my Americano and Rafik orders a cappuccino. We take our coffees to go, as we have a schedule to meet and need to be on the mountain by 10:00.

I get in the car and buckle up for the hair-raising ride ahead of me. He reminds me that I don't have to buckle up. I say, *"Yes, I do with you driving."* He laughs at me and buckles up too. I'm thinking, *"If he's buckling up, what the hell am I in for?"* He floors the gas.

Away we go into the left lane. He crosses two or three lanes at a time, passes about 10 vehicles, and slides between two cars just in time to miss the oncoming traffic. He punches the gas again and crosses a few more lanes to the right, passing a lot more cars. As I try to sip my coffee, it spills out from the little hole on the lid. I start slurping it, trying to catch it before it ends up all over me. Rafik calls out to me, *"We're going to be on the mountain by 10:00!"* I don't have any doubts.

There's no order to the driving in Lebanon. There are stripes in the city that divide the lanes, but people are driving on the lines, outside the lines, and between the lines. There are a few red lights along the main highway through town and the cars seem to totally ignore them. As we get out of the city and start the ascent into the foothills, the lines disappear. What appears to be a two-lane road now has four vehicles across it. As we are flying up the hill, Rafik moves over to the far right, and three vehicles are side by side in the oncoming lane. I brace myself for heart failure. Sometimes we are side by side, passing another car while there are two cars in the oncoming lane. There are four fucking vehicles taking up two lanes of road. As we climb the winding roads, I notice there are no guardrails. I'm beginning to think my life is in more danger riding in Rafik's car than it is living in a war zone.

At one point, we're flying down the road and Rafik opens my window all the way down from the driver's side electronic button. He pulls the vehicle to the far right, pulls up to some trash dumpsters, and tosses his empty coffee cup in front of me, out the window, and into the dumpster while the car is still moving at a pretty good clip. We both shout out, *"Yeah!"* As quickly as I observe what he's doing, I follow his lead and toss my cup toward the dumpster. My cup catches the top back corner of it, bounces off the edge, and flies behind the dumpster. Oops. Rafik rolls up the window and floors the gas again, and we fly back into traffic. I don't feel like I'm in a car. I feel like I'm in a mini space shuttle. He's flying low.

I tell Rafik his driving is like playing a video game. He says, *"But this is the real thing!"* He punches it some more and we fly by a few more cars. Rafik keeps looking over at me and asking, *"What?"* His question just makes me laugh more. If he only knew what's going through my head.

We finally arrive in Faraya in one piece, thankfully. We stop at the ski shop. Rafik is like a celebrity in Faraya. He grew up here, so he knows everyone and gets me his "discount price" for my rental equipment. Just $27 gets me the skis, poles, boots, jacket, and snow pants for the day. Not too shabby. Not shabby at all.

We get back into the car and continue farther up the street at a much slower pace. Rafik pulls into a little bakery and orders us handmade Lebanese bread called *man'oushe* (more commonly known as *za'atar*). It's baked to order right here in front of us. It's freshly grilled on a hot upside-down wok and smeared with olive oil and a mix of Middle Eastern fresh herbs of oregano like basil, thyme, marjoram, and savory. The bread, olive oil, and herbs just melt in my mouth with a delightful zest on the palate. We split two different kinds before we leave.

Rafik and I step outside onto the patio that overlooks the hills to finish our tasty breakfast. Off in the distance I can see the snow-covered mountains towering over the foothills. Beautifully terraced, the foothills remind me of the Tuscany region of Italy. Everything is dormant, but I can just imagine how marvelous and vibrant it must be in the spring and summer.

We finally make it to the ski resort. As we approach, there are cars and buses parked everywhere along the road. People are lined up and marching single file up the mountain. The entrance seems so far away and a pretty long walk. Rafik keeps driving. I have my doubts we're going to find parking any closer.

Alas, we get to the jam-packed parking lot in front of the chalet. Rafik rolls down my window from the driver's side console and starts speaking Arabic to the parking attendant. Arabic always sounds like they're arguing. I think they are exchanging a few bad words, but then the attendant flags us through. We narrowly squeeze through the rows of parked cars until we get to the very front. Rafik goes up a snowbank and parks the Jeep right smack in front like it's reserved just for him. Maybe it is. Hell, I don't know.

I look at my watch and the time is 9:58. Rafik was right: We're on the mountain by 10:00. The brochures say it's a two-hour drive from Beirut to Faraya. Ha! It took us less than an hour, and that included stops at Starbucks, the ski shop, and the bakery.

The snow on the mountains is glistening from the sun. This place is enormous. There are three or four mountains of slopes above the tree line and trails on all sides of the mountains. Who would've ever known this about Lebanon? I certainly didn't until Rafik told me about it.

Of course, the lift lines have no kind of order, just like the highway traffic. It is a solid mass of people shuffling toward the lift, sliding inch by inch on their skis. We wedge our way to the far right and to the front. After we get off the main mountain and onto another, it is much more enjoyable, but when we get off the lift, Rafik is constantly texting or talking to someone on his phone. What's up with that? Leave the damn phone in the car!

I continue to make my way down the mountain, concentrating on my solemn skiing and dodging moguls all the way to the chairlift. Rafik is wearing a fluorescent-orange helmet. I can spot him on the top of the mountain as he zips down top to bottom in what feels like 10 seconds at probably 160 miles per hour. It takes me about 10 minutes to do the run. Sometimes he stops to help or coach little kids, or pick them up and put them back on their skis. There are a lot of kids on the slope who look like they can't be more than three or four years old. I love to see little kids learning a fun new sport at an early age. They are fearless, flexible, and resilient.

We ski throughout the day almost nonstop. It's gorgeous. There are so many awesome trails and grades. At the bottom of one of the slopes, there is a huge party with loud electronic music playing. There are free drinks, as it's sponsored by a vodka distillery. I don't see any kind of mixer with their vodka. I think they're drinking it straight, and there are a lot of empty Vodka bottles stacked up along the wall. The people look like they are having a really good time. We don't stop, but it strikes a nerve with me that all these folks are drinking and will be driving down the mountain of winding, narrow roads with no guardrails. But, well, there are a lot of happy people.

The wind starts to pick up in the early afternoon. The resort closes a few of the slopes because the chairlifts are bouncing up and down. People are leaving the slopes, but we keep going until they kick us off the last one. I surprise myself that I still have quite a bit of energy after my long flight the day before and a day on the slopes, not to mention the roller coaster ride from Beirut to Faraya.

There's about an hour and a half of daylight left. Rafik recommends we go for a snowmobile ride in the backcountry. He asks if I want to get my own machine or ride on the back of his. Since I'm not familiar with the terrain or the snow, I opt to ride on his machine. Plus I haven't driven a snowmobile in probably 30 years. Before we take off, Rafik instructs me that if he leans to the right, I need to lean to the right too. Same with the left. And finally I'm told to hold on tightly to him. Those are the three rules. He says it just like that and then ends with, *"That's it."* Before I can start to think—*"What the hell am I thinking? First his driving in the Jeep and now I'm letting him drive me on the back of a snowmobile?"*—off we go, full throttle!

If Rafik's Jeep driving is a hair-raising experience, his snowmobile driving doesn't compare. No roads, no trails, no lines, hills, dips, no limits! There are a few times I think we are going to flip the machine. When he said to lean my body to the right, I didn't know that he meant to lift my whole body up and to be perpendicular with the machine. As he's zipping through the snow full throttle, up and down ravines, he turns back to me and yells, *"We have too much weight. The machine is a little sluggish."* *"Amen!"* I'm thinking. All I can imagine is crashing out here in the middle of nowhere with nobody else around. I wouldn't even know which direction to go to get help. My trust and faith are all in Rafik's hands.

After an electrifying 40- or 50-minute ride of nearly plummeting to our deaths a few times, Rafik drops me off at the snowmobile place and takes off on the machine by himself. As he takes off, the front skis of the machine are in the air at about a 90-degree angle from the ground. I think of one of my bosses back at Bagram saying in his Southern Mississippi accent, *"Sweet Jesus, Hail Mary."* I'm surprised this man hasn't killed himself.

He returns about half an hour later. The sun has gone down and the temperature is dropping. I'm standing there shivering when I see the headlight of his snowmobile coming toward me. He returns the machine, we get back to his Jeep, and he cranks up the heat.

We drive a short distance down the mountain to his family's home. It has been in the family for a couple of generations, with multiple additions of other family members. His parents occupy the main house, with his uncle's family next door and across the driveway. Plus it looks like a few more rooms are being added to the main house. Each residence looks like a tall, narrow, three-story structure.

We pull up to the house and Rafik waves to his uncle, who is walking down the long driveway. The house is dark and cold. The wood-burning stove in the center of the living room is not stoked. Nobody is home.

We unload Rafik's equipment and change into warm, dry clothes. About the time we get ready to leave, his parents come in. I greet them in Arabic with, *"Ah salemma."* Rafik and his parents converse in Arabic. Rafik turns to me with a grin and tells me that his mom is wondering where I am from because they don't use the greeting that I just used. (I learned it in North Africa.) They use the greeting *"marhaba."* Rafik introduces me to them in English and then interprets the introduction of me in Arabic. I can't remember the phrase *"pleased to meet you"* off the top of my head in Arabic, so I say it in French, *"Enchanté."* Both his parents' eyes light up and they smile at my response, indicating that they understand. They each repeat it back to me, shaking my hand.

I check out Rafik's parents. They're both so short and cute. I wonder where Rafik gets his height. Certainly not from either one them. Rafik's mother goes to the kitchen and makes us a blackberry fruit drink that's exceptional. Rafik can't remember the name of the fruit in English, so he says it is called *framboises* in French. I tell him the English equivalent. His mom tries unsuccessfully to repeat it. It's cute to hear her try.

We finish our drinks, stay a little bit longer, and head back down the mountain into Beirut. The drive is much more relaxing going back. I know we are both tired after a full day of skiing and fresh air. We stop to drop off the equipment and then go get something to eat.

We go to a local restaurant that is a huge, family-run business. It's packed to the brim and the smell of cigarette smoke slaps me in the face. I remember we're not in America and nonsmoking sections don't exist. We follow the waiter through the smoky room to the very back of the restaurant and to our table. The nonsmoking sections in the U.S. are one of the things that I miss the most when I'm overseas. Even better, the completely smoke-free facilities everywhere.

The restaurant has a set menu and everything is served family style. We have salad, hummus, olives, pickles, bread, kabobs, and rice. It seems like too much food for the two of us. The waiter keeps bringing us more and more. The Lebanese start with a plate of fresh lettuce, a whole lemon, a whole cucumber, a whole tomato, slices of carrot, and sometimes radishes. At the table, someone cuts up all the vegetables and serves it. I usually go for just the tomato and the cuke if I'm by myself, especially since they seem to be garden ripe off the vine and handpicked. I save my appetite for the hummus, fresh pita, olives, and grilled meats. I love Lebanese food. It's fresh and flavorful. There are many different textures for the palate.

I can also order my meal with shisha or without. It's convenient to have a smoke or no smoke with your meal. Shisha is the molasses-soaked tobacco with carnation petals that is smoked through a hookah pipe. It's very sweet to smell and comes in many flavors: orange, lemon, rose, and mint, to name a few. I've tried it a few times and my favorite is either the strawberry or the apple.

We pass on the shisha, but the tables around us are toking away on their hookah pipes and cigarettes. My heart seems to beat extra hard from breathing in the secondhand smoke. I don't like it. I don't like it all. But I don't have much of a choice. Fortunately neither Rafik nor I smoke. In fact, we're both militant when it comes to smoking. Neither one of us wants to be around it, so Rafik must've requested a table toward the back of the restaurant, away from it all, in that determined, guttural, Arabic tone.

I am exhausted by the time I get back to my hotel room. Rafik is too and spends the night instead of making the journey back to Faraya. We sleep 10 or 12 hours. It's a great day to sleep in, as the weather turned in the late evening and we awake to a gusty and rainy day.

Church bells awaken me at 6:45 a.m. It's another reminder that I am in a Christian nation. I think it's odd that they ring the bells at 6:45. They usually ring on the hour or half past the hour. Maybe my clock is slow. Or maybe it's their call to prayer for mass about to begin. I doze in and out of sleep until the second set of bells rings at 9:00. The first chimes must've been the symbol that mass is about to begin. Did I sleep through a set? I doubt that because the church is right outside my hotel and across the street. There is no way I could've slept through the loud gonging of the bells.

I can't remember the last time I heard church bells echo through a town or city. I remember as a teenager living in downtown Green Bay on Madison Street, all the church bells would ring about the same time on the hour every Sunday. I would count the number of rings. That's how I knew the hour of the day. Noon was always the grand finale. I always enjoyed hearing the clamor of those bells. I couldn't hear anything else but the loud, rhythmic ring that somehow brought solace to my soul. It could be a beautiful, sunny wedding day or a windy autumn day with leaves blowing down the street. The dong always brought comfort and warmth, assimilating my chakras, life-force energy . . . the basic component of my subtle body, energy field, and the entire chakra system. It's the key to life and source of energy in the universe, as believed in Hindu practices. That's a concept! Catholic Church bells triggering a Hindu phenomenon.

As I lie cuddled next to Rafik, I reminisce about my Catholic upbringing and the church bells I heard often from my apartment in downtown Green Bay. The Van Morrison song "Gloria" plays in my head and quickly transcends into the riveting Patti Smith version: "And I heard those bells chimin' in my heart, going ding dong, ding dong, ding *dong, ding dong, ding dong . . . chiming the time when you came to my room and you whispered to me and we took the big plunge . . . and oh, you were so good, oh, you were so fine . . . and I've got to tell the world that I made him mine, made him mine, made him mine . . . the tower bells chime, ding dong, they chime."* Those bells chiming in my heart is how I feel when I'm with Rafik.

Rafik and I finally get up and set out to explore Beirut. I love knowing someone from the local area to guide me as his or her host. Beirut surprises me. My impression of it is not one of Paris, but more of San Francisco. Its topography and climate is very hilly and built along the Mediterranean Sea. The city maintains a cooler climate with a constant sea breeze. Less than an hour outside the city are snow-coated mountains and ski resorts just like in California.

It's nice to watch people on the sidewalks, all dressed up in their Sunday best. I guess that's the "Paris" part of Beirut. They love their clothes, jewelry, and fashion. It's a joy to see young couples and elderly couples alike walking hand in hand. The young people dress chic, stylish, and sexy; the elders dress elegantly, conservatively, and traditionally. It reminds me more of Venice—the city of love—than Paris. I guess they're both cities of love. I'd add Beirut to that list too.

As I watch the people, I wonder what kind of life they have here and where they live. There are people from all over the world in Beirut. Many are from other Arab nations, the South Pacific, and India. It seems like Filipinos and Indians are leaving their homelands and spreading their roots in any other country that will take them. I don't see many Caucasians.

The architecture of Beirut is a mix of historical, old, modern, and war-torn ruins. Some of the buildings are blown out from the war and left abandoned. Others are brand new and built around the ruins.

After our day of touring the beautiful city, Rafik heads back home. He has a family dinner to attend. I'll see him tomorrow.

The next morning, I venture to a coffee shop a couple blocks away from my hotel. The barista obviously knows I am American by my cowboy hat and says, *"My cat's name is Farika."* I think, *"Okay, what does that have to do with coffee?"* She looks me in the eyes and says, *"You look very exotic."* The young guys at the table close to the counter turn around, look at me, and start laughing. One of them says to me, *"She's hitting on you."* One looks me in the eyes and tells me that they don't see blue eyes or cowboy hats very often around here.

That's another part of the Lebanese culture that surprises me compared to many of the other Arab countries that I've visited. In most other Arab countries, a woman doesn't dare make eye contact with a man. They'd be treated as a whore if they did. It's sad but true. The Lebanese are more liberated, thankfully. I guess they're more like the Italians when it comes to Christianity—or does that even have anything to do with religion? Maybe it's more of a cultural thing.

I smile at the guys and then turn to the barista and give her my coffee order. It's too early in the morning for me to be flirting. I haven't had my first cup of coffee yet. I usually like two big cups to start my day.

By the time she whips up my coffee, three other girls at the counter are checking me out and smiling and talking. One of them comments, *"That's a very nice hat."* I reply, *"Thank you."* I become a little anxious and shy as they make me the center of attention, so I quickly scoop up my coffee and sit at a table on the sidewalk outside, away from the smoke-filled store.

The smoke—yikes! Lebanon must be one of the worst places that I've been to as far as smoking in public places. I've found only one restaurant that is smoke-free. It's close to the university and I've eaten there twice. I even noticed that McDonald's isn't smoke-free here, when I walked by their storefront window.

Back at the hotel, the receptionist greets me. We make small, friendly conversation as I wait for the elevator. I make a comment to him about the smoking in Lebanon. He tells me that they just passed a no-smoking ordinance at the airport, but it's not enforced. Rafik tells me that they have all sorts of rules in Lebanon, but nobody pays attention to them. That's for sure. Just like the road signs and stoplights.

My time in Beirut goes quickly, and before I know it I'm taking a cab back to the airport. I get my boarding pass and head toward the security scan. I set my bag on the conveyor belt of the scanner. The security guard is looking at his computer screen while lighting up a cigarette, with an ashtray full of butts next to his keyboard. So much for the new no-smoking ordinance in the airport.

My return flight is on Middle East Airlines. Fortunately the airlines are the only place the no-smoking policy is enforced in the Middle East. As they say in Arabic, *"Il hum du'allah!"* Praise the Lord.

And off into the friendly skies, I fly back to Dubai.

Frank

I'm amazed at the number of stories I'm hearing of how guys are working their asses off over here only to send home the paychecks to their families; they return home to a wife or girlfriend who has spent all their money on a drinking or drug addiction. I guess for many, love is a feeling, marriage is a contract, and relationships are work.

I never met Frank, but I heard his story a couple of times. Janet Atkinson told me her side of the story, which lines up with other versions I've heard. Frank worked for Barron for a long time. In fact, he was in Afghanistan and Iraq for a couple years and must've worked different task orders of LOGCAP. He enjoyed the life and money of being a DoD contractor. He was married to a lawyer who was home holding down the fort and going about her business. Frank had direct deposit to his account back home and was stashing it for retirement, which didn't look too far off for him.

Frank decided it was time to quit working and enjoy his life with his lovely wife. He packed up his bags, left Afghanistan with a big smile, and headed home only to never look back. Upon returning to his home in the Carolinas, he opened the door to an empty house. Everything was gone: his wife, every piece of furniture, the bed he was looking forward to sleeping in, the TV to kick back and relax and watch, every knickknack, every stitch of clothing, and even his car.

Frank went to the bank to check on his accounts. There was no money left in them. While working overseas for a few years, he probably sent home several hundred thousand dollars. There wasn't a penny to be had. A second mortgage was taken out on his house and the financial debt was more than he could bear. Frank let the house go into foreclosure and moved into a travel trailer that his son owned.

Frank was living in the travel trailer without a job and without any money. A few months had passed. He hadn't heard from his wife who had abandoned him and wasn't able to locate her. To make matters worse, the IRS sent him a letter claiming he owed $66,000 in back taxes. Apparently his wife also had his power of attorney. While he was working overseas, she changed his exemptions to the highest amount possible to collect the most money from his paycheck.

Frank had a lawyer or an investigator working on his case and eventually located his wife and took action. I'll never know if she was still in the States or if she took all the money and left the country. I wonder what her motive was. Why was she so cruel to Frank? What did he do to her? They were obviously in love at one time and he still loved her. Nobody knows, and I guess we'll never know.

Music of a Navy Seal

Trigger and I are walking to the DFAC to grab breakfast. As I'm checking out the strapping young men in uniform walking ahead of us, Trigger darts ahead and taps one of them on the shoulder and says, *"Hey, man, your weapon isn't on safety."* I'm thinking, *"Safety?"* I don't even know where the safety switch is on a rifle. The soldier quickly thanks Trigger and makes the quick adjustment on his rifle.

We eat breakfast and return to the office. Trigger tosses me a thumb drive with a bunch of music on it. He directs me to a specific genre of music that he plays while he works out. I'm expecting some upbeat, lively music. It definitely isn't dance, rock, or hip-hop. It's definitely not the blues or country. It certainly wasn't the theme from *Wonder Woman*. Not that I listen to that, but I can just imagine some Navy Seal listening to the theme from *Wonder Woman* and fighting off imaginary bullets as they lift weights and look at themselves in the mirror.

I don't recognize the form, style, or names of the artists. Trigger gives me a surprised look when I tell him that I've never heard of any of these groups: The Prodigy, The Chemical Brothers, Gorilla, The Crystal Method, or Buckethead. Both Trigger and I are almost the same age: I was born in '61; he was born in '62. I feel like I missed a trend of my generation, or maybe he was hanging out with the wrong crowd. It wouldn't surprise me if I missed out, as I traveled out of the U.S. for more than half of the 1980s and missed most of that era. When I hear and see people my age get into the eighties music, dress, and hairstyles, I can't even relate to it because it's something I missed during that decade.

I select the band The Crystal Method. The name alone sounds gripping. It looks like a good place to start. I'm not sure what I'm about to expose my delicate ears and mind to with a band name like that. I imagine it's some tweaked, psychedelic, nerve-hitting, fast-paced music associated with a psycho-stimulant drug.

I hit select, then play, and a slow, steady, hypnotic beat of a sound box and DJ artistry penetrates my ears and brain waves as I fall into a trancelike rhythm for the first several minutes. A few bass chords and sliding electric guitar strings are added to the rhythm. Add the fierce beat of some drums and entrancing honeyed lyrics, causing me to drift off into another mindset as the convulsive electrical chords nudge and jerk a dark place in my soul. Maybe that's what crystal meth does, but instead of being drug-induced, this is music-induced.

Then comes the sputtering, agitated hip-hop verse, "*Not gonna get a piece of that! No, ain't goin' out like that. Motherfuckin' true caliber pimps,*" and then back into the trance and repeat. Yeah, I envision a lethal fight and nobody's going to take me out, so take that, you motherfucker! I can see Trigger grooving to this music during his workouts, hitting a euphoric psyche from the "meth"-induced chords causing excessive feelings of power and invincibility.

The next song: "*Wild, sweet, and cool . . . let me do my thang . . . let me do my thang . . . let me do my thang . . . sweet, sweet, cool.*" I picture Trigger listening to this on a mission. The mission is something so wild—it seems surreal—but it's the real thing and causes an adrenaline rush where he wants to move quickly against the enemy. The music and words drive and push him, but he tells himself to remain sweet and cool. "*Let me do my thing. Do what you gotta do. Sweet and cool.*"

Moving forward comes deeper, faster moving, grinding bass filling my ears. After about 20 seconds of earth-riveting bass, the churning of "lyrics," the lead singer yells, "*Listen all you motherfuckers!*" The pulverizing beat of the bass guitar continues, deeper and more intense. Again, "*Listen all you motherfuckers! That's the name of the game . . . calling all freaks now! That's right! That's the name of the game!*" I imagine a group of Seals on a ground mission, walking through tall, grassy fields in their camouflage BDUs (body dress uniforms) and boonie hats outfitted with high-tech equipment. They're walking slowly and softly, making sure not to snap a blade of dry, straw-like grass that could blow their cover, each of their movements signaled by a nod of the head, eyes, and hand signals. The music sounds like a hybrid genre that mixes the intensity of heavy metal, the beat of dance music, the insomnia of a rave, the zone-out of trance, and the lyrical tone of hip-hop and rock.

"I can't ever stop working hard. Each day I feel I have to improve. Hard work. Determination. I've got to keep pushing myself. I can't ever stop working hard" brings me to a dark, hidden place in my brain. It starts with a little amateur drumming, like practicing in a garage, before the electric grind of guitar strings. A pulsating drumbeat created with force. Voices echoing. Set out on a mission. The adrenaline rush. Drumroll and ear-ripping chords of the guitar. Angelic voices: *"Smack my bitch up."* More heavy, resonating, grinding bass. Serial thrills. Overpowering sound. Explicit lyrics. Is this what it's like to be a Navy Seal? The music and words take me to a dark, hidden place in my head and nudges at the reality of it . . . the deep-down secrets. Speed up, slow down. Start off energized, body frozen as everything passes before my eyes at supersonic speed and then slows way, way down. I don't know where I am, but I keep moving. Now I can't move. I tumble into the mind and body of someone taking an LSD trip . . . controlled schizophrenia. Then the angels start humming and singing. I see a dim light in the long, shadowy distance and follow it. The iron curtain comes crashing down and I'm listening to the penetrating beat. The sound of engines from above . . . galactic spaceships speeding through the air.

I love this music! It creates some uncensored visions and artistry in my mind. Some of it is dark. It strikes a nerve with me, going to places I've heard about, never seen, but makes me feel the motion and emotion. This is music that I can run and work out to. It does add an extra pump and push to keep me moving. I can see me running on the treadmill with my arms up in the air and pretending I'm playing the drums. Reminds me of someone from the past.

The Dirt

People never cease to amaze me. I'm not sure if it's the environment that we're working in that causes people to do crazy things or if they're just stupid and think they can get away it. These infractions are not just with the company I am working for but across the country with other contractors, subcontractors, military personnel, and the locals. There are plenty of articles published by the military as well as reports by the different military branches and the Pentagon addressing alcohol, drugs, sexual abuse, and other issues on base. Plus, every trip to Dubai, the security manager, Kyle, gives us the lowdown on the "One Percenters" who break the rules or the laws.

Word is that two upper-level managers are being terminated for inappropriate behavior. Both were investigated and found guilty of touching women subordinates in improper places. I hear one consistently slapped one of his female employees on the ass "to motivate her." Unbelievable. It's sad that many women working here come from countries where the only way they'll get a raise or be promoted is to sleep with their boss.

I've heard of a few supervisors who did just that too. They were terminated for sleeping with their employees who reported up to them. Some of them promised raises and promotions in exchange for sex. From speaking with a few women from former communist governments, I've also heard that it's common for a woman to sleep with her boss to get ahead. Sex scandals are exposed all the time. The ones that get the biggest exposure are the ones in higher-ranking positions. But it happens at every level. We see that in American politics and it seems like you can always find someone who will talk or sling mud at someone else for their own personal gain.

While I was at Cherry-Beasley, there was a female RSOI tent two doors down from mine. A male soldier snuck into the female tent, stood at the edge of her bed while she lay there sleeping, and ejaculated on her. He ran out of the tent before he could be caught, but apparently the female soldier knew her assailant, as there was a picture of the accused on the nearby bathroom door, looking for his whereabouts.

Allegedly, this guy went AWOL. The military believes he may be hiding outside the wire. That's kind of creepy. There are so many stories of sexual abuse—not only against women, but men too.

I've read that the Pentagon reported that one in five females and one in fifteen males in the U.S. Air Force report being sexually abused by other service members. How sexual abuse is defined, I don't know. Is it abuse or assault? Verbal or physical, or both? The Pentagon also estimates that 80 to 90 percent of sexual assault cases go unreported due to repercussions, embarrassment, and confidentiality issues.

Most squadrons and some of the bases have a buddy-system policy where another service member or coworker must accompany you. It makes logical sense, but there are so many areas of base that are so dark that even a quick, casual walk to the restroom can result in unwelcomed confrontations.

We've had several cases involving alcohol and drugs. General Order prohibits alcohol consumption. My colleague Roy got a copy of a military brief that reported 365 DUI cases on base for the year: one a day. Of course, that doesn't mean that contractors don't drink when it's prohibited. Some were caught and terminated.

We've had cases where people failed a random drug screening. Not so much while working on base but as they return from R&R. Those who were caught partook in some recreational drug use while on leave. That shit stays in the body!

Health and welfare inspections are required by the military. The inspections are random. Alcohol, steroids, and other drugs have all been found. We had a couple guys get into the beer storage of one of the planes coming from Dubai to Bagram and did some binge-drinking during their flight. Of course, they were reported, caught, and terminated when they got to Bagram. There have been a few groups of employees who decided to throw a little after-work party in their B-hut, and they've been busted. But my favorite alcohol-related termination is a few guys who were busted for diluting alcohol sanitizer with a flavored-mix packet and drinking the concoction to get drunk. I'm not sure if they got drunk, or how drunk they got, but it got them terminated.

People have been found with possession of narcotics or dealing or taking drugs. I've been told that drugs in Afghanistan are easy to come by since they produce the largest poppy fields for opium production in the world. In many other countries you can buy any medication, including narcotics, over the counter. We had one guy bring back a supply of narcotics with him from his home country. He didn't think there was anything wrong with it because he could buy it over the counter back home.

A bus driver tested positive for heroin use after he crashed the bus into a T-wall while carrying a busload of soldiers. I've even heard that one of the B-huts was used as a meth lab. They bought all their meth ingredients from the PX. Now the PX keeps a lot of that stuff under lock and key. Of course, all of this is word on the street, but as we know, there's a portion of truth to many rumors.

A few people were found in their rooms dead from drug overdoses. The locals or the military brings in most of the drugs when they're working outside the wire. Considering the locals are searched prior to entering the base, they smuggle it in from their "back door"—they pack it in their ass.

Pornography is also prohibited under General Order. There seems to be quite a bit of that being downloaded and shared, even from our own IT people. A group of them were busted and sent home. One worker was reported for watching pornography on his work computer.

A worker walked by his office window as he was watching it with his curtain open, computer on his desk, and his back toward the window. He obviously forgot to close the curtain behind him. Either that or he just didn't care.

I'm surprised at the number of fraud cases: people falsifying government documents, timesheets, and credentials. My team tracks and verifies skill craft licenses 100 percent. Initially we were recruiting skilled crafts from other countries, but we could not verify their licenses. If they were offered a job, we could only hire them as a helper or an apprentice who required direct supervision of their work. We discovered multiple cases of employees Photoshopping their IDs, licenses, and other credentials to make it look like they had updated their license.

Those who manipulate a card or license are terminated. The crime is serious, especially if a governing authority issues the credential. Not only do we take action, but also in correspondence with state licensing boards or the U.K. Joint Industry Board (JIB), the employee may be stripped of their license or punished with jail time. I've seen it happen in cases with both the U.S. and the U.K., and that's after telling employees that we verify 100 percent! Go figure! Our motto is *Trust, but Verify.*

I recently heard another rumor about a guy in our cost department who was caught sharing proprietary cost estimates to a competitor. I'm not sure if he was selling them or just sharing them. When investigated, there was a ring of employees who were exposed and terminated. The department was wiped clean.

There was a corrupt hiring ring taking place involving one of our HR people. It was three cousins. Two of them would recruit back in their home country, create a fictitious resume, and be on the receiving end of a phone interview in English, and our HR guy would fill the job requisition with the name. They had a huge pool of people willing to pay them for a job where the unemployment rate in their home country is around 35 percent or greater. I heard some of them were paying 5,000 to 8,000 EUR, and half of them didn't speak English.

The U.S. military requires that all personnel on base speak English. Some of these guys have zero qualifications to do the job they are hired for! Site managers are catching on to this quickly and returning the newly hired employees back to Bagram to be returned home. If they can't understand English, they are a safety threat and a liability when there is incoming. They are easy to pick out and we even end up administering English tests to entire groups, both written and verbal, to weed them out.

Rumors arose that one of the Balkan men who was determined unfit to perform his duties, due to the lack of English proficiency, spilled his guts. He threw others under the bus by laying out the scam in detail and naming names. He even had written evidence from conversations he had on Facebook. Yes, Facebook! It doesn't get any better than that! In addition, he exposed a group of heavy truck drivers who were selling their fuel to locals outside the wire. Internal investigations showed they were all guilty and sent home.

I love hearing the stories of stupidity and the risks people take. You just can't make this shit up. I can understand the people who are desperate for a job, but for the people out to make an extra couple bucks on top of a six-digit figure they're already making, is it worth it? If they're going to do the crime, then they should expect to do the time. I don't feel sorry for them.

BagramBody

There's a workout craze sweeping across the U.S. called P90X. Trigger recently got the DVD series and we've been doing a few of the workout sessions at night in the conference room, but the ceilings are low and the class is growing quickly. Plus the floor can get slippery after working out in a puddle of sweat. We're moving our class to the utility shop.

The utility shop is a huge, open space. We set up a projector and a large screen at the front of the shop. A few carpenters have made pull-up bars that are suspended from the rafters of the building. A lot of folks order their own workout mats, weights, and resistance bands. Our classes have grown from three of us to about 25 to 30 people. We've even got a couple of soldiers to join us in our regular workouts.

Juliet Alpha starts to lead the class, but somehow I take it over. I think I got elected to the lead position because my voice carries. Trigger goes around the shop during the class to ensure people are in proper form. He's a good teacher to show people the correct form and how to get the best out of their workout. Juliet Alpha always helps the newcomers.

Beachbody is a registered trademark for the P90X fitness program. BagramBody is our trademark here on base. The group talks and laughs about our BagramBody program, and someone mentions we should have T-shirts made. I go back to the office, look up the Beachbody attire, and create a similar shirt design with "BagramBody." Nearly everyone in the class wants at least one shirt.

I order the shirts and distribute them to the class at cost. I'm not out to make money on this—I just want to build the camaraderie and keep the momentum going. Within a day or two, after I receive the shipment and start to distribute the T-shirts, I'm called into the HR office. I'm informed that I'm being investigated for my shipment because it was reported to HR that I am doing it as a profitable business, which is against the General Order. Ludicrous! I assure our HR manager that is not the case at all and show him the receipts, orders, and costs. He finally understands and lets me continue about my business.

I make my rounds to deliver the shirts with Juliet Alpha in tow. I swing by Randy's office and deliver his shirts. I tell him how I've been reported to HR and investigations about the shirts and ask, "*How and why would anyone report that?"* Randy looks at me and whispers, *"Josef, look who's behind you."* Yes, of course. Juliet Alpha. The company mole. The snake. She always makes sure everyone is following the rules. She knows the motivation behind ordering the T-shirts, yet she still has to have her nose and say in my business. *Shit!*

The Legend of Bunkerhead

I assigned Bunkerhead a project, but she hasn't been providing updates or weekly reports. The project is scheduled for completion in just a few weeks. I mention this to Trigger, and he demands that she show us her progress or she'll be walked to HR for insubordination. She doesn't have much to reveal.

Trigger moves her into our dinky, crowded office. She's to report her progress daily. Juliet Alpha and I jump in to pick up her slack and guide her along on her project. Not long after Bunkerhead moves into the office, Trigger injures himself during one of our intensive P90X workouts and has a hiatal hernia. Dr. K confirms the injury and submits a medical leave request. He's out for the next 60 days.

While Trigger has his surgery and recovers at home, Juliet Alpha and I work diligently with Bunkerhead to complete a computer-based training. We have our casual conversations in the office about our personal lives and some of our accomplishments. Juliet Alpha and I are talking about training for the upcoming marathon on base. Bunkerhead pipes up, *"I ran a marathon."* I look at her with disbelief in my eyes, thinking, *"You ran 26.2 miles? Girl! I know you didn't run no 26.2 miles with that Pillsbury body of yours!"* I glance over at Juliet Alpha, who is looking at me with an expression on her face that spells out *L-I-A-R*. Of course, as quick-witted and sharp as Juliet Alpha is, she starts to ask Bunkerhead all sorts of questions. Which marathon did you run? Where was it? How did you train for it? Bunkerhead just stumbles over her words, making them up as she spews them out.

Over the next few weeks, Bunkerhead jumps into numerous conversations with us and seems to have an endless list of credentials. A bird perches on our outside windowsill and Bunkerhead states, *"Oh look, there's a yellow-bellied sparrow."* Yes, it's small like a sparrow and has a yellow belly. Bunkerhead pipes up, *"I know my birds. I was a park naturalist."* I look over at Juliet Alpha and she has that expression on her face. Once again, she starts with her amusing series of questions that has Bunkerhead stumbling for words.

We're talking about books and I share that I send home a monthly or quarterly newsletter to family and friends about my life over here and that a few of my friends suggest that I turn my stories into a book. Bunkerhead interjects to inform us that she's an accomplished writer. Juliet Alpha giggles like Betty Rubble from *The Flintstones* and repeats, *"Accomplished writer."* Bunkerhead reaffirms her words of choice and says, *"Yes, I am an accomplished writer. I've written children's books."* This time, instead of asking Bunkerhead a list of questions, Juliet Alpha gets on the computer and googles Bunkerhead's name (using her real name, Merissa, of course). She flips around in her office chair at Bunkerhead and says, *"If you're an accomplished writer, how come I can't find you on the internet, Merissa?"* But Bunkerhead always has a response. *"They're no longer in print, so they wouldn't be on the internet."* Juliet Alpha chalks up one point for herself for catching Merissa in a red-handed lie.

Over the course of the next few weeks, Juliet Alpha keeps a list of all the professions and accomplishments of Bunkerhead's: a marathon runner, a naturalist, an author, a nurse, a teacher, a caregiver, a master gardener, and a slew of others. She's quite the accomplished woman for being in her early thirties! I'm surprised she hasn't cut an album recording yet. She's quite the Renaissance woman. She manages to leave out one of her accomplishments: a sociopath—a person who believes their own lies.

Not long after Trigger's return, Bunkerhead leaves the project.

The Finish Line

Henry Ford once said, *"Whether you think you can or you think you can't, you're right."*

This spring there's a lot of runs, sometimes two or three a week. I try to participate in all of them. I manage to recruit a few new folks. I even convince our ol' Texas friend, Miss Mona Lee Cartwright, to run her first 5K. Well okay, maybe not *run*, but she did walk it. Not bad for a lady in her sixties.

A 5K is a piece of cake when you're usually running three miles in less than 30 minutes before work several days a week. What an awesome way to start the day! It's so easy, so rewarding, and makes me feel good. It's a phenomenal way to wake me up. It's also great to see all the other runners first thing in the morning with their motivation, high moods, and excitement. Rain or shine, it's a great day!

A specific military unit sponsored one of the runs. I don't remember which one it was because there are a lot of runs sponsored by various branches and units. This run I remember because one of the soldiers I met was photographing the event. I didn't see him until I crossed the finish line, when he yelled out my name to get my attention and snapped a series of shots. I saw that he had a nice camera and was taking pictures, so I asked him if I could have a copy of the pictures. He agreed. We exchanged names and numbers. His name was Carlos. We met up later and I handed him a compact terabyte external drive to download the pictures.

About a week later, Carlos finally returns the drive and tells me he also downloaded some music and movies for me too. *"Cool,"* I think to myself. When I plug my external drive into my Mac, I spot a ton of files. No wonder he had my external drive for a week. It probably took him that long to download it all.

I go through the music files first. I play some of it as I scan the rest of the library. Carlos has pretty good taste in music—or at least we like the same kind of stuff. I'm impressed. I come across a file named Fort Bragg Underground. That sounds interesting. The files have video extensions and the titles are quite intriguing. They actually sound a little dirty and risky. Did he download porn onto my external drive? I must find out. Sure enough, they're all short porn flicks of Fort Bragg soldiers that were filmed off base in some sleazy dive hotel.

Porn doesn't do a whole lot for me, but I know plenty of others who really enjoy it. I enjoy just checking out the good-looking men and their bodies in these flicks, not so much the sexual content. Some of the sex looks pretty lame and amateur. It also appears the producer filmed these to see just how far a guy will go if the opportunity is there. I have to check the other folders. He's loaded me up with a ton of porn. There's every kind of flavor and combination imaginable. I don't want the porn because it's against General Order 1B, so I delete it.

I believe pornography has its benefits. It can be a learning tool, create a sexual comfort level for you and couples, and expand sexual creativity. In addition, it can rekindle a sexual relationship and intimacy or create delightful and fun fantasies. It really can help you get in touch with yourself. This day and age, I see it as nothing different than music to the ears, from pleasant and soothing to pure raunchiness, much like G-rated and X-rated movies. The U.S. military comes to these countries and it's usually their government that dictates what is and what is not allowed. It undermines what American freedom is and what it's all about. But we must be culturally and politically sensitive. Bullshit! Not when it comes to freedom.

The porn business in America is an insanely booming business. If there's that much demand for porn, then why not allow it? Here on base, if porn is not available, people resort to creating their own pictures and amateur videos using Skype and webcams to post them on the internet or exchange through phones and email. I've been asked—more than once—to be in a couple of video calls with a few soldiers, with their wives watching on the other end. That's not my thing and I declined.

I believe prostitution is another issue that should come out of the closet and not be treated as a social evil. Empower the women and men! In many countries, it's enabled women to rise out of poverty and increase their economic mobility. For others, it's helped them pay their way through college and more. It has the potential to be lucrative, flexible, and independent.

I believe red-light districts and brothels can also be advocates for sex education, as well as promote healthier and safer sex practices. I've seen this in other countries. Their government registers and monitors the profession through regular licensing, medical tests, and health certifications. They set prostitute and escort restrictions, guidelines, and zones to make it safe and unobtrusive. Legalizing the prostitution business could potentially reduce the need for police services and increase revenues in the hospitality, retail, medical, and security industries. Additionally, a labor union in this field may be beneficial to protect workers. I believe keeping prostitution illegal and in the closet does more harm than good to society. It's time to open this door. How's that for job creation?

As far as the running pictures I was looking for when I came across the porn on my external drive, I can't find any of them. I think he forgot to download them because he was distracted with his porn collection. I wonder if Carlos is trying to send me a message. Was this deliberate or accidental? I really don't think this is by accident. I'm sure it was downloaded intentionally. Now that I got his message, I'll confront him when I see him next. The confrontation became an invitation for sex and, of course, I couldn't say no. I'm here to serve! Sir, yes, sir!

The Intruder

I've been corresponding and flirting with a 38-year-old Marine named Rob who is deployed in the Helmand Province of Southern Afghanistan. It's a very hot zone (heavy fighting and climate) for military activity. His one-year tour is up and he's coming to Bagram as part of his end-of-tour briefing and out-processing. I tell him if he can find me, he can have his way with me.

I give him my B-hut building number. I test his Marine mapping and directional skills with subtle hints of where he can find me amidst this airfield labyrinth of T-walls, B-huts, and 40,000-plus personnel. He texts to inform me that his show time to depart Kandahar is 2230. He will arrive sometime after midnight. I tell him my door will be left unlocked.

In the vague hours between midnight and dawn, he quietly enters my room. Between the wall A/C unit and a low setting on my fan in my room, I don't hear a noise. I lie sound asleep on my back with my face tilted toward the sky and resting comfortably on my soft, fluffy pillow. The B-hut is already very dark before another layer of darkness is cast upon my eyes with a blindfold. He quickly ties the blindfold from the side and turns it so the knot is behind my head. I'm in a dead sleep and I don't know if this is a dream or if it's really happening. Seconds later, my lips are sealed with his mouth, and my wrists are restrained with his upper body strength.

My palms are upward and pinned to the bed alongside my head as he vacuums short puffs of tepid air from my mouth, followed by his warm and succulent tongue. I'm receptive and I play along with our tongues dancing together. My body goes into a trance as I enjoy the powerful kisses being planted in and around my mouth.

His hands restraining my wrists are weakened, and the sheet covering my body is slowly pulled away. He saddles his naked body over me, and I feel his jewels on my waist. He leans forward and rubs his body against mine. His scent has a woodsy, manly smell with a slight undertone of soap. I can feel the definition of his muscular chest against mine.

He leaps off the bed, grabs a cord from his pants lying on the floor, and ties my hands behind my back. He shifts my body onto my back and spreads my legs, kneeling between them. He runs his whiskered chin up and down across my body and down to my toes, caressing my limbs and stigmatizing my skin with the path of his lips. He lifts my legs and gallantly sniffs and explores my cracks and crevices with his warm, moist tongue before moving up the inner thigh and socket joint to my groin. I am totally aroused.

I teeter on the brink of having no movement or control of my hands. I so much want to touch and caress the master of my domain, but it is forbidden and that lowers me into total submission. He dictates which parts of his body he wants me to explore orally by how and where he positions himself. He's in control.

He's standing next to the bed, rubbing the tip of his soft and spongy organ across my lips. He dictates his motion for me to open my mouth. I do and he gently enters. There's an instant sensation of his shaft pulsating as he slowly releases controlled squirts of cum. The warm fluid tastes like chamomile tea as it streams down my throat and I swallow with small gasps. He engages his tongue into my mouth, and I share the vapors of his inner soul he just sowed upon me. I get lost in time with our perpetuating kiss and unending sensual touch. He pauses briefly to moisten his fingers with his own saliva before using them to manipulate and massage my asshole.

Anticipating what may be coming next, I send hand signals to God, and angels fall from the heavens and earth. The skies to the universe break open and luminescent stars swivel and swirl in cosmic patterns while the midnight stars sing together and all the angels shout with joy. I feel him inside me and we become one. He's penetrating my soul with his. Light echoes and travels through our bodies as a stellar explosion of color pulsates at superluminal speeds. My words are heard and the angels ascend the two of us to heaven and above the tops of the clouds. They raise our throne above the stars of God, where we become a ray of light moving in dimensions.

Our escapade goes on for a couple of hours. After we push our bodies to sheer exhaustion, he finally unties me. When he removes the blindfold, sitting in front of me on my bed is the sight of an angel with Keanu Reeves's eyes, a Kevin Costner smile, short and cropped dirty-blond hair, and a cleft chin under a couple days of stubble. As we gaze at one another, both of us smile. He's a hot fuckin' stud and I'm glad to have had him.

We lie next to each other side by side on my twin bed for another hour, falling in and out of sleep with his arms wrapped about mine. We're not lying there long when he whispers into my ear that he has to get rolling before the sun comes up and people start to move about. As I lie in my bed and watch his every move, he gets up, gets dressed, and is ready to leave. Before he heads out for the day, he bends down next to me and whispers, *"See you tonight?"* I smile and agree. He kisses me one last time and departs.

All day, I can't stop thinking of him and the wonderful evening we shared. He returns later in the evening after I'm done with work, but our evening is not as intense as the night before. We're both so exhausted that we spend most of the night cuddling each other. With his arms wrapped around me, I think of our escapade from the night before, smiling and recalling how it was one of the most extraordinary sexual encounters I've ever experienced. I drift into a deep sleep, beamish in my dreams.

May 2, 2011

Osama bin Laden, the founder and head of the Islamist militant group, al-Qaeda, is killed in Pakistan. The news of bin Laden's death spreads like wildfire on base. The first person I see on my way to work is Timmy Dwayne. After I shout my good morning to him, before entering the headquarters building, he quickly yells back asking if I've heard the news of bin Laden. I tell him no and his news captures my attention, so I move closer and into better hearing range to get the details. He says, *"I'm serious as a heart attack."* Timmy provides all the details as I look at him attentively.

I walk into my office and Janet Atkinson is just waiting for me to walk through the door. The first words out of her mouth are, *"They got bin Laden."* Janet Atkinson has a few more details than Timmy and has a plethora of websites up on her computer screens, scanning them for new information.

People are affixed to the television news networks and internet to learn the details. The spread of the news is good to the U.S. military and NATO forces serving in Afghanistan and received favorably by the United Nations, the European Union, and other governments as well. I absorb as much as I can about bin Laden and his life during the day.

Bin Laden was just a few years older than me. He was born in March of 1957. His father was a wealthy Saudi businessman, Awad bin Laden. His mother was Awad's tenth or eleventh wife. He had a total of 22 wives but divorced many, having only four wives at once in accordance with Muslim law. Osama became one of 50 children by his father. He was the firstborn and only son of his mother. Fifty children! I can't imagine. Now what kind of father-son relationship did they have, if they even had a relationship?

Bin Laden studied economics, business, and civil engineering at the King Abdulaziz University in Jeddah, Saudi Arabia. He was already a pious Muslim and advocate of Sharia law. He also began to show and express his hatred toward Western practices, Judaism, democracy, and communism. Upon leaving the university, he traveled to Afghanistan to help fight the war against the Soviets.

At one time, it was supposedly rumored that bin Laden was pro-American and claimed to have had ties with the CIA when it armed jihadist groups against the Soviet Union during the Soviet war in Afghanistan. I have my doubts. While bin Laden was in Afghanistan, he met another Islamic fundamentalist who, between the two of them, set up an organization to funnel money and arms, and to recruit soldiers from around the Arab world to support their cause in Afghanistan.

In 1985, Soviet troops withdrew from Afghanistan. Bin Laden moved to Pakistan, where he supposedly drew a huge following of young Muslim men with his similar pious Muslim, anti-Western, and anti-Semitic views.

In 1990, he returned to Saudi Arabia, the same year Iraq invaded Kuwait. The Saudi government asked for assistance from the U.S. military to protect their oil fields. Bin Laden was so outraged by his government for using "infidel" troops that he publicly denounced the Saudi king. In 1994, the Saudi government ousted bin Laden and withdrew his citizenship from the kingdom. He fled to Sudan. While in Sudan, it was believed that he started his al-Qaeda terrorist camps, and Sudan received so much international pressure for hosting bin Laden that he was expelled in 1996. It was after his expulsion from Sudan that he made his second visit to Afghanistan, where he became a staunch ally and friend of Taliban leader Muhammad Omar.

After a decade of being the world's most wanted man, bin Laden met his fate today with U.S. Forces.

Watermelon Head

I walk into the office and Janet Atkinson informs me in her direct and organized speech, *"FOB Shank is on lockdown. A female Barron employee from Serbia was brutally raped and beaten."* She continues, *"Employees became concerned when she didn't show up for work yesterday morning. They went to check on her and found her beaten and unconscious in her B-hut."*

I imagine Janet Atkinson has been on the phone and emailing people already this morning. She continues with more of the details, *"Someone told me that her room was splattered with blood and the victim's head was swollen like a watermelon, beyond recognition. Her condition is life-threatening and medics don't think she'll make it through this. She's been medevac'd and is here at Bagram Airfield. She's listed in critical, but stable, condition. FOB Shank is on lockdown. Nobody can come or go until the military completes their investigation."* I stand there in shock.

I've heard of assaults and domestic violence reports on the bases. Barron has a zero-tolerance policy for physical assault, sexual assault, domestic violence, and stalking. People lose their jobs from these aggressive acts. I've seen guys with black eyes and cut lips from fighting get sent home. I've heard of a few cases of domestic violence between boyfriends and girlfriends, and even husbands and wives, and they've been sent home too.

FOB Shank is on lockdown for about five or six days before the military lifts the restriction. There's dozens and dozens of people waiting to leave that FOB for R&R. It's a major hub for that region, so it affects about a dozen other bases in the area. What a mess! People missing their flights home or to some other destination, canceling hotel reservations, or missing special events. I guess in this day and age with cell phones and computers, it's difficult to contain information.

We get the news of the assault as details unfold. The Serbian woman is flown to the U.S. military hospital in Landstuhl, Germany, where she makes a full recovery. She refuses to talk to investigators to identify or provide details of her assault or assailant. Word on the street is that she must know her attacker. Another rumor or piece of information we heard is that there was no forced entry into her room, indicating she knew her attacker(s).

She occupied a room in an all-female, eight-room B-hut. It's strange that nobody in that B-hut heard screams or a body being slapped and slammed around. Maybe there was more than one person involved: one to hold her down and keep her quiet while the other one bludgeoned her.

I read blogs on the assault. I think a lot of it is speculation. One report I read is that her husband in Serbia found out she was seeing another man while she was working on base. He contacted some of his friends who were working with his wife and asked them to beat the living shit out of her. I've heard of some damn horrifying cases of domestic violence, and that story would not surprise me. I haven't heard what really happened. It's a sad tragedy when something like this happens on base and it affects the entire community.

Spain and Morocco

Spain is in the Union of European Football Associations (UEFA) playoffs. Greg is meeting me in Barcelona and we'll embark on our trip from there. One of the conditions we agreed upon when I took this position is that we were going to travel. Since I'm on this side of the globe and there's a major IRS tax credit if I stay out of the U.S. for 330 days a year, most of our R&R destinations will be outside the United States.

When I meet Greg in Barcelona, there seems to be a little disconnection between us. I'm on my regular daily schedule, but he's still on U.S. time. So even though it's 11:00 p.m. here now, it's only about 3:00 p.m. in the U.S. I go to bed and Greg stays up.

He's on the computer most of the night. When I wake up the next morning, he starts an argument after befriending and conversing with Rafik on Facebook. This doesn't sit well with me. I don't know what they exchanged, but he's umbrageous and calling me a liar. The tension levels are high between us. It sounds more like jealousy to me. Why should he be jealous when he has a boyfriend back home? What's good for the goose is good for the gander! I just want to relax, be happy, and have some fun. Instead I get snotty remarks and jabs taken at me over the next couple of days. At one point, I want to bring Greg to the airport and send him back home, but we resolve things and it takes a couple more days to reacquaint ourselves. We kiss and make up.

Once the tensions dissipate between us, again, we have a wonderful time exploring the treasures of Barcelona, driving aimlessly through the Pyrenees Mountains for several days, exploring their beauty and splendor. We love watching as the autumn foliage turns to deep colors of red, yellow, and orange the higher in elevations that we drive. We turn here, there, and wherever the road less traveled takes us.

We stop along the road to watch and listen to the cows jingle their cowbells as they meander in the pasture. One evening we come across a beautiful stone hotel that looks like a castle overlooking a peaceful lake with reflections of the colorful trees and azure sky on the water. We believe this picturesque place will be way too expensive and out of the question for us to stay, but when I inquire about a room, we are pleasantly surprised at how reasonable it is. We spend the night sipping wine and watching the moonrise above the trees and reflect on the dark, placid lake water as we sit in rocking chairs on the hotel porch.

Afterward we travel to the coast, where we spend several days in the coastal town of Sitges and walk the cobblestone streets, eating tapas and sipping wine through the town. We head to Marrakesh in

Morocco and live the Aladdin fantasies of snake charmers, acrobats, hookah pipes, genie bottles, and magic carpet rides in Jemaa el-Fnaa—the main square and marketplace in Marrakesh's medina quarter. We wind down our journey on the Grand Canary Island, where we rest and relax for our final days of this trip, and then it's back to Barcelona for a few days before we head our separate ways.

The Spanish proverb *"como agua para chocolate"* describes an emotional state: boiling over in either anger or passion. The saying pretty much sums up this trip.

Our next trip, we are taking Kamal with us on a weeklong Caribbean cruise.

Unbalanced

"He ain't right," says one of our site managers, Alan, regarding one of our young engineers. He's walking around wearing a white bathrobe over his clothes and saying stuff like *"Jesus loves you"* and *"May God be with you, brother"* to anyone who looks at him. This is not ordinary with Daniel. He's always been very logical, direct, analytical, and professional in his thinking and speech.

I met Daniel at the gym a while back when he was attempting to bench press about 300 pounds without a spot. He freaked me out, so I went over to his bench to spot him. He works for Barron. After seeing him and talking to him a few times, I got him to take part in a few of the 5Ks on base and found that he's very athletic. He's a former college boxer and he has a hard, muscular body and is very well proportioned. He's a handsome guy and he has some of the bluest and most captivating eyes I have ever seen.

Daniel just came back from an R&R and a few people told me he was acting weird. I saw him the previous day, walking around with his white robe over his clothes, but I thought he was just heading to the showers. Others must have reported him to our employee assistance program (EAP) to check on him. Our EAP team is a group of professionals trained to help employees deal with personal problems that may adversely affect their work performance, health, and well-being. I swing by the EAP office to address my concern. I'm told that people have come forward and that Daniel's been evaluated and will be heading to Dubai for further evaluation.

The next morning, I walk into the headquarters building to go to my office. My office happens to be right next door to the EAP office. In the hallway is a big, black, cushioned chair for employees to wait for the availability of an EAP counselor. Daniel is sitting in the chair, still wearing his white robe over his clothes. I say hello to him and when he replies, I know something is wrong. I can see it in his eyes. He's either experiencing post-traumatic stress disorder, under the influence the drugs, or just completely lost.

He keeps calling me "brother." From just a few short sentences of our conversation, I think he believes he's Jesus Christ or the second coming. He is saying things like *"May God be with you, brother"* and *"Jesus loves you."* It's way out of character for Daniel. He's nonthreatening but certainly a little off balance.

He checks in with our EAP counselor, and the next day they send him to Dubai for a mental evaluation. By then, whatever is going on has ceased some and he's able to get checked out on his own. I've heard people claiming that he overmedicated himself with over-the-counter medications for sleep and allergy. Apparently that triggered this bizarre reaction. I'm not sure what he took or how much. I've heard stories of people having side effects from a mixture of drugs, from drowsiness to dizziness to hallucinations. This is the first time I've seen it affect someone I know.

A week later he's back. Seeing him back at work, I know everything is okay and back on track. I'm glad.

I Don't Want to Go to DFAC

It's July 23, 2011. Amy Winehouse is dead. I'm not familiar with her music except for one song that I really like, "Rehab." That song is running through my head and since I'm heading to the DFAC, I change the lyrics to what's going on at present: *They tried to make me go to DFAC. I said, "No, no, no." The food is probably GMO. Thought you should know, know, know. I've got the time but it's really not fine. They're trying to make me go to DFAC. I won't go, go, go.*

Of course, I go to the DFAC because it's the only place to get some grub. Or shall I say, free grub. There are plenty of fast-food restaurants on base, but we all know what those are like. It's rare that I shy away from food. I love food. The dining facilities (DFAC) on base serve everything buffet style. It kind of reminds me of Golden Corral restaurants, belly up to the trough with their low-quality foods at a low, low price to feed the average 300-pound glut who usually frequents and gorges at a place like this.

The DFACs are very well maintained and under constant scrutiny by the contractor, military, and DCMA. After all, they must maintain the highest and strictest of standards because can you imagine a foodborne-illness outbreak in a place like this?

All the DFACs are white-tiled walls, white-tiled floors, and white-painted walls and ceilings. All the kitchen appliances are stainless steel. I guess everything is white so they can tell if any part of the DFAC is dirty. The DFACs remind me of hospitals: very sterile. They always have someone checking the temperatures of the food and wiping down the counters. I'm always very glad to see that. Clean, clean, clean.

If the military has 100,000 troops and 50,000 contractors in Afghanistan served three meals a day, that would equate to 450,000 meals per day, every day. It's a massive operation. Our base houses about 35,000 to 40,000 personnel, or around 120,000 meals a day. Huge cargo planes arrive all hours of the day and night bringing food and amenities.

Sometimes I feel like I'm at O'Hare or JFK with all the air traffic coming and going with the loud noises of the planes and jets.

Presentation is a big deal. Everything looks so appetizing and delicious. In the morning, there's a buffet of freshly cut fruits, breads, cereals, juices, and every kind of flavored milk. There's a huge crockpot of oatmeal with all the fixins. There's always a hot buffet of scrambled eggs, hard-boiled eggs, sausage, bacon, ham, waffles, French toast, whole-wheat toast, white toast, English muffins, and bagels. There's strong coffee and light coffee. There's every kind of soda and coolers stocked with energy and mineral drinks. And bottles of water are everywhere—not only in the DFAC, but all over base. Bottled water is the only drinkable water on base. Not all bases are as well equipped as BAF, but considering we're the largest base and hub of all military activity in Northern Afghanistan, we stay well supplied.

Lunch and dinner menus change daily and there is a short-order grill that serves burgers, hot dogs, fries, onion rings, pizza, and wings every day. One of the DFACs specializes in BBQ. They serve BBQ ribs, chicken, brisket, and sausage with all the traditional BBQ fixins. They also serve homemade chili and soup every day. That's one of my favorite DFACs, but it's a hike from the office.

Friday nights are surf and turf, offering lobster tails, crab legs, salmon, baked trout, crab cakes, and deep-fried shrimp, or a combination. The lines are always long, as there is a tendency that the DFAC will run out of lobster; it's first come, first served. There's hot soup and a salad bar. For dessert, there's always a huge selection of baked cookies, pies, and cakes, and ice cream. And for those who want a nice, cold beer to go along with that pizza or burger, there's near-beer in the fridge. No alcohol is allowed on base because we are in a Muslim country. So much for diversification and sharing cultural differences! I tried the near-beer once. It's pretty bad.

It all looks so good, but looks can be deceiving sometimes. The first few days, I think, *"Oh, this is pretty good."* I check out the posted menu each day and plot out what I'm going to have. One morning I had hard-boiled eggs, but the yolks looked fluorescent orange and I couldn't eat them. Another morning I switched to scrambled eggs, but they were cold. Now I wait for the short-order grill and order an egg-white omelet to my liking. Sometimes the lines are long. I hate waiting in line, so I settle for a bowl of fruit that I top with yogurt and some cereal.

It's always like a roll of the dice. Sometimes it's good; sometimes it's mediocre. It also depends which DFAC you eat at and if there have been any cargo planes diverted from delivering goods. I think everything comes out of a frozen bag or a can. Some of the cooks are pretty good about adding some spice or flavorings, but not always. I've had overcooked steak, rubbery seafood, boiled and seasoned chicken, and tomato soup that tasted like watered-down catsup. I don't get too excited about going to the DFAC anymore.

After having a meal at the DFAC, a few of my coworkers and I fill our pockets to bring snacks back to the office so we can skip a meal or too. When I go to the DFAC, I always make a sweep through the cafeteria, filling my pockets with items. One of my coworkers, Scott, loves to wear his cargo pants because he has more pockets to fill. Another coworker of ours would rather eat in his office and has a set with jacket, pants, and shirt that has 64 pockets to fill! As we exit out the door, there's a big sign next to it that says, *"Civilians are not allowed to take food out of the DFAC."* I feel like we're Laverne and Shirley making the sweep and score.

My Balkan friend, Arian, observes me making my daily score of goods. He's an auditor and he ensures the rules are being followed. He observes me making my way down the hallway of the headquarters building. He sees that I have two cans of soda in my hands and decides to follow me to my office. I empty my pockets and start to fill our fridge with all the goodies I brought back. He suddenly appears and I look up at him standing in the doorway of my office. He nods his head and reminds me we are supposed to take only two items. He sarcastically remarks, *"You HR folks are the worst for not following the rules. You're supposed to be leading by example."* I'm busted! Oh well, I need to stock up so I don't have to go to the DFAC for every meal. This becomes a game for us. He'll tease me, but if he's looking for a snack or something to drink, he knows where to come. And he's been known to show up time and time again.

I call Arian "The Warden" or "The Hall Monitor."

0400 Sharp!

All work and no play makes Thomas . . . a runner! The last marathon I ran was when I turned 40, 10 years ago. When I turn 50, I decide to run another marathon. Janet Atkinson has run 60-plus marathons—one for every year of her life. I've been sticking to 5 and 10K runs, but she convinces me to go for the longer distance. I do.

I manage to recruit a few other runners from the Baserunners team to train and run the upcoming Air Force Marathon on base. There are about 10 of us who will go for it. As one of my workout and running buddies, Randy, would say, *"Extreme, man!"* to run 26.2 miles or 42 kilometers. Every other Friday, I'll do two laps, or about 16 miles, and do three laps a few weeks before the race.

The first Friday of long-distance running around base, a handful of runners show up. By the second and third meet, a few change their running schedules or drop out. It seems 0400 is way too early for most.

One of the newer LOGCAP employees is Stella. She makes it to the first meet but not to the second one. When I see her, I ask where she's been. She says, *"I was just a few minutes late and you all were already gone."* I reply in my drill-sergeant tone, loud and clear, *"0400 does not mean 0402 or 0405. We leave at 0400 sharp! Now drop down and give me 50 push-ups for the team!"* She's late again for our third meet! She obviously didn't learn her lesson. So when I finish my run, I go right to my office. I take out a pad of sticky notes and start writing memos:

- 0400 is not 0401 or 0402!
- You snooze you lose!
- 0400 SHARP!!!
- Don't forget to set your alarm!
- What's the story, morning glory?
- Lazy Daisy, drive me crazy!
- Fail to prepare . . . prepare to fail!
- If you arrive early, you're on time; if you arrive on time, you're late!

Before Stella reports to work, I post a sticky note on the front door of her office B-hut. I post memos all over her office, at her desk, on her computer screen, and inside some of her books.

After my shower, I go back to the office. I still haven't heard from her. So I get on Sametime—the Barron interdepartmental instant-messaging system—and start to ping people at other FOBs. I feel like I'm sending an all-points bulletin through Afghanistan to send messages to Stella about being late and missing our training runs. A lot of my messengers don't know Stella but want to get in on the fun and follow my instructions and plea.

Within an hour of our workday, Stella comes bouncing into my office and yells, *"Josef!"* I look at her with a big smile. She rants in her high-pitched voice, *"I have people from all over Afghanistan pinging me on Sametime and have no clue who they are!"* Everyone in the office bursts out with laughter. My practical joke is working! She continues, *"I'm going to be finding sticky notes weeks and months down the road. You even put one on the bathroom door and in the bathroom stalls!"* Yes, I did. I knocked before I entered the women's bathroom. When I got the all clear, I quickly added sticky notes to each of the stall doors.

Well it worked. From that day on, Stella wasn't late for another run. Of course, everyone she didn't know who was pinging her on Sametime had to meet her when they came through Bagram, so she ended up meeting a lot of new people and making friends. We call that a win-win.

Team Texas

It's 0359 and from the lighting of the building, I can see Stella's silhouette. Her tall, slender body and long legs are stumbling about; I'm sure she just crawled out of bed. Her hands are all up in her hair as she is fumbling with it and trying to put it up. She sees me looking at my watch like I'm timing her with a stopwatch. She shouts out, *"I'm heeeere!"* The only other runner joining us is Randy. By now, all the other runners either changed their running schedules, dropped out, or are currently on R&R.

Neither Stella nor Randy is a morning person. I hand them each a bottle of an energy, sustainability, and muscle-recovery concoction— another one of my secret potions for working out—that I whipped up with a little wild berry powder packet for extra flavor. Stella opens it right away and takes a big swig. She likes it.

Safety check: I check to make sure Randy and Stella each have on a reflector belt, a flashing light, tied shoes, and an optional sweatband. We turn on our flashing lights and start off with a brisk walk from Barron Village to the corner of Disney. We hang a right on Disney and begin a light jog at a conversational pace on the sidewalk for the first mile. Conversing during a run helps me to monitor everyone's breathing. If they can talk while we're running, it's a good pace. If they're gasping for air and can't finish a sentence, then we need to slow down.

Stella is originally from Austin. I graduated from the University of Texas at Austin and have been residing there for the past 25 years or so. Randy is from San Antonio. Randy names us "Team Texas" and starts to sing, "*The stars at night are big and bright . . . deep in the heart of Texas.*"

Team Texas hangs a left on the corner at ECP-1 and heads toward Warrior Village. We pass by a lookout tower on the right perimeter wall, ECP-3, another lookout tower, CDC on the left, and 77 Construction Company on the right. We stop at mile three by Warrior Village to take a good gulp of my concoction and walk for about a minute. Randy tells us to stay on the road and keep running as he dashes off into the darkness. I think maybe he's going to relieve himself. The sun is starting to come up, but it'll be a while before it clears up and over the mountains. Stella and I get a ways up the road when Randy reappears with three bottles of ice-cold water. I ask him where he got them and he says he knows where all the hiding places with cold water are. Of course he does. He's the man! Randy travels all over the base with locals, so I'm sure he knows all the locations where the cold water is stored. We guzzle them down.

We continue straight ahead, where we hang a left and the road turns to dirt for a short distance. It seems like it never fails, but when we get to this corner, there's always a bus or truck that's kicking up dust everywhere. I've learned to wear a bandana around my neck and pull it up to cover my nose and mouth until I can get by it. The dust clings to the sweat on my face, arms, and legs.

The run and concoction must be waking up Stella and Randy. They're finally feeling alert and talking a little more. I guess four miles into the run, it's about time. Randy dashes off again to get Team Texas another bottle of cold water. We stop by the bus stop to drink it. Between the warm, dry conditions and our long, sweaty run, we are extra thirsty and our bodies are really craving the water. Randy even pours some over his head.

At the end of Smacktown, we take another sip of our concoction. We hang a right and run parallel with the airfield. Fields on each side where wild poppies grow surround the road. It's the kind of poppy cultivated for opium. The military chops them down before they flower. We cross a creek and proceed up a small hill. The road becomes an alleyway of T-walls to protect the airfield.

Stella starts to quiz us with Texas trivia. What is the state bird? Mockingbird. What is the state flower? Bluebonnet. What is the state tree? Pecan. Then she goes into Texas music trivia. I fail miserably and she accuses me of not being a true Texan. I've failed at worse things. She and Randy get into a long discussion and question-and-answer session about Texan musicians. Of course, they get on the topic of Willie Nelson and start singing at the top of their lungs. They're quite a hoot. I know the two of them are wide awake now. I guess that energy powder mix that I added to the concoction must've really kicked in.

After the long section of T-walls on both sides of the road, we're at the old Russian bunkers, arsenal storage, and a deserted two-story building. Randy asks Stella if she's ever run through Russian Hills. There are mounds and mounds built for bunkers and arsenal storage that resemble small hills. Stella has never been through, so we hang a quick right to take the loop through there.

Randy asks, *"Do y'all know the history behind the two-story dilapidated building?"* Stella and I tell him, *"No."* Randy starts to tell us the history that took place here. He factually states, *"On February 15, 1989, the last of the Russian soldiers held their ground here in the hills with the last 129 soldiers fighting to the end when the Taliban ambushed them. All of the soldiers were killed except for two of the higher-ranking Russian soldiers named Vladamir Bykovsky and Ludvig Novokof."*

Randy pronounces their names perfectly and without a stumble and continues his story without missing a beat. *"The Taliban killed off all the remaining soldiers. They used this building to interrogate and torture* their enemies. But they knew that Bykovsky and Novokof were still at large and must be hiding in one of these bunkers or storage areas. The Taliban had to figure a way to lure Bykovsky and Novokof out from their hiding. So they . . ." Just as he's telling us the suspenseful, historical story, a feral cat out in the fields lets out a big, loud, startling cry Randy states, "They lured them out from hiding by making cat sounds from the field." Then Stella and I knew he was pulling our leg, and the three of us burst into laughter. Stella slugs Randy to stop his silly bullshit.

We do the Russian Hill loop that adds maybe a half-mile to our run. I'm so proud of these two for taking the longer route because we're not slackers! We continue to run along the length of the east side of the airfield. We hear the first F-16 fighter jet rev its engines and blast off down the runway. The sound is piercing and we cover our ears. About a minute later, the second one takes off and up and over the mountains. I love to watch the jets take off with the sunlight starting to illuminate our day. I can see the trail of flames from the empennage. It must be 0430 at this point and the pilots are doing a test exercise. They seem to do them quite regularly at this early hour.

We continue straight along the road until we come to a T-intersection. Trash builds along the roadway as we get closer to the landfill. I raise my bandana again over my nose and mouth as we get closer. The toxic smoke billows high above the landfill and into the sky. It's a good day for running; the nasty smoke is not hovering low. We try to pick up the pace to get by the landfill quicker. We can see parts of the outskirts of Bagram through the wire, with mud-brick homes, a mosque, and a few trees that tower above the rooflines. I was told to be careful along this stretch of road, as Taliban can open fire into the base. I forget to tell Randy and Stella that, but I've never heard of anyone getting shot over here. But with that thought in mind, I scan the ditch along the road for cover, just in case. You can never be too careful.

We loop around the end of the airfield and come to a lookout tower. Here, we take our final swig of the concoction and toss our empty bottles into a trash can nearby. We have maybe one more mile to go. We wind along the road running parallel again with the other side of the airfield. We pass a few more lookout towers and a long stretch of running on partial rock roads. Stella lags behind, far behind. That's what she gets for missing our other long runs.

Randy and I stop and wait behind a waist-high cement barrier on the side of the road before we make our final dash down Disney. We see Stella making the bend as she's getting closer. Coming from the opposite direction off Disney Drive is an Army squad out for their morning run and PT. Stella and the squad are about equal distance from us. As they both get closer to us, Randy sees some big chunk of solid mass lying on the ground, picks it up, slams it back on the ground, and yells to Stella as the squad jogs by, *"Damn it, Parks! You're lagging behind and holding up the team!"*

Stella slows down some more as she gets close to us. She starts to whine about her legs hurting. We're so close. We shuffle by the north end of Disney Drive, where the North DFAC and Cherry-Beasley are located. We sidestep from the part-road, part-gravel with lots of potholes to a nice solid stretch of pavement for the end dash. Disney Drive feels smooth to the feet after the run across the rocks. We can pick up our pace a little quicker. Well Randy and I can pick up our pace a little faster. Stella is still lagging. Every minute or two we yell back at her. Randy starts jogging backward to slow down and keep an eye on her.

We are approaching Craig Hospital on the left, and up ahead in the distance is a communications satellite tower that's by the Clamshell gym. That's my target. When I reach it, I pick up the pace at full speed for the last half-mile. I zip past Camp Montrand, the main PX, and Koele DFAC, and we're done!

Randy and I high five each other at the corner of Disney and California Loop. We wait for slowpoke Stella to come strolling up the sidewalk to the finish. We high five her and make our short walk to Barron

Village. Great run for Team Texas! Every run is a great run. What a great way to start the day!

As we head toward The Village, I see our project manager (PM) and an entourage from the second floor walking toward the DFAC. The PM and his assistant have been nicknamed "Mr. Burns" and "Smithers" from *The Simpsons*. The PM kind of looks like Mr. Burns: old, thin, frail-looking, gray hair, and bald on top. I can picture him in his office, tapping his fingers together, gazing out the window, and watching the workers: *"Another defiant employee? You'll soon learn your lesson, friend!"* Or as we walk by him and the buses dodge past us: *"I'm too good to ride the bus! I hope you asphyxiate on your exhaust fumes and die a horrible death!"* I shout out good morning. Everyone acknowledges me but Mr. Burns. Good ol' Monty.

After finishing the run, taking a shower, and reporting to work, I think I'd better whip up a recovery drink for Stella. I know she's going to be hurting and I need to take care of my running buddy. Plus she should be rewarded for showing up on time and finishing the run. I have a rocket blender in my office just for this purpose. I deliver the drink to Stella and get a hug and a smile in return. Worth it.

The Resort

"Mr. Josef, your schedule for the day at the resort is as follows: Your wake-up call will be at your requested time of 3:45 a.m. Mr. Ward and Ms. Stella of Team Texas will be joining you precisely at 4:00 a.m. for your marathon training. You will run eight miles this morning, according to your training schedule. After you shower, you'll be served complementary coffee and a continental breakfast of fresh fruits and yogurt. Our seasonal selection today is pineapple, strawberries, cantaloupe, and kiwi. We have some additional extra toppings that we know you'll enjoy, like raisins and sunflower seeds. After breakfast, you may drop off your laundry. Your first meeting is at 0700. Around midmorning, Ms. Stella will accompany you for a refreshing and frothy

cookies-and-cream smoothie. A lunch buffet is served in our dining room starting at 11:00 a.m. until 2:00 p.m. In the evening, you are scheduled to instruct the P90X class in our fitness center starting at 7:00 p.m. You have 20 people signed up for your class."

For most people that may not sound like an appealing way to spend time at a resort. But sometimes, if I imagine and pretend hard enough, working and living at BAF isn't so bad and I think of it as an all-inclusive resort. It's all about attitude and the journey for me. I imagine really hard, but there are a number of things to be desired and appreciated. These are some of the things that I like about working and living over here:

- Seeing the daily beauty of the Hindu Kush Mountains that surround Bagram Airfield
- Diversity of people from all over the world and the many different looks and languages of the people
- Meeting new and different people nearly every day
- Hearing people's many and interesting travel experiences and life stories
- Time to enjoy reading books
- Living simplistically
- Casual work atmosphere
- Casual "Friday" every day
- Workout opportunities
- Very fit and active community
- No cooking
- Laundry service
- No humidity, higher elevation
- No grocery shopping
- Cut, fresh fruit most mornings
- Adult community—no screaming kids

- Walking everywhere and no long commutes or traffic jams
- No suffering from Texas Hill Country allergies

The Work Team

Trigger and I are able to get our staffing and budget approved. After most of the short-term, adopted folks from the transition team leave us, we lay out our dream team consisting of 10. Trigger is taking the helm. I am his second-in-charge sharing the management, development, and instructor responsibilities. Janet Atkinson will assist with development, teaching, and special projects. Assisting us are a graphic artist, Jason, and another classroom instructor, Mark, to develop and deliver training. Because office space is very limited on base, we end up with two offices. Trigger, Mark, Juliet, and I will share one office. The database cell will occupy the other. Jason takes a desk wherever he can because we're short one desk.

The database cell is challenged with creating a hybrid learning management system that will interface with other department databases and networks. It'll generate customized reports through a web-based link. Agim, Jeton, and AJ will run the database and enter the data for the 10,000-plus Barron employees in the country. There's the specialist, Tina, who is already on board, as well as Byron, who resides in the U.S. His job as a software developer is to bring all the training together and to be able to program CBTs for training certification and verification online. He'll pull our storyboards and narratives in the field and put them into a computer-based training (CBT) format that will be accessible on our internal portal.

Our tasks are unique for the LOGCAP project because the work environment is different in a war zone. We are subjected to four levels of training requirements: 1) military; 2) corporate; 3) project specific (LOGCAP); and 4) departmental. We are limited in many ways. First, there's almost no road structure in Afghanistan and ground travel is forbidden for civilian personnel in a hostile environment. To get from base to base, the only way is by air travel: small prop planes or helicopters. Therefore, doing any kind of instructor-led training would be very difficult and costly. Second, there's limited facilities to deliver training. They're almost nonexistent. Third, there's limited bandwidth. Anything done in cyberspace is slow. The internet here is awful and can cause dropped connections or freeze up our laptops. You learn to deal with it and adjust.

The preliminary work of a "needs and gap analysis" were conducted with the materials and assessments we gathered from the various functional areas, many of which Sissy managed to gather for us with her Southern charm and good looks before she left the project. We want to build a library of computer-based trainings so any employee can access the training anywhere at any time in the country. We will develop leadership training with subject-matter experts from senior management as an instructor-led course and face-to-face interaction. There's plenty to do, which will keep the team very busy in the coming months and into 2012.

All our new recruits were already serving in the field in different capacities. Trigger first pulled Mark into the group. He was one of the spokespersons for Air Operations. He's obviously very comfortable talking in front of large groups and striking up conversations with people from all walks of life. He's outspoken and transparent, and has a comment on just about everything. He's sociable and likable, so I can see how Trigger thinks he'll be a good fit. He's a couple years older than me, a Texan—and boy can he talk! I dubbed him "Motormouth" after watching a John Waters flick with a character named Motormouth Maybelle.

As a former Navy Seal, Trigger's only life is military, and he introduces the team to a lot of military processes, procedures, resources, and tools. One of the tools he introduces first is the military phonetic alphabet. Nobody else on the team has a military background, so the phonetic is new to us but not completely foreign. As entertainment in the office, we quiz with the letters and words or create code words. Trigger's big thing is using code names when talking about people. My initials are JT so my code name is "Tango Juliet" Trigger's is "Tango Mike." Mark's is "Mike Echo." Valentina's is "Victor Juliet," or since she goes by Tina it could be "Tango Juliet" like mine. Janet's is the best-sounding code name: "Juliet Alpha." When it comes to company policies, procedures, or contacts, Janet always has the answers. Our department is the information center because if someone needs to find something out, they know they can get the information from Janet. Of course, the rest of us will gladly get the answers, but Juliet Alpha always seems to know things off the top of her head. When our department is publishing a newsletter, we decide to include an "ask and answer" column titled "Ask Juliet Alpha."

Juliet Alpha is our sharpshooter for the team and the company. She is a long-term Barron employee with an established network of connections and knows who to contact for what; she knows who the shakers and movers are; she knows the insides and outsides of the business; she knows processes, policies, and procedures (perhaps a bit too well); and she is a quick learner and proficient with computer software and proprietary systems. She's a workhorse. I also think she's a mole for the company, so her code name fits her well. She's a spy and we begin to treat her like one.

Wedding Bells: July 30, 2011

It seems like we just got back from our Spain and Morocco trip, and now we're off to meet in Vancouver, Canada. Greg and I chose Canada to get out of the sweltering summer heat of Texas and Afghanistan. There's a huge momentum in the United States for supporting same-sex marriages. Since Canada already recognizes same-sex marriage, Greg and I decide to tie the knot. We've been together for 13 years.

Our wedding is atypical and impromptu. First, the closest marriage license office in Chinatown is about two miles from where we're staying. The office is like a government office I would picture in China. All the workers are Asian and there are papers stacked on all the desks. Applying for a marriage license is mundane: fill out the paperwork, sign, and pay. That's it. It's like filling out a housing application. I also learn the marriage is not complete until a service is conducted by a justice of the peace, a preacher, or an officiate. After we get our receipt, we ask the clerk to take our picture to cherish the moment, the memory . . . the process. We go to enjoy some dim sum for lunch and then walk back into town near the high-rise condo where we're staying. We find a jeweler and buy matching white-gold rings.

I search for Vancouver justices of the peace, also known as wedding commissioners or wedding officiates. I scroll through dozens by location, checking out their profiles, philosophies, and pictures. I finally come across one who interests me and share it with Greg. We both agree that her secular approach to life would make her the perfect officiate. We call her and she tells us she can perform our ceremony the next day.

Since both Greg and I are informal people, we wear jeans and dress shirts for this notable occasion. We jump on a city bus that winds along the shores of Vancouver and through some foothills about 30 miles out of town. The last stop is in front of the officiate's house.

She's patiently awaiting and expecting our arrival. She scoops up her little Pekingese dog, Fluffy, and we all jump in her car to go to a nearby park along the shore. The day is a bit cloudy, but the temperature is very nice. We walk along a park trail and across some massive boulders until we come upon an open area along the shore. There's a couple playing classical music nearby and there's a light breeze coming off the water. Perfect. This is the spot. The officiate tells us that Fluffy will be our witness and maid of honor. She picks up the dog and hands her to me to hold her during the ceremony—probably so she doesn't run off. Fluffy is so sweet and tries to lick my face when I hold her. She sits in my arms quietly as the officiate starts our ceremony.

The officiate wrote the readings by herself and from her heart. She spoke eloquently and meaningfully. As the cellos play, her words flow something like this:

> "Before this moment, you have been many things to one another: acquaintance, friend, companion, lover, dancing partner, and even a teacher, for you have learned much from one another in these many years. No relationship is perfect, ever. There are always some ways you must bend, to compromise, to give something up to gain something greater. The love you two have for each other is bigger than these small differences. And that's the key.

> "Love can be a temporary madness, and it erupts like volcanoes and then subsides. It can be a crashing ocean wave and then placid waters. It can be a thunderous storm, but the sun will shine again. You must work out whether your roots have so entwined together that it is inconceivable that you should ever part. Because this is what love is. Love is knowing each other's most intimate thoughts that are not just skin-deep but rooted deep and intertwined like a hundred-year-old tree.

> "Love is not breathlessness or excitement. It is not the promulgation of promises of eternal passion. It is not the desire to mate every second minute of the day. It is not lying awake at night imagining that he is kissing every cranny of your body. No, don't blush, I am telling you some truths. That is just being 'in love,' which any fool can do. Love itself is what is left over when being 'in love' has burned away, and this is both an art and a fortunate accident."

Everything she says in her readings relates to natural occurrences—mostly calm, sometimes disruptive. It's always beauty in the end. Her readings almost make me want to cry because they're so poetic and beautiful. They fit both Greg and me very well. After the readings and our vows, we kiss and smile. We're both very happy.

Fluffy was the perfect maid of honor. I set her on the ground. A couple comes by as we finish up and the officiate asks them to sign our wedding papers as witnesses—complete strangers. After the signing, the cello players come walking by as well and we express our thanks and enjoyment of their music during our wedding vows. They're flattered.

The officiate recommends a quaint local restaurant on the harbor near the park. She departs to another wedding. Greg and I go to the restaurant to celebrate. Informal, short, and sweet is our wedding. Our relationship has been recognized by both of our families for many years. Now if only the government of the United States can recognize it.

After we depart Canada, we head back to the States to spend a few days to witness and celebrate another wedding between my nephew and his bride.

Air Force Marathon, Bagram Airfield

Today's the big day for about a dozen of the Baserunners. We've been training for months to take part in the Air Force Shadow Run at Bagram Airfield to run a half marathon or full marathon. The main event is at Wright-Patterson Air Force Base in Dayton, Ohio. Runners at BAF receive a lot of the same perks as runners in Ohio: T-shirt, cap, patch, medal, and a few other goodies.

About 450 runners are registered for the event. Our show time is 0330 with a start time of 0430. For about 90 percent of the runners, this is their first marathon. Like any other running event, before the starting gun is loud upbeat music, fruits and drinks, and people registering, stretching, taking pictures, and talking in small groups all over the place. Excitement fills the air. People are gung ho and ready to go. I know I am and so is my Barron team.

We're an interesting group of folks. Our group of runners includes my boss Trigger, my coworker Janet Atkinson, and Team Texas: Randy, Stella, and me. There's also the lieutenant colonel dressed in his Marine-green training shorts and shirt, as always. As a Marine, he doesn't need any supplements or training beyond a 5K.

Under the lieutenant colonel's command is one of his staff, Paul. Paul's come a long way to prepare for this event. He smoked and was overweight, but he's quit smoking and dropped quite a bit of weight while training. I really admire people who kick some bad habits for better health. Poor Paul hurts from all the training. He has his knees wrapped up in compression bandages and is wearing black compression socks over his calves. He looks like Forrest Gump as a kid in his leg braces. But that doesn't make any difference. He's set out to complete his first half marathon regardless.

Another runner is Milena from the project controls department. Milena is a tall, alluring young lady from Bosnia. She always looks her best. Her hair is usually tied back into a braid without a strand out of place. She has a lovely complexion and looks nice even in her running attire. Her mother was the first woman to run a marathon in her country. Like mother, like daughter.

Two of Milena's colleagues join us, Alex and GP. Alex is usually at all the runs. He's my competition to see who can get the most T-shirts. I think I'm ahead by a few. I look for Alex at every race, but he's not a morning person. I know he'd rather roll over in his bed when that alarm clock goes off. He always seems to manage to show up right at the start. The starting gun will go off and Alex goes from walking, sometimes running, down the sidewalk and eases right into the mass of runners taking off from the starting line. I caught him once jumping midway into a race after he overslept. He was hiding behind a tree along the race route, and when the crowd of runners ran by, he jumped in and blended right in with the pack. What a sneak! And he still got the T-shirt.

GP is from India and is a dedicated runner. He lives on the east side of base and works on the west side. He runs the four miles to and from work just about every day. He used to work in the materials yard. His real name has about 25 letters in it and nobody can pronounce it or remember it, so his coworkers nicknamed him GP for "Government Property" after his department.

The youngest in the group is Aaron. Aaron is a lanky college graduate. He worked for Barron as a college intern for the past few summers. He's not a morning person. Sometimes I see him walking to work looking like a zombie. He's usually sporting bed head. I guess that's also the style now though. We've been pressuring Aaron for weeks to run with us in this event. The farthest he's run was a 5K. He's going to hang with Janet Atkinson, who usually picks up the rear of the racers and has a slower pace. For Janet, it's not about the speed or the race time; it's about doing it and finishing it.

Janet is bouncing around all over the place like a little butterfly, giving last-minute advice and handing out nutritional supplements to fuel the body for this 26.2-mile event. Janet has completed more than 60 marathons, including a couple 50-milers and 100-miler endurance runs. She knows exactly what to do. She's set up training schedules and diet plans to prepare people and knows how to build their confidence. Now she's handing out extra energy gel packs. She's a bundle of energy. She takes not just a few but a handful of supplements a day. She doesn't eat much, so it seems like she lives on those supplements. It's no wonder she doesn't sleep either. If one of her kids were feeling sluggish when they were going to school, Janet Atkinson would probably give them a handful of supplements and say, *"Take these. They'll get you through the day."* Okay, mom. Gulp.

Thirty minutes before the start, the emcee makes an announcement and gives a safety briefing with route information. The announcer is a jerk. Instead of sharing the enthusiasm of finishing the marathon, he's up on stage with his microphone, announcing to the group that we have only five hours to complete the marathon instead of the normal six. To make the arduous task less desirable, he continues to tell us that if we are still running after five hours, there will be the ugliest bus of shame to pick up any runners still on the road. I doubt the guy has ever run a marathon, and for all these first-timers, those aren't the words they need to hear. Even the lieutenant colonel scuffled at his announcement, showing a little snarl. That's the lieutenant colonel: He's not much for words, but you can see it in his expressions and actions. Since the run is a half or full marathon, I hear a lot of runners deciding at the last minute to do just the half.

Since I've been training with Randy and Stella, we start off the race together. Randy needs to finish in less than four hours because he has a work meeting he must attend. What work ethic and dedication! Randy has a lot of spunk and I know he'll do it. Trigger, Janet, and I already got our approvals to take the day off to recover and reward ourselves afterward. Randy's also carrying a camera to document this event and his accomplishment with pictures and video. I don't want to be carrying a camera for 26.2 sweaty miles. No way, not even a pocket-sized point-and-shoot.

At the starting gun, we watch all the rookies dash ahead at full force and know they'll probably burn up a good amount of their energy before the half. We start off slowly for the first mile or two, just kind of taking it easy. Randy is busy taking pictures of the crowd and chatting with everyone he knows. He knows a lot of people. *"I'm fired up, man, because I just downed an espresso energy gel with caffeine! I just love these gels!"* he exclaims to us. The kid is a bundle of energy even without the espresso gels. He's running sideways, backward, ahead of us, and behind us to snap photos. He's hopping around like Rocky Balboa. I'm beginning to think he's had more than just one caffeinated espresso gel. That boy is wired! I hope it lasts for the entire race. We have about 23 more miles to go!

Stella starts to lag a little behind, but Randy and I continue at my pace. Randy's pace is faster, but he's going to hang with me for the first 10 to 12 miles. He turns to me and says, *"Hey, man, since I'm going to be the champion of this race, you want to hear my acceptance speech for the trophy?"* I smile and nod with a yes. *"First, I'd like to thank the Air Force for putting on this terrific event. I'm really looking forward to being swept away after the race on an F-16 to compete in my next race. I'd also like to thank the Army for their tactical support along the race route to keep us safe from the Taliban. You guys are badasses! Next, I'd like to thank my sponsor, Nike, for providing me with this awesome performance running wear, from my T-shirt and shorts to my socks and headband. I couldn't have completed this race without my favorite bands playing along the route . . . my favorite Texas homeboy, Willie Nelson. Willie, I love ya, man! The song 'Me and Paul' helped push me to the finish line. Also playing great music along the way were Paul Simon, my man Buddy Guy, Dave Matthews, and so many other fantastic musicians. I'd also like to thank my terrific coaches, Trigger and Thomas Josef, for keeping me pumped. I'd like to give a big cheer for Team Texas! 'Hook 'em Horns!' We rock! I also want to thank my drug dealer, Janet Atkinson, for supplying me with some of the best Hammer Nutrition products ever. Extreme, man! This stuff rocks! Last, I'd like to thank all my fans who lined the course, cheering me on the entire way. Your support, enthusiasm, and cheers kept me pumped the entire race."*

I have the pleasure of listening to him build and rehearse his speech for a few miles. He also flips on his camera and takes a quick video of himself to let the audiences know that he's feeling great at the halfway mark. After sharing his acceptance speech and video clip with me, he decides he needs to bolt ahead so he can finish the race, collect his medal, and go to work. After Randy wins the marathon and works his 12-hour shift, he wants about 20 of us to gather for a dinner that he's going to whip up. Not really, but Randy has that kind of energy.

As Randy darts ahead and loses me in his trail of dust, I continue at my regular pace, taking nutritional supplements, energy gels, and gulps of water every few miles. At every mile is an aid station, and I walk through them to down a good drink of water to stay hydrated and prevent my muscles from spasms. At alternate stations I hydrate with liquid electrolytes and water. I always take a few seconds to thank all the volunteers. If it weren't for the number of volunteers, the event wouldn't be as successful.

After the halfway mark, other less-experienced runners are starting to fade. I pass up a few of them. I continue running at a leisurely pace—or at least as leisurely as one can get while running. I run at conversation pace—talking to myself in my mind and jamming to tunes on my iPod—without huffing or puffing. My pace seems consistent with a few runners ahead of and behind me. I keep my pace in check with theirs and we stay together for a while. Eventually I pass up the three ahead of me around mile marker 22 or so when a lot of runners "hit the wall" and their legs don't want to cooperate with their minds to finish. When a runner hits the wall, it's the greatest mental challenge. I hit the wall running my first marathon a decade ago. From that experience, I learned how important it is to fuel the body along the entire course.

Another running buddy I know, Ed, is manning the last aid station with a small group of others. Ed is just a few years older than me and sticks with running shorter distances. He knows what it's like to run a marathon or do a triathlon. He's done plenty in his days. He's still in great shape. He knows the monstrosity of putting on such an event, and he's always willing to volunteer where he can during a race. Volunteers rock!

Ed sees me coming up to his station, looks at his watch, and grabs a cup of water to hand me. I stop to drink the water and Ed informs me, *"You're doing great, Thomas. You're under a 10-minute pace. Make the last mile your strongest!"* Ed's little pep talk has me stoked to get to the finish line. I manage to pick up the pace just a bit when I come across a young 20-something soldier. As I'm about to pass him up, I look at him, and he looks at me. I say, *"You're not going to let this 50-year-old man beat you to the finish line, are you?"* That is enough for the young kid to pick up his pace along with me and we run across the finish line together. Ed was right. I come in right at four hours, almost on the dot. What a feat of accomplishment!

After crossing the finish line, there's an Army master sergeant on a low platform holding up a medal. I stop before him and bow my head as he places the medal around my neck and says, *"Congratulations!"* and shakes my hand. Awesome! Completing a marathon is a victory. Chalk another one up for Josef!

Paul, who ran the half marathon, has already showered and changed. He's here to congratulate me and a few of the other runners. I see Randy is still hanging around. He must've decided to bail out of work or go in late. I join Paul and Randy and stand along the sidelines near the finish line to congratulate and cheer on the others crossing the finish line. We stand proud for the other Barron Baserunners as they cross. After me comes Alex, then Milena, then the lieutenant colonel, Stella, GP, Aaron, Trigger, and last but not least, Janet. I think Janet comes in last because, like a good mom, she picks up the rear to make sure everyone is in good spirits mentally and physically.

We all finished! I'm so proud of our group! After a shower, it's time to celebrate with a recovery drink, chow, and rest. Mission accomplished!

Mogadishu

On October 3–4, 1993, in Mogadishu, Somalia, two Black Hawk helicopters were shot down during a battle to capture the leaders of the Habr Gidr clan, led by the self-proclaimed president and warlord Mohamed Farrah Aidid. The battle ended two days later. U.S. forces were finally evacuated to the U.N. base by an armored convoy. While leaving the crash site, a group of Rangers and Delta operators realized that there was no room left in the vehicles for them and were forced to depart the city on foot to a rendezvous. This has been commonly referred to as the "Mogadishu Mile." The Battle of Mogadishu is also known as "Black Hawk Down" or "The Day of the Rangers." *Black Hawk Down* is the title of the movie that portrays the event. I got a copy of the movie about a week before the race to watch it and replay the incidents that took place that day.

In memory of this historic military event, the military sponsors a "Mogadishu Mile" run that has been held the past two Octobers. The Mogadishu Mile is a 5K (or 3.1 miles). Participants are expected to wear their full battle rattle and uniform that adds probably an extra 35 pounds or so.

I didn't do the run last year, but I try to get some of my fellow Baserunners to take part in this year's event. There are no takers. Nobody wants to run in their PPE, and some of the runners are still recovering from our Air Force Marathon two weeks ago. After the marathon, I drank a recovery drink and took some post-workout supplements. I was up and running (pun) without any soreness or stiffness. I think I've mastered the training and post-marathon recovery.

I feel I need to run the Mogadishu alongside our military to show my support. It appears that I'm the only civilian to run in the event with my black PPE. I'm wearing my running shorts and a T-shirt with my ballistic vest loaded with armored plates. The military men and women are wearing their uniforms, boots, PPE, and helmets. They're even carrying their guns just as they would if they were in battle. There are military K-9s running it alongside their handlers. Even these military dogs are wearing their battle rattle.

I stand out in the crowd of desert camo uniforms, helmets, and tactical gear. Service men and women come up to me and thank me for taking part in the event with them. They probably think I'm a retired vet. I'm even the center of attention in a couple of photos, balanced by the camo men and women on each side of me.

Running with an extra 25 or 35 pounds or more certainly gets the heart pounding quicker. I've never run with body armor and my weight load is much less compared to the other runners. Because of that, even though I am running a slower pace, I still manage to stay out in front of quite a few. The macho, athletic men and a few women who pass by me with their entire garb impress me. I'm blown away by their endurance and incredible stature.

During the run, all I can think of is *Black Hawk Down* and the events that unfolded that day. It was a horrific battle that ensued and left 18 American service members dead and 73 injured. The finish line is somber and cheerless.

Morning Faces

Our cheap housing units don't have indoor plumbing. Everyone walks to a community bathroom or uses a porta potty. If there's been any kind of improvement to the living conditions here in the past two years, I haven't noticed it. It's the same old slum-weathered and worn B-huts.

The spring thaw of the Hindu Kush Mountains causes flooding in the valley. There's standing water everywhere. It's flooded in the back 40 where my B-hut stands. The Village looks more like post-Katrina District 9. In a thug's life, The Village is "da hood."

It's always interesting to people-watch in "da hood" or anywhere on base. There are more than 60 nationalities on base and I often wonder if the hood is a higher standard of living for them. It is common practice in many countries to have a one- or two-bedroom home that is occupied by five or more family members. Here, they have the luxury of their own room all to themselves.

The bathroom and hygiene habits are always interesting to observe in a community bathroom. Of course, they can also be disgusting. The Americans come into the shower room with their nice necessity bags filled with soaps, shampoos, colognes, deodorant, etc. The Balkans remind me of the 1950s American male. Many are good-looking men with short hair and solid, medium builds, and they also smoke like chimneys. I swear they all smoke. The Kosovo men spend more time in front of a mirror than any other nationality I know, trimming their facial hair perfectly, pulling nose hairs, applying facial creams—and if one isn't up to par like the others, they'll let him know.

As people are creatures of habit, I see a lot of the same faces at the same time in the shower room. I usually don't talk to them; I just say good morning. As often as I see the same faces, I nickname a few in my head.

First, there's "Beak." Our alarms and shower times must be synchronized, because we arrive almost every day at the exact same time. Beak is Bosnian and has a very big nose—hence the name. He's tall, lean, and toned. He's actually a nice-looking man, but his shnaz really stands out—so do other parts of his body. He's nicely endowed.

Then there's "The Gagger." I think The Gagger is the caveman in the Geico Insurance commercials. He looks just like him. I'm not sure where he's from, but my guess would be India. He has long, scraggly hair with Neanderthal-type features. I'd love to take a scissors to that mop of hair on his head. What he lacks in beauty, he makes up for in cleanliness. I nickname him The Gagger because every morning he brushes his teeth like he's testing his gag reflex. He gags himself until he chokes on his toothbrush over and over. I'm pretty sure he's brushing his tonsils.

"The Hippie" has long hair and hauls a hair dryer with him to the showers so he can blow-dry his pretty hair afterward. When he plugs it in, our lights go down a few volts. That poor guy is stuck in a time warp, sporting his 1980s big hair design. He even styles it with his 1980s hair dryer. The lovely gold chain around his neck adds to the decade's charm. I bet he was a hit on the dance floor back in the day. Now he looks like an old porn star.

I love it when the Marine comes in. Yes, another one. I'm pretty sure he served in the Marine Corps since his shower bag has the Marine emblem embroidered on it. He strips down to nothing and neatly folds and stacks his clothes on the bench like a good soldier. His years of service are defined in his physique that shows a lot of self-discipline. It's perfectly shaped and toned to show off his muscles. His upper body is the work of some massive pull-up training. He's nicely branded with a tasteful tribal tattoo on his shoulder and upper arm. Not only does he have a fabulous body, but he also has the looks. I can't keep my eyes off him but do it nonchalantly. He, too, has been blessed in other areas.

The Indians are always fun to watch as well. They tote their shower necessities in a plastic bag. Why spend money on a nice bag when a plastic one does the job just fine? Shorts, towel, shower shoes . . . they wear an array of colors. Whatever is the cheapest and the most colorful will do the job—that seems to be their motto.

There are three little Indians who come in around the same time as the rest of us. It reminds me of the little nursery rhyme, *"One little, two little, three little Indians."* They all look so young. The three of them enter the shower room together. I can be the only one on that end of the shower room, with my belongings on the far-right end of the bench, but the three little Indians come in and butt their stuff right up to mine. There's plenty of room to spread out, but nope, they crowd in like sardines.

They wear their flashy colored Crocs and shorts. One has a red pair of Crocs with orange shorts. Another has pink Crocs with light-blue shorts. The last little Indian is wearing lavender Crocs with his lime-green shorts. If I could look in their plastic bags, I bet I could find every color of the rainbow.

I listen to them talk. I'm not sure what language or dialect they're speaking, but it almost sounds like a clucking sound with a lot of tongue hitting the roofs of their mouths. I find them to be very interesting and fun to observe and listen to.

There's generally competition for the first shower stall. It has the best water pressure and showerhead. It seems like only Beak, the Marine, the three little Indians, and I know about it—and whoever is the first one there claims it by putting his towel on the hook beside the shower.

Also, part of the morning crew is "Nic"—short for nicotine. Usually, when I'm walking to the shower room, I see Nic having an early-morning smoke. There's nothing like jumping out of bed, getting dressed to head to the shower, and stopping at the smoking pit to light up. I walk through the smoking pit to get to the showers and it nauseates me. Nic typically comes strolling in as I'm at the sink shaving. As he walks by me, he smells like a dirty ashtray. Even worse, when he's showering the smell permeates the air. I am stigmatized by his nasty habit.

This type of work and the environment seems to attract a lot of smokers. As I make my way to the office and walk by the Bagram company headquarters, I will always see three senior managers outside smoking. Two are retired Marines, "Mean Gene" and "Leatherface." Both men work out regularly and still have good shapes considering they're both pushing 60. The other is retired Army. I call him the "Bulldog." I've worked directly with him and Mean Gene. Leatherface, not so much.

Leatherface is a quiet man. His eyes are always probing the scene like he's in combat and ready to fire off a machine gun. Whenever I walk by the headquarters building and he's standing out there sucking on his cancer stick, he looks at me like he's got me in his crosshairs. I never see the man smile. Hell, I hardly ever hear him talk. However, once when I did hear him speak, he spoke very intelligently. I call him Leatherface because his face is baked like a hide drying in the sun from all those smoke breaks outside.

Mean Gene is a stern man with an unpredictable temper. I approach him like I'm walking on glass because I'm not sure if he'll laugh and smile or blow up. His short-fused temper is exactly how he got his name. One of the female managers went to him with an issue and he flung a stack of papers at her. I don't recall why or remember the details, but that's Mean Gene for you.

Bulldog, on the other hand is . . . well shit, I just think he's a very ugly man. He has a pitted, hard-featured face with bloodshot and watery eyes that look like they're exuding an overflow of last night's gin consumption. His chain-smoking adds to the combination and leaves him emitting a funky smell. I don't like the guy and I don't like the way he treats people. I've had managers under him send me copies of email responses that were degrading. One letter he sent to all his managers started with the line, *"All of you have failed as managers."* I guess that's a direct statement of his own management and leadership.

These are many of the faces I see daily. Some I have never and will never speak to. We just happen to be at the same place at the same time.

The Kabul Seven

Everyone is waiting patiently for the news and details. In this type of instance, it's corporate policy not to release any names or information until the families have been notified. The only information we are given is that seven of the casualties are Barron employees. It includes five Americans, two Brits, and a Kosovar. The number of casualties is higher because there were military personnel and other contractors on board.

News like this isn't generally communicated from the top downward. If we want any information of the news, we get on the internet or tune in to CNN. I'm told the military and contractors withhold the information because they don't want the Taliban or outsiders to know that deaths have resulted from their attacks. A lot of it is secondhand news from people talking. I can't get a definite number, but apparently the attack on the Rhino was caused by an improvised explosive device (IED) attack. The Taliban later claim responsibility for the attack, saying it packed a four-wheel-drive vehicle with 700 kilograms (1,500 pounds) of explosives. A later report also verifies five International Security Assistance Force (ISAF) members, four Americans, and a Canadian were among the dead, bringing the death toll to 13.

It's always tough news within our community when we lose one of our own. I can't imagine what it's like in the military as a warfighter. It has such a personal and emotional effect on everyone. It's another reality check that we're working in a war zone and we can be a target at any given time. Though I feel relatively safe where I'm at, there's always the possibility that my time can be up in a blink of an eye. For most of us here, I'm sure we all think about that.

The military and Barron both conduct a flight-line service for each of the deceased. The night is cold and windy with sprinkles of rain. There are a number of Barron employees who have never been to a flight-line service, so Janet and I lead the group down Disney Drive to the medical helipad entrance at Gate 13. I think about how ironic it is that the medical helipad to Craig Hospital is located at Gate 13, a not-so-lucky number. Each of us presents our ID to the guard to get access to the airfield. We walk along the fence and through some three-foot-high barriers to the flight-line fire station. Just on the other side of the fire station is where the ceremony will take place. There's a crowd of people already present.

There is a military aircraft parked on the runway apron to load the caskets. I count 13 caskets lined up perfectly, side by side. Each of the American caskets has an American flag draped over it. First, the military conducts a ceremony for the service members. Then they load the caskets into the awaiting aircraft, and the band performs some music. When they are finished honoring their fellow perished service members, they pack up and leave. It seems very awkward to me. It displays a separation of them and us. Yet we are all here together for the same reason and at the same time. I think a little more compassion could've been exhibited, but another part of me understands that after attending many of these, you just want to get it over with, move on, and grieve in your own way. Only a few people in uniform remain for the Barron service. I know one of them is the Army chaplain.

Barron conducts its own ceremony for our fallen. A number of Barron personnel have served in the military and seem to have the ceremonial protocol down perfectly. I'm impressed by the actions and detail that go into the service. There are eight pallbearers for each casket, plus a leader to direct the lift of the casket, the walk to the plane, and lowering of the casket. It's a production of 63 people. It's orchestrated harmoniously.

There's a prayer given at the loading area of the plane, but many of us are instructed to stay on the sidelines of the flight line. We aren't close enough to hear the sermon, but when it's finished, we're summoned to come to the plane to pay our last respects. We walk up the loading ramp and into the plane. It's extremely quiet. All I can hear is the wind blowing. The inside is massive and I feel like I'm standing on a football field. The floor is a stainless steel, perforated metal grating; the walls look like an imitation stainless steel and are probably fiberglass. Each of the caskets is locked into place and in a perfect line.

Nobody seems to know what to do next. Some people kneel in front of a casket, touching it with their hand, their eyes closed, and saying a silent prayer. Others stand quietly and observe. If there's ever a feeling or time of being lost, this seems to be the moment—a loss for words, a loss of ritual, a loss of solace. Some people hug each other side by side. Some rub the back of a coworker, as if reaching for a touch to confirm that this is not a dream.

After five or ten minutes of silence and hundreds packing into the plane to pay their last respects, a man breaks the silence by resonating the tenor sounds from his diaphragm and oxygen-packed lungs, and boasts the lyrics of "Amazing Grace."

> *"Amazing Grace, how sweet the sound*
> *That saved a wretch like me!*
> *I once was lost but now am found.*
> *Was blind but now I see."*

He sounds like an opera singer and has a beautiful voice that echoes and fills the plane. Most of the others join in and sing the song in its entirety. When the song gets to the line *"that saved a wretch like me!"* I think, *"A wretch! Really?"* All these people and the soldiers were here to serve in the name of democracy and freedom. They're not wretches! A wretch is some miserable, unfortunate, or unhappy person! They were somebody's children, brothers, and sisters! They were heroes! They were awesome! I hate that word in the song.

After the song ends, silence resumes. People start to slowly file out of the plane; we disperse. The bodies will soon be returned to their homelands.

Broken Ankle [written prior to the U.S. legalization of same-sex marriages]

Greg calls to inform me that he fell last night and can't walk on his foot this morning. He's waiting on a friend to come by the house to pick him up and take him to the hospital to have it examined and X-rayed.

Hours later, he's home in a foot cast with crutches. X-rays reveal a break in the ankle and they put a pin in the leg along with the cast.

The orthopedic surgeons highly recommend that he keep his foot elevated and stay off it for about six weeks for it to heal properly.

Greg can't drive. He can't walk to the mailbox. He can't put out the garbage cans. He can't walk the dogs. He can't go to the grocery store because he can't drive. He can't do anything. He's homebound. There is no food in the house. Basic chores turn into an ordeal and he really has nobody to help him. He won't ask for help either. His mom can't get there for several days.

I feel horrible. This is the love of my life . . . my world. There's not much I can do being on the other side of the globe. I really need to be there for him. I'm about two weeks away from heading home for R&R, but I want to be there now. I check with our human resources department to see what my options are. Married couples can take emergency leave and be home during a minor crisis such as this. In fact, a manager's wife recently broke her leg and he was home with her within 72 hours.

Because we're a same-sex couple and the state or federal governments do not legally recognize our relationship, or marriage, that policy does not apply equally to me. The way the policy is written is that it must be your spouse, parent, sibling, child, grandparent, or in-law to qualify for emergency leave. There is no personal leave for the project.

I try to challenge the policy to let me go in my favor, but the only compromise is to allow me to take my R&R early. Emergency leave does not count against our R&R time either, and the company will fly us to our point of origin. For me, the R&R is time counted away from work and the airfare comes out of my own pocket. What a great way to enjoy an R&R! I can't put Greg on my health and medical insurance like other married couples. He's self-employed and pays a very high premium for his health and medical insurance that increases every year he turns another year older.

It really upsets me that my relationship is treated differently from a man and woman's marriage. Equally frustrating to me is knowing half the guys over here are leading double lives with a girlfriend here and a spouse back home. They're great examples of embracing the sanctity of marriage. It's nothing but deception and bullshit. It's estimated that nearly 50 percent of all married individuals will engage in infidelity during their marriage. Half of marriages end in divorce, so that statistic sounds accurate, maybe underestimated. There are people who get married and divorced multiple times. Liz Taylor, Zsa Zsa Gabor, and Mickey Rooney were married eight times each. Britney Spears was married for 55 hours after a wild and crazy night in Vegas. Kelsey Grammer was married four times and has five children. Seriously, will gay marriage really affect straight marriage? What is the sanctity of marriage? I bear witness to many dysfunctional heterosexual marriages, and their families are living proof.

Greg and I have a great relationship, partnership, friendship, marriage—call it whatever you want. What matters to me in marriage is the love for one another, friendship, health, harmony, happiness, and quality of life. Greg and I have those things and many friends and family to share it with. In our eyes and to all of our friends and family, our relationship is a marriage. That's what matters the most.

I decide to wait to go home until my scheduled R&R. In the meantime, I contact family, friends, and neighbors through Facebook and email to let them know what's going on with Greg's situation. I tell them that he will not reach out for help and ask if they could stop in or call and check on him for the first week until his mom can get there. The response is amazing. Neighbors and friends drop by with all sorts of food, and Greg says he hasn't eaten that well in a long, long time. They also help to walk the dogs, take the trash out, collect the mail, and even take him to doctor appointments. We are so fortunate to be surrounded by cool neighbors and great friends and coworkers. It's heartwarming for me to know that he's being taken care of and to hear about the compassion from so many people. Of course, Greg also manages just fine on his own for the week he's by himself. He calls another friend of ours who installs media rooms and has him pick up and put in a 42-inch television for the bedroom. If nobody stops by with a delightful meal, he picks up his phone and calls to have food delivered.

As for my company's leave policy, it is what it is. Businesses, politics, cultures, and societies are in a constant state of evolution. Marriage has been since the Stone Age. I hope during my lifetime that I will be able to marry Greg (in my own country) and have it recognized by all people and all governments.

For now, I'll be heading home in a week to take care of him.

Sheikh Samir

I always look forward to the lead security guy, Kyle, giving us the security brief on the bus at the company hotel. He's always calm, cool, and collected, and he gives us the rundown of the latest terminations. He reminds me of Joe Friday from *Dragnet* reporting his detective work. No smile, just the facts. Most of the terminations are due to high alcohol consumption, disorderly conduct, and public intoxication that are against the law in Dubai.

Kyle boards the bus. I can pretty much recite his greeting and opening because I've heard it so many times. *"Welcome to Dubai, everyone. I hope you have a restful stay here at the hotel and enjoy the city. We've had a few incidents that I'd like to share with you, where people were sent home."* That's his segue to revealing the dirt on people, so ears perk up. We usually hear about the typical drunk and disorderly incidents, but it's how they get caught that makes the stories jaw-dropping: passed out in the lobby, pissing in a hotel planter, pissing in the elevator. Everyone knows there are security cameras everywhere. Why do they do this? Obviously they're beyond a state of conscious mind.

There are a few other incidents that are grounds for termination: arrested during a brawl over a prostitute, and a boyfriend physically assaulting his girlfriend in the hotel room. I'm surprised to find out that the Brits have a higher percentage of termination due to alcohol-related incidents than the Americans. As Rupert would say, *"Them bloody Brits love their bloody beers. Damn bloody drunks."*

The total number of people caught breaking the rules is less than 1 percent, and Kyle always sums up his brief with the question, *"Do I have any one percenters on the bus?"* Sometimes I want to jump up just for the fun of it and say, *"Hell yeah! Me, me, me! Let's go party!"* But we all sit quietly in our seats. After Kyle's spiel, we are released and go through a line for our assigned rooms.

There are usually three things I want when I check into the hotel: a long hot shower, a scrumptious meal, and an adult beverage. I usually order a few drinks from room service and drink them after my shower. Then I set out to one of my favorite restaurants.

Today I'm heading to a Moroccan restaurant that I really like. It's midafternoon, so the restaurant isn't busy. I'm glad about that because adjoining the restaurant is a shisha room, and when it's busy the smoke billows into the dining area. There are just two women at a table and a single man across the restaurant at another table. The host seats me next to the man.

He's an Arab man, dressed in a traditional white *thobe* that is freshly pressed and stiff with creased long sleeves. He's wearing a *keffiyeh* and *ogal*. I'm guessing he's from Saudi or Kuwait. Protruding from his *keffiyeh* is a well-manicured beard and mustache with a princely appearance. I greet him with, *"Saalem alaikum."* His amber honeysuckle eyes look up to meet my baby blues. He replies, *"Walaikum Saalem."* I go into my friendly Arabic greetings and stance. As we converse, I feel like I'm talking to a prince from some sort of fairy tale.

We're sitting side by side at our tables. I can't help but look out of the corner of my eyes to watch this magnificent man. As he lifts his cup of tea to his lips, I notice his long fingers and polished nails. There's something very hot about a well-dressed and manicured man. As I look over the menu, his food is delivered in a North African earthenware pot called a *tagine*. He lifts the lid and a billow of aromatic steam rises from the bowl. The smell is heavenly to my nostrils. I ask the stranger next to me what he ordered. He replies, *"This is the tagine lamb served with couscous."* He follows up with, *"Would you like to try it?"* Flattered by his gesture to a complete stranger, I smile, put my hand on my heart and say in Arabic, *"No shokron."* I tell him I will order the same dish myself.

Throughout our lunch we converse. My suspicions are right. He is from Saudi—or more specifically and appropriately, Riyadh, Kingdom of Saudi Arabia (KSA). His name is Samir. In my mind I call him "Sheikh Samir." He looks like royalty from the way he's dressed to his nails to his delightful mannerisms. We talk about the delicious food, the marvel of Dubai, and our various travels around the globe. When he asks me what I'm doing in Dubai, I just tell him I'm a contractor. I'm sure he knows what that means and I try to divert the conversation to something we have more in common.

Samir orders a small plate of various bite-sized Arab desserts: dates stuffed with almonds and feta, a dumpling-like pastry filled with cheese, butter biscuit cookies that melt in your mouth as soon as you eat one, baklava, and others made with honey and pistachio in different shapes and layers of crispy phyllo. We share the desserts and a pot of Moroccan mint tea. He rattles off the names of the desserts in Arabic, but the only one I know and remember is the baklava because of its popularity and the many times I've had it.

After our delicious lunch, dessert, and tea, Samir asks me if I would like to join him for a shisha. I normally don't smoke, but I'm enjoying his company and hospitality, so I accept his offer. I'm thinking we're going to go to the shisha room next door, but he says, *"My car is parked downstairs. We can have a shisha at my house."* At first I'm hesitant, but at the same time I'm excited at the thought of going with Samir to his house. I also think he's offering it out of politeness and comradery, and as a cross-cultural experience. He's not the first invitation I've had to go to an Arab home for dinner, tea, or shisha. It's the Arab way of showing their kindness and hospitality to travelers. Knowing a few lines of Arabic or being able to converse a bit also breaks barriers to a cordial welcome.

We go downstairs and Samir hands a ticket to the valet attendant, who walks to the other side of the circle drive to get the car amidst a couple of Lamborghinis, a Bentley, a few Mercedes, and some BMWs. A minute later, the valet pulls up in a shiny battleship-gray car. I don't know my cars, but at first it looks like an older, sporty Jaguar with the longer coupe body. But it's much too new to be of that body or style. It's not a Mercedes or a BMW. I know the looks of those vehicles. I don't recognize the emblem on the car either. It has a very sporty grill in the front with a style of luxury. I look at Samir with a smile and a raised eyebrow. He smiles back at me and winks. As I go to the passenger door, I see the make of the car by the front wheel. It's a Maserati. *"Holy Crap!"* I think. *"I've never ridden in a Maserati."*

The interior of the car is sleek with red and gray leather. It's incredibly sharp and I feel like a million bucks. I'm thinking Samir is going to show me how powerful a ride this car is, but with Dubai traffic, we take our time as we journey 30 or 40 minutes across town to his townhouse.

We walk into his home and my eyes are automatically drawn to a large crystal chandelier hanging from the ceiling. There's a big Persian rug with imprints of blue, gold, and white below that stands out on the wood floors. A white leather sofa rests in front of a wall of glass overlooking the water, and a clear glass coffee table with two traditional Arabian blue chairs accents the space. His house is immaculate and beautifully designed.

I think Samir has other ideas on his mind and it's not shisha. He tells me that he's going to take off his *thobe* and slip into something more comfortable. He offers me the option to get out of my jeans and to join him in more comfortable attire. I follow him to his bedroom, where he hands me some navy-blue shorts. I hope they fit me since he's leaner than me. I watch him as he carefully removes his *keffiyeh* and *ogal,* which exposes his jet-black curly short hair. He then unrobes his *thobe* and carefully places it on a hanger in his closet. As he disrobes, I look to see what's underneath. He's wearing a *sarwal* or *pyjama*—a white fabric wrapped around the waist to hide and support the male genitalia. Samir has a moderately hairy body, nicely toned with a rippled stomach. He catches me looking at him and says, *"Please take off your clothes."*

I do as I'm instructed and as I lower my jeans without wearing underwear, I flaunt my jewels at him. He removes his *sarwal* and does the same back at me. He walks over to me entirely naked and puts his arms around me. He plants a soft, gentle kiss on my lips. Then another and another.

After a long session of exploring our bodies and making love, we lie on the bed, side by side, holding hands, talking in low tones with an occasional snatch of a kiss. Samir is a married man. He's in his mid-thirties and he has one son. He tells me that if he was back home and someone found out about his homosexuality, he could be killed. Hearing him tell me this breaks my heart. I ask him, *"Why do you do it then?"* He replies, *"Women are for having babies. Men are for fun."* He's not the first Arab man to tell me that. He confides in me to share his true feelings toward men and how much he wishes he could be with a man rather than a woman.

We talk, cuddle, and rest until the sun goes down. Samir hands me a glass of water, but I never do get the shisha. Samir confesses that he doesn't even smoke. He really doesn't care for it but just thought it would be a good way to invite me to come over. Sly dog. I guess situations of single men traveling alone are targets of sexual prey. I would not have suspected that with Samir, but his feelings and intuition toward me must've set something off in him to pursue me.

It was a lovely afternoon to spend with this sweet, gentle, masculine man. I leave to head back to my hotel and then the States to take care of my number one . . . but it won't be the last time I see Samir.

EOD Memorial Run

For the past two years I've participated in the Explosive Ordnance Disposal (EOD) Memorial 5K. It is a great way to pay tribute not only to those who currently serve on the EOD team but also to those who lost their lives in the line of duty at an enormous cost to themselves and their loved ones.

Before the run starts, the EOD team sets up a couple of demonstrations. A popular one among attendees is the bomb suit. I try it on for size. It weighs about 65 pounds but looks and feels heavier than that. The bomb suit is designed to withstand the pressure released from a bomb and any projectiles. EOD technicians provide demonstrations of miniature army-tank robotics equipped with high-tech cameras and delicate instruments to deactivate or detonate a bomb from a distance.

While I wait for the race to start, I see a few EOD team members suiting up in bomb suits that they're going to wear during the run. This is a tradition among them and they try to beat previous record holders. I guess the reward is bragging rights for doing it.

In the same center where the robotic and bomb-suit demonstrations are taking place, a wall is lined with easels propped with a large framed picture of each EOD member who lost his or her life in the past year. I walk down the line of easels and stop and look into the eyes of every soldier pictured, each of them posing with a smile in a crisp, new uniform. I note that many of the deceased soldiers are under the age of 25, a couple in their thirties, maybe one in his forties. Some are shown with their K-9 partners who also lost their lives in the line of duty. One day they're here; the next they're not.

Tables in the center are set for a banquet ceremony later in the day. Biographies of each soldier lie on the tables. I walk through the rows of tables and read many of the biographies. Some of them give a very good sense of the lives each of these individuals lived—military, school, new family. Some left behind young children. One of the soldiers was a new dad and passed before meeting or holding his newborn.

A lieutenant colonel, clergy, and a few others take center stage to welcome the people. They give a presentation to recognize those we're remembering. The center is completely silent as the names of each soldier are read. I can feel the grief and mourning sweep through the crowd. After the names are read, music video clips of each of the young lives are presented—a collection of photos of their lives at home and as soldiers and parents, some with their K-9 partners, who added to their everyday companionship and joy.

The presentations are done very tastefully. I imagine all the people coming together to collect photos, stories, and memories of their comrades. By the end of the presentation, I feel like I'm part of each of their short lives. I sense a very emotional moment, as the crowd remains quiet and joyless. The clergy says a prayer and the crowd heads to the starting line.

During my run, the music video clips continue to play in my head. The pictures and time spent studying each soldier's set of eyes passes through my brain. I imagine how different their lives were compared to mine, but also how we are bridged together as Americans and serving overseas in Afghanistan in different capacities. My 5K run is a tribute to the soldiers and a celebration of their lives.

The sun has barely risen and I have another run under my belt. I head to the shower and then the office. In the office I get wind that a runner was found dead in a ditch on FOB Kandahar. It's being investigated as a hit and run. Nobody stopped to render help. It's believed a passing military vehicle hit him and the driver probably never knew he hit the guy.

Closed Borders

A NATO airstrike kills 24 Pakistani soldiers on November 26, 2011. It's the second time in about a year that an attack like this has occurred. Supposedly the attack was unprovoked, at least according to the Pakistani government. Stories differ.

Our ally, Pakistan, immediately and permanently closes its borders to NATO convoy troops taking fuel and supplies to forces in Afghanistan. Almost half of the NATO-led force supplies come through Pakistan. Both sides blame each other and this will have deep diplomatic consequences.

I'm not sure what to think of Pakistan. I don't believe any country that runs its politics under any religious law should be supported by the U.S. It's against our own constitutional beliefs of separation of church and state—not to mention the dichotomy of religious belief systems in this world. Of course, there are plenty of right-winged Christian fundamentalists in the U.S. who would love to make the U.S. a Christian nation. If that ever becomes the case, which I doubt it ever will, then I guarantee we will see more wars.

Pakistan is a member of the United Nations, the Commonwealth of Nations, the Next Eleven Economies, South Asian Association for Regional Cooperation (SAARC), Economic Cooperation Organization (ECO), the Developing Eight or D-8, and the Group of Twenty (G20) developing nations that account for 60 percent of the world's population, 70 percent of its farmers, and 26 percent of the world's agriculture exports. It all sounds wonderful and Pakistan is moving forward. If Pakistan is part of all these great global organizations and partnerships, why does the U.S. afford them billions of dollars in aid? They sound self-sufficient. I wonder if any of the other countries that are members of some of those organizations give any financial support to Pakistan. I have my doubts.

The U.S. pays Pakistan billions of dollars intended to support counterterrorism efforts. Yet there's no proof the Pakistani government uses these funds for their intended use. Pakistan is the largest recipient of Coalition Support Funds as part of a counterterrorism effort by the Bush administration launched in 2001. Pakistan has received more than $5.5 billion of the nearly $7 billion distributed to 27 countries over six years from 2001 to 2007. Let's face it, Pakistan has their own share of Islamic fundamentalists, they have an open back door with Iran, and they harbored Osama bin Laden. Someone in Pakistan had to know bin Laden was there.

The more I learn about U.S. Coalition Support Funds to Pakistan, the more I'm troubled by this in terms of waste, fraud, and abuse of a huge amount of U.S. taxpayer funds and their failure to achieve vital U.S. security objectives. Now they shut down the borders to stop the flow of supplies to NATO troops? Some ally!

It's time the U.S. quits breastfeeding these questionable countries and starts weaning them off our aid. We expect the same thing from American citizens: to be taxpayers instead of tax users. So why not make the same expectation for these developing countries?

We need to hold them accountable and make sure they set out to do what they agreed to. Otherwise, it's nothing but a U.S. taxpayer's welfare check to a corrupt recipient.

Thanksgiving in Northern Afghanistan

This Thanksgiving, the 57 DFACs combined in Northern Afghanistan served more than 48,000 pounds of whole turkey, 13,000 pounds of ham, 172,000 servings of stuffing, and more than 130,000 servings of pie and cake for dessert! That's a lot of food and a lot of people served. One of the great sights and memories I will cherish from my Thanksgiving holidays here is the number of "brass" serving the men and women in uniform, as well the civilians here providing services. I'm thankful for all who have and are currently serving in our armed forces. Thank you.

Morning Joe

I'm always one of the first folks to arrive at work. Sometimes I grab a cup of coffee and sip on it outside the main entrance and watch the people muddle throughout The Village going about their morning business. I enjoy the morning skies and temperate climate. The mornings and evenings are gorgeous about nine months of the year, with moderate temperatures in the sixties and seventies and low humidity. Perfect. I walk to work toward the sun as it rises above the eastern horizon and pampers me with its warm rays of light shining on my face—and the same when I leave work and the sun is setting in the west and shining on my face.

The afternoons can heat up, but not as hot as the West Texas desert. Most afternoons reach the upper eighties or low nineties. In the summer, the hot afternoon temps may peak a little over 100 degrees. When I hear people complaining about the heat, I say, *"It's not as hot as Texas."* The Texans often comment how wonderful the temperatures are here.

Afghanistan does not exercise daylight savings time. The sun sets around 7:30 p.m. The sunrises and sunsets are beautiful. As the sun sinks behind the western ridge, the sky and clouds light up in an array of pastel colors—peach, pink, lavender—against the luminous white clouds and deep-blue sky. The temperatures can drop quite a bit this time of day. I laugh at some of the foreign nationals from hotter climates as they bundle up in sweatshirts and jackets. They feel chilled while so many more of us purely enjoy the moderate evening air.

Winters can be harsh and bitter cold. Temperatures will go below freezing when the sun sets and the frigid air rolls down the snow-covered mountains and into the valley. The temperatures are just as cold at dawn and for the first few hours of daylight. Midday will warm up some, enough to melt any snow or ice on the ground, but it freezes again during the night and the base becomes one big ice rink. After our first snowfall of the season, we had five or six people fall and break bones. They had to be treated here and repatriated for recovery.

John Paul shows up at my door one night just before midnight. He says, *"I can't stop shivering."* His lips are practically blue. I'm sure he's showing signs of hypothermia. I tell him to remove his clothes and jump into my bed under my blankets. He takes everything off except for the lacy red underwear that he's wearing. He likes to wear his wife's panties because it makes him feel closer to her. I cuddle up next to him naked on my twin bed to help bring up his body temperature.

John Paul is a British Special Forces officer and just got off a helo flying from his remote base to Bagram. I see him about every eight weeks during his rotation when he comes through Bagram. His barracks for the night is in the neighboring village. He looks like he lost weight since the last time I saw him.

As I hold his beautiful, tight body close to mine, he tells me in his quivering voice, *"We had to fly with the hatch open. That helicopter ride was so fucking cold. That ride was supposed to be 35 minutes and felt like hours."* I whisper to him, *"You're safe now. I'll warm you up."* I pull him closer to me and hold him snug. My body is like a furnace and I can feel his body warming up from my radiating heat as he falls asleep in my arms.

Christmas 2011

I've traveled to a couple dozen countries across five continents over the past few years. Everywhere I've been, there's an overwhelming Indian population. There were swarms of Indians standing outside the airport doors of Dubai and Beirut. They're a major labor force in the service industry. Many of them are grateful for the job opportunity, well educated, courteous, and polite, and are always smiling and willing to help you. It's Christmastime and I keep thinking of Johnny Mathis's song. Because I see so many Indians working on base, I switched the word *Christmas* to *India*: "*It's beginning to look a lot like India . . . everywhere I go.*"

Bagram is no exception. We use some subcontract labor companies based in India. Now my company is hiring Indian labor directly. Of any labor group, they appear to be one of the more loyal workforces. They do just about any job without question, they work hard, and they do their work with pride. Most of the Indian workers I know work in IT. That doesn't surprise me. Many of them are here to improve the quality of their lives as well as support multiple people within their family. They're also here because back home there's high unemployment and low wages. They work 12 hours a day, 7 days a week, and get one 30-day R&R per year, compared to the expat 21-day R&R every 10 weeks.

Nearly every contractor starts their assignment in Bagram by living with sometimes hundreds of individuals in a transient tent. After a few months, one continues to upgrade into smaller tents and eventually into a room in a plywood B-hut. The ultimate goal is to get into a container with solid walls, your own HVAC unit, your own thermostat, and your own door entry. The average time in country to get into one of those units is five or six years. It seems like a lot of the subcontracted labor force never gets out of tents.

12 Days of Christmas

Bee has a beautiful voice and loves to sing. She's been singing for a few special events and regularly at church on base. She has this fabulous idea of spreading Christmas cheer by creating a flash mob to sing "The Twelve Days of Christmas" at the DFAC. She asks me to be part of the singing flash mob. I think, *"Seriously? Have you heard me sing? I do not sing!"* Since she's participated in a number of running events with my running group, she springs quid pro quo on me.

She explains her plan to me: *"We'll create a group of singers and all meet for lunch. We'll spread ourselves throughout the DFAC and for each line in 'The Twelve Days of Christmas,' the singer or small group of singers will jump up and sing their part. Of course, the verses are sung 12 times, so whoever gets the first verse . . ."* as she wistfully sings, *"and a partridge in a pear tree' gets to sing that 12 times; 'two turtle doves' 11 times; 'three French hens' 10 times; and so on. Whoever gets 'twelve drummers drumming' only has to sing one line."* When she mentions that, I spark up and say, *"That's the one I want!"* She shoots back, *"That one's already taken."* Damn it! She continues on, *"And you don't have to be a perfect singer. Most of the verses are just one line and you can chant, yodel, or vocalize your line. You can do it alone or with a group."* The keyword is *group*, I think.

Okay, so I'm suckered into singing. Since Bee is such a sweet and nice person, I tell her that I'll help her recruit singers for her event. I know quite a few people, and plenty of them love to be heard and love attention. My sly recruitment strategy is to find some singers who are worse than me to make me sound better. I don't know if that's possible, but I'm sure there are plenty of folks who can and can't carry a tune or sing harmony. Perhaps if we sing in small groups like Bee suggested, we won't sound so bad. Or maybe I can get a small group together and I'll lip-sync my verse. Ha! I'm not sure about the singing part and how I'm going to convince people, but right now I'm going to focus on getting as many people as I can.

I think I must've been the third or fourth person Bee asked to do this. The first had to be Mark, because he got the twelfth verse, that bastard! Bee's two other friends—and extroverts—Keisha and Tara took two verses to sing themselves. Tara opted for *"a partridge in a pear tree"* so she could sing it 12 times. Keisha also took a verse for herself.

I send email messages and make my rounds to offices recruiting folks. I get my two coworkers from Kosovo, Jeton and Agim, to take a verse and my friend Mohit from India to take another. Stella says she'll sing with me. She has a high-pitched voice, so I won't be able to lip-sync. And if I did, she would kill me.

By the end of the next day, I have 25 singers ready and willing to spread Christmas cheer. We have a quick meeting with all the singers, and Bee explains how we are going to meet and pull this off. We follow up with a quick little rehearsal.

The day of the flash mob, we all meet at the DFAC at our prearranged lunchtime of 1:00 p.m. Bee goes around greeting all the singers and taking note of where everyone is sitting in the DFAC and which verses they have. By the time Stella shows up, she's recruited two more singers to help us with our part, Adam and Paula. Both are soft-spoken and I'm still thinking, *"Boy, we are going to need some help because these three can't belt out any lyrics. Their voices will never carry through the DFAC."*

In a full dining room with a few hundred folks eating lunch, Bee and Keisha start banging on the table to get everyone's attention and asking everyone for silence. Bee hurdles to the middle of the room, wearing her festive bright-red Christmas sweater, and bursts into the first line of the song, *"On the first day of Christmas, my true love gave to me . . ."* Then, across the room, the lovely and talented Tara stands up and finishes the line with her cheery melody, *"A partridge in a pear tree!"* Verses two, three, and four move along smoothly. Then we get to verse five, and Kenny stands up solo and belts out in a dramatic libretto like an opera singer, *"Fiiiiive goooooldeeeeeen rings!"* Everyone in the room can feel the power of his voice starting from the diaphragm. The crowd starts whistling, clapping, and cheering at his performance. After Kenny is Keisha. She has a tough act to follow and decides to do a modern hip-hop acapella on her verse: *"Six . . . geese . . . a' . . . layin'!"*

Verse seven comes and goes, and then it's Mohit's turn. Mohit is a former model from India. He loves the attention and stands alone, wearing a bright-red long-sleeved T-shirt. He's been waiting for this moment. He's been practicing his line for days because he has a heavy Indian accent. I can see the glow on his face as he yells out, *"Eight maid milking!"* The crowd laughs, charmed by his accented version. *"Nine ladies dancing"* is my verse with Stella, Adam, and Paula. We knew we wouldn't be getting any standing ovation or whistles and cheers, but we did it and it wasn't too bad.

Following us are Jet and Agim from Kosovo. Of course, those two are at a table full of Albanians. I'm hoping all of them will jump up and sing the verse, but just Jet and Agim rise from the table and sing in their Balkan, deep-voice ensemble. The two of them roar out their verse like they are a couple of lords, with Agim harmonizing his arms like a music conductor: *"Ten lords a-leaping!"* I'm so impressed with their masculine accord. I'm also impressed with and proud of Jet, Agim, and Mohit because they're not Christians, they don't celebrate Christmas, they're not American, and English is not their native language. They're fantastic!

Moving along to verse 11, and then finally 12 is Motormouth Mark. He managed to recruit another guy named Adam. Adam has a voice like a DJ—very manly and animated. I think he could do professional voice-overs. Mark and Adam sound great together and end the song with, *"Twelve drummers drumming!"* We've pulled it off.

During our performance, most people stayed seated; some got up from other parts of the DFAC to get closer to hear and watch us sing.

The turnout was great and so was the audience's response. I'm glad we could add a little cheer to the season, especially for all of us away from home who miss being with our families. It was also a great team-building experience for all of us who work together across many different departments. In the end, the word gets back to our managers and we're asked to do it again in the other DFACs around base.

We're going on tour. Live from the DFAC!

12 K's of Christmas

"If it's not broke, you can run!" commands the lieutenant colonel after hearing one of the runners complain about legs cramping. He looks at me to see if I heard him. I just smile and nod my head from side to side when I hear the Marine lieutenant colonel talk so tough. He walks the talk. The temps are below freezing and he shows up in his Marine-green shorts and a sweatshirt for our bitter-cold Christmas run. Once a Marine, always a Marine. I bet when he gets to the shower the water feels like stinging needles all over his body. Of course, the lieutenant colonel may like that.

For Christmas, our department received some cases of hand and foot warmers from people back at the home office. They probably heard we were freezing over here. I bring a box of the warmers to the Christmas Day run for our group. It's so damn cold outside that the turnout is small: me, Dr. K and his colleague Dr. Jose, Trigger, Tom, Ed, and the lieutenant colonel. I grab the microphone, hold up the box of warmers, and announce that if anyone wants a mini heat pack or two to drop into their gloves or socks, they are welcome to help themselves. They go like hotcakes. I feel bad that I didn't bring more of them.

A few of us wear balaclavas over our faces to keep warm, but it restricts my breathing and I strip it off shortly after we start the run. The air is so cold that when I start, I take short, frequent breaths. If I breathe too deeply, my lungs feel like they're going to crack. Even though I have the heat packs in my gloves, my fingertips freeze and are numb by the time I finish the 5K. A few guys look like yetis with icicles hanging from their beards by the time they cross the finish line. Nobody hangs out at the end today. Everyone leaves quickly to go seek warmth.

News hits the base that an Afghan family died of carbon monoxide poisoning. Some of the local households burn their trash or anything they can find to keep their houses warm. Forty more Afghans died from freezing overnight in the Kabul-area refugee camps. There's a winter vortex over Bagram. Hell has frozen over.

The news of the deaths sparks the need for a blanket drive. Our Afghan First program takes on the initiative. One of the first to respond to the blanket drive is the Polish Army on base, and they donate almost 9,000 blankets that they have stored in containers and will be distributed among the local community and refugee camps. Humanitarianism at its best.

Our turnover rate plateaued for a while around 22 percent but has recently jumped up to 27 percent. It's tough to be in this environment and people are missing their families. The work here is a job, not a career. There are all sorts of reasons for people leaving the project, but after doing this work for a couple years, most folks are ready to leave, be with their families, and have a normal life again. Especially around the holidays.

Good Old Bird

The novelty of being in Afghanistan must be wearing off for my family and friends back home. It's my third Christmas in Afghanistan and I receive just a few Christmas cards and letters. I can always count on the annual box of homemade rum balls sprinkled with a little extra tonic from my former coworker Arian. Those are always a hit in the office. It seems odd that I haven't heard from my Peace Corps journalist friend,

Marg. She always sends me her Christmas newsletter with highlights of her year accompanied by a newspaper clip of some sort.

I contact a few former Peace Corps volunteers from my group to see if any of them has heard from Marg, but no one has. I last saw her a few years ago in San Diego. She was living with her son for a while. I know she moved back to Vancouver, Washington. She wrote me a letter stating she got a fabulous apartment in a medium-rise building in downtown and took on the job of groundskeeper around her complex. That's also the time our correspondence picked up.

Fearing the worst, I decide to Google Marg's name. The first website link to pop up is a link to her obituary. My heart sinks. I'm not shocked. I know Marg was up there in age, but she was always so active, mentally and physically. I guess I thought that she would be around a lot longer. I open the link to her obituary and read it. She died a tragic death earlier in the year while crossing the street. She was in the crosswalk, with the right of way, when a city bus hit her. She was hit and dragged by the bus and died instantly. The bus driver said the sun was glaring in his eyes and he couldn't see her. My eyes well up with tears. I feel horrible having to read the news. I'm going to miss her.

I email another close friend of ours, JoAnn, to pass along the news. The three of us were in the same Arabic language class during our Peace Corps stint. She and Marg were martini buddies during our stateside training and classmates in Tunisia. They were both close to the same age. During one of our Arabic classes, I nicknamed JoAnn "Azuza." It means "old lady" in Arabic.

Azuza replies to me and says, *"She was a good old bird."*

Game Over, Man!

As the year winds down, more folks have left the project. The young former Army captain, Brian, is leaving as skinny as he came. I've seen the boy eat—and he can eat—but he doesn't put on any weight. He was offered a job back in the Greenville home office and is going home to get married.

My running buddy Alex, who was trying to beat me in the number of running-event T-shirts, was just offered a position on a Barron stateside project. That's the nice thing about working for a corporation that maintains a network of offices in more than 25 countries spanning across six continents. Since I'm here longer, it looks like I'll win the T-shirt contest!

Erin, who coined our running team "Baserunners," decided to leave to pursue her passion of scuba diving. She left for the Philippines to obtain her master's and instructor-level certifications. After she left the Philippines, she took a job in Thailand with a scuba diving company and is now in Australia. It's always sad when people leave the project, but it's also great to hear what's next in store for them in the journey of their lives.

Sam, who gave Cookie her nickname, also left. He took a job with another company and will have offices in Dubai and Istanbul.

Sissy, Will, Grumpy, and Huggy McPherson all left. Tina moved to a different department. So many people come and go, I can't keep track. But still going strong is Team Texas! I have met so many wonderful, adventurous people—with more to come!

2012

Bagram Prison

The base is becoming more and more like a prison and I'm singing "Folsom Prison Blues" by Johnny Cash with my own twist: "*I hear the MRAP comin'. It's rollin' 'round the bend. And I ain't seen the sunshine since I don't know when. I'm stuck in Bagram Prison, and time keeps draggin' on, but that MRAP keeps a-rollin', on down to Kandahar.*"

The entire chain-link fence has been replaced by 10-foot-high concrete T-walls, creating a border completely around the perimeter of the base. The walls are topped with razor wire to prevent outsiders from scaling them. Nobody can see in or out. Of course, I don't think any civilian would want to go outside the wire. I'm sure we'd be rounded up by the Taliban, be tortured, have our throats slit, be dragged behind a pickup truck, get shot at point-blank range, or a combination of any of those draconian methods. The Taliban has done these things to their own people. The locals who work on base are often a target. If not tortured and killed, many are robbed of their measly earnings. Word on the street is that eight locals didn't make it to work. They were later found dead in a ditch, tortured and shot execution-style.

The Pakistan border closure, from November 2011 and this year's harsh weather, has had an impact on receiving shipments. The PX shelves are bare. The military gets priority the first two hours of business every morning, and the few goods that are received are wiped clean immediately. It leaves nothing for the contractors. There's no snacks, no canned soups, no peanut butter, no popcorn, no creamer for coffee, no chocolate, no jerky, and no gum. The shelves are literally empty. I can't remember the last time I saw basic bathroom necessities on the shelf. Fortunately I keep bars of soap in my shoes that I can use as backups if necessary.

Employees on base will email or call the employees returning from R&R to pick up any necessities in Dubai before returning to Bagram. Some are given a shopping list by others. I just like to make sure I have my shower necessities and coffee. Surprisingly the PX always seems to have an endless supply of cigarettes and smokeless tobacco. Tobacco products are probably flown in by plane instead of by convoy. I can't imagine some of these folks without their nicotine. Yikes! Of course, it'd probably do this place well and improve health if military bases were tobacco-free.

It's a cold, cold winter unlike the past two I've experienced in Afghanistan. The past two were wet and moderately cold, yet warm during the day. This winter feels like the thermometer doesn't go above freezing even during the afternoon. The air is horribly dry and creates a lot of static electricity in my clothes and my bedding. My skin itches when my clothes rub against it, which is all the time.

There seem to be endless days of moody skies that look incredibly fierce, with shades of gray and dark blue against the bright-white snowy mountains. Many of the outer FOBs are experiencing delayed or canceled flights due to heavy snowfall or poor visibility. Some have not been able to make movement for days and people are stuck there. That would really suck to be scheduled for an R&R or expecting food supplies. Employees are warned of this and told to be flexible. We're told to buy refundable airline tickets, but most folks will roll the dice and take their chances. Then they'll get upset when they find out they're screwed.

To survive in this prison, you need to join a gang. I belong to two: my workgroup and my running group. Both are gangs of fantastic people. My coworkers have become my family. We spend an awful lot of time together: work, eat, and play. We've gotten to know each other quite well, and we live and laugh a lot.

Sadly the running group has dwindled down quite a bit with this cold winter. The runs keep only the die-hards going. We're down to about five of us who show up regularly. We're all collecting our gang colors of T-shirts from our completed runs. The rest of the Baserunners are waiting for spring and warmer temperatures.

Regardless of the temperatures, running in the cold helps me shake the winter blues, boosts my energy level, shows my support to our military as I run alongside them, and keeps me in shape. Life isn't so bad in this hellhole. I guess it is like a prison: All we do is work, work out, eat, sleep, and repeat all within the parameters of a mile or so. It's monotonous and the days can seem long when it's gloomy.

The Basics of the Big House: Food, the Yard, the Gang, and My Cell

FOOD: Breakfast is my favorite meal, especially during these cold days. I always feel better with something warm in my stomach: an egg-white omelet made before my eyes and hot off the grill. After a morning run and a nice warm breakfast, I'm ready to start my day.

When I go to breakfast, I usually go with Stella and some of her coworkers from HR. Considering Stella has only been here maybe six months or so, she's well known everywhere she goes. When we walk into the DFAC, she spreads her wings and flutters around the place like a butterfly, saying hi to all the workers and giving a few of them hugs. Her big smile and squeaky voice just light up everybody's day.

The other mealtimes and food in the chow hall are not as festive as they are in the morning with Stella. After having a made-to-order omelet for breakfast, lunch and dinner look bleak. It's not uncommon to see four different kinds of rice dishes or a pasta bar for the main courses in the chow hall. The leftover vegetables become vegetable soup. The roast beef for lunch is beef stroganoff for dinner. Sometimes they don't even hide it. It really doesn't matter because so much of the food is tasteless, maybe old or freezer burned. It's prison food. I am thankful for fresh fruit and salad when we get it.

THE YARD: *"Josef! Look at all the frozen loogies on the sidewalk,"* Stella points out during our lovely stroll down Disney Drive to the DFAC. It's gross and our walk ends up in a game of hopscotch trying to dodge the nasty frozen slugs on the sidewalk. I'm not sure where this breed of folks comes from, but there are a lot people who spit in this prison yard. They spit their saliva and their chewing tobacco. It's everywhere. It may be days, weeks, or months before they are thawed and washed away by the rain. They'll probably end up on the bottom of someone's shoes or boots and end up dragged into the office and B-hut rooms. I can see why spitting is against the law in Singapore.

THE GANG: *"Trigger, are you leaving us?"* asks Juliet Alpha. Trigger replies, *"No, why do you ask?"*

Juliet Alpha obviously knows something we don't. She points out that a training manager is on the flight manifest scheduled to come to Bagram. Something's up and, as usual, the company is calling the shots from headquarters and leaving us in the dark.

Within weeks, Trigger is moved into a new role and position as industrial relations manager for the corporate office. Taking his place is Dipper. He has an identical twin brother, so I call them "Dipper One" and "Dipper Two," or just "One" and "Two." One is my new boss; Two works in and runs project controls in the B-hut near us. I'm dismayed by this move because if Trigger had any intention of leaving, I was hoping to fill his spot. He's groomed me well for the position and his are some pretty tough shoes to fill.

I call the new boss "Dipper" because he always has a clump of dip packed in his cheek or behind his lip. Of course, with the dip comes the spit bottle. He carries it with him everywhere he goes. During conversations, he talks in a gargled tone thanks to the dip in his mouth. He hangs on to the spit bottle in his hand as though it's part of his body. He also leaves the nasty dip-filled bottles—clear water bottles—on his desk or lying around the office. Sometimes I'll see one in or on top of the microwave or in a bathroom stall. What a nasty habit.

I hope to garner some support from upper management about creating a policy against not just smoking in the office but against all tobacco products. They have it in the military and at the corporate office, so why not here? I go up the chain of command. The HR manager says he doesn't feel it's an issue in the office but feels it's more in line with poor manners or hygiene, like having body odor or bad breath, or snapping gum. Seriously? And we allow that? He says he'll speak to the country manager, Mr. Burns, about it if I want him to. Of course I do.

I present my complaint from the viewpoint that it shows a lack of dignity and respect to the staff. In addition, it's extremely unprofessional. We have policies against facial piercings, tattoos, T-shirts, and other unprofessional appearances. What's professional about a wad of cud in your mouth? Plus it smells like Dipper's sucking on a dried piece of cow shit, man.

I take my complaint to the next level, Mr. Burns, but to no avail. As "managers support managers" in this business, our country manager gives it back to our HR manager to take care of and supports his decision on the basis of a "manners" issue. Fucking feeble Mr. Burns has no balls. I could and probably should go farther up the ladder with it to the corporate level, but I feel if it can't get resolved at the country manager's level, it's probably a lost cause. Plus I've heard that Dipper One will not be in the position for long. Upper management has their eye on him for a site management position, with his military background.

I tell a friend that I have a new boss and talk about his identical twin brother. He recognizes the last name but isn't positive who he is. To verify we are talking about the same person, he asks, *"Do you mean the guy who chews tobacco and usually has flecks of it on his teeth?"* Bingo! I'd hate to be remembered for that.

Dipper One quickly acclimates into his job, but less than 12 weeks into his position, a site management position becomes available and our director of operations shuffles site managers around and assigns Dipper One to a regional hub of FOBs. After One moves to his new site, I take over the lead of the training and development department.

Motormouth Mark is always the first into the office. Juliet Alpha usually sleeps from 2:00 to 5:00 a.m. and then goes to breakfast right when the DFAC opens their doors. I'm sure she has a reason to be the first one at their door. She probably goes through the DFAC to do an inspection.

When I get to the office, Mark is usually talking on the phone to his mom and girlfriends back home. Yes, girlfriends. Plural. Mark is a charmer and womanizer. He also has a couple girlfriends here on base. I'm sure one day that'll get him into trouble. I wouldn't be surprised if he gets caught in a woman's B-hut.

Mark is from Texas and speaks the state lingo. I'm a transplant of Texas, like most people who live in Austin, and I've never picked up the lingo. In fact, speaking Texan is slaughtering the English language, and it has its own form of Ebonics. However, a Texan would be the first to tell you that everyone else speaks funny and that Ebonics is just awful and *"bless her little heart for speaking that way."*

Mark will ask someone, *"How's ya mom 'n them?"* And when Juliet Alpha gets on a tizzy with Mark and starts slinging orders, he'll say something like, *"I'm fixin' to do that right quick. I'll go down yonder while y'all just stay here."* Most Texans drop the G with verbs that end in "-ing." Texans are talkin' or singin'. They're dancin' and walkin'.

Juliet Alpha and Motormouth sound like an old married couple in the office. They're constantly bickering back and forth, jabbing one another comically. Juliet Alpha always makes sure Mark has plenty to do and will walk on his coattails to make sure he follows through with the orders she's given him. She's a go-getter, and when she wants something done or she's ready to move on, you'd better be ready to jump. Chop, chop! Juliet Alpha has many names and one of them in our building is "Command Sergeant." We can hear her in the hallway slinging orders all the time. She fits the part. She's also referred to as the "Pit Bull" and "Chihuahua." I gave her the name Chihuahua because of her tiny stature and big yap.

Mark is generally a gentleman, but he'll let Juliet Alpha know she's out of line. One of Mark's favorite lines that I've heard him say repeatedly is, *"Juliet Alpha, we're goin' on R&R together to Aruba and I'm buyin' you a one-way ticket!"* He always follows up with something like, *"Yeah, we're goin' scuba diving on our first day in Aruba and I'll have the room booked for single occupancy after that."* I have to send the two of them out to some remote sites for assignment. They are assigned to go in opposite directions during one. I make the comment that maybe they should meet up at a base hub and fly back to Bagram together. Mark, who is always quick with his witty responses, says, *"Yeah, maybe we'll be on a helo together, and they always fly with the door open. I'll hand Juliet Alpha my camera to take some pictures from the door and keep tellin' her to get closer and closer to the door until . . . oops, she fell out."* I can just feel the love between them.

Their conversations become a game to see who can outdo the other to be more evil, conniving, and entertaining. Their act is a very entertaining piece in the office. Though they have their differences, Mark is still a Texas gentleman. He'll greet Juliet Alpha at the luggage truck to help her carry her things back to her room after R&R. He'll help her carry boxes of mail or make sure the office is always neat, orderly, and well stocked. Mark has OCD. Of course, Juliet Alpha and I like that. I think the two of us have some level of OCD too. Mark always has a wall of bottled water stocked for us that's always perfectly balanced and placed. Our little refrigerator is well stocked with additional waters, juices, sodas, milks, yogurts, and more. They're all neatly arranged with all the labels facing outward.

One man's junk is another man's treasure. Juliet Alpha and Mark both like to dumpster dive to see who can find the best trash and recycle it. Those two are always hauling tables, cabinets, drawers, chairs, and whatever they can get their hands on. Plus all the little stuff like nails, latches, hooks, and any kind of hardware imaginable. Motormouth is a handyman. He's always fixing, nailing, or tinkering with something around or near the office. Obviously, it's always with Juliet Alpha's uninvited supervision to make sure the job is done right. They're a match made in heaven.

We also share the office with our graphic artist, Jason. He's responsible for making our training materials look pretty and creating safety posters and other ad hoc projects in the field. Now, Mark and Juliet Alpha may poke fun at each other in a cheapening and unworthy way, but Jason and Juliet Alpha bump heads. There are a lot of people who do not like Juliet Alpha, but after Jason couldn't meet a deadline on a project a while back, she's had it in for him ever since. Jason always claims the racist card. Juliet says it's his work performance, and she's right. His work is mediocre and he can't meet most deadlines, so we have to pick up his slack. Eventually Juliet wins the battle and I let Jason go. Not only because of the poor work performance but also to keep some peace and harmony in the office.

The rest of our group is the data cell group. Because Juliet Alpha, Motormouth, and I are old enough to be their parents, we refer to the data cell group as "the kids": Agim, Akhjoltoy, Jeton, and Regala.

Agim is the lead and the oldest of the data cell group. He's well spoken in multiple languages, he's very diplomatic and polite, and he would make a great politician one day.

Akhjoltoy is from Kazakhstan. We call him "AJ" for short. He spent his high school years in the States. He's always gentle and kind.

Jeton is from Kosovo and came to us from our health, safety, and environment (HSE) department. He's very analytical, scientific, and smart. I always enjoy listening to him give our morning safety topic in his firm and assertive voice. I think he has a bright future ahead of him.

Regala is the youngest of the group and the only female of the data cell, also from Kosovo. She's tall, slender, and pretty with a contagious laugh. I'm surprised how often she laughs at my dry sense of humor. When Regala is laughing in the office, everybody is laughing. She's fun to have around and is the fastest keyboard typist I know.

They are all sharp kids, but slobs. They get their work done and do a good job, but they don't keep their office neat and tidy at all. During one of my absences, they were written up by our health, safety, and environment (HSE) department for poor housekeeping. I'm sure Juliet Alpha had something to do with instigating that HSE audit. They deserved what they got with their overflowing trash cans, spilled coffee and coffee grounds on the floor, used cups, and empty cans and bottles all over the place. It makes a great place for rodents to hang out at night. That's unacceptable.

A few times a week I pop in on the kids to make sure they are doing what they're supposed to do. I always tell Motormouth to send the kids an instant message that I'm coming down there and that their office better be spotless! Sometimes he'll send them the message, but I'll never stop by. I just like to keep them on their toes.

MY CELL: I've been moved to a new room, or maybe I should refer to it as my cell, since this place is more like a prison every day. It's a little bigger than my previous B-hut. Not that much bigger, but maybe two feet wider. It has its own private door to each room and it's on the boardwalk. I've been told that it's one of the original B-huts left from Russian occupancy.

One of my first nights in my new digs, we have an incoming attack. As department manager, Trigger must account for our staff face to face. He can't find my room but settled for a cell phone check. There are no numbers on the doors of my B-hut. The next morning, Trigger asks me to show him where my room is. We walk over to it and he pulls out a military decal and places it on my door. After he does it, he says, *"Now I'll know which room is yours."* But that doesn't last too long because Trigger hands over the accountability task to me. As soon as he does, I walk with everyone to their B-huts and take note of who is where. There's not much space in these rooms—enough to hold a twin bed and a small wardrobe for clothes. As for me, I mainly use my cell just for sleep. And sex.

The Revolving Door

We're at the height of the surge and I could have a fucking revolving door on my cell with the number of men coming and going. I've got a new smartphone. Between that and the number of new dating apps, finding a piece of meat around here is easy and plentiful. As I tell the military personnel, I'm here to serve!

Life is like a box of chocolates and comes in all shapes, sizes, and flavors—just like my men: white chocolate, milk chocolate, dark chocolate, caramel and truffle, sweet and bittersweet, hard candy, and cream filled; short, tall, thin, toned, muscular, curvy, and smooth; Army, Navy, Marines, corporals, specialists, sergeants, major sergeants, and master sergeants. From the U.S., U.K., Poland, France, Italy, and Australia. Mild to wild. Sometimes two or three in a day. Sometimes a group. I'm like a kid in a candy store, and I've become quite the whore.

But I'm not alone. Everyone's a whore in this place. I see the married men prancing around with their new young girlfriends trying to act like nothing is going on between them. They can't hide that shit from me. I see it their lustful, bottomless eyes and through the smirks on their faces. I see them at lunch together or sometimes at the gym. I see men and women sneaking into rooms. Some of them are hiding the fact that they're sleeping with a subordinate. I've heard of sex orgies with both men and women present. The sad part about it is that they were sent home not because of the sex part but because they broke the housing rules.

I've allowed a married couple to have conjugal visits using my room. They're separated for nearly three months because they work at different bases. So when they finally get together and need a place, *mi casa es su casa!* I don't hand out my key to just anyone, only a select few I can deeply trust. I just have three rules: use your own sheets, leave the place spotless, and be quiet.

Mona Lee Cartwright even totes up a few of her escapades. She's gotten some action and shared a few stories with me about her fine pickings from the smorgasbord. She's had a few young ones and she laughs when she talks about being a cougar. I don't even know what a cougar is until she tells me: an older woman who scores with a much younger man. She also boasts to me that she's seen and been with a general while assigned to another base.

I'll see my man Cliff with one of his lady friends. I call him "Cliff-banger." Sometimes he's with the same one. On the other hand, he'll see me escorting a soldier through The Village and be nodding his head and smiling at me. Of course, he only has filth on his mind, but sometimes I do escort military personnel through The Village to help them find a training room, conference room, the self-serve laundry—and yes, sometimes my room.

There's one guy on base—or at least only one that I know of—who has two wives. He has a wife in the States and one in the Philippines. He carries two cell phones, one for each wife. His American wife doesn't like to travel overseas, so he uses the tax credit as his excuse for not returning home and for spending his time outside the U.S. He tells his Filipino wife that he needs to return to the U.S. for medical reasons or some other bullshit. He's a cunning fella. Others—and there are plenty of others—head off to somewhere in Southeast Asia, mainly Thailand, looking for a girlfriend or wife or newfound love.

Yes, there's a lot of action taking place and sex going on.

Groundhog Day Run

"I didn't know there's a Groundhog Day run," says Randy. I tell him, *"Of course there's a Groundhog Day run. The military will use any holiday to host a run."* I give him the usual details: 0530 show time, 0600 start at the Clamshell. *"I'll send you the flyer."* Randy exclaims, *"Cool, man. I'll be there!"* with his usual enthusiasm and excitement, and he starts hopping around like he's in a boxing ring.

I quickly return to the office with a big grin on my face. Without a second to waste, I whip up a flyer on my computer. Picture of a groundhog. Check. Date, time, location. Check. Military logo. Check. It looks good and it looks official. Randy is always talking about playing practical jokes on people, so I think I'll give him a taste of his own medicine. I hit send.

I tell my partner in crime, Stella, what I'm up to and she gets in on the action. I follow her back to her office and she jumps on her computer to send Randy a Sametime message. I'm standing over her shoulder as she starts off with the girlie stuff: *"Did you see the cool shirt for tomorrow's run? It's hanging up at The Rock."* Yup, it's all about the shirt. She tells him he'll definitely want this T-shirt for his Bagram collection. They casually converse and she starts to whine about the early-morning run in February and how cold it is. Perfect. Randy barks back at her, *"Parks! Josef is depending upon us! Team Texas! We're tough!"* She has a comeback line and types it super fast on the keyboard, *"Yeah, Josef. He's such a drill sergeant!"* We burst into laughter. She's making it sound so real and convincing. Of course, I didn't like her rant following that about how she would pay the price with me if she didn't show up. She thought those sticky notes were punishment? Ha!

The day goes by as the three of us work diligently at our desks in different offices. Toward quitting time, I ask Stella if I should tell Randy that we're playing a practical joke on him, especially since I know how much he'd rather sleep in. Stella says, *"I don't think he'll show up anyway, so don't worry about it."* She's right. He has been slacking lately. So I forget about it. I go to bed and sleep well.

The next morning, I get to the office and as I'm enjoying my morning cup of coffee, Trigger enters and asks, *"Have you seen Randy yet?"* I tell him no. Trigger bursts out laughing. From Trigger's bellowing laughter, I'm thinking, *"Oh, shit! Randy showed up for the race and I'm sure Trigger's heard the entire story already."* I've completely forgotten about the joke. Trigger adds, *"Thomas, Randy is out to get you now."* Just a couple minutes go by and Randy comes flying through the door. I thought he would be mad at me, but instead he has a big smirk on his face. He says, *"Josef, you got me!"* And he's so proud of the fact that my practical joke is the biggest and best joke ever played on him.

Randy tells us how his day unfolded: *"I jump up out of bed at 0515, throw on my running clothes, and make a dash to the Clamshell."* I assume that's definitely true. He generally shows up as runners are taking off from the starting line. He continues, *"Well when I get there, nobody is there, so I'm thinking I have the location mixed up and run about a mile down Disney to the North DFAC."* The North DFAC is another common starting place for races. *"Nobody's there either, so I ask a couple of soldiers if they know where the Groundhog Day run is being held. The soldiers look at me like I'm crazy. They tell me they don't think there is a Groundhog Day run. We all agree that it must be starting at The Rock fitness center."* The Rock is in Camp Cunningham, not far from the Clamshell. *"So I hightail it to The Rock. Still, there are no runners to be seen. I become very suspicious and walk into The Rock to ask the attendant. She says there's no run today. She even shows me on the calendar that nothing is scheduled."* Randy starts shaking his head up and down, and finishes up his story, *"I knew I'd been had. Damn Josef."*

I wish I could've been a fly on the wall to see his expression right there and then. Now he's standing in front of me with a smirk and his head nodding. He adds, *"I took one for the team. But I can't believe my beloved Team Texas running buddies could do such a thing."* But we did.

As he's finishing telling me the story, Stella comes bopping into the office. We get all fired up about what just transpired, so Randy tells his story all over again to Stella. He adds, *"Despite the fact that there was no scheduled run, I still probably ran a 5K!"* When he gets back to his room, he takes an old plain white T-shirt and, with some markers, makes his own Groundhog Day 5K T-shirt and wears it with pride.

Midnight Marine

Jake and his squad all do their laundry at the same time every week: Mondays at 11:00 p.m. They use the self-serve laundry located in Barron Village near Infantry Village where they're staying. After Jake's squad gets their clothes from the washer to the dryer, the rest of his squad continues to watch a movie, play cards, or grab some midnight chow. They have about an hour before their clothes will be dry. While they're all occupying their time, Jake sneaks over to my room nearby.

I know he's coming, so I leave the door unlocked. When he enters my room, I may get a glimpse of him from the outside light. His uniform is tan, unlike the Army green. He removes the M4 or M16 military assault rifle strapped around his body. He unties his boots and removes them and then his shirt, pants, socks, and underwear. There's something about a man carrying a gun and stripping off his clothes in front of me that intrigues me.

Jake is a tall guy all of 22 or 23. He's lean and has a full head of black hair buzzed evenly all around. He's such a good-looking young stud. He's engaged to a woman. I asked him once why he pursues sex with men, and he said he was tired of jacking off and was curious to experience sex with another guy, without any attachments. He told me he likes the tenderness of being with a woman and the firmness of being with a man. I can understand that. As a young man in his early twenties, he surely has a pretty high sex drive and no place for a release except with his hands or another man.

Other than a few email exchanges here and there, we really don't talk or communicate much. I guess the mysteriousness of who I am with is also appealing to me. All I really know about him is his physical appearance, uniform, and behavior in bed. I don't care to learn too much more because I know his stay at BAF will not be a long one. I respect his discretion.

I can tell Jake is still new to all of this and still in an exploring stage. But what comes naturally he does very well: the kissing, the touching, and the massaging. He tends to follow my lead. I'm patient and "vanilla" with him until he's ready to try something new and different. Because of this, I know he enjoys his time with me. I'm old enough to be his father and I'm a good teacher. Whatever I do, he reciprocates. Each week it may be something new or different, but it's always friendly and affectionate. I tell Jake I've been with two other Marines in the past few days. He laughs and responds, *"I guess it's a rite of passage for us."*

The fun lasts six or eight Mondays until he is reassigned to another forward operating base. I don't keep in contact with the young stud.

Desecration of the Qur'an

So how did a bunch of Qur'ans end up in a burning landfill in February of 2012? Muslim prisoners held at the detention center at Bagram Airfield used the Qur'ans. They used their Qur'ans to pass messages back and forth among each other. For that alone do extreme Islamists commit desecration of the Qur'an. Was that mentioned in the media? I didn't see any mention of the origination of the desecration of the Qur'an until today, five days after the incident started. And even then it was a tiny article hidden among larger news stories.

The Qur'ans from the detention facility were given to soldiers to be disposed of. They were brought to a burn pit and landfill located just outside of base. Here is where the Army made several mistakes: 1) any type of documentation is supposed to be concealed and burned at an incinerator inside the base; 2) specific direction of how the materials were supposed to be disposed of should have been communicated by the soldiers' chain of command; and 3) in all due respect to the Muslim religion, consultation from the mullah on base should have been sought.

So someone screwed up. Locals scavenge the landfill every day. One man's junk is another man's treasure, and that's particularly true when Americans are big consumers and don't give much thought about throwing out something they no longer use. This is especially true to a civilization that has very little or nothing, to people who have just one set of clothes, to children who have no shoes or jackets, to households that have no running water, electricity, or heat. There is very little infrastructure and prior to the U.S. occupation of Afghanistan, there were few schools and limited access to health care.

The landfill is part of the base, but it's located outside the wire. Locals are hired to sift through all the trash to take out materials such as plastic that will become toxic in the air we breathe if burned. And amidst mounds and mounds of debris, there are the Qur'ans. Pictures are taken and word spreads through The Village, the country, and the world.

After five days of protest, 30 people have been killed, including four Americans. Over 200 people are wounded. International condemnation follows the burning from the library that is used by inmates at the base's detention facility. The protests include domestic riots, which cause at least 41 deaths and around 270 injuries.

The Protests

It's a cold, cloudy day at Bagram. Locals are combing the landfill and come across the Qur'ans charred and burning in the landfill. In America, where we can practice freedom of speech, we might turn our heads or shrug our shoulders when hearing of the burning of Bibles or U.S. flags. Not here. Holy hell breaks out. The word spreads across the Parwan Province and hundreds, maybe thousands, of locals gather in outrage outside the Bagram entry points in protest by starting fires and throwing rocks. Again, another act of violence to prove their point.

The seeds seem to be sowing across the North Africa and Middle East regions of Mali, Tunisia, Libya, Egypt, Yemen, Bahrain, Iraq, Syria, Iran, and Israel. The problems, the protests, and the violence appear to be erupting like someone swatting a beehive. Every day there seems to be a new development, a new crisis, and a new outbreak of something. It's pandemonium.

Immediately the base is put on lockdown. Nobody can come or go. Bagram Airfield employs about 5,000 locals who fulfill necessary services such as food service, laundry, and cleaning. Some of the locals try to enter and come to work but are stoned or beaten by others, like crossing a picket line during a strike. Some manage to get in and are not able to leave as a safeguard for their lives.

All water is transported onto base and all the gray and black water is transported off base. Those services cease during the protests. Water restrictions are put in place. No water means no flushing toilets, no showers, and no self-serve laundry. We use porta johns that get nasty quickly.

People are starting to bitch about the water restrictions. Attitude is everything. I'm not so bothered by the lack of water. I just pretend I'm camping for a few days. I wear the same clothes for a few days in a row. I have baby wipes to clean myself. I brush my teeth outside my B-hut and spit the rinse from my mouth onto the gravel ground since the bathrooms are closed. What's the big deal? Who cares if you don't get to shower every day?

A contingency plan is put into effect. Civilians and some soldiers are asked to cover essential duties that are generally performed by the local workforce. Our entire department is asked to cover different shifts and duties. There's talk that the contingency plan may be in effect for the next few weeks, possibly through the month of March.

I sign up to cover in the dining facility one day and do a 12-hour shift of laundry on another day. Everyone in the department signs up for two shifts per week as long as this goes on. I'm one of the first to volunteer and select decent shifts because I don't want to get caught on latrine duty. Yuck!

My dining room foreman is one of the local Afghans, who is staying on base, as is his second in charge. Their names are Muhammad and Ahmed. They dress in American clothing and speak very good, clear English. They pretty much blend right in with all the other nationalities. They are very delighted and grateful that we're here to help. They are singing and humming between meal hours as we clean the tables and floors, stock condiments, and refill napkin holders and salt and pepper shakers. It's actually a nice change from working in the office.

Before the 1700 dinner hour, we're all able to take about a 15-minute break. We sit around a large table. The five or six Afghans who are here sit separately from the rest of the group and are talking up a storm in their native tongue. I'm thinking, *"I wonder if they're planning an interior attack or where they're going to meet after work to launch the next missile at us."* I hate to think that way, but I'm sure some of the Taliban are working among us or that we have workers threatened by them to carry out acts. On the other hand, many of the locals also serve as intelligence sources to the military. They will inform the military who's planning and doing what on the outside of the base.

Water for laundry is considered high priority, as our contract with the military states we must maintain a 72-hour turnaround on laundry. I'm sent to do laundry again on the fourth night of the protests. By the end of my shift, a large group of locals come in to return to their jobs and take over.

On day five, water trucks are coming and going from base again and tanks are being filled and dumped once more. We're able to flush toilets and take showers again, but there's a three-minute time limit for the showers and there's someone in the shower room timing people. I usually don't take long showers anyway, so this doesn't bother me.

When the lockdown lifts and locals return to work, I hesitate to eat in the chow hall. If they're prepping and serving the food, I can only imagine what a pissed-off Afghan might do to it. I choose my dining selections wisely. I almost always choose foods that I can see being made in front of me and cooked to order.

Incoming

It's not very often that Bagram gets hit with incoming rockets or missiles. In fact, if there is incoming, rarely does it reach the base. It's more of an annoyance than anything else. When The Big Voice and base alarms go off, people are desensitized to it. The smokers find it to be an opportune time to go outside for a smoke break as others continue to work.

For the most part, one or two rockets may be lobbed toward base and that's the extent of it. Our military readiness and technology can zoom into an exact location of where the rockets are launched and counterattack. Of course, the locals wised up after their launch pads were immediately blown up when they launched their rockets. Now they set up contraptions such as ice blocks (in the summer) to slowly melt and set off the ignition or ignite by cell phone. As my Vietnamese friend Ha says, *"Then they go and have tea in the field and laugh at the Americans and watch them scramble."* Ha fought side by side with American soldiers in the Vietnam War and said the Viet Cong would do that all the time. To this day he gets all fired up about it when he tells me the stories. Sometimes I just like to egg him on to get him going.

The day of the protests, we knew we were eventually going to be a target. The first night there are two separate attacks. The military requires 100 percent accountability of all personnel on base after an attack. I prepare my staff beforehand to call me immediately for accountability. They all know the drill. For those who do not have phones or don't answer their phones, they must come to the office and report face to face, or I must track them down. Half of the time this is the only option because the military will jam radio frequencies so the enemy can't communicate. This affects communications inside and outside of base, so it obviously affects us. The first attack is around 9:30 or 10:00 p.m. No problem. Almost everyone is still up or hasn't gone to sleep, and they all show up at the office for accountability.

The second attack takes place around 2:00 a.m. Nobody shows up at the office. I know they're not going to drag their asses out of bed to check in, so I make my rounds and go to each of their billets. First I check on Jeton. I pound on his door and shout in a stern voice, *"Accountability! Jusufi, are you here?"* No response. Then I pound on the door again and repeat, *"Accountability, Jusufi, are you here?"* Still no answer, but as I knock on his door, it opens ajar. I push his door open a little more and shine my headlamp on his bed. I see him bundled up under his orange sleeping bag, sound asleep. I remember that he told me he sleeps with earplugs in his ears because his neighbor snores so loudly and keeps him awake. Either he must be a sound sleeper or those are some damn good earplugs!

I go to Agim's B-hut next. I'm not sure which room is his because none of the doors are numbered, so I shout, *"Accountability! Agim Ajeti, are you here?"* A voice from the room across and down the hall answers, *"Yeah, I'm here."*

Next is Motormouth's room. He flings open his door like he's experienced a night terror. He sees me and responds, *"Oh, hell no!"* in his Texas twang.

Next up: AJ. He's easy to check on because he's in an all-male tent, first bunk on the left. I just open the tent door quietly, shine my light by his headboard, and see that he's there without having to wake him up.

Tracking down Regala can sometimes be a challenge because she's assigned to a women's tent with about 60 other female occupants. If I enter the tent, I announce my presence in a loud voice, *"Male on the floor!"* and wake up everyone and proceed to check on her. I don't like to do that and I think I've only done it once. I usually wait outside her tent and ask one of the other women doing accountability to check on her for me. Fortunately Juliet Alpha will usually help me with accountability, so she'll check on Regala.

I get 100 percent accountability for my team and report it to our HR department lead. We hunt down anyone not accounted for in the maze of plywood buildings and tents, going from room to room, or bunk to bunk. After we have full accountability of our department, it's reported upward to operations. Generally it takes about an hour or two to get full accountability for all the employees on base, unless people are shacking up and you don't know where they are. That's happened a few times and people have been terminated as a result. Accountability is taken seriously here.

We have incoming the next two nights.

After five days of violent demonstrations, more than 30 people are dead and dozens are injured. Most of the deaths are from Afghans killing Afghans, but we've lost four soldiers. What I don't understand is why the demonstrations turn so violent, especially under the name of Allah. I bet most Afghans have never heard of the teachings of Gandhi or MLK and nonviolent protests.

The Announcements

U.S. Commander in Afghanistan, General John Allen, publicly apologizes and orders an investigation soon after the discovery of the Qur'an burnings. President Obama also apologizes to help stem the violent demonstrators. I believe both men are sincere in their efforts. Afghanistan President Karzai publicly accepts their apologies. The Taliban replies to the situation by stating, *"You should bring the invading force's military bases and convoys under your brave attack, kill them, capture them, and teach them a lesson that they will never again dare to insult the Holy Qur'an."* The Taliban is as ruthless and ignorant as they come.

Newt Gingrich and Rick Santorum make public announcements denouncing Obama's apology. Just more idiots at a time of violent demonstrations who can create greater and more harmful consequences to our soldiers and set back U.S.-Afghanistan relations by years. They should either be standing behind our president and troops or keep their mouths shut. Better yet, if they can't stand behind our commander in chief and our soldiers, maybe they should try to stand in front of them. Soldiers on base are not happy with the Gingrich and Santorum comments and can see the increase in tensions and fighting outside of base. Neither man has ever visited a U.S. military installation. The good news is that it's had a negative effect on the Republican Party and their presidential runs.

The Dalai Lama says, *"Where ignorance is our master, there is no possibility of real peace."* With that said, the Taliban has mastered ignorance.

Coffee with the Lieutenant Colonel

The lieutenant colonel is the Baserunner who shows up in freezing rain and snow in his Marine-green running shorts. I'd say retired Marine, but he corrected me by stating that once a Marine, always a Marine. He's the epitome of a Marine. He's a few years older than I am—54 or 55—and lean, muscular, smart, determined, and clean-cut, and he still wears a Marine-style haircut. He bleeds green.

He's also one of my running buddies. He still runs about a 07:30-minute pace and is trying to get to a 07:00-minute pace. I tell him he's not 21 anymore and he responds, *"But I have more experience."* I say good luck, man. He stops by my office occasionally just to shoot the breeze over a cup of coffee, or if I have a cold nonalcoholic beer in the fridge, he may crack that open. Once, he snuck quietly into my office and told me how he could've taken me out along with my four coworkers. How sweet.

One afternoon we're walking back from lunch and the lieutenant colonel makes the comment, *"Man, those are some big Army boys."* He's not talking about their height. He's referring to their overall size. Then he continues with his experience, *"Yeah, when I had to hand out uniforms to my new Marine recruits, I would hand them a size smaller. Then they'd complain that their uniform wouldn't fit and I'd tell them they'd be fitting into them within two weeks."* I can just see a smug look of pleasure on his face as he did it.

The lieutenant colonel also gives me a hard time about my dress. He'll say, *"Josef, you're out of uniform!"* I'll ask him what's wrong. He'll roll his eyeballs at me and shake his head, *"Your belt is not aligned with the gig line and it's too long."* I'll ask him, *"What the hell is a gig line?"* He rolls his eyes again. A gig line is when your zipper flap, belt buckle, and buttons on your shirt are all aligned. I tell him if it was up to me, I'd be wearing a tank top and sandals. Who comes up with this stuff? He and a few other former military guys just laugh at me. They give me a lesson on how to salute properly. Another lesson on rank. I tell the lieutenant colonel, *"I don't know what all the stripes mean. I just know the more you have the more important you are. I address everyone in uniform as sir or ma'am."* He looks at me like I'm a damn rebel.

One morning we're sitting in my office, drinking our coffee and solving the world's problems. I ask him point blank, *"Do you think we should be in Afghanistan?"* He replies sternly, *"Why should we be here? This society has nothing going for them. They live in extreme poverty. There's been no progression in the past several hundred years, maybe thousand years. It's so damn primitive. There's no industry or infrastructure. There are no roads to open commerce or communications. They're not educated. Most of the population is doped up on opium. They don't use half of their population to their benefit [women]. All they do is breed and pray to a higher deity. I'll give them credit for that . . . they're highly dedicated to their deity. That's it. But what good is that to the American people and our tax dollars being spent over here? You want to know why we're really here? It's the perfect strategic location to quickly counterattack any threats in the Middle East. We're right on the heels of Pakistan, Iraq, and Iran. Afghanistan has no infrastructure, which puts us at a high advantage with our military air superiority, and no country in the Middle East could compete with us there. I don't think we'll be going anywhere for a long time."*

The lieutenant colonel makes some very interesting observations and a solid case for being here. I can honestly believe what he said. And if that's our government's intent, why not share that with the people? I often wonder if we'll ever pull out of Afghanistan. Bagram has grown tremendously in size since I've been here. The military has gone from plywood huts and tents to hard-structure buildings and improved runways, drainage systems, roads, and electrical power poles instead of just power generators. Structures are being built here to last for a long time and to withstand missile attacks. Or is all that for the Afghan National Army?

The Taliban among Us

We have locals working in our water treatment plants, and I'm hearing that a couple of them were caught pissing and shitting into our water tanks. The water is very highly chlorinated here and I know why. It's labeled disinfected non-potable water. You can smell and feel the chlorine in it when it comes out of the shower or the faucet. A short shower dries out your skin horribly. Long, daily showers would probably bleach your hair or make it fall out. Thankfully all our drinking water is in sealed bottles and from the U.S.

The laundry facilities and service use a harsh detergent to kill anything and everything. I can understand that, considering some people's hygiene around here, and who knows where they've been or what they've been up to. My skin breaks out if I have my clothes washed by the laundry service provided on base, so I do my own laundry with a less-abrasive, allergy-free detergent at the self-serve laundromat in The Village.

I don't mind doing my own laundry. What I don't like is waiting for a washer or dryer. There are only eight washers and eight dryers at the self-serve, and when you have dozens of soldiers or people with multiple bags of laundry, you wait. Most folks come prepared to watch movies, play card games, read books, zone out to music, etc. My skin has healed within a short time of doing my own laundry.

There are reports that food is being tampered with in our DFACs. Some of the reports include bleach poured on fresh fruit, metal shavings in a casserole, and even nuts and bolts in another. So this raises questions. Who's doing it? Are they acting alone or as a group? Are they locals or other country nationals? Where are they getting the items to tamper with the food? On base? When are they doing it, and how are they getting away with it?

There are plenty of locals who work on base and serve our food in the chow halls. Some are involved in the direct preparation of the food. I know some are very grateful of our presence in their country—others not so much. Some of them downright hate us. So why do we hire locals to work in our chow halls to prep and serve our food when they can easily tamper with it? The locals go through a metal detector and are searched upon entering the base. That means if they are the culprits of the food tampering with metal shavings, nuts, bolts, screws, and nails, they're collecting the objects on base. The base is a nonstop construction zone. Those items are lying all over the place. Pick it up on the walk to work, put it in a pocket, and slip it into the food while working in the kitchen.

Does the Taliban work among us on base? I'm sure they do. Security briefed us from our first day on base. We are constantly being reminded to be aware of our surroundings and what we say. We can't be complacent; we break up our routines and walk with battle buddies. But for the many local men who work on base, they're just family men who want to provide for their families. I think some of them would prefer to stay on base rather than return to their homes outside the wire. They see how we live. We have running water, hot water, sinks, toilets, electricity, and vehicles. Things that we consider to be very basic necessities of life appear to be luxuries to them. We teach them about dignity and respect, health, and hygiene. They better themselves by learning English and a skill or trade. They're given proper safety equipment to do their jobs and to show the locals that the employer and military care about them; we care about everyone. Many of them arrive to work in their traditional dress of light cotton pants, a long shirt, and sandals. When they get to their job site, they change into Western clothing of cargo pants or jeans, a button-down shirt or T-shirt, and shoes or boots. The Western attire helps them fit in among the general population and is more appropriate for the type of work they're performing.

Most of the local Afghan men are Muslim. Maybe all of them are. Five times a day a Muslim is bound to perform the fixed ritual of the Islamic prayer and worship. There are a couple mosques on base as well as a mullah (Islamic leader). The mullah calls out on each occasion four times, *"Allahu Akbar"*: God is great. Before going into a mosque or worship, Muslims must perform an ablution, so they stop what they're doing, grab bottles of water or a bucket of water, and wash their faces, wash their hands and arms to the elbow, rub their heads with water, and wash their feet to the ankles. The ritual is set out in the Qur'an. I've never seen any of them wash with soap, and it shows sometimes.

After the washing ritual, they proceed into the mosque. They remove their shoes before entering. Nearly every day, I walk by the utility shop near my office and see dozens and dozens of shoes outside the entrance at lunchtime for their noon prayer. Inside the utility shop, they temporarily clear their space, lay down their prayer mats, and pray in unison. Sometimes the prayer looks like a yoga class, all together in total submission to God. I think the unity of a fixed ritual of prayer that joins all Muslims is one of the beauties of their religion. After the prayer, they continue what they were doing and go back to work. Instead of a smoke break, they take a break to pray.

When it's time to leave base for the day, the men will switch back from their Western clothing and into their traditional attire. Blending in with local tradition and clothing helps not to set them apart. When they leave base, they face a lot of dangerous consequences. Some have been robbed, beaten, or even murdered because they are working on base with the Americans. Some have had family members kidnapped or held captive until they can produce a ransom or pull off a malicious act on base (like the food tampering). It's a rough life. They're damned if they do, and they're damned if they don't.

The Taliban: How It All Began

Prior to September 11, 2001, few Americans had even heard of Afghanistan, Osama bin Laden, the Taliban, or al-Qaeda. And still fewer had heard of Sharia law or kafala.

We are 11 years into this war in Afghanistan. In October 2001, the U.S. and supporting countries launched Operation Enduring Freedom. The war was organized and launched by the U.S. in response to the terrorist attacks of September 11 in the United States. The U.N. Security Council established the International Security Assistance Force (ISAF) at the end of 2001, and NATO assumed control of ISAF in 2003, including troops from 42 countries.

There were two main objectives of invading Afghanistan: The first was to dismantle the terrorist organization and base camps of al-Qaeda; and the second was to remove the Islamic fundamentalist Taliban regime from power. The Taliban protected and harbored al-Qaeda as well as Osama bin Laden, where it is understood that he drew a great following from Pakistan of young Muslim men with strong anti-Semitic and anti-Western views as early as the mid-1980s, after the Soviet troops withdrew from Afghanistan.

After Osama bin Laden's expulsion from Sudan, he made his second visit to Afghanistan, where he became a staunch ally and friend of Taliban leader Muhammad Omar. Omar fought in the anti-Soviet *mujahideen* (freedom fighters)—whom the U.S backed during the Soviet war—and later in the Afghan civil war. During the civil war between 1986 and 1989, Omar was wounded, disfiguring his face from extensive burns, and lost an eye.

Omar went on to study to become a mullah (mosque leader) at the Islamic seminary in Pakistan. He gained a large following of young

Afghan orphan refugees. In 1994, he returned to Afghanistan with some of his students, known as *"talib,"* where they overthrew the corrupt rule of the country. Omar named his regime the "Taliban" (the students) where he immediately introduced and enforced Sharia law, his own rules and regulations. Taliban law is about as fascist as Hitler's rule.

To disobey any of the restrictions is punishable by beheading for men and public stoning for women. A law forbidding women to wear male clothing was introduced due to women who had no male relative to go out and provide for them. They were forced onto the street in male clothing in order to buy food or gain medical assistance for single or other women. Female doctors who lost their jobs when the Taliban took power were forced to run secret underground hospitals for women or to walk to the homes of sick women, where they would dress in men's clothing.

The suicide rate for women in Afghanistan is at an all-time high now. As it goes against Islam to take one's own life, women favor the act of setting themselves on fire using cooking oil. This way they can call it a kitchen accident if they do not succeed, thus escaping punishment by public flogging.

The disturbing part of the coalition forces leaving Afghanistan is the fact that we will be doing a full 360 degrees since our invasion in 2001. What have we accomplished in 12 years? What have we learned? History tends to repeat itself. How do we overcome this current situation?

Sharia

Most Islamic countries are under the pretense and practice of Sharia law. Sharia is the moral code and religious law of Islam that varies substantially between sects, schools, states, and cultures. I look at it as a city, state, and federal law. Sharia is comprehensive and, by definition, without limit in its ambitions and scope, and it also includes legally mandated, recommended, permitted, discouraged, and prohibited practices that are strongly biased and discriminatory against women, homosexuals, and non-Muslims. It rules over and above any fundamental human right.

As far-fetched and extreme as Sharia may sound, the U.S. wasn't too far from the same type of injustices not very long ago. For decades and even today, U.S. conservatives have tried to use biblical verses to defend their views on slavery, segregation, voting, civil rights, poverty, marriage equality, clean air, and clean water. Today they use the same biblical viewpoints to defend any progress against the LGBT community. Decisions are being upheld based on Catholic belief rather than knowing logically what is right for humanity. One discussion the conservative side presents is how same-sex marriages and adoptions will destroy America and its values. U.S. politicians who share the same Christian beliefs and practices have introduced and passed legislation against the LGBT community. This is an example of Christian Sharia law in America: advancing laws based on religious beliefs, not our basic human rights.

An eye for an eye. Islamic Sharia law provides a legal framework for violence up to and including legalized murder against homosexuals, blasphemers, and women. I've read stories of family members— usually the brother or father—who killed a female member of the family due to suspicion of adultery or premarital sex. Oftentimes, the female is set up. There is one story I remember reading about where a father beheaded his daughter because she dishonored the family by committing adultery. He pranced around the community holding the bloody, severed head of his daughter by her hair and showing the people that he killed her to restore honor to his family, as though murder is an honorable thing. I remember the crime did not take place in the U.A.E., and I think the father got a mere two years in prison for the murder. He may have been set free after pleas made by the rest of the family. The U.N. estimates the number of honor killings in the world is about 5,000 per year. Middle East and Southwest Asia women's groups quadruple that number to 20,000 per year.

Another story out of Iran made huge headlines recently when a married woman, who supposedly committed adultery, was sentenced to death by public stoning. There were international pleas to stop the stoning of the mother of two. Supposedly her husband and some local men fabricated her act of adultery, but it was too late for her.

Up until recently there were certain crimes in America that showed leniency in the sentences of certain crimes that were motivated against race, religion, sexual orientation, ethnicity, and disability.

In 2009, the Matthew Shepard and James Byrd Jr. Hate Crimes Prevention Act was passed. It expanded the 1969 U.S. federal hate-crime law to include crimes motivated by a victim's actual or perceived gender, sexual orientation, gender identity, or disability. James Byrd was dragged behind a pickup truck along an asphalt road by three white supremacists. In one police report, it stated they found Byrd's body parts in 81 different spots.

Matthew Shepard was targeted because he was gay, tied to a fence, tortured, and left to die in Laramie, Wyoming. It was reported that Shepard was beaten so brutally that his face was completely covered in blood, except where it had been partially washed clean by his tears. A cyclist found him 18 hours later and initially mistook him for a scarecrow. He died three days later.

Both deaths riled many around the world, including me. Reading about them brought tears to my eyes; and even as I write this, it still brings me immense sadness. How can humanity be so cruel and full of hate? Byrd's lynching-by-dragging gave impetus to passage of a Texas hate-crimes law. Texas previously had no such laws on the books.

In 2007, the Matthew Shepard Act was introduced and passed in both the House of Representatives and the Senate, but then President George W. Bush indicated he would veto the legislation if it reached his desk. The amendment was dropped because special classes of people would receive preferential treatment. How about special protections? Some minority groups and classes *do* need special protections. To me, that sent a message that hate crimes were okay against race, religion, and sexual orientation. In 1990, Congress passed the Hate Crimes Statistics Act and, according to FBI statistics, of the more than 113,000 hate crimes since 1991, 55 percent were motivated by racial bias, 17 percent by religious bias, 14 percent by sexual-orientation bias, 14 percent by ethnicity bias, and 1 percent by disability bias.

Currently in Iraq, there's been a rash of gay bashings and killings. Homosexuality was not criminalized under Saddam Hussein. In fact, Iraq in the 1960s and 1970s was known for its relatively liberated gay scene. A London-based human rights group reported almost 700 deaths due to violence against gays since 2004.

Their perpetrators hunt down gay men. The killings are brutal and victims are ritually tortured. Oftentimes, extremities are dismembered, genitals are cut off, rectums are ruptured from a projecting device, and the anus is filled with glue. Bloodstained notes are left on the doors of family members or roommates to let them know where to find the bodies. Islamic hardline extremists who feel Islam is being destroyed by acts of homosexuality do all of this. And under Islam Sharia, these acts are considered honor killings. What will the world remember as being worse: homosexuality or unfathomably brutal murders?

There are varying degrees of Sharia that are accepted in Islamic countries. Blasphemy—the act of cursing or reviling God—is the most common punishable act under Sharia law in 21 Islamic countries. I feel like we're living in the Stone Age. Blasphemy is punishable, from imprisonment to death. Yet some Islamic nations include some level of Sharia that shows lenient sentences for honor killings, spousal rape, girls married before puberty, ban on new churches, floggings, caning, and more.

Perhaps Sharia serves as a deterrent in some respects—outlandish in others. The corollary to the Islamic rule against disclosing anything disadvantageous to Islam is Sharia's prohibition against blasphemy. This requires that infidels refrain from engaging in discussions about Islam that extend beyond what is permitted of them or would give offense to Muslims. It is probably the reason why some of these laws remain on their books. They're not allowed to criticize the law.

My analogy of Christian Sharia versus Islamic Sharia brings up three points:

First, Sharia is based on Islam—their religion is the law. Islam is the second-largest religion and the fastest-growing religion in the world. America is seeing Sharia law being introduced in Muslim communities across America, and there are current cases being reviewed by the U.S. federal courts to ensure legal proceedings are upheld. How will our U.S. politicians think and react if Islamic beliefs are introduced into our legislation? Will they share the same views as their Christian supporters?

Second, the United States of America is not a Christian nation and was never founded on Christianity. People from Europe fled to the U.S. to avoid religious persecution. The United States of America was founded on freedom, and one of those liberties is the freedom to practice your religious beliefs however you like and, in addition, to be free from religion if you so choose.

Last, don't politicians take an oath to uphold the U.S. Constitution? And if so, why do they swear on a Bible instead of the U.S. Constitution? Why do they allow their religious beliefs to interfere with the liberties of others, particularly minorities and the powerless, whom the Constitution specifically states to protect? Where is the separation of church and state? What that means is that our government is designed to express not only the will of the majority (democracy), but also to simultaneously protect the unalienable rights of minorities and the powerless. It is the constitutional protections of minorities and the powerless that add civility, humanity, and decency to what could otherwise be a barbaric nation—democratic or not. Human rights should reign over religious rights any day, no matter what.

The Big Five

"Incoming, Incoming, Incoming!" The Big Voice announces as I sit and wait on the bus to take us to the flight line so I can get the hell out of here. Along with three full busloads of passengers, I'm heading to Dubai. We freeze in our seats as we hear The Big Voice and wait for the impact. There's dead silence on the bus. Nobody is saying anything. Nobody is moving. Nobody is trying to get off the bus to run to a bunker for cover. We listen for the whistle of the missile that usually follows 10 to 15 seconds after our warning. There's a big boom. Then another. There are two missiles, and they hit somewhere on base close to us.

Our flight has already been delayed by 15 hours. It's close to midnight and we've been waiting all day to board this bus. Nobody wants to get off it now. Still, nobody is moving or saying a word. No other missiles are detected. Hopefully this is it. Finally an Air Operations representative boards the bus and tells us to stay seated. Within 15 minutes, we get an "all clear" from base operations and we can proceed with business as usual.

It's after midnight when we finally get on the flight line and almost 1:00 a.m. when our wheels are up. The one and only time that I book a flight out of Dubai without a layover is this trip. Because we've been delayed so long, I might miss my connecting flight.

I'm heading to South Africa to meet Greg. I'm registered to run in the Big Five Marathon on a wildlife refuge. In Africa, the big five game animals are the lion, the leopard, the rhino, the elephant, and the Cape buffalo. The term "Big Five" was coined by big-game hunters and refers to the five most difficult animals in Africa to hunt on foot. Subsequently the term was adopted by safari tour operators for marketing purposes and is used in most tourist and wildlife guides that discuss African wildlife safaris.

When we get to the Dubai airport, I immediately call South African Airways to tell them I'm not going to make my 5:00 a.m. flight to Cape Town and explain why. The representative is friendly and understanding, and reschedules me on a flight later in the morning free of charge. It's a 10-hour trip and I'll miss my prearranged pickup in Cape Town to drive me two more hours west to the wildlife refuge. I make more calls to re-coordinate a new pickup time, and our guide and the staff are so friendly and accommodating.

It's June and the beginning of the South Africa winter. There's no snow, but it's cold. The dark evening air is very cool and crisp. I'm greeted by one of the park staff rangers, who goes by the name Finn—a middle-aged, sturdy black man dressed in a park uniform. He grabs my backpack and tosses it in the back of a convertible jeep. Finn will be our safari guide for the next few days before the marathon.

As we converse during the drive, the brisk evening air is whipping my face. After spending long, hot summer days in Afghanistan, I feel susceptible to the cold. I crouch down in my seat and under the short windshield of the jeep so the air blows over me. It helps a little bit to get out of the direct path of the wind, but not much. The drive to the lodge seems to take forever because of my discomfort. Now I know how John Paul felt riding in the helicopter with the hatch door open in the middle of winter.

As we finally pull up to the lodge, our guide, Greg, two sisters from Australia, and one of the kitchen staff greet Finn and me with a warm welcome. They're all aware of the long journey I've been on.

I plop down in a comfortable leather chair with a fire blazing in the enormous stone fireplace. The kitchen staff brings me a cup of hot tea, a bowl of piping-hot soup, and some homemade bread. I warm up quickly as I tell them about the adventure I've been on for the past 36 hours. As I talk, my eyes scan and study the massive room of the lodge and the beautiful furnishings made of natural woods, stone, glass, and textiles. The fire in the fireplace, the subtle lighting, and the candlelight all add to the warmth and ambiance. I feel comfort and ease as I experience cordiality and homeliness in my new surroundings. My rough departure from Bagram quickly settles as a distant past.

For the next several days, we adventure off on predawn safaris, followed by a morning feast, a midnoon lunch, another safari at dusk, an evening meal, and socializing in front of the fireplace. One of the days, we even get in a quick 5K in preparation for the full marathon coming up.

The safaris are very impressive. Finn knows just where to go and points out a lot of interesting facts and tidbits to arouse our sense of wonder. The beauty of a winter safari is that there's more to see easily, since there are no leaves on the trees and fewer hiding places for animals. We watch lions hunt giraffes and wildebeests, elephants graze on bamboo, hippos and rhinos bathe in ponds, and warthogs run amuck and flaunt their heavy tusks. We learn about the different personalities of the animals just by observing their behaviors and laugh at how the *Madagascar* movie is right on key with the characters and personalities. Every outing is spectacular and fascinating. I feel so fortunate to experience and cherish these moments, especially with the one I love and the new friends we've made.

The rooms are set back from the main lodge about 100 yards. As instructed, every morning we call the front desk to verify that the coast is clear of wild-game animals and that it's safe to make the walk up to the lodge for breakfast. One morning, we get the thumbs-up that the coast is clear. Greg and I open our front door and start walking toward the lodge. We get about 50 feet and Greg quickly turns around, bumping into me and practically knocking me over to get back into our room. Straight ahead of us is a family of lions with three cubs. They're off in the distance, playing in the grass, but close enough to make one of us a tasty meal. We get back to the room and one of the park guides comes down with his rifle in hand to escort us to the lodge.

As the weekend approaches, more runners join our group. There are various lodges throughout the refuge, and this one holds about 20 to 24 guests. Our group consists of people from the U.S., Australia, Belgium, Brazil, Mexico, Denmark, and a few other destinations. It's a great group of people. Of course it is, because we're all runners!

On race day there are 250 registered runners. That's the cap to ensure the least impact on the environment. Rangers with high-powered rifles are strategically placed throughout the running course to ensure our safety. Greg delivers the exciting news that he's going to run the half marathon with our guide. He's never done a half marathon before. I tell him nutrition is the most important factor to stay fueled. I hand him a couple packets of supplements and know he'll be just fine. Our guide sees him taking the supplements and asks him what he's taking. He tells her, *"I don't know. Thomas just told me I should take them at mile 4 and mile 8."* Such a good husband. He does as he's told.

We are running up hills, through sandpits, across plains, and through thick forest areas. The number of runners across the open plains makes a few herds stir in stampedes. We are running amidst the wild beasts: ostriches, elephants, rhinos, zebras, giraffes, warthogs, gazelles, and others. It's a tough course. One of the hills has a 48 percent grade for three to four kilometers. It's a thigh buster that sets off my quads into spasms, and I end up having to walk about six kilometers before the spasms cease. At one point, we are rerouted because of an elephant invasion at one of the rest areas. I get the rest of the story at the finish line: The elephants were in defense mode, flapping their ears heavily in defense to get some bananas.

There are snacks and food and drinks at the finish line. In the evening, there's a celebration. We meet many of the other runners and make some good friends. We connect closely with the Australian sisters and a New York couple. We are heading to Cape Town after the refuge and agree to meet there for dinner and drinks.

We check into our B&B in Cape Town and set off to explore the area. Cape Town, with its towering seaside cliffs, large rock beaches, and crashing waves, makes it one of the most beautiful cities I've been to. Add Stellenbosch Wine Country just 25 miles away and I'm in heaven. Greg and I end our trip by becoming certified scuba divers in preparation for another upcoming trip to the Great Barrier Reef of Australia.

The Dark Side of Dubai

In one of the Dubai newspapers, I read many stories where it's evident that Sharia is practiced and protected. There's an actual "Lost and Found" column in the paper that lists "lost" housekeepers. Really? A lost housekeeper? Where did they lose her? At the mall while shopping? I don't think so. These housekeepers are most likely victims of verbal and physical abuse, forced submission, sexual assault, and/ or being held against their will without pay. Where do they go? They usually end up in a prostitution ring. Prostitution is rampant in Dubai despite being illegal. It's one of those Sharia laws where heads are turned. Or maybe Sharia doesn't have a law against prostitution. I don't know.

Rafik is an architect and working on a project in Dubai now. He picks me up for lunch and takes me to this wonderful Turkish Arabian restaurant in Jumeirah Beach. We sit outside to enjoy the early spring air, sipping on our mint lemonades. Rafik orders for us. I love it when he does the ordering. He knows all of the foods listed on the menu and has a silver palate when it comes to taste. He orders a lot of small plates of lamb and chicken kabobs, tabbouleh, hummus, sun-dried tomatoes with olive oil, balsamic vinegar, walnuts, and lots of fresh hot pita spread out on a white tablecloth with clear glassware. The food is abundant, colorful, and beautifully displayed.

During our lunch conversation, I talk about an article that I read called "The Dark Side of Dubai." The article uncovered all sorts of Sharia laws and *kafala* (in-country sponsorship or immigration law). It talked about the high rate of construction deaths, noting that many of them are suicides.

Rafik tells me about his short experience here, *"Thomas, many of the laborers are treated awfully here. I've been to camps where they are housed to pick them up for work. Many live in tents or cement dwellings without floors, in the middle of the desert without any form of transportation. It's horrible. Employers recruit from India, Bangladesh, Pakistan, the Philippines, and other countries, and tell the workers what a paradise it is to live and work in Dubai. When they get here, it becomes a living hell for a lot of them. Their passports are taken away. They live in squalor—crowded conditions that smell of sweat and sewage. They're required to work 14 or 16 hours a day in the high heat with few breaks and barely enough food to live on. Some don't even get paid. They can't leave because the employer has their passports and their money. Their alternative is to accept what they're doing or commit suicide. They're treated like shit. I can't stand it and I don't think I'll last here very long."*

In 2005, during the construction boom of Dubai, the Indian consulate registered nearly a thousand construction deaths due to heat exhaustion, overwork, and suicide. Those numbers have dropped significantly in recent years. I'm not sure if it's due to the slowdown of construction, better safety practices required by the U.A.E. government, or how numbers are being reported. Maybe the U.A.E. government is enforcing tougher penalties against construction companies that have reported incidents of not paying workers or holding employee passports, which is considered human trafficking.

During another visit to my cosmetologist, he tells that me he shares a one-bedroom apartment with 15 other Filipino men. I can't imagine. I ask him if he's getting paid. He says he does. I ask him if his employer has his passport. He says he doesn't. He informs me that most of them scrunch up together to work, live, save money, and send it home. After he tells me this, he bursts out laughing and asks, *"Are we crazy or what?"* Yes, that is a little crazy. I can't imagine their lives being any better here if they live that way.

When I hear these stories—not the honor killings but people working in a foreign land in pursuit of a better life and happiness—it's no different than some of the stories that I've heard in the U.S., with illegal immigrants. I had a landscaping company at one time and used a lot of day labor. A few of my workers told me how they were victims or knew of someone who had been held against their will. They were held captive and not paid in remote farming areas. Their lives were threatened if they tried to leave. If they were paid, they were subsequently robbed—usually by their own kind. It's so sad because, just like in Dubai, these people are only trying to make a better life for themselves and their families. In the U.S., because we have migrant workers who are undocumented and there illegally, many of these types of situations and crimes go unreported. Fortunately, in Austin and some other major cities, partnerships with local agencies, private businesses, and the police have worked together to address and alleviate some of these issues and crimes. But I hate hearing stories like these. Humans can be so cruel.

Call to Prayer

My running buddies and I meet at 0400 to run the eight-mile loop around base three times a week. As we run the last mile, I can hear the predawn call to prayer from a little mosque just "outside the wire" and right next to the base. The imam's voice vociferously echoes across base. Day after day, week after week, month after month, we hear the first call to prayer just before sunrise.

One morning, I'm dragging. I just want to roll over and go back to sleep, but I get up anyway to run the loop. As my mind is still thinking about my head on my pillow, I hear that call to prayer. I think to myself, *"Wow, there must be some very devout Muslims to get up this early to pray every day, week after week, month after month, year after year."* They get up every morning to pray before the sun comes up. I don't know if I could do it. I wonder if they ever sleep in. Do they ever just lie in bed and think, *"I'll sleep another hour or so and get up to pray when I'm ready,"* or do they jump up out of bed every morning just to pray? Even if they get up to do their prayer ritual and then go back to bed, it's just not the same as being able to sleep in without a worry or disturbance. I wonder if some lie in bed and just pray from there. And the mornings are cold. I can just imagine sticking my foot out from my nice warm blankets and feeling that cold air biting my foot. That alone would make me want to crawl back under the toasty covers and stay in bed longer.

One time I asked one of my Muslim friends to interpret their call to prayer for me. It sounds like a lot of *allaaah, ilaaha, illallaah, salaah.* If you get a good imam with a wonderful voice who sings the prayer with passion, it sounds delightful.

Allahu Akbar

(Four times: "Allah is Most Great.")

Ash'hadu an laa ilaha illallaah

(Twice: "I bear witness that there is no god but Allah.")

Ash'hadu anna Muhammadar-Rasulullah

(Twice: "I bear witness that Muhammad is the Messenger of Allah.")

Hayya alasssalah

(Twice: "Come to prayer.")

Hayya alal-Falah

(Twice: "Come to the good.")

Allahu Akbar

(Twice: "Allah is Most Great.")

La ilaha illallah

(Once: "There is no God but Allah.")

My Muslim friend who translated the call to prayer told me that there's an extra verse for the morning prayer. The kicker is that the imam cries out an extra verse for the predawn prayer that translates to *"Prayer is better than sleep."* Brainwashed! So I guess if you're a devout Muslim, you have no choice but to drag your ass out of bed and pray. I'd be praying for uninterrupted sleep!

I'm wide awake and close to the home stretch of my run when I hear the call to prayer. My brain and heart is my temple. I love it when my temple is outdoors, my feet pounding the pavement, my lungs filled with the cool morning air, the sun on my face, my heart pounding, my head clear of heavy thought, and my body sweating out the toxic energy. *"I'd rather be running and thinking about my health and life than be in church thinking about running."* The Dalai Lama says, *"If you have a particular faith or religion, that is good. But you can survive without it."*

If I Were Religious, I'd Be Buddhist

The war within Islam between the Sunni and Shia is about whether their religious beliefs and convictions are better upheld by the Prophet Muhammad's descendants or a caliph and successor of the prophet.

What I find more interesting about Islam and the Prophet Muhammad is his marriage to Aisha. According to Sunni scriptural Hadith sources, Aisha was six or seven years old when she married Muhammad, with the marriage not being consummated until she had reached puberty at the age of nine or ten. Child marriage may not have been uncommon at that time, but at age six or seven? Really? To put it bluntly, Muhammad was a pedophile. How can Muslims turn their heads at that and praise it like it's a good thing?

Christianity is no better. They worship a god who sacrificed his only son by torturing him to death. What kind of sick god are people worshipping? *"Oh, but Jesus was sacrificed and died for our sins."* Tell that to the courts in a modern-day killing of sacrifice. I'm not buying it. The Muslims don't either. They believe in the teachings of Jesus Christ but don't believe God the Almighty Father would choose such violent means to prove his point. He couldn't choose a nonviolent means?

If I were religious, I'd be Buddhist. Many believe Buddha is a god, but he's not. Buddha is not a deity or a supreme being like the Christian God or Muslim Allah. For Buddhists, what and how you practice is more fundamental than what you believe. Enlightenment is obtained through righteous conduct, wisdom, and mediation. I take this thought and try to live by what I believe and what society believes is the right thing to do.

But I'm not Christian, Muslim, Buddhist, Hindu, or any of the other 4,300 religions or deity beliefs in the world. I'm an atheist. I don't believe in organized religions. I don't believe in God, but I believe God is man's greatest idea. I don't believe in the devil. I don't believe in heaven. I don't believe in hell. I do not believe in the power of prayer. I prayed until I was blue in the face to be a straight man, but my prayers were never answered. It's my belief that one can be spiritual, but they don't need religion. I believe religion is a curse and distorts freethinking and progressive thought. So why did God create atheists?

As atheists, we exhibit the true lesson of compassion and humanity. We perform acts of deed, due diligence, and charity, and help those in need. We don't do these acts of kindness and caring from religious teachings; we do them from an inner sense of morality, humanity, and integrity. We do them from the heart.

I run in organized events because the proceeds generally benefit nonprofit organizations or a cause in need, such as cancer research and care, children's hospitals, animal shelters, the environment, etc. I was a Peace Corps Volunteer and continue to volunteer at animal shelters and events, and for meaningful causes—not because God tells me to but because of my morality and humanity. As a human, it's my purpose and objective to help others and society and the world become a better place.

I'm donating proceeds of this book to the Wounded Warrior Project because after working nearly five years side by side with these warfighters, I've seen the inflicted pain, injuries, and hardships cast upon our injured soldiers and their families, and our government continues to cut aid, benefits, and pay to these warriors. The U.S. government doesn't give a shit about our own people. I have gained tremendous respect for our military while serving as a military contractor in Afghanistan. I'm doing it out of a human act of compassion and empathy. Again, thank you all that have served or are serving.

Pogs for Peace

I open my email and in the attached document, a fellow employee is asking me if I will print some colored posters for him. Colored printers are a rarity in the field, but my department happens to have one because we also do a lot of graphics and public relations work. So if it's needed in color, we're asked to produce it.

I open the attachment and it's labeled "POGS for Peace." Pogs are our substitute for coins here on base. They're basically a cardboard printed token that carries the equivalent value of a U.S. coin: nickels, dimes, and quarters. They don't fuss with the pennies.

The attachment is a picture of seven children from the Bibi Sarwari Sangari Orphanage in Kabul. An Afghan doctor is involved with one of the local shops on base and collects money for the orphanage. I think his family runs the shop here. The past two years, employees contributed to the orphanage during a charity fundraiser in the month of November. Last November, we collected more than $2,000 that was used to purchase sewing machines for the orphanage. The doctor organized with local women to voluntarily sew clothes for the kids. The initiative was a success.

The picture of the four girls and three boys (ages 7 to 10) strikes me with sadness and delight at the same time. Sadness because each of the kids looks terrified and depressed. I recall a portion of a story in the book *The Kite Runner* that written by a U.S. doctor born and raised in Afghanistan. In the book, his character returns to Kabul in search of his childhood friend's son. He describes walking through the dark and poorly funded orphanage, where they barely had enough food rations to feed the kids, let alone clothe them. The picture in the flyer triggered stories of these kids and how they ended up at the orphanage.

The little girls are all wearing headscarves. I'm sure it's in preparation for reaching adolescence and covering their bodies from head to toe. It saddens me to see this because I know how women are treated in this country, and these poor little girls won't have much of a life ahead of them unless the perception of women changes and the Taliban is kept from power. As the lieutenant colonel said, *"They don't use half of their workforce."* Women.

On the other hand, I'm delighted because they are neatly clothed and clean, have shoes on their feet, and are holding boxes of clothes delivered by the U.S. Postal Service. Not only did we—as contract employees—raise funds to help the Afghan needy, but many of the military platoons, companies, and battalions adopt schools, orphanages, hospitals, etc. to help the local population. I've seen many pictures and drives for backpacks, clothes, jackets, and blankets, and military personnel delivering them to local children and families. It is the altruistic value that I see in other Americans that makes me proud to be an American. I'm proud of the difference we can make. It would be nice if more stories like this were shared in our media instead of all the turmoil and killing of war.

The Informant

"Muhammad, what were you doing in that Hummer with the military guys this morning?" I ask. He's surprised that I saw him and he hesitantly says, *"I tell them what's going on outside the wire."* I'm sure Muhammad wouldn't share that information with just anyone, but we've built a great deal of trust between each other over the past couple of years. I reassure him, *"You're a good man, Muhammad. Helping out our military helps to keep everyone safer."* *"I think so,"* he replies.

"You know, I'm jealous," I follow up. *"Why is that, Mr. Thomas?"* he asks inquisitively. *"Because I never got to ride in a Hummer, like you."* Muhammad chuckles at my comment. *"You will one day, Mr. Thomas."*

Muhammad is tall, dark, lean, clean-shaven, and handsome with dark, amber-colored eyes. He's 28 years old and married with three kids: two boys and a girl. He's always dressed in traditional Afghan attire, and he has a very nice smile that shows his perfectly aligned white teeth. Seeing him get into the Hummer military vehicle with a couple of military personnel this morning is not typical of military personnel and a local Afghan. I figured out right away that he's an informant for them. I know Muhammad wants to do what is right for the Afghan people. He's been through war with the Russians and now the U.S. presence here in his country. He also knows the evils of the Taliban and what would happen if the country fell under their power.

Muhammad is a supervisor over a labor group of local Afghans. His group has very limited English, but Muhammad speaks quite well and can converse on most topics. When I see the group, I acknowledge them all, sometimes with a hello, a good morning, or a handshake. Our team keeps a drawer full of chocolate candy bars that I occasionally share with Muhammad's them. They love American chocolate!

In the morning, when Muhammad and his group show up to clean, he and I share a "word of the day" in Dari. Since Dari uses the same alphabet or script as Arabic, I try to write out the word as it sounds, trying to remember the Arabic script that I learned many, many years ago. Muhammad is always so patient and kind. He's a good teacher and he helps me with pronunciation and spelling. I learn best from being able to hear it, see it, and then speak it.

I see Muhammad outside sitting in the sun. I can tell his mind is preoccupied about something. I sit down alongside him and we start to talk. He asks me, *"Mr. Thomas, how can I get a visa to go to the United States?"* I'm sure he's heard plenty about America from communicating with us on base. He tells me he would work in a restaurant or do anything to be able to leave Afghanistan. I know he'd be a great worker too, but I don't know the selection criteria. I don't even know what the process is to sponsor a foreigner. I tell him the process is long and difficult. I wish I could take him back to the States or arrange a plan for him, but it would be a long-term commitment, and considering I don't know what's in my future from day to day, it would be very difficult. I find out about other Afghans on base going through the visa process. Most of them applying are very sharp guys with technical school or college education. I ask one of them if he'll help Muhammad through the process and he agrees.

Dr. K

My finger is bulging, red, and painful. I go to the medical clinic and meet Dr. K. He's a young doctor from Kosovo. He's in his mid-thirties, stylish, amiable. When he checks out my finger, the first question he asks is, *"Did you get a pedicure from the salon recently?"* Yes, we have a salon here that offers haircuts, massages, manis, pedis, and waxing.

Just what every soldier needs! I'm thinking, *"I wonder if the doc noticed how nice my nails look from the manicure I had there."* I reply, *"Well as a matter of fact, yes. It was about three or four days ago."*

I like going there occasionally to treat myself to a manicure and a pedicure, sometimes a back wax, or sometimes a massage if I pull a muscle from working out or running. I get a peculiar pleasure and fascination watching men in uniform packing M9s or M16s as they get their heads shampooed and receive manis or pedis. And yes, they really do all that, especially the younger ones. I get a kick out of the guys who get their brows waxed for the first time and leave with big ol' grins on their faces, looking and feeling real *purdy*.

The doc goes on to tell me that the clinic sees this type of infection quite frequently. I contracted a staph infection on my finger, possibly from unsanitary equipment being used during my manicure. That doesn't make me happy at all, but when I think of my last visit, I don't recall Rosie sanitizing her tools before or after using them on me. I'm not sure if there are health inspectors to oversee or inspect the salon's hygiene practices. Can you imagine some kind of outbreak on base from the military personnel getting haircuts? I call the salon and make a complaint. They claim to have strict standards on hygiene health and safety, and say they do random inspections. I don't know where else I could've gotten the infection.

Dr. K cuts open the staph infection with a razor blade, drains it, cleans it, and puts antiseptic on it. During all of this, I ask him his name and where he's from, and make small talk. As part of an office visit protocol, he takes my vital signs. He comments on my low heart rate and tells me that I have a sport heart. I've never heard that phrase before, so I ask him what he means. He informs me that a low heart rate is common among athletes and runners. Our conversation broadens to our mutual interests and we move to a first-name basis. His name is Gezim (the G is soft) and the others in the office call him "Jim"—so typical of Americans to give their foreign coworkers American names.

After my office visit, I see Gezim all the time. We work out, run, and attend P90X classes together to stay fit. Occasionally we meet for coffee or lunch. Gezim is married with three kids and a fourth on the way. His wife must have an eye for photography because she sends him some beautiful photos of their kids and he displays them on the wall of his office. He's here in Afghanistan, like the rest of us, to get ahead financially. His plan includes finishing building his house. I don't know if Kosovo has a banking system that offers mortgages, but as he has the cash, the house gets closer to completion.

One evening I ask Gezim how and when he decided to become a doctor. He's very passionate about his profession. He tells me that during the Kosovo conflict, Muslim Albanian-Kosovar families had to hide their young men to avoid ethnic cleansing by the Serbs. He returned home one morning to find his parents murdered and his little sister clinging to their dead mother. He had to pull his sister off her. She was "One Ply" traumatized, and he knew from that day forward that he wanted to become a doctor to help others. He finished raising his sister and worked with her to overcome some of the emotional trauma.

Gezim speaks highly of his family and knows the importance of being at home with them. He gives BAF about a year and plans to head home after that. Time will tell.

The Electrical Engineer

This morning, a man in his early fifties comes into my office to inquire about an online electrical engineering program offered by Barron University. He's a nice-looking fella and he speaks clearly and eloquently with a slight accent. I can tell he's well educated.

As I listen and advise him of the process he needs to follow for course credit, I finally ask him where he's from. He replies, *"I'm from Houston."* He elaborates on how much he loves living in Houston because of the educational and engineering opportunities that have been offered to him. He continues on about working for Barron and discusses the educational programs through Barron University. He's very grateful for the opportunities bestowed upon him.

I mention that I can hear an accent in his voice. He tells me that he's originally from Bosnia and he sought refuge to the United States in 1998 at the onset of their war. He shares his background of how he became an engineer. I can tell he's very proud of his accomplishments. When he came to America, he was sent to Houston and many of the schools or corporations would not accept his credentials from Bosnia. As he's telling me about the obstacles and challenges he encountered, his story starts to unfold. I can see the expression on his face change from pride to frustration to pain and grief.

His journey from Bosnia to the U.S. began when his wife and children were killed as the result of the war. When he tells me he lost his children, I can see the energy drain from body, his voice quiver, and tears well up in his eyes. I'm not sure how they died and I don't want to go down that path. I can't imagine holding in that grief for so long or revisiting the situation over and over. It's obviously so vivid in his mind, and the way he tells the story is emotionally draining. I almost feel like he's on the verge of having a breakdown. It's making me feel uncomfortable and I'm not sure how to handle this situation. I pat him on the back and give him my condolences. I quickly switch the topic back to our original focus to keep the conversation professional.

I don't know why the situation makes me so nervous and uncomfortable, but it does. I guess it's just an unexpected scenario. I've just met the man and he walked into my life with this heartfelt story. I wonder how many others who walk by me have similar stories here in Afghanistan and how many of the people ended up here from other countries.

In a war zone, one can't help but think of death. We come into this world and we will all leave it one day. I often wonder what is going through a soldier's mind when faced with combat. Is the combat life like playing a game of Russian roulette? Do they think, *"What if today is my last day?"* Have they thought of the consequences? The impact that their life will have on family and others? For some, life is way too short.

The Biggest Loser

Gambling comes in many forms. We're most familiar with poker, slot machines, and craps—all those Vegas-style games. There's even football game bets that take place. Of course, buying a lottery ticket is also considered gambling. One day there is a multi-state Powerball lottery that is up to several hundred million dollars. About a dozen of us want to purchase numbers, but it's brought to our attention that it's a form of gambling and against General Order and Barron policy. So we can't play a little game of lotto fever to test our chances of winning. Oh, to win that jackpot would be so sweet!

A group of people—both contractors and military—decide to challenge each other to see who can lose the most weight and body fat percentage in a specified amount of time, kind of like *The Biggest Loser.* That sounds harmless, and to make it more motivating they decide to place bets on who can outdo whom. To be part of the competition, each person pays an entry fee. After the course of eight or twelve weeks, the winner takes all.

The word of this competition for money gets out—again, people thinking of it as no big deal—and an investigation is conducted. Investigators discover that 12 Barron employees are involved in *The Biggest Loser* sweepstakes, and all 12 of them are terminated. Most people think that's harsh. The punishment really does not fit the crime, if you can even call it a crime. The military or Barron could've just said it was against General Order and asked them to stop. Of course, the entry fee *was* high. I hear it was $500 per person. That would make it one hell of an incentive to get in shape if you had a dozen folks competing for $6,000.

Then I think that with all the runs I participate in, there's usually a prize given to the top runners. It may be in the form of a medal, a trophy, or gift cards. Here, the prize is paid for by a sponsor, but what about the innocent game of *The Biggest Loser*? They all just pitched in for the grand prize. Personally, most of us think it was a great incentive for a group of them to get in shape, but the military and Barron didn't see it that way. The verdict seems unjust to most of us, but we don't make the policies; we're just expected to know them and follow them. But who would've thought that was gambling? I didn't.

The Sweep

Tonight the military comes through Barron Village, banging on our doors to search our rooms. We're always subjected to random and unannounced health and welfare inspections. I can hear the banging on the doors from one end of the B-hut to the other and then onward to the next B-hut. As soldiers are banging on the doors, I can also hear them ordering people to open up and exit the room. It sounds like we're in the fucking Nazi Germany roundup.

It's about 10:00 p.m. and I'm in bed when I hear all the commotion going on outside my door. When they bang on my door, I open it shirtless and in my shorts. A woman officer asks me my nationality and requests to see my military ID. I tell her I'm an American and hand her my ID. She apologizes for waking me up and tells me I can go back to bed.

The military is sweeping through The Village, searching other country nationals (OCNs) rooms for electronic devices. A new amendment to the General Order that went into effect a few months ago prohibits OCNs from having any electronic device that can carry, send, or retrieve information. This includes personal computers, cell phones, cameras, thumb drives—even iPods! I consider most of those devices a daily part of my life nowadays. I can't imagine trying to function without one of them. For most people today, these items are our lifeline here because we use them to communicate with our families back home. Because of bandwidth issues, we can't use a work-issued laptop for social or communication purposes with family or friends. The company and the military have many social sites blocked.

I find the treatment of OCNs by the U.S. military unfair. It's like how there was the supposed suicide bomber with explosives in his shoes and now everyone must remove their shoes at the airport. I'm not sure what instigated the amendment to the General Order, but there must be good reason. Or is it just paranoia and fear? I'm more fearful of an American pulling a stunt like that than an OCN. Sometimes we treat our other country nationals with distrust, lack of dignity, and lack of respect. I see it all the time—Americans who think they're better. But all the OCNs are here for the same reason as their American counterparts.

Some of the OCNs, like the Brits, are part of NATO and denied electronic devices and gym privileges. That's another one of the privileges that I see as being very discriminatory. Why deny someone the benefit of working out, especially in a stressful atmosphere like a war zone? Are these decisions being made as a show of power? Do they really affect the safety and well-being of our military? I don't see the reasoning or logic in either of the two cases. If Americans were on a Brit base, I wonder if they'd be entitled to work out at the gym and possess electronic devices.

The sweep causes quite the stir in the office the next morning. People are talking about how their rooms were searched, questions they were asked, and who was caught. Among the many who were caught in the sweep—I can't believe it when I hear this—were two guys I know, Bojan and Martin. Both are from Macedonia.

Bojan was a professional soccer player and worked here because sport players don't make much money in his country. He reminded me of a junior Tom Jones, with black curly hair, a beautiful smile, and probably the nicest-looking soccer ass on base—firm and pronounced. He was one sexy young man. I tried to get him to join our running network and he tried to get me to join his soccer team. They played their game too late at night—way past my bedtime. Our runs were too early in the morning for him.

Martin was a cutie I used to tease and flirt with all the time. He took it all in stride and always laughed and smiled. He was always so well groomed and manicured. He cut his hair weekly, and it was never out of place and always looked perfect. He always wore a pressed shirt and jeans. He never stopped smiling and had a deviant laugh that I loved to hear.

I'll miss those guys. In the end, 56 OCNs were caught with electronic devices and ordered by the military to be terminated and repatriated.

Insurgent Attacks

In April, forward operating base (FOB) Finley Shields is attacked. Even though base defenders quickly repulse the attack, an explosion caused by a suicide bomber destroys a number of buildings. When fire breaks out from the explosion, a couple of B-huts catch fire and start a chain reaction. To stop the fire from spreading, the site manager jumps on a bulldozer and bulldozes down a row of B-huts. The heroic move saves 12 other buildings, a generator, and a fuel tank from igniting.

Sixty soldiers and dozens of civilians working on the base lose everything except for the clothes on their backs. A lot of soldiers and civilians know what it's like to lose everything in a war zone. We hear the stories over and over again.

The word gets out quickly and a clothing drive is in place. I go through my closet and donate some cargo pants, long-sleeved dress shirts that are too big for me anyway, some performance-wear gym shirts and shorts, and some shoes. When I deliver them to the drop-off point, the room is full of bags and tables are loaded with donated clothes. Again, our people come through for the others in need. That makes me feel good and makes me feel like I'll make a difference in someone's life.

Later, on a nice, sunny afternoon in August, members of the Taliban launch a coordinated assault that breaches the perimeter of FOB Salerno. This is the site to where Dipper One has been reassigned. Several of the Taliban are wearing suicide-bomb vests. One of them rams his explosive-packed vehicle carrying about 1,500 to 2,000 pounds of explosives into the base's fence, and the attackers enter through the gap. Fourteen insurgents, two U.S. troops, and five Afghan civilians are killed in the attack.

The large blast causes considerable damage to the base's DFAC and PX. Back at Bagram, we are receiving up-to-date messages about the blast from employees; people are crawling their way out of the DFAC to get to a bunker. Fortunately most people get out of the crumbling building with just minor injuries.

FOB Salerno's PX and DFAC will be shut down for a while due to the damage. That means they'll be eating MREs (Meals Ready to Eat). Toiletries, snacks, and other goods that we purchase at the PX will not be available to personnel for a while either. A small group of us on BAF take up collections to buy comfort foods and some necessities from our PX and forward them to our fellow employees at Salerno to help them get through this difficult time.

Streak of Luck I

I'm in bed and Juliet Alpha is calling me on the phone. It's past 10:00 p.m. I pick up and say hello, and she states, *"Thomas, I think you have a family emergency and you should come to the office."* My first thought is that something is up with one of my parents. They've been married for 55 years and they're up there in age. One never knows. I jump out of bed and quickly check my personal email account from my room. I have email messages from both Greg and my brother. The one from Greg has "emergency" in the subject line and in the email, and it says to call him as soon as possible. My brother's email has "your sister" in the subject line. I open the email and find out right then that he's sorry to inform me that our oldest sister is in the hospital with a terminal prognosis.

I call Greg. He tells me that my sister is in the hospital and had a couple of unexpected colon surgeries and that she's not going to make it. I call my brother and he tells me the same news. She's on life support and the doctors don't know if she'll live two more hours or two more weeks.

The only way to get out of here on an emergency leave is to receive notification from the Red Cross. I pull up the Red Cross document on my work computer and give my brother the instructions to notify them with the appropriate and required information I need submitted.

From phone calls I make back home, I find out that my sister was having abdominal pain for several days. She waited until the pain was so severe and had to be rushed to the hospital. Tests revealed that she had a blood clot to the colon. Surgeons removed a good portion of her colon, which caused subsequent complications, resulting in two more surgeries. A portion of her colon was already dead and it was causing other organs in her body to shut down. She was conscious when doctors told her she was going to die with all her family around her except me: her husband, kids, grandkids, siblings, and parents. The news of her medical condition is unexpected and takes me by surprise.

I contact our emergency response team (ERT) to let them know what's going on. They receive the Red Cross notification during the night. ERT and HR are already in full action to get me out of theater and back home. It's 7:00 a.m. and I'm on the flight manifest for the 9:30 a.m. flight to Dubai. Motormouth Mark helps me get country management's approval, all the necessary signatures to out-process, and an airline ticket out of here. And the Texas gentleman that he is, he walks me to the base terminal, carrying the bag he helped me pack.

I am hoping to make it to my sister's bedside to hold her hand one last time. I need to let her know I love her.

I'm instructed that I have a ticket to Dubai and that Air Operations is still working on a flight from there to my birthplace of Green Bay, Wisconsin, where my sister is lying in a hospital bed. I get to the Dubai Airport and two of the Barron Air Operations personnel are waiting for me when I come through the exit doors. They quickly take my bag, put it in a van, and whisk me away from Terminal One to Terminal Two. From there I manage to make my connecting flight to Detroit without a whole lot of time to spare.

The flight from Dubai to Detroit is when reality sets in that I'm heading back home. I may be attending a funeral. I didn't sleep the night before and I try to sleep on the plane, but I can't. Because her death is inevitable, I start to jot down some thoughts of my beloved sister and write a eulogy.

During my layover in Detroit, I receive word that my sister has passed. There would be no last touch. There would be no last words.

When I arrive in Green Bay, my two other sisters have most of the funeral arrangements made. Everyone seems to be handling the death quite well. I can tell her young grandson is having a difficult time understanding everything that's going on. My mom is also grieving. Like all parents, she expects her children to outlive her. My sister is cremated and we have a memorial service in her honor. My two sisters, two brothers, and I all contribute to her eulogy.

Streak of Luck II

The CrossFit instructor is in his early thirties and built. He starts the class by barking an order, *"Drop and give me 30 burpees!"* Stella looks at me with her big brown eyes that clearly sends a message: *"Are you frickin' kidding me? Thirty burpees!"* But Stella, who always has a quick-witted solution to everything, pipes up in her squeaky voice, *"Josef! We can do it! We'll just count by fives."* She drops down to do a burpee and calls out softly to me, *"Five, ten, fifteen . . ."* I love her! Not surprisingly, she's the first to finish her 30 (six) burpees, jumps up, and shouts, *"Done!"* Wonder Woman here.

We do all sorts of running, jumping, pull-ups, box jumps, deadlifts . . . and the young instructor continues barking one order after another. He must be a drill sergeant. I tell Stella, *"I don't like the way this young whippersnapper is conducting the class. He doesn't do any warm-up and somebody's going to hurt themselves."* I'm sure I'm the oldest one in the class and, sure enough, right after I say that while jumping back and forth over a long barbell bar with 45-pound weights on each end, I feel something rip in my knee. We're almost done, so I don't tell Stella and just hope it's a temporary affliction.

I head to the office in my gym shorts for something cold to drink. I tell Juliet Alpha what happened in CrossFit and show her my knee. She thinks it's swollen. Like a good mom, she fixes a bag of ice and plops it on my knee.

My knee is in painful discomfort for a few weeks. When I return to Dubai from my sister's funeral, I decide to have it checked out. I waited until now because if I would've had it done in the U.S., I would've acquired a hefty medical bill for the treatment. My international medical plan covers 100 percent on my medical expenses if I have it done outside the U.S. Anything I have done in the U.S. is subject to a $3,000 deductible and 20 percent of the bill. Yeah, I'll go for the 100 percent coverage.

Americans who believe the U.S. has the best medical in the world are misinformed. According to the Commonwealth Fund report, the U.S. has the most expensive health-care system in the world and ranks the worst among industrial nations in terms of efficiency, equity, and level of performance. Results of the study rely on data from the Organization for Economic Co-operation and Development, the World Health Organization, and interviews from physicians and patients.

As greedy as American insurance and pharmaceutical companies are, I won't be surprised at all if non-life-threatening medical procedures in the U.S. are eventually outsourced to other countries like India, Thailand, and China. The U.S. already hires medical doctors from these countries. Why not recruit and hire them to practice their professions in their home countries? It's cheaper for the insurance companies to fly a patient and significant other abroad to have a procedure done, go through recovery, and fly back home for about 50 to 80 percent of the cost in the U.S. A $100,000 open-heart surgery in the U.S. will cost maybe $20,000 in India. This is not new news to the insurance companies. In fact, I've heard one of the major insurance companies has already set up shop in India for this very reason. The common denominator being profit—the bottom line. I can see this happening more and more, especially with so many countries surpassing the U.S. in education, particularly in the fields of mathematics, science, and medicine. Doctors even graduate there at much higher rates than the U.S.

As for my knee, my suspicions are correct. I have a torn meniscus. The orthopedic surgeon states the tear is small and he thinks it may heal on its own if I continue to lay off it for the next four to six weeks. I opt to try this over the surgery. He writes me a medical release and checks a box stating I need to do sedentary work, which I do already working in an office.

I become aware that the Barron medical staff in Dubai interprets this as a restriction. I'm put on medical hold for six weeks to have it corrected. I can't believe it. I try to appeal the decision, but it sticks because of the Afghanistan environment that I work in. Much of the walking areas are gravel, and it's easy to have poor traction that affects your ankles, knees, and legs. It bugs me a little because there are plenty of people on base who do not disclose their procedures, medications, or illnesses and get away with it. I've heard of a couple who paid off their medical doctors to give them a clean bill of health or a waiver so they could go about their work.

I plot out my next move. If I spend the entire six weeks back in the States, I'll lose my foreign income tax deduction, which saves me about $20,000 in taxes a year. I really don't want to do that because it's a nice chunk of change. I have 21 days left out of 35 to spend in the States. I start to check around for an apartment to rent in Dubai for a month. Even paying around $2,000 a month for an apartment to rent would be worth the savings on my tax return. I also check into flying to less-expensive places like Nepal, Thailand, or Sri Lanka, but it's the monsoon season in each of those places. I'd rather stay in the fiery, baking heat of Dubai than the inundation of rain. I spend the day checking the region for cheap airfare and inexpensive places to stay.

I chat with my friend AbuBakr, who lives here in Dubai, and he insists I stay with him. He lives in Sharjah, the third largest and most populous city in the U.A.E. It merges with Dubai and overlooks the Persian Gulf. I'm thinking of taking him up on his offer until I can plan my trip back home and figure out what I'm going to do about my knee.

Abu is from Iraq. He and his extended family fled to Dubai during the uprising in Iraq in 2006. They are Sunni Muslims and a minority in Iraq that was protected under Saddam Hussein's rule. Under Saddam's rule, Shia opposition to the government was brutally suppressed, resulting in the genocide of tens of thousands of casualties and successive repression by his forces.

Iran is unique in the Muslim world because its population consists of an overwhelming 92 percent Shia compared to just 8 percent Sunni. It's believed Iranian Shias crossing the border inflated the Shia population in Iraq. In 2006, militia-dominated government death squads were reportedly torturing to death and executing hundreds of Sunnis every month in Baghdad alone. Many Sunnis were arrested at random.

After the fall of Saddam, some of the worst Shia-Sunni sectarian violence occurred. Abu's family feared for their lives because all their first names are affiliated under the Sunni doctrine and belief, and would warrant their execution. They sought refuge in Dubai. Abu's father worked for the Iraqi government and was a high-ranking official of the Saddam regime. He may have bankrolled the Iraqi government to flee the country. None of the boys work and they seem to be living quite comfortably.

After the sun sets in Dubai, I take a taxi from Dubai to Sharjah. Abu greets me at the front of his building. He's a gorgeous, masculine man. He's all of 25 but looks much older with his wondrous, full beard, shortly trimmed hair, and those beautiful russet eyes that pop from razor-thin tattooed eyeliner.

His apartment overlooks the beautiful Persian Gulf. It's modern and sleek, outfitted with suave-leather white furniture, with the white walls displaying large prints of his personal photography all strategically hung like a fine-art gallery.

Shortly after I settle into his apartment, his three brothers show up for a visit with one of their friends from Iraq, Sayeed. Abu is the best-looking of the four. One is older, two are younger, and all of them are wearing traditional Arab robes. Abu is also the tallest and fittest of the four. His brothers call him "The American" because he wears the latest style of Western fashion and dreams to work and live in the U.S. or Canada.

He's also open to his family about being gay, and they all accept it and love him for who he is. Sharia law condones honor killings of homosexuals in many Arab-Islamic cultures. It's also more of a cultural and emotional issue rather than a religious one. I say that if a religion preaches killing of any human being, then find a new religion. Fortunately for Abu, he also comes from a well-educated family.

Like most Arab families that I know, they are very close-knit and family oriented. So close, in fact, they all live within about a four-block radius of each other and their parents. They hang out for a couple of hours talking, horsing around like brothers do, taking pictures, and sipping coffee. Around 2:30 a.m., they decide it's time to go grocery shopping! We all march down to the parking garage and jump in a new silver BMW 7 Series. We journey over to a grocery store to buy groceries for dinner for the next day.

I now realize that Arab culture comes to life late at night when the average daily temperature in Dubai reaches 130 degrees. The grocery store is packed and the streets are lined with cars. Abu takes charge of the grocery list and his brothers start putting things into the shopping carts—two shopping carts—as he marks each item off the list.

We finally go to bed around 4:00 or 5:00 a.m. One of his brothers and Sayeed spend the night. The next day, I wake up around 9:00 a.m. because that's the way my body is programmed. I tiptoe around and make some coffee, read parts of a book, and check emails and Facebook. The others start to get up around noon, and Sayeed and Abu's brother take off.

Abu tells me that his Lebanese friend, Tariq, is coming over and we're going to go to the beach. To the beach? It's 130 degrees outside and we're going to the beach in the middle of the afternoon. There's not a cloud in the sky for sun cover. I'll go along with them to be polite, but if worse comes to worst, I'll take a taxi back to the apartment.

Tariq pulls up in front of Abu's apartment building and calls Abu's cell phone. We grab our beach garb and head down. Tariq is in his car with all the windows rolled up and the A/C on, smoking a cigarette. Abu starts to cuss him out for smoking in the car with all the windows rolled up and rolls them all down to help air out the car. Abu doesn't even smoke the traditional Arab shisha. I'm proud of him for setting his own standards and not being peer pressured.

We take off to the beach in Tariq's car. His driving reminds me of Rafik's driving in Lebanon. Of course, they're both Lebanese, so maybe it's a cultural thing to drive like maniacs! I'm sitting in the back seat and as we make the curve on the roundabout on two wheels and a quick right, Abu turns around and asks me how I like Tariq's driving. I reply, *"He drives pretty fast."* Abu and Tariq laugh and then Abu tells me that Tariq got his driver's license two weeks ago and just picked up his new car three or four days ago. I think, *"Oh great! Not only am I driving with a maniac, but he's also inexperienced."*

We make it to the public beach. I see only one other car in the parking lot. There are no taxis in sight and it'd be a long walk to get one off the main roadway. Well at least we'll have the beach to ourselves. I open the car door and get blasted by a thick wave of heat. Shit. I know I'm not going to enjoy this.

We walk toward the beach with our stuff and I notice there are no trees for shade. There is one beach attendant, and Abu and Tariq ask him for three lounge chairs and an umbrella. He kindly obliges and sets us up. We lay out towels and head for the water, only to find that it's almost unbearable. We go from 130-degree air temperature to about 105-degree ocean water. It's basically a fucking hot tub. There's nothing refreshing about being outdoors in the heat of the Dubai summer.

After I get out of the water, I lie down on my lounge chair under the umbrella. I can tell I'm dozing off here and there because I keep waking myself up with a few snorts and grunts. Abu and Tariq pay no attention to me and let me go in and out. They get up and go for a walk along the shore. I'm left there to nap. Between the night before and jet lag from returning from the States, it's all catching up with me. I don't think we're at the beach more than an hour before we're back in the car heading to Abu's place. We go to the nearby gym to work out after the sun goes down, and then we go to his oldest brother's house for dinner.

At his brother Mustafa's home, the four brothers are given place settings from the ladies in the kitchen to set the table: pitchers of a fresh-squeezed fruit drink, plates, bowls, and platters of food. It's Arab tradition to sit on a rug and eat at a low table that we would call a coffee table in the States. You either kneel or sit Indian style. The Iraqi traditional meal is fabulous and some of the best food that I've had in a long, long time. Abu sits next to me and keeps filling my plate. His brothers reach over the table to add food to my plate too. We have fresh fish and side dishes made with herbs and vegetables. Everything is so mouthwatering and delicious. I never knew Iraqi food was so wonderful.

During the meal, Sayeed decides to start up some conversation about his brother being killed in the Gulf War. Abu interprets for me because I don't understand the Iraqi Arabic dialect. Sayeed blames the U.S. for killing his brother during the Gulf War, and because I'm an American, I'm also blamed. I tell him that I'm not the embodiment of the U.S. government or politics but that I agree with the removal of their ruthless dictator. I apologize to him that he lost his brother and tell him that most Americans are people just like him. I can see the hate toward Americans in Sayeed's eyes, his scathing voice, and his facial expressions. Abu's brothers look surprised and somewhat embarrassed by Sayeed's behavior and opinion. I don't want to debate or argue the point. I can also tell that he is not well educated, so I choose to sit there and let him blow off steam while still trying to be nice and polite. Fortunately Sayeed is heading back to Iraq tomorrow and this dinner will be the last time I see him.

The routine is the same for the next five or six days that I spend with Abu, but instead of going to the beach, we go to Mustafa's apartment and swim in the pool for a good portion of the afternoon. The pool is well shaded by surrounding skyscrapers, and the water is nice and refreshing.

I take it easy for the week at Abu's. He's a great host and a sweet man. As I look out his wall of windows overlooking the skyscrapers and mesmerizing gulf, I contemplate the weeks approaching and the next journey. Greg and I have our next trip planned to meet in Germany. I'm registered to run in the Berlin Marathon, but with my knee injury, that no longer looks possible.

Streak of Luck III

While at Abu's and counting my days before I return to the States, I get a phone call from Greg informing me that we lost our sweet chocolate lab, Java. My heart sinks as he tells me. This is the third streak of bad luck within the month. Java was 15 years old and we raised her since she was a pup. I am horribly sad to hear the news, but I also knew it would eventually come one day.

Greg and I rescued Java as a puppy. She led a very active life yet had a pretty rigid routine. Her life evolved around mealtimes and walks: 6:00 a.m. she was fed; 7:30 a.m. she was walked; 6:00 p.m. she was fed again: 8:00 p.m. she had another walk before bed; and 9:00 p.m. she would look for her big pillow and sleep for the night.

She loved taking road trips, swimming, and running. She trained with me for 5Ks and 10Ks. When she was a pup, I trained her to run alongside my bicycle for our morning routine so I could tire her out for the day. She also loved to hunt squirrels. The squirrels in our yard would taunt and tease her, but she outsmarted a few of them.

One day I was working in the yard and she saw a squirrel starting to run across our fence. She charged the fence and hit it hard enough for the squirrel to lose its balance and fall on our side of the fence to the ground. Java quickly snapped its neck and brought her prized possession in her mouth and laid it down by my feet. She was so proud of herself. Good girl.

We have a house with a pool, and Java was in the pool all day long while we were at work. During the summer, she never seemed to dry off and sometimes it was funny to watch her act like she accidentally fell into the pool.

The life expectancy of most labs is about 10 years and Java was completely blind by then. She was a stubborn dog and determined to be independent as long as she could be. The last year or so, we knew she also suffered from dementia. She couldn't find her way around the house and would get stuck behind the kitchen bar stools and couldn't get out. She knew to bark and we'd come help her.

Then two summers ago, she had a seizure and suffered from Bell's palsy and could not keep her head up straight. Swimming became her worst nightmare. If she fell into the pool, we'd have to fetch her out because she was no longer able to hold her head above water. The morning she died, she got through the pool barrier, fell into the pool, and drowned. Usually we could hear her when she fell into the pool, but that morning Greg didn't hear her at all. He saw her floating, pulled her out, and tried unsuccessfully to revive her. Again, I wish I was at home with Greg to grieve our loss.

She brought so much joy and happiness into our lives. She was like our child. I only wish I could've made it back home just one last time to lie down beside her and hug her, rub her chest, and give her one last kiss on the ear. It's going to feel very different to be greeted by just one dog instead of two.

Ladies of the Night

It's very late at night and the side street of Abu's complex is dimly lit. I see a few women wearing black burqas and they're walking alone, weaving between parked cars and along the sidewalks. They're walking with their heads down so their faces are not seen. They're not together but walking alone. A woman walking alone is not common in the Arab world, especially at night. These are ladies of the night.

As in other cultures, it's not uncommon for men to have a mistress in the Arab world. Mustafa uses Abu's apartment to entertain his mistress. He's married with a couple of kids. One evening Abu and I return to his place after a late dinner to find Mustafa and his mistress sitting on the couch. At first I don't know who she is. I'm thinking she's some relative. She's an attractive woman with a beautiful face. She has heavy eye shadow that glistens and she's wearing long, dangling, silver earrings and a pearl-white necklace that contrasts her black knitted shirt and black *burqa*. I see Mustafa present her with a gift—maybe more jewelry or perfume? She smiles and puts the small, ribboned box in her shoulder bag. When she leaves Abu's apartment, we follow her down in the elevator. As she leaves the building, her long, draped black *burqa* flutters with the evening air and she disappears and blends into the café-noir night, dispersing among the other ladies of the night

Desert Warrior

A 14-minute movie trailer over an anti-Islam film that mocks Islam/ Prophet Muhammad is being aired across the Middle East and North Africa. It's going viral on the internet. The original title of the film is *Desert Warrior*, but it's eventually retitled *Innocence of Muslims*.

Protests are erupting in Egypt. In Benghazi, Libya, a mob of protesters scale the U.S. embassy walls and storm the consulate by force, killing the U.S. ambassador and three other U.S. nationals. It's not certain if the protest that went awry over the film is to blame or if it may have been a terrorist attack on the anniversary date of 9/11. In Pakistan, the chaos spirals out of control as mobs ransack banks, cinemas, and government offices, leaving 15 dead. It's just my luck that these violent protests are taking place as I prepare for my journey back to Bagram.

Bagram is on high alert and the Afghan government is blocking the film. The military is requiring us to don our IBA (individual body armor): a tactical vest and helmet. Military security is beefed up around base, checking IDs on street corners, the sidewalk, the PX, and the DFAC. Military police are turning people back if they're not wearing their IBA. I'm sure they've gathered some intelligence and are monitoring activities outside the base to warrant these actions. What a nice homecoming after being away for six weeks.

Is my knee any better? No, not really. I didn't have the surgery. It's a small tear, but the doc thought it might heal on its own. I have my doubts. It still hurts, but I can run to a bunker if I must. The doc and I can't understand why the company put me on a medical hold, but I'm not going to fight their decision, so I decide to ride out the time.

I notice there have been a lot of changes in the six weeks that I was gone. Surprisingly, this time it's not as much about people as it is about the structures and the environment. Most of the same faces are around. I guess our workforce is stabilizing. We're the diehards. I haven't heard any earth-shattering news or gossip. Everything seems to be low-key.

I notice our New York City-sized sidewalks are all torn up and most of the trees lining Disney Drive have been chopped down to install a new water and sewage system. Farther north on Disney is a whole new compound being built. It looks like a new joint operations center made of sturdy concrete and a few windows. There are new housing units set up all around the area. Closer to Barron Village, several areas have been flattened and the lots have been cleared. Several more new, large buildings are going up. I'm not sure what the buildings will be, but I'm impressed by the metal framework and brick-and-mortar structure. They're obviously being built to last a long time.

The days following my return have been quiet. The fall weather is upon us with cool evenings and refreshing mornings. The afternoons warm up, but not even close to the sizzling heat of Dubai. The days will be getting shorter and the nights longer. I just hope that no incoming breaks the silence for the days and weeks ahead.

Also upon my return, Team Texas is officially done. Randy is leaving the project to return to his hometown of San Antonio. He has a lot of reasons to leave: job offers, new business developments, and his girlfriend and kids. Stella is packing her bags to head back to the States to take a job in the Greenville headquarters office. She wants to be closer to her dad, who is dying of cancer. I'll still be able to stay in contact with her through our interoffice instant messenger and emails. I'm not sure when I'll be running again, with my knee not healed. But I hope one day Team Texas will reunite back in our home state, and maybe we'll go for a run for old times' sake.

Euthanasia

No, euthanasia is not about the youth in Asia. It's about intentionally ending a life at a scheduled place and time to relieve pain and suffering. We do it with our animals when their poor bodies physically give out or when they are in dire pain or suffering, so why not do it for people? We treat our animals better than we do fellow humans.

I'm at the age where I have friends and family watching our aging parents suffer through life with Alzheimer's or a debilitating disease like cancer. Sometimes it's difficult listening to what they are experiencing and going through. Many live the final days, months, or years of their lives bedridden or in pain. They've lost their quality of living and the best thing we can do is make sure they're safe and given the best care we can provide. But the suffering extends to the families socially, emotionally, and financially.

Elderly Americans have the highest suicide rate of any age group, and few of them talk about killing themselves before they do it, at least according to surveys. Some theories attribute elderly suicide rates to illness, pain, and depression. Many elderly people do this by starving themselves to death or by deliberately stopping their medications. Rather than have them go through the grave consequences, why not make euthanasia legal and end the suffering? Dying should not be a crime. I believe Dr. Kevorkian was ahead of his time to illuminate an ideological belief within the euthanasia movement and a freedom of choice. If there's a right to life, then we should also have a right to die—death with dignity!

Currently, the Netherlands, Belgium, and Luxembourg are the only countries to legalize euthanasia. Euthanasia is responsible for about 2 percent of the deaths annually in the Netherlands. Euthanasia in the United States, with its for-profit health-care system, will be a big issue because of economic reasons for the pharmaceutical and medical industries. Euthanasia is illegal in most states of the U.S. Physician aid-in-dying (assisted suicide) is legal in Switzerland and in the U.S. states of Washington, Oregon, and Montana.

If we trust our fellow humans to choose their occupations, significant others, political persuasions, and stances on religion, we should also defend their right to dispose of their most valuable possessions—their lives—even if disposing of life is precisely the choice they make.

I hope to see this effort to change government policies during my lifetime. We need to release the imperative power of logic to push us toward the humanist nirvana of a dignified death by choice, instead of a life of increasing indignity and misery.

Malala

All she wants is to learn and get an education, but on October 9, 2012, a Taliban gunman hunts down teenager Malala Yousafzai of Pakistan on her school bus. The young girl is attracting attention across the globe for blogging on life under Taliban rule and speaking out against the jihadist group's policies toward women's education.

Malala is a symbol of courage, bravery, hope, and inspiration. She's a modern-day Rosa Parks by standing up for her rights with the world behind her, expressing their outrage toward the Taliban. Hopefully this incident will spark some deep soul-searching and reform among the people of Pakistan and their neighboring countries, within Islam, and around the world, where women are often treated as less than human. I share the optimism of a better world for women and a world without repression and violence.

My Balkan Friends

The days are cold, stormy, and wet. The only good thing about winter in Afghanistan is that it seems to deter the Taliban from insurgent attacks. It's been quiet for weeks until this morning. The Taliban has been saving some of their missiles and energy for today.

I arrive at the office at 0530. Shortly after my arrival, around 10 consecutive missiles hit base. They sound close. This morning is the first time on BAF that I've heard this many launched at one time, seconds apart. Later I hear that the missiles did some minimal structural damage and injured a few soldiers, but no civilians.

The next morning I'm getting ready for work when we have a repeat of the day before: missiles launching into the base. Again, around 10 seconds apart and too close for comfort. There's no telling what's going on or if there will be more. My PPE is right by my bed. As instructed in safety awareness classes, I don my PPE and hit the floor—arms along my body and legs close together to protect my organs and main blood vessels from shrapnel.

We get the all clear but remain on high security alert. We're instructed to continue to don our PPE when outdoors going from point A to point B. As I head to the office, I see my Balkan friends standing in the smoke pit, having their morning cigarettes and coffee. I grab a cup of coffee and join them, and we talk about the morning's incident. My good Balkan friend, Arian, has an office just around the corner from mine. Shortly after Stella departed for Greenville, our department moved offices to bigger and better. I love the new office design. It's the most room we've had per employee since I've been here.

Since Stella left, I've been hanging out with Arian a lot. Instead of a morning smoothie with Stella, I drink copious amounts of coffee with Arian. He's a supervisor for the audit and compliance department and a really smart guy. When I first met him, I thought he was American because he spoke English so well—better than most other Americans on base. Because of his position as an auditor, he reminds me of a prison warden or a high school hall monitor checking students for bathroom passes and making sure they're not cutting class. His job is to ensure that rules are being followed and that the U.S. government is not being defrauded. I dub him "The Warden."

The Warden sees me coming back from the DFAC. Most days, as usual, I take a few extra items than what we're allowed. The Warden knows this because he's observed me filling my pockets. He follows me back to my office to see how many items I'm going to unload from my winter jacket. It's become a challenge to see how many items I can bring back. I pull out a handful of sugars packets, two handfuls of creamers, a few cans of soda, some yogurts, soy milks, juices, fruit . . . and he always tells me facetiously, *"You HR people are always breaking the rules. You lead by example."* I laugh at him and tell him to be quiet and enjoy a nice cup of coffee loaded with the sugar and cream that I just took from the DFAC. I tell him it would be rude if he came to my office and I had nothing to offer him. We laugh.

When I see Arian, I always say, *"Hello, my Balkan friend."* And he replies, *"Hello, my American friend."* After we make our connection, I walk into his office area and say, *"Hello, my Balkan friends,"* addressing half of his team, who are mostly from Bosnia and Kosovo. Here in Afghanistan, your coworkers become family. We spend so much time working together, eating together, working out together, and watching movies together. We congregate for morning and midafternoon klatches and share teas, coffees, and chocolates. Arian's family owns a tea manufacturing company and he's always down to share some good teas with me.

His coworker, Dragan, is from Bosnia. He's also the office barista and he always offers me a cup of coffee when I come into their domain. Dragan sees Arian and me exchanging coffee and teas all the time. One day Dragan asks me why I never bring anything for him. I know he doesn't like American coffee. He likes his Turkish coffee strong and thick enough to stand a spoon in. I remind him of that and he claims he's just a poor little Bosnian always being neglected. *"You know what, I'm going to start calling you 'LB' . . . short for 'Little Bosnian,'"* I tell him. Everyone in the office calls him that now.

After one cup of coffee, Arian says, *"Shaky, shaky?"* He knows my hands are a little shaky after the fuel-injected cup of mud that Dragan just served us. I don't see how these guys can drink the stuff nonstop all day long, but they do.

I enjoy hanging out with the guys from Kosovo and Bosnia. Most of the time they are jovial and make it a good time. They have a social element in their culture that seems to be lacking among the Americans around here. The Americans always seem so serious, always talking about work or bitching about someone or something. As for my Balkan friends and me, we just like to hang out for 10 or 15 minutes, drink our coffee, and shoot the shit with one another.

Drama Momma

Word on the street is that Motormouth's running of the mouth has finally gotten him in trouble.

Debra and Karen are corporate managers from the Greenville headquarters office, and they came over at the same time last August. They're both in their late fifties, a little overweight, and they always dress professionally—even in a war zone. They seem to be the breadwinners in their relationships, and it sounds like they're both running from their lousy marriages back home.

Debra is the friendlier of the two. I can't pinpoint it, but Karen puts off some bad energy. Ah hell, she's a bitch. I'm not sure if it's the stress, her marriage, or being in Afghanistan, but her aura seems to be heavily weighed down with a lot of personal baggage. Being near her makes me feel uncomfortable. I'm not going to be her friend. I have to do business with her and keep it at a professional level only. She's also Debra's boss.

Motormouth Mark knows how to attract the attention of most women. He's in his fifties, pretty good-looking and fit for his age, and quite the talker and schmoozer. He's always complimenting Debra and Karen on their long, gorgeous hair and their clothes, jewelry, and perfumes. I guess neither lady gets compliments from her husband back home, because the three of them act like a bunch of high school kids.

Motormouth, Debra, and Karen are hanging out together quite a bit lately. The three of them go to breakfast and lunch, and they take evening walks together. Debra has dropped some weight and is looking more and more attractive to Mark. I hear him talk about it the office, but he tells her that he won't date a married woman. That appears to be the final straw for Debra to push forward with a divorce—and she does.

Motormouth and Debra are a couple. They always claim to be just friends, but it's an easy facade to see past. Since I'm Motormouth's boss, I'm informed by human resources that he's been in Debra's room and seen in the hallway by other female occupants. He's also been heard talking and laughing in her room after 2200, which is during our "lights out" policy. He's breaking the rule twofold. When I hear this, I remind Motormouth of the rules and to be careful of what he's doing. Of course he denies the allegations. I can't believe I have to address this issue, but I must. I don't want to be in the middle of their love affair.

Debra swings by the office to get Motormouth to go to breakfast and lunch every day. She jumps at every possible opportunity to engage him in helping her with something or stopping by her office. He's the man. He can fix things and drive nails into the wall, and he lifts and moves heavy objects. Her appearance in our office becomes intrusive. She always seems to have a training inquiry for which she thinks Juliet Alpha or I will have an answer. I think she's really checking up on Motormouth to make sure he's in the office and not flirting with another woman.

Their friendship seems to become more involved and enigmatic. If they aren't together, they seem to be spending a lot of time texting and chatting. He'll receive a text message and minutes later I'll see him and Debra outside together. When he plans his R&R break, Debra's R&R dates are the same. It's more than just a friendship; they're inseparable, but I think she has more feelings toward Mark than he does toward her.

Eventually Motormouth confesses to me that their relationship is one-sided and that he really isn't interested in her intimately. I can see that she's always doing more for him than he does for her. It's no secret in the office that Motormouth has multiple friendships with women. I don't know how in-depth or to what extent, but he's a womanizer.

One time, after I left Afghanistan and Dubai to go home for a break, I ran into the two of them in the Atlanta airport. They told me then that they were headed in different directions. Motormouth was heading to Texas and Debra was going to South Carolina. I observed that their next few R&Rs had the same flight plans. Both always insisted that they were heading in different directions on their R&Rs and just happened to be leaving at the same time. Yeah, right.

Motormouth tells me that he'll book his flight and then Debra finds out and books the same one for the same date and time. She always wants to know where he is, whom he's with, what he's thinking, and where he's going. She's obsessed with him—stalking him.

Karen comes to my office and informs me that Debra is spending way too much time at my office with Motormouth and vice versa. Most of their time is not work related. She goes on to tell me that Debra's work performance is declining and that she is not setting a good example for her staff.

Perception is everything when you work and live together. The person you're working with may be your best friend but can turn on you at a moment's notice. I've seen this happen over and over on this project. Debra and Karen came over to Afghanistan together and were pretty good friends when they arrived, but now both their friendship and their work relationship are really starting to suffer. Drama.

Over time Karen becomes very distant. Debra has lost weight, she's friendlier and more outgoing, she's ended her unhappy marriage, and she now has something going on with Motormouth. Karen sulks over all of this. She puts on more weight and becomes moodier, unhappier, and bitchier.

Karen's jealousy reaches a high and she eventually manages to get both Debra and Motormouth terminated. I hear rumors that Motormouth threatened her, and that sparked the investigation on him. She must've spilled her guts to management and investigators because the ground for termination is not related to a threat. So they dig deeper and the investigation is extended another week.

IT runs stats and reports on computer use within our department. Motormouth is off the scale when it comes to the number of hits on non-work-related sites. I try to defend his position because we do a lot of research on various topics and sites. I know he's a news buff, and those sites refresh and ping up new ads and articles all the time.

Debra and Motormouth are scheduled to leave Bagram on or after Christmas Day. They'll be back home in the United States for the New Year. Motormouth will go to Texas, and Debra to South Carolina supposedly. I'm ambivalent about seeing them go. Motormouth was just dragged into a vicious love triangle, so it's sad to see it work out this way. The other part of me is glad to see the two go. Finally, the end of the gossip and drama.

Debra is terminated from the project but not the company. Shortly after their departure, Debra contacts me to tell me she has a couple of prospects for jobs on other projects within the company. She's trying to get Motormouth on with the company too. She asks me to write a reference letter for him, but I tell her that he's a big boy and if he needs a reference, he can ask me directly for it. I've still never heard from him.

Eventually Debra takes a job on another project in Texas only 45 minutes from Motormouth's hometown. She rents an apartment there. Motormouth always claimed not to have had an intimate relationship with her on the job, but circumstantial evidence is looking otherwise. She's a stalker.

As the story develops and unfolds, she needs to be in constant contact with Motormouth whether it's in person or by email, text, or phone; she follows him back to his hometown to work nearby; she buys him gifts and flips the bill; and he probably won't let go of her. It's a fatal attraction . . . just like the movie.

Prison Break

A few of my fellow colleagues managed to break away from this prison for good. One of my data cell employees, Jeton, decided to go home on R&R and has chosen not to come back. I don't blame him. He's young and probably homesick. He's put in his time here.

My running companion and good friend, Dr. K, left the project about six months ago to be home with his wife and five kids. Family is very important to him and a high priority. He put in his time here and it was time to be together as a father and husband. We correspond through email and Facebook.

Back home, Kamal ended his relationship with Greg. It's back to just the two of us—but the three of us was fun while it lasted.

2013

Surviving Bagram

Death hits in many forms. Combat casualty stories are the worst, but we also hear about other forms of death. Word on the street is that a young athletic man didn't report to work this morning. Security was notified and entered his room to find him stiff and cold. The young bodybuilder's death is being ruled an accidental overdose from steroids. Steroids are illegal and prohibited on base but accessible from the outside. And if the drugs are being brought in from the outside—usually by the locals—it's usually in their anal cavities.

This will be a challenging year ahead. The military has changed our scope of work and will be transitioning some of the bases over to the local Afghanistan Army. In some cases they'll just close the bases. Our timeline is to significantly reduce the number of bases we're servicing and maintaining. As the primary contractor, we peaked at 85 bases in Northern Afghanistan and we're told to reduce our footprint down to about 20 by the end of the year.

My team consisted of 10 during the height of our scope of work. I'm down to five. Besides losing Motormouth and Jeton recently, I also had to let go of our stateside computer programmer who put everything into web format and programmed our library of computer-based trainings onto the company portal. I'm not authorized to replace any open positions. We're reducing staff and the team now is Juliet Alpha, Agim, Regala, AJ, and me. Finally, the five of us share one office space. It only took nearly four years to accomplish that. But the five of us will soon be four, then three, and so on until we're all gone.

As our team works together, Juliet Alpha needs someone to pick on and smudge her finger against. Now her target is Agim. She's very good about sneaking behind my back to do her malicious work. Agim brings this to my attention. He points out that she has always had to have someone to pick on: Harvey, Sharon, Bunkerhead, Tina, Jason—I'm not sure what her problem is. Is this the objective of a mole?

I have high respect for Agim. After a conversation I have with him about Juliet Alpha and her behavior, I immediately walk over to talk to the HR manager. He gladly accepts my unscheduled interruption to talk about what's on my mind. I lay out the scenario and tell him the only way to stop this chaos is to send Juliet Alpha home or assign her to an office by herself without windows. For some reason, she's untouchable. The company will not terminate her no matter how many complaints are filed against her to HR. Alfred knows how she is and immediately assigns her a "special projects" role in her own office with no windows. My team is saved and we're down to four.

Arian gets wind of Juliet Alpha's move because now she's almost next to his office. I tell him what transpired and what I did. He says, *"Man, you should get a huge bonus for putting up with that Pit Bull. Nobody can tolerate her . . . and you worked the longest with her. You need a raise, man!"* It's true. Nobody else has worked with Juliet Alpha for more than a year. I had a few years with her and the longest tenure. I should get a bonus, goddammit! I love the woman on a personal level, but from a career standpoint, she's a major roadblock—she stirs up shit and creates havoc.

Mona Lee Cartwright is still hanging around. Her room is practically across from my office. She stops in to visit me frequently. We reminisce about home in Texas and she fills me in on the latest gossip and word on the street. I can usually hear her voice or distinct laugh outside when she's talking to people in passing. I enjoy her company.

Over the course of the past three and a half years, I've seen the base go from something new and exciting to looking like a trailer park. Now it just feels like an oppressive, enclosed prison. This environment is not for everyone. In fact, it takes a certain personality. I hear conversations of people stating there are more type A personalities here. That may be true, but I'm more type B. I've adapted to the many and constant changes that are common in this environment. I've always welcomed change and I thrive more in these types of surroundings. I'm less focused on competitiveness and more on enjoying the journey. That journey continues.

The Lottery

Word on the street is that the flight is delayed for leaving Bagram today. Not only do I anticipate the delay, but I expect it. The weather is always unpredictable leaving base. In the summer months it can be dust storms or high heat. In the winter months it's the freezing rain or snow. Some flights are grounded due to military operations, mechanical problems, or unavailable plane space. Plus there's only one flight per day. On occasion, if the flights are too backed up, Air Operations arranges to have a second plane or a second flight. I've learned to give myself a few extra days in Dubai to catch a connecting flight. Today's delay is for several hours and we'll arrive in Dubai after dark.

I love Dubai! There are so many wonderful restaurants and hotels. I love the modern and innovative architecture and engineering wonders. It has some amazing, futuristic mega-projects, like the only seven-star hotel in the world, the tallest building in the world, the largest mall in the world, the largest manmade marina, the largest dancing water fountain with almost 7,000 lights that can be seen 20 miles away—Dubai is luxury and opulence. So after working 12-hour shifts seven days a week for 90 days, Dubai is a paradise. Of course, poor people need to live somewhere, so there are all sorts of places and accommodations to fit most budgets—even in Dubai. But this amazing city is known for luxury nonetheless.

As the plane descends into the city, I swap out my phone's SIM card, from service in Afghanistan to Dubai. As we approach the landing and I gain phone reception, it starts to go off like a winning slot machine. I feel like I've just won the jackpot. I'm being pinged and dinged by a menu of Arab men. For such a homophobic society, they have plenty of men seeking other men. And hell, not just Arab men but men from all over the world. Though I'm open to many different walks of life, nationalities, and types of guys, I do lean more toward men of the Arab persuasion. So with all these options, I'm like a kid in a candy store, going through all the profiles and pictures. Pick and choose. Who's going to be lucky tonight? One, two, maybe three of them.

I have a couple of favorites I've seen repeatedly over the years. One of them is Ali. He's another Iraqi and a doctor. He's toned, clean-shaven, and dapper. He lives on an upper floor in one of the towers in the Marina District. It's a corner unit with a wall of glass doors looking out over the incredible skyline that reflects light and colors onto his white marble floors. Beyond the glass doors is a massive balcony to take in the views.

I always make it a special point to bring a bottle of vodka from Duty Free to Ali. Bulk alcohol is not available in Dubai. It's only sold by the drink in hotels and certain restaurants. After I enter his apartment, he closes the door behind me, wraps his arms around my hips, and gives me a kiss. I offer the bottle of vodka to him and he sets it next to his huge display of liquor bottles on his kitchen island. Ali likes to entertain and he likes to drink. He fixes us each vodka and tonic, and we walk out onto his balcony. I feel like we're so high in the sky that I can reach out and touch the stars. We drink, we talk, we smile, and we laugh as the sky changes color from the neon lights reflecting among us.

Ali and I spend a few hours together. Since the nightlife in Dubai starts around midnight, he usually has plans to go out to meet other friends. This trip will be the last time I see him. He's moving to London.

Another one of my favorites is Mahmoud. He's Syrian and he speaks English with a British accent. We usually arrange an afternoon rendezvous, as it's easy for him to break away from work. He's always very courteous with a high standard for hygiene. When he arrives to my hotel room, he always asks to use the shower. Sometimes I join him. Other times he's picked me up and the two of us have gone to another guy's hotel for a three-way. He's certainly a lot of fun.

I recall speaking with another Arab man about being gay in a Muslim country. He had an interesting perspective that I never heard before. He told me that homosexuality is only a sin if you are married and made it sound as though many men played with men during their adolescence or before marriage. Perhaps it is that way in a gender separated society. I really don't know, but found that to be rather interesting.

On this trip I take a stroll along the boardwalk of the Marina that stretches for seven or eight kilometers (almost five miles). Fortunately it's early February and the outside temperatures are moderate, so it feels great to be out here walking. The Marina area consists of a series of interconnected channels that feed into the Persian Gulf. Area towers and condo high-rises keep it well shaded from the blistering-hot sun during the summer. There's an abundance of shops and good restaurants on the street level. On one side of the boardwalk are the residences and businesses, and the other side is the water. Tremendous, elegant yachts line the canals and the bright neon lights reflect on the ripples of the water at night. It's easy to take in so much of the beauty and fun that people watch along the Marina Walk. The thriving businesses and high occupancy among tenants are evidence of the master plan. I spend the afternoon walking the Marina Walk to Jumeirah Beach.

It's early evening and the sun won't go down for another hour or two. I decide to head back to my hotel for a rest. I walk toward the nearest metro stop, Jumeirah Lakes Towers. The metro in Dubai is a monorail system and I love it. It's incredibly clean and no food or drinks are allowed on the transit. It's super quiet and stops at some incredible landmarks in Dubai.

As I walk toward the Jumeirah Lakes Towers tram station, a sapphire-blue Mercedes-AMG GT pulls up next to me on the sidewalk. The horn toots at me, and the passenger window rolls down. I look in at the driver, but I'm not sure who it is. As I take a closer look, the passenger car door pops open. All I see is an Arab man in his starched *thobe* wearing a black-and-white checkered *keffiyeh* and an *ogal*. I recognize his regal appearance. He pulls down his gold-framed aviator sunglasses and I see those mesmerizing honeysuckle eyes. It's Sheikh Samir.

He tells me, *"Get in."* I obey his order and off into the falling turquoise sky we drive.

The General

Out with the old and in with the new! Word on the street is that a four-star retired general is replacing our project manager, Mr. Burns. I am also told that Mr. Burns's departure is nonvoluntary. He's being asked to leave by the military brass. As soon as "The General" arrives, Mr. Burns takes off so quickly that I only see a trail of dust from the vehicle driving him to catch the next plane out of here.

The General is a short, staunch man—maybe all of 5'4"—with a round little belly. He reminds me of Danny DeVito. Thankfully The General's character is friendly and outgoing. He makes his morning rounds, shakes hands, and stops and talks to people. He's the complete opposite of his predecessor. Within a week or so, he knows just about everyone in the main headquarters buildings. I like the change and The General already.

$70,000 Check

Word on the street is one of our employees needs to be medevaced for a life-threatening condition. Apparently, she went to Thailand for her last R&R and had some cosmetic surgery—breast implants and a tummy tuck. The wounds became highly infected and she was first brought to the military hospital on base. The military made Mean Gene write a check for $70,000 to have her airlifted off base to Dubai. When she heels and gets through this, she'll lose her job because any kind of surgery while working on a military base must be reported. Hers was not.

More shit going on:

Louie Risotto is getting ready to leave for R&R and he's camped out in our office. He has a Japanese wife, and they have a home and a child in Japan. The stories he tells me about his wife are unbelievable. They met in the U.S. during his last R&R so he could withdraw a large sum of money to hand-carry back to Japan. He says the amount was $250,000 and they had to have special documentation from the bank to take that amount of money out of the country. I thought that's what wire transfers were for.

Today he's heading back to the U.S. for his R&R because his wife doesn't want him to visit or come home. What? The man just gave her $250,000 in cash to carry back to Japan and now she doesn't want him to come home? Love comes in many strange forms. She must be a total control freak. I can barely stand Risotto hanging out around the office for a few hours, so I can't imagine living with him.

Motormouth used to mention another guy—another Frank—and talk about his mail-order bride. Listening to Motormouth tell the story was quite funny: *"Frank shows me a picture of this beautiful woman from the Ukraine and tells me he's going to marry her. I look at the picture of this woman who looks like she could be a model. I hold it up, look at Frank, and think something can't be right. I hate to sound mean, but Frank is butt ugly. There's just no way in hell this woman is going to marry this butt-ugly man."*

Frank meets this pretty woman online through some Ukraine dating service. Most guys know these are fraudulent sites and scams, but not gullible Frank. Frank pursues his dreams with this lovely woman. He flies to the Ukraine, they meet, and they fall in love.

When Frank's next R&R is scheduled, she calls him to tell him not to come because her mother is sick and she must take care of her. Her medical expenses are in the thousands of dollars. She asks for money, so Frank sends her $2,000. Next R&R, the mother has taken a turn for the worse and his future bride isn't sure she's going to pull through. *"Don't come. Can you send some money?"* she says. Frank still has hope and is clueless to what's going on.

Frank decides to take matters into his own hands. He flies to the Ukraine and shows up at this girl's apartment unannounced. Her husband answers the door and beats the living shit out of Frank. He's hospitalized. Motormouth knows this because he was working in HR at the time. He knows the whole story and how the company had to get involved with the medical insurance.

Frank isn't the only one to fall for the marriage scam. There are a whole slew of men over here who have fallen for Thai or Filipino wives. Some of the relationships are legit, but most of them are just arrangements. Thai women know these men are contractors and make good money, so they play the good housewife part when they come around on R&R. Many will marry, but soon after a house is paid for in cash in Thailand, the marriages dissolve. Under Thai law, the woman who has birthrights in Thailand ends up with the property.

The Fruit-Bowl Challenge

While most offices have a bowl of chocolate or candy, our office has a fruit bowl. We eat healthy! I turned Regala onto smoothies a couple months ago and now she's hooked. I usually whip up one or two a day with a dose of protein powder for pre- and post-workouts. Regala joins me with a midmorning smoothie just because they're so refreshing and healthy. We have also taken on the fruit-bowl challenge.

Because we go through an enormous amount of fruit every day, we try to keep the fruit bowl full. And where do we get our fruit and yogurt to make our smoothies? From the DFAC, of course. And how many items are we allowed to take out of the DFAC? As always, only two. Well two is not enough. Most people don't snack on fruit, so I don't think it's a big deal to take a few extra pieces. Arian is sure to remind us of this and point it out at every opportunity he gets.

Every morning I go to the DFAC, I order my usual egg-white omelet and bring back several pieces of fruit. Regala follows suit and even gets Agim to bring back a few pieces for us occasionally. With each passing day, the number of pieces of fruit becomes a challenge. I come into the office with my proud four or five pieces of fruit and a few small containers of yogurt. But Regala takes it to the next level and comes back with a grocery sack full of fruit. She gets extra bonus points for her snatching of special fruits like strawberries or raspberries. I think she has a special connection to the kitchen refrigerator.

One day Regala comes back to the office excited and barely able to keep her composure because she's scored so big. She enters the office with a serving tray of fruit: 21 pieces of fruit! And she doesn't stop there. She starts to empty her pockets, pulling out containers of yogurts and boxes of juices. I ask her how she managed to walk out of the DFAC with a tray full of fruit. She reenacts her performance for me. She says, *"I put all the fruit on my cardboard tray and placed another tray on top of that. Then I walked toward the exit like I was going to throw away the trays . . . but I just walked out the door."* And just outside the door one of her friends had been waiting in a pickup truck. The getaway car.

I'm sure from her beautiful good looks that any soldier policing the takeout policy was checking out her body and pretty face, and not paying attention to what she was carrying. Score!

Pet Peeve

Agim's office chair is practically in the middle of the room. Every time he gets up he lets his chair glide halfway across the room and leaves it there instead of pushing it back under his desk. Our office is pretty tight quarters and sometimes his chair bangs into the back of mine. That doesn't seem to bother him, but it's my pet peeve!

Agim comes prancing back into the office after a jaunt to the bathroom. Before he stops and grabs his chair, I say, *"Ajeti, I have a pet peeve with you!"* He responds quizzically, *"Pet peeve? What is a pet peeve?"* Regala—who is sitting at her desk close by—turns toward me to learn about this new American phrase that is foreign to their Balkan ears.

I tell Agim that a pet peeve is something that a person finds particularly annoying, like people cutting their fingernails at work or chewing gum loudly, or people who don't silence their smartphones when playing video games in public.

"Do you understand?" I ask. *"Totally,"* he replies. *"Good,"* I respond back and continue, *"my pet peeve is when you leave your chair in the middle of the room and you don't push it back under your desk."* Agim replies, *"Well I'm used to my wife picking up after me and doing those things for me."*

Regala pipes up, *"Yes, she waits on him hand and foot. He thinks that's a woman's job. He's worse than a child."* Agim knows he's pushed some buttons with Regala, so he adds, *"It IS a woman's job. My wife loves to wait on me hand and foot, as she should. She loves to clean and whenever she's vacuuming, I just lift my legs up from the couch and let her vacuum under my feet."*

I know exactly where this conversation is going, as I've had many with this young male chauvinist, so I quickly add, *"Well your wife doesn't work here and she's not here to clean up after you. You're going to have to do it yourself and do more around here to show some respect to your coworkers. I expect your desk to be clean at the end of every day, and I'm going to create a daily cleaning schedule to sweep and mop our office floors daily. I'm tired of doing it myself, so I'm going to have everyone pitch in."*

Regala has a half smile on her face and a squint in her eyes. Agim catches this too and barks, *"But that's a woman's job!"* I snap back, *"That comment just put you on the cleaning schedule for the first seven days!"* Regala blurts out a laugh, as she knows I chalked one up for the girls' team.

Agim replies, *"C'mon, Josef!"* I warn him not to say any more or I'll find plenty for him to clean and organize around here and I'll turn up my EDM loudly in the office, which he despises.

Then he smiles at us with half a laugh and agrees to the cleaning schedule. His level of cleaning is pretty low, so I tell him I'll be walking through the office with a white glove to inspect. Regala continues to laugh, as she knows I will and she'll be glad to assist.

Agim leaves for lunch and Regala quietly gets up to clean the office whiteboard. She starts to write line item after line item on the clean slate. I ask her what she's doing. She replies, *"I'm writing down my list of pet peeves for Agim."* I smile at her actions. Man, she's a quick learner! I quickly look it over: biting his nails . . . touching other people's computer screens when explaining something . . . not closing computer files when he's done with them . . . not responding to work emails in a timely manner . . . not putting things back where they belong . . . never taking out the trash . . . using counter space like it's a communal meeting room—she has a list of 10 items. I read each one out loud and we burst into laughter.

The next morning, I have to show Agim how to properly sweep and mop. I don't think the guy has ever cleaned his room or house in his life. I even take some pictures to send to his wife back in Kosovo. It's time he needs to start pitching in—enough with classifying duties by gender. Regala and I go grab a cup of coffee while Agim finishes up and lets the floor dry. When we get back to the office, I hand a pair of elastic gloves over to Regala and ask her, *"Shall we inspect?"* She blurts out her contagious laugh and we laugh together. She's having some fun with this and enjoying it very much. Agim did a good job. Of course, if he didn't, he would be on the cleaning schedule until he got it right.

Harper Valley P.T.A.

I have thousands of songs downloaded on my iPod. Agim likes some of the folk music that I have and the country and western genre. He tells me he likes that style of music because he can understand the lyrics. He listens to music from his native land and shares some of it with me. I don't care for it. It sounds rather amateur and rough. He describes the music and how many of the various groups are older men. *Old man* in Albanian is *plako*. I tell him I don't care for his *plako* music. Then he starts calling me *plako*.

He sings along to Jeannie C. Riley's "Harper Valley P.T.A.": *"I wanna tell you all a story 'bout a Harper Valley widowed wife . . ."*

As Agim is singing along to the lyrics, I ask him, *"Agim, do you know what a P.T.A. is?"* He smiles and says, *"No. What is a P.T.A.?"* I tell him a P.T.A. is a parent-teacher association and elaborate a little more about what they do to advocate education and the well-being of children. He nods his head.

He continues to sing along and he whips out another part of a verse: *"Well this is just a little Peyton Place, and you're all Harper Valley hypocrites."* Then it dawns on me that he probably doesn't know what a Peyton Place is, so I ask him. No, he doesn't know. So I explain that a Peyton Place is based on a 1950s novel and TV show of the same name, used to mean a small town or a group with scandalous gossip and secrets. He catches on quickly and responds with a smile on his face, *"You mean kind of like here?"* Exactly!

Agim says, *"Well now that song makes a lot more sense to me knowing that."* He follows up with a question to me, *"Do you know what my favorite part of that song is?"* "No, what?" I ask. He sings, *"When Mrs. Johnson wore her mini-skirt into the room . . . and the day my momma socked it to . . . the Harper Valley P.T.A."* Of course, he knows what a mini skirt is!

When I leave the office for the day, Agim says, *"Shimi plako"*—see ya later, old man. He says it every night as I walk out the door. He tells all of his Balkan friends, so when they see me, they all call me *plako* now. It's an Albanian phrase I will never forget.

O Mire Dite, Ardi! (Tell Us, Ardi!)

The phone rings just about every day at 1600 with a 513 area code. That's the area code from Agim's home using a magicJack. A magicJack allows the other country nationals to call our U.S. phone numbers free of charge. It's usually his 10-year-old son, Ardi, so all of us in the office gather around to listen. He's just learning English, so when I answer the phone, I put him on speakerphone so his dad and Regala can test his English skills.

After working and living in an adult-only environment, it's quite pleasant and charming to hear a young boy's voice over the phone.

When I answer the phone I speak slowly and clearly for the young student. Ardi asks, *"Can I speak to Agim Ajeti please?"* He says it so clearly that I would've guessed that his English proficiency is much higher than it actually is. I reply, *"Yes, Mr. Ajeti is here. May I ask who is calling?"* Ardi replies respectfully, *"This is his son, Ardi."* I continue, *"Oh, Ardi, how are you? This is your dad's boss."* He responds, *"Can I speak to my dad?"* He doesn't know that his dad is listening and that we have him on speakerphone. I ask Ardi another question, *"Ardi, how old are you?"* He says, *"I am 10, but can I speak with my dad?"* So far, so good. I know he really wants to speak to his dad, but I ask him another question, *"Ardi, do you know my name?"* He says he doesn't, so I tell him, *"My name is Mr. Thomas. What is your last name?"* He doesn't understand and starts seeming frustrated. *"I don't understand. Can I speak with my dad?"* he asks once more. I finally give up and let the little guy speak to his dad.

Don't Ask, Don't Tell

I see the first OutServe flyer above the handwashing sinks in the DFAC. I am noticing them more and more around base at the rally areas. OutServe is a meet-up group of gays and lesbians in the military. I praise the people who have taken a stand in the military to end the "Don't Ask, Don't Tell" ban and educate and advocate equality.

I mention this to Max, and of course—not surprisingly—he already scoped out the group a few weeks ago. We agree to investigate it further together and walk by the Green Beans Coffee shop where they're meeting tonight. Max and I nonchalantly walk by a long table of what is obviously the group. Most of them are women, and the few guys who are attending look like new recruits. We pass on attending the meeting, but we're glad these young comrades are joining forces to be heard and seen.

The ban on "Don't Ask, Don't Tell" was lifted on September 20, 2011. Gay service members said they felt relief that they no longer lived secret lives. Pentagon officials have since said that recruiting, retention, and overall morale have not been affected since the change. None of the dire predictions of opponents, including warnings of a mass exodus of active-duty troops, occurred.

The U.S. is seen as a world leader, but not so much when it comes to the topic of human rights or equality for gays and lesbians. Why is there so much resistance in the U.S. to address the issues in an intelligent, diplomatic way? Marriage equality idles steadily at the forefront of U.S. politics. What does love mean if we deny it to others? Love has no gender. I wonder at what point the people fighting to protect "traditional marriage" between a woman and a man will realize that traditional married couples haven't exactly been doing a good job at it. That's why the U.S. divorce rate hovers around 50 percent. I grew up and around many broken households due to divorce and the single-parent syndrome.

Other countries—like Germany, the Netherlands, Finland, and Canada—allowed same-sex marriage nearly a decade or more before the U.S. Even Mexico and Ecuador signed same-sex-marriage bills into law long before us. I wish the U.S. would take a better stance in leadership.

With same-sex marriage in debate, one of the most beautiful speeches that I've heard and read is from the Spanish prime minister nearly a decade before the U.S. acted. His speech comes from the heart of humanity and is eloquently worded. I'm glad this is shared with the world:

> *"We are not legislating, honorable members, for people far away and not known by us. We are enlarging the opportunity for happiness to our neighbors, our co-workers, our friends and, our families: at the same time, we are making a more decent society because a decent society is one that does not humiliate its members.*

"Today, the Spanish society answers to a group of people who, during many years have been humiliated, whose rights have been ignored, whose dignity has been offended, their identity denied, and their liberty oppressed. Today the Spanish society grants them the respect they deserve, recognizes their rights, restores their dignity, affirms their identity, and restores their liberty.

"It is true that they are only a minority, but their triumph is everyone's triumph. It is also the triumph of those who oppose this law, even though they do not know this yet: because it is the triumph of liberty. Their victory makes all of us (even those who oppose the law) better people, it makes our society better. Honorable members, there is no damage to marriage or to the concept of family in allowing two people of the same sex to get married. To the contrary, what happens is this class of Spanish citizens gets the potential to organize their lives with the rights and privileges of marriage and family. There is no danger to the institution of marriage, but precisely the opposite: this law enhances and respects marriage.

"Today, conscious that some people and institutions are in a profound disagreement with this change in our civil law, I wish to express that, like other reforms to the marriage code that preceded this one, this law will generate no evil, that its only consequence will be the avoiding of senseless suffering of decent human beings. A society that avoids senseless suffering of decent human beings is a better society.

"With the approval of this bill, our country takes another step in the path of liberty and tolerance that was begun by the democratic change of government. Our children will look at us incredulously if we tell them that many years ago, our mothers had less rights than our fathers, or if we tell them that people had to stay married against their will even though they were unable to share their lives. Today we can offer them a beautiful lesson: every right gained,

each access to liberty has been the result of the struggle and sacrifice of many people that deserve our recognition and praise."

—Spanish Prime Minister José Luis Rodríguez Zapatero

July 1, 2005

This is leadership—bringing hope and unity to all people.

50 Shades of Gay

Ben Dover, Slut Whisperer, Hole Puncher, Hot Poker . . . these are just a few of the profile names that I see on the smartphone apps. Men are pigs. Do they truly seek out their deepest, darkest sexual desires? What's so dark about them if it's an instinct? Alfred Kinsey said, *"The only unnatural sex act is that which you cannot perform."*

It's late. Usually I'm in bed at this hour, but after my typical day of work, then workout, I'm hungry so I head to the DFAC for a bite to eat. I'm not tired and I wander around my room before I head to the shower. My usual shower room is temporarily closed for maintenance, so I head over to the double-decker connexes with three cells of showers.

I notice there's someone in a shower and the curtain is partially open. I must investigate. As I take the shower stall across from that one, I glance at the young man showering. He's lean and toned with white pearl skin that glistens from the water. His frame looks like he's a runner or messenger, and he has a beautiful bubble butt. Our eyes connect and lock. As I put my towel on the shower hook, I turn around to take a second look. His deep, sensual eyes are sending me a telepathic message. As they fasten with mine, his eyes follow my hand and I slowly rub my hairy chest down to my groin. I stroke my cock a few times to send him the message that it's his if he wants it.

I enter the shower and leave the curtain half open as another gesture of interest. He enters my stall, closes the curtain, and positions his body up against the wall with his arms raised and his legs spread as though he's expecting to be frisked. I slip both of my arms underneath his armpits and lock my hands behind his neck, pushing his head forward against his chest. He squirms and lets out a muffled moan of pleasure as I lick on his earlobe. My warm breath and moist lips make a trail from his ear to the middle of his neck as I lean in closer to his body. My hairy chest is pressed tightly against his lean, hairless back.

I release one of my arms to reach around to his front side and with a feathered touch, I run my fingertips down his chest and stomach, and grab his cock with a firm grip, stroking and tugging it a few times. I bounce his balls lightly. He's hard as a rock.

I massage the head of his cock until it feels like it's ready to explode. I know he wants to blow a load, but I'm not ready. I back off a bit and tease him to let him know I'm just starting to warm him up and won't let him ejaculate.

He has a sweet white puree dripping from his spout. I wipe it with my fingers and feed it to his nourishing lips, rubbing it across his gums. I remove my finger from his mouth and position my face at the crack of his ass. I spread his cheeks and spit. I know what he wants. He wants to feel me deep inside of him.

Eventually I swirl the head of my cock in his back door as I unhinge it and ease my way in slowly. I park in him and he sighs a moment to relax and embrace my manhood. I gradually pick up the tempo, faster and deeper. We are being blessed with the warm sprinkling of water that trickles down our bodies and between us, creating a rhythmic, slushy sound as our bare skin rubs and slaps together. He murmurs with pleasure and I quickly cover his mouth with my hand. His moans and groans are deeper and louder, and I press harder onto his mouth to muffle his sound. I feel the growls pulsating in his throat.

As I cover his mouth with one hand, I work his cock with the other. He jerks off onto my hands and the shower wall, and I quickly switch hands to continue covering his mouth. I smear his cum on his face and lips. He wants to pull away, but I don't let him. I want him to feel and remember me from this night and into the day with a soreness of passion and lust that he highly craves.

When I am done with him, he steps back over to his stall to quickly soap up and rinse off his body. No words are exchanged and he exits the shower cell for the night.

A few days later, I see the boy during lunch at the dining hall. I catch a quick glance of him in uniform, looking at me, and he immediately looks downward to avert my gaze. I watch where he sits and after he finishes his lunch, I follow him out the door. He walks through a maze of B-huts, and when I get close to him and nobody else is around, I say, *"Did you enjoy the other night?"* He freezes and turns around. *"Yes, I did."* I know he did. I hand him a prescribed piece of paper with my name, number, and email address. I tell him we should do it again. He tells me his name is Sean.

It's about my bedtime when he lightly taps on my door. I've been expecting him. He's not much for words or talking, and when he enters my room we barely exchange glances. He strips off his uniform and lies down on my bed with his face down.

He's a good-looking guy who looks about 22 to 24 years old with buzzed brown hair, a smooth face, and brown eyes. Considering we didn't speak a word in the shower cell nor here, I find him a bit strange. But it's an erotic kind of strange. I know he just wants his hole drilled. I give him what he wants.

As he lies there on the bed, I snatch a web belt hanging from the back of my door hook rack. It's flexible and easy to bend and tie. First I grab his left arm and pin it behind his back, and then the right. He asks me, *"What are you doing?"* I lean into him and whisper in my deep Midwestern voice, *"Just trust me."* I place both palms facing each other as I begin to wrap webbing binding his wrists and tighten the belt.

I prop him up on the bed and instruct him to suck me soft and easy as I grow hard inside his warm mouth. I grab his legs by the ankles and swing them to the side of the bed, where they now hang over with his knees on the floor and his ass at the perfect angle. This time I'm not as slow and gentle with him. I spread his legs and then his cheeks, spit on his hole, and ram myself inside. He yelps and then starts to moan. I push his head into the pillow to soften the sound. As I penetrate him at different angles, I push his head deeper into the pillow to subdue his congenial wails. I do my business and when I'm ready to blow my load, I pull out, flip the boy over, and shower his face.

He's lying there naked with a stiffy, cum dripping on his face, and his hands tied behind his back. At that moment, the loud voice announces, *"Incoming! Incoming! Incoming!"* Just our luck. It's happened to me before. I grab some tissue and wipe his face before I untie him. The big voice orders *"Shelter in place"* meaning to stay put where you are until we get an all-clear. More people are injured running to a bunker during an alert than if they were to stay put. The *shelter in place* is more commonplace for that reason.

I look at the boy. He has a look of lust in his eyes, wanting me to finish him off, but I order him in a low, soft voice, *"We have to take accountability. As soon as we get the all clear, you need to go. You need to wait and come back here in a couple more days and we'll do it again."* Then I order him to get dressed and leave. He replies, *"Yes Sir."*

Two days later the boy returns. He tells me how turned on he was by our last visit and shared some of his fantasies with me – one to be totally bound and gagged.

I order him to strip. As he stands there naked, I blindfold him. I order him to raise his arms as I wrap his wrists with a bandana and then duct tape that I had there from the office. I place him on the bed and do the same to his ankles. After my night with "The Intruder" a while back, I've been fantasizing and researching the alpha role. As The Intruder did to me, I start to explore the boy's body with my hands, lips, tongue, and mouth as he lies there helpless to stop me. I flicker and twitch his nipples, licking and nibbling on them. The boy is immediately hard. I reach for a few clothespins that I have on a clothesline in my room and clamp them in his armpit and upper arm, taking my time to watch the boy squirm with pleasure and pain endurance. The boy's cock is standing at attention now and he's leaking cum.

I run my fingers up and down his body from his forehead to his toes. We kiss again and again. I ask him if he likes being my boy . . . my bitch. He replies, *"Yes, sir. I love the way you make me feel."* I pull away and clench his lips on each corner and lower his jaw. I spit forcibly into his mouth. I rub my cock around his face and smack it a few times. I let him lick it and suck it enough to know it's there. I ask him again if he likes being my boy. *"Yes, sir,"* he weeps. I taunt and tease up and down his body, every crevice, every orifice, and every projection for nearly an hour. When he finally can't take it any longer, he explodes with an eruption of white lava that shoots to his chin and flows down his volcano.

Sean is older than he looks, but I call him my boy. Days and weeks go by and we continue to see one another until he's reassigned to another base. Sometimes it's for a quick hookup; other times it's an elongated session, but it's always interesting and there's never much talking.

Kinsey

There's a lot of sexual energy here. Abstinence? Phoo! Humans need sexual contact. We are designed and wired that way. It's not bad or dirty or perverted . . . it just is. Man's need for sexual release is based on actual physical, hormonal needs. We relieve ourselves by masturbation, but that only seems to work temporarily if you're by yourself. Most men—and women too—need and want the physical contact and human touch. Without it, we become irritable and bitchy.

As we navigate our way through a landscape of social networks, dating sites, ubiquitous porn, designer sex toys, Craigslist hookups, and more access to information about sexual relationships, our needs have gotten a little more complicated. Technology and media have certainly changed attitudes toward sexual liberation and experimentation. In places where the male-to-female ratio is significantly higher or where few women are present—like in a war zone, military camps, man camps, prisons, or gender-separated societies—there's opportunity to act out a fantasy or innate inhibitions or experiment with the same. The longer I'm here on base the more I'm aware of doors opening.

Cybersex using cam-to-cam features has contributed to voyeurism and exhibitionism around the world. The media in recent years has portrayed many different relationships from all walks of life. There are open marriages, mate swapping, swinging, same-sex exploration, and communal sex. I had my first sexual experience at age 12. At 18, as some count sheep to fall asleep, I remember counting my sex partners—it was over 200. Was I just a hormone churning adolescent? Perhaps. Was it the need to search for lust or love? I didn't know what love was. I didn't feel loved. I didn't love myself. But I had a sexual drive and energy to seek human touch and bodily contact. But not just anyone's touch. It was the other touch of a man. The dire need to be with a man. It is my innate being. I was born and wired this way.

Sometimes I blame society, culture, and religion for the philanderer that I am. I grew up during a time when homosexuality wasn't talked about, and if it was, it was only negative. So men like me were expected to keep it a secret or keep it "in the closet." We couldn't express our love without consequences. So, for sexual gratification I went from sex partner to sex partner. It was easy to find. No names. No dates. Just sex.

I've had many escapades here on base. A hundred would be putting it lightly. Several hundred, sure. I've had offers on base for cybersex, three-ways, and communal sex parties. I've even been offered money to perform sex with a soldier I was not interested and turned it down. Fortunately most of my encounters practiced safe sex. It's how I survived the AIDS epidemic through the 1980s and beyond. If someone's actions were questionable, I mentored them on safe-sex practices.

We've heard the saying *"What happens in Vegas stays in Vegas."* Well that goes the same for here. What happens in Afghanistan stays in Afghanistan . . . until now. Everyone has different circumstances, needs, and desires, and how they communicate it and express it. I don't hide it from my lifelong partner, but I also don't volunteer what's going on or provide details unless he asks. He tends to ask a lot more than I prefer. I don't like to kiss and tell. He knows he's my number one.

I talk to both military men and women. Some separate their home life and deployment. While home, they are with their spouse and kids. During deployment, they may hook up temporarily with another person. It may be a woman and a man, or a man and a man, or a woman and a woman. The same-sex relationships tend to be much more secretive. Hetero relationships may be more obvious and they think they're being secretive, but most of the platoon knows. Perhaps that is also the reason the military divorce rates hover around 75 percent. Long-distance relationship, frequency, and independence all factor into military couples splitting apart.

As for the contractors, there are many married folks on base and very, very few are here with their spouses. Sometimes it seems like a lot of people stay over here in this job not just for the money but to get away from their spouse or kids. Hearing conversations, I think many of them are running from something and haven't yet figured out what that is.

The doors open for many people to shack up with someone else while they're on tour or working over here. We work and live with the same people day in and day out. We know who's hooking up together. We call it friends with benefits, like anywhere else.

I wonder if the Generation X culture developed a more open and lenient attitude toward relationships because they saw their Baby Boomer parents or their friends' parents going through divorces and dating. Sometimes these kids are referred to as the "Ignored Generation" or the "Turnkey Generation." As they were growing up, both parents were working. They were told to go straight home from school and lock the door when they got home. They were ordered not to talk to strangers. They were conditioned to detect danger in and around everything. I picture these kids with built-in antennas on their heads. I wonder if the fear, loneliness, and being raised in single-parent households led them to a journey to find temporary love to help them heal their wounds later in life. They were left to fend for themselves. They became highly skeptical of many different circumstances and questioned trust. Some, perhaps many, observed and concluded that the family life and commitment is overrated.

For some soldiers, same-sex hookups are easier than hooking up with the opposite sex. They want it with no strings attached, no emotions, and no judgment. They're single, married, engaged, divorced, dating, or seeing others. Many have families back home. They span across all military branches and all ranks. They are men and women of different nationalities, cultures, skin colors, religions, and ages. I applaud them for being open-minded, exploring their sexuality, and being true to themselves.

In a human sexuality class that I took in college, I learned about the Kinsey Scale of sexual orientation. The scale attempts to describe a person's sexual tendencies and experiences, and to better understand the complexity of sexuality. The scale ranges from zero to six, with zero meaning exclusively heterosexual and six meaning exclusively homosexual. Three on the scale is bisexual. I'm pure homosexual. I've never dated a woman or been aroused at the thought. Pure heterosexual would, of course, be the complete opposite of homosexual: seeking relationships with only the opposite sex.

My thought is that if homosexuality is about 10 percent of the world's population and at one end of the spectrum, then I would predict that pure heterosexuality is about the same. This forms a bell curve and a balance in the scale of sexuality, which puts about 70 percent of the world's population in the incidental situation categories, meaning that they've at least had thoughts of sexuality outside their predominant sexual orientation. I believe the bisexual community is much bigger than what populations are led to believe. I also believe religion plays a major factor in condemning one's sexuality. Many are stigmatized and will not act upon their own true feelings and what is natural. There's a saying, *"If all the people who had same-sex relationships turned lavender for a day, the numbers would astound people."*

For some of the men who pursue sex with other men, I don't believe that they're all gay. Many may think about it; some act upon it. I highly believe most humans are bisexual and it's all part of the balance of gender, just as I believe homosexuality is nature's way of trying to balance the world's population. Again, take the "hetero" or "homo" off of "heterosexual" and "homosexual," and you're left with "sexual." Humans are sexual beings. Abstinence is a self-enforced restraint and unnatural. To me, abstinence is like telling yourself not to eat when your stomach is empty and growling.

Sometimes I make love to another man for no reason, and I think it's the best thing. I may not know his name, where he's from, or what he does for a living, and I have zero history with him. Sometimes it's not about the look or the body, but the feeling—to touch his soul. I become intoxicated by the passion of the unknown and feel there is nothing more than an artistic expression between us to love each other in that moment. During the past four years, I've had hundreds of sex partners. Of the several hundred sexual contacts that I've had, I would estimate that 85 percent of the men said they were married with kids. About half claim they're bisexual, and the other half declare that they're straight. Those I have fooled around with who claim to be straight are just kidding themselves and in denial of their truest and innate feelings.

The Boston Marathon

It's April 15, 2013, and a double bombing near the finish line of the Boston Marathon has killed three people and injured hundreds. The word on the street spread like gasoline on a wildfire. Juliet Alpha and I are tuned in to CNN and the internet to see if we can find out the latest news coverage.

Both of us take this to heart, as not only is the Boston Marathon the world's oldest and best-known marathon, but both of us ran last year's shadow run—also known as a satellite run—on BAF. We trained and trained for that marathon. It paid off for me because it was a personal record and best marathon performance for me at 03:42:00. I'm not sure if I would've qualified for the real Boston Marathon, but I'm proud of this one: 26.2 miles with about an 08:30-minute pace.

We even got Motormouth Mark to run in that marathon. He actually didn't run, but he's a fast-paced walker and in good shape. He finished just under six hours with no prior training or running. He speed-walked the entire course. The day before the run, our coach Juliet Alpha went over to the PX and bought Motormouth a pair of compression shorts. I think they only had them in women's, or at least that's what Juliet Alpha told us and we laughed about because as masculine and womanizing as Motormouth is, he still wore them under his shorts and claims it really helped him. When he called his sons to tell them of his victory, I don't think any of them believed their dad did this race, but he had the T-shirt, certificate, and medal to show for it.

I volunteered for the 2011 Boston Marathon shadow run on base. I got Barron to sponsor an aid station and recruited fellow employees to volunteer in shifts. We had a lot of great people working our station and cheering the runners. Among the runners that year were Trigger and Juliet Alpha, and they were my inspiration to run the 2012 event.

This year's satellite race in Afghanistan was finished by the time we received word of what happened in Boston. It's so unfortunate that we have people on this earth who want to inflict pain and do harm by using weapons of mass destruction to terrorize people, but this is the world we live in today.

The Department Meeting

Every Friday, I take part in a human resources management meeting at 9:30 a.m. The departments under the HR umbrella are country HR, Bagram site HR, human resources information system, employee assistance program, employee relations, strength management, industrial relations, public affairs, and my department: training and development. I hate attending these meetings. Over my career, I've been amazed how many managers don't know how to conduct or lead a meeting, or keep it on track. They schedule a weekly meeting just to have a meeting. Most of them are not very productive, including this one.

I scan the faces around the table. Everyone on this team worked for RBK in Iraq or Afghanistan except me. Six of the eight are white males all over 50, plus one black and one Hispanic. The two senior men are in their sixties. The Hispanic of Puerto Rican descent is the youngest of the group and just turned 40.

Alfred is the country HR manager and has been leading these meetings for the past few years. Alfred is a mediocre boss at best. His philosophy is *"If it's not broke, don't fix it."* He doesn't want to ruffle any feathers if he doesn't have to. As far as continuous improvement, don't bother.

I guess all of this showed from his formal education. He doesn't have any. He never went to college, but he has 30 years of experience working his way up in HR with corrupt RBK. That never sat well with me. Barron couldn't find a better-qualified candidate? I guess nobody wants to commit to the job in a war zone.

The meetings are nothing but a report out of the week's activities. I talk to most of these guys, so I know what they're going to say. Alfred doesn't take the opportunity to motivate, inspire, develop, coach, or build the team. It's humdrum to say the least.

I recall one time when he was reporting on taking over a campaign from public relations on dignity and respect. Alfred rated himself a C+ and seemed to be pleased with that. I'm a perfectionist. I like to make a difference, engage the people, and strive for an A+ and notable recognition on most things that I do. But that's the bar that Alfred has set for himself and for others. The excuse is always *"This is Afghanistan!"* I don't give a shit if I'm in Afghanistan, Timbuktu, Geneva, or D.C., I can shine much brighter than the standard he leads by—and I have.

The HR topics never seem to vary much. I can't believe we're still discussing a unique assignment provision change or an exception to this policy or that policy. We've been talking about the same damn thing for the past six weeks! We've all given our input on the issues. Alfred leans back in his faux-leather chair with his hands raised at chest level. He's touching his fingertips as he gazes up toward the ceiling. Can't this manager make a fucking decision? I think I'm going to scream.

In the two and a half years that I've worked under Alfred, he's never made a site visit to any of our eight hubs or 80-plus forward operating bases. He doesn't get up and out from behind his desk unless it's to smoke and the smoke pit is right outside his office door. He could walk by one of my staff and not acknowledge them or know who they are. It took him nearly a year or more to remember some of the names on my team and we're all under the same umbrella. But he only knew them by name, not by face.

Next to Alfred, we have our Jerry Falwell graduate of Liberty University, Tony Tomorrow. Tony earned his master's degree online from Liberty University in Lynchburg, Virginia, while working in Afghanistan. I'm sure it was quite convenient for him to have his own office with the door closed to do his studies while on government time. I'm sure it's very Christian-like to screw our own government by declaring fraudulent hours of work in place of school time. Tony is wearing his Liberty University sweatshirt. It makes me cringe to see him wearing it. The teachings of an ultraconservative university really don't seem to go hand in hand with the diversity and inclusion principles and practices that are supposedly advocated and supported in a corporate environment.

Tony is a smart guy but not management material. I've seen him lose his cool several times. If others chime in to give their viewpoint that challenges a process he has written, his face lights up from a blush color to a beet red and he explodes. He won't let people finish their ideas or the discussion. He always needs to be right and in control. He treats his wife and kids the same way, from what I've heard of his conversations with them. I bet they're glad he's over here and away from them.

Next to Tony is Roy. If there's one weekly report out that I listen to, it's his. He's a good guy and I've always thought he should be running HR. He has a master's degree, is one of the more experienced LOGCAP guys of the group, and is a heck of a lot smarter than some of the clowns amidst us. He always has good information to share. He's direct and factual. He gives numbers and statistics. I like that and I can easily draw a picture or graph in my head. I can plot where we've been, where we are, and where we're going.

Standing next to Roy is Darnell. For over three years, Darnell's report out is the same: *"I have nothing for the group."* Week after week, he has nothing for the group. I'm not even sure what his job duties entail. I think he runs the country HR office, second under Alfred, but has nothing to contribute. Ever. Another fine example of our HR leadership: no expectations. It must be top-secret HR stuff or he's drawing an easy paycheck! Why even show up to these meetings?

My old boss, Trigger the Navy Seal, is the philosophical one and calls out the BS or any questions. He's now over industrial relations for Afghanistan and is part of this meeting. He's usually the one who will generate worthy discussions. I've always liked Trigger and his management style. I'd work for him again in a heartbeat.

Then there's the Puerto Rican—the pretty one and the youngest of the group: El Niño. His hair is perfectly in place and set with hairstyling gel. I had to touch it once just to see what it feels like. It feels like plastic with all the gunk hardened to each strand. I dread getting on an airplane and thinking someone before me had that crap in his or her hair and on the headrest. I think it's gross and I'm not sure how or why it ever became popular.

I've asked El Niño how his wife likes to run her hands through it. He dodges the question every time. Actually El Niño tends to dodge a lot of things, including showing up for meetings on time, creating reports, and making deadlines. For the past three years, someone usually fetches El Niño or calls him to come to the meeting. He has most of upper management snowed by embellished information, and they fall for it. It's becoming more and more obvious: the late arrivals for meetings, the missed deadlines, and the made-up numbers, statistics, and events. If he has the floor, he'll talk in circles for an hour if he's allowed, and no one has a clue what he's trying to say.

Fortunately El Niño is one of the last people in the meeting to speak, and he's learned—after three years—to be brilliant, be brief, and be gone. That boy loves to hear himself talk. I've coached him to keep it short and simple. He generally sits across from me and I give him the hand gesture across the throat to cut his speech if he gets a little long-winded.

We end the meeting with the most senior of the group, Russell. Russell talks extraordinarily slowly. He's from Texas, I'm from Texas, and so is Darnell. We all speak in different tempos. Russell may be slow in speech, but he's always to the point. He's confidential, consistent, and very calm. He's excellent at what he does.

The Friday meetings end with an alibi—a justification or an explanation of any given topic. Once in a great while, somebody in the group will have an alibi, but most of the time the meeting is adjourned.

I'm glad it's over. It's become an arduous task to make myself go to these grueling meetings. I'm tired of being here. I'm tired of listening to the news and politics of the world. I'm tired of listening and reading the news of the heinous acts humans do to other humans. It's not just war. It's the way we live and treat one another and how we define humanity. So many stories surface constantly to remind me of what an ugly place the world is. The act of war is endless and ruthless. September 11 was horrific, but does the U.S. reaction to retaliate make it right? The U.S. has been involved in war in some form or another ever since I was born. Hell, the U.S. has been involved in war since its independence was claimed.

It's not just war; it's the news that I'm reading about today and every day:

Poor orphans left by war were swept up by human traffickers and led into lives of drug trafficking, prostitution, and sweatshops.

An Iranian woman was sentenced to death by stoning for allegedly committing adultery. Her husband and his friends fabricated the story because he wanted to marry a younger woman. He faced no repercussions.

A Pakistani father beheaded his two teenage daughters and pranced around the village holding their heads to restore honor to his family name, all because he felt his daughters had dishonored the family name with their flirtatious behaviors with teenage boys.

A prostitute in India tossed her newborn infant from an upper floor of her brothel and into a burning building next to it because she didn't want it.

I hear and feel the cries of the Chinese woman who lost her purpose for living after being forced to abort her eight-month pregnancy due to the violation of the one-child laws in her country.

An eight-year-old Yemen girl was sold off to a 40-year-old man for a measly dowry to the family. She died on her wedding night when her new husband brutally raped her and ruptured her uterus.

There's the gay-bashing in Iraq by the Islamic fundamentalists who solicit the encounters, gang up on their victims, and then rape and torture them with a broomstick or other foreign object up the ass. They inject silicone into the victim's crack to glue it shut and leave them to die.

This is the world we live in.

Cleaning House

The General hit the ground running in high gear. He's visited more FOBs in his first month than his predecessor did in three years. He stops to talk to everyone and he knows he can find the truth at the lower end of the totem pole about management, coworkers, scams, unethical business practices, or anything else. With a major downsizing to occur over the next year, a lot of people will be leaving.

When The General arrives, Mean Gene decides it's time to bail out while he's ahead. He leaves on good terms and has had several accomplishments during his tenure here. He helped to build, service, and maintain bases and the workforce with a very good success rate.

The rest of the senior management on the second floor of the headquarters building quickly dwindles. Leatherface isn't far behind after Mean Gene's departure. With the reduction in force, both Mean Gene and Leatherface are reassigned to different projects.

Bulldog is hanging on by a hair. I can't understand why the man is in the position he has. I guess he's part of the good ol' boy network, but many of the managers who reported to him now dislike him. Word on the street is that Bulldog was previously terminated by RBK for drinking and having sex with a subordinate. I feel The General needs to know this because senior managers are generally put in positions based on integrity and their accomplishments. Bulldog may have had some significant accomplishments under his belt, but he doesn't have integrity.

I don't want to be a Juliet Alpha and run to The General with this information. Instead I create a secret email address and send The General some facts that I gathered from workers who worked with Bulldog in Iraq. I detail his actions, such as having sex with a subordinate and possession of alcohol. I send the email from my personal laptop with an anonymizer proxy so it can't be traced. The General requests an investigation, but before the entire findings surface and more mud is slung, Bulldog resigns.

Our HR manager, Alfred, may not like The General's tactics or directives either, especially when I show up for The General's weekly management meeting to represent HR instead of Alfred. Alfred asked me to attend on his behalf, and when The General sees me at the table instead, shit hits the fan.

Alfred resigns and leaves the project, replaced by a slower-tongued Texan, Clayton, who manages to make the already agonizing Friday meetings even more agonizing by talking in slow motion. I must admit that I admire the man. For as slow as he talks, you will never hear him raise his voice or get upset.

RIF

"Thomas, your department will be gone by March. I need you to reduce your team by one in November, another one in December, and the last one in January. You'll be gone in March."

At a billion dollars a day, the wars in Iraq and Afghanistan are fruitless and pointless. Many soldiers I talk to believe this war is an unnecessary waste. I do too. I believe Obama would love to end the legacy of this U.S. conflict and occupation of Iraq and Afghanistan, and bring our troops home. I believe war is just a symbol of world leaders losing their ability to solve conflicts with intelligence and diplomacy. Peace by power is a fallacy. It only generates disdain and hate. The rich folks love war because they profit greatly and greedily. Former Vice President Dick Cheney is a prime example. Before becoming vice president and before the Iraq War, his previous profession as a CEO was awarded $39.5 billion without any bidding from other firms. Tell me that wasn't a plot to get rich quick. How many frickin' millions or billions does a person need?

Obama orders us to reduce our footprint here, so the U.S. is transferring many bases over to the Afghan National Army or shutting them down completely. As I'm instructed to reduce my team, I'm also told not to tell them until it's their time. I guess HR is always afraid of some sort of retaliation or deviant behavior that may occur. But I know my team very well. We're like a family and I've always held them to the highest regards and watched out for them for the past few years we've been together. I know their families, I know the way they think, I know the music they like, and I know what makes them laugh and tick. They all know we're contractors and our contracts can be terminated at any time. We've been preparing for this for a long time. We've expected it.

I don't waste time. Despite what the HR manager tells me not to do, I immediately gather my team to deliver the news. These are my people. We've built trust. They're my Bagram family and I will take care of them. As always, being the professional and the diplomat, Agim says, *"Thomas, thank you for telling us so we can plan. If we can find another job on base, will you give us an early release?"*

"Absolutely," I tell them. *"Anything I can do to help you out, let me know. I'll also keep my eyes and ears open and let you know."*

Jebel Hafeet and Gokyo Ri

This is the last overseas R&R for Greg and me. We're heading to Nepal to hike in the Himalayas. Because of the long distance of the trip and flight time, we decide to break up Greg's travel with a stop in Dubai. We do our usual day at the spa, gallivant around the city, and rent a couple of Harleys and drive to Jebel Hafeet, the U.A.E.'s most famous mountain. Who would've thought there were mountains in the land of desert and blowing sand?

Greg grabs a cab from the Dubai airport and meets me at our hotel. As always, he's looking good, working out regularly, and is as handsome as ever. He's learned to pack super light. This time he has just a couple pair of clothes and a collapsible duffel bag that he uses to fill on a shopping spree in Dubai for the latest fashions. He's a bit jet lagged, so we spend the first day just resting and catching up.

The next day we decide to treat ourselves to a spa day. I think there are more men's salons in the Arab world than women's. It's no wonder many of the Arab men look so manicured and pretty. The salons are also very segregated. A woman can't go to a men's salon and vice versa. I know this because after many of my wonderful experiences with

Regala at Diva Salon in Dubai, she tried to go there and they denied service to her because she's a woman.

Diva Salon offers all sorts of services for men: haircuts and styles, beard trimming and shaving, manicures, pedicures, facials, massages, and back waxing. I'm sure there's a list of other services they offer, but these are the ones we go for. On the second floor are rooms for all the services, so up we go and we each sit in a barber's chair and get our heads and faces shaved.

One guy around us is having the whiskers of his beard removed by a Turkish process called "plucking." It uses two thin, floss-like strings and a technique using his teeth and fingers to thread out the facial hair from the follicle. I heard it stings and I've seen men leave the salon afterward with red marks on their faces from the treatment.

A popular grooming technique here is waxing of the ears and the nose to remove hair. It looks more painful than it is. A Q-tip is placed in warm wax and properly applied to the ears and nose. The recipient has Q-tips sticking out of their ears and nose while the wax hardens. After a minute or two, the barber yanks the waxed Q-tip from the ears and nose along with all the hair. I wish it was practiced in the U.S.

The barbers finish us up with a neck and shoulder rub, and then we're instructed to go upstairs to the second level for our other requested beauty services. The barber downstairs rings the staff upstairs to signal them we're on our way up. A line of sheboys—at least I think they're mostly sheboys—greet us at the top of the stairs. They're all young men by assigned gender but as feminine and girlie as they can possibly be. There are six of them and three will work on each of us.

As we get to the top of the stairs, they remember me. I come through here every 90 days and I tip them well. They greet me and I smile at how they enunciate their vowels and words with emphasis like they're speaking with a diphthong: *"Ohhhhh Meester Thomas, HOw are YOU? It's so GOOoood to see you again."* After one girl takes the lead introduction, they all chime in. They know Greg is my husband and ask me to remind them of his name, so I introduce them. *"Ohhhhh Meester Grag. How are YOU?"*

The girls get all chatty and lead us each to a different room, where one is set up to do the manicure, another the pedicure, and the last one the facial. The girls ask all sorts of questions and are very chatty throughout the service, sometimes talking in English and sometimes their native Filipino language of Tagalog. When I tell them that Greg is a salon owner in Austin, Texas, they all want to come and work for *"Meester Grag."* I'm entertained during the one hour of services by their personal questions, conversation, jokes, laughter, voices, and gestures. I feel like I'm being worked on during a drag queen show. I wonder how the Arab men react to all of this.

After the mani, pedi, and facial, we wrap it up with a long massage. All these services in the States would run several hundred dollars; in Dubai it's just over $100 or $150 for each of us. I guess the Arabs benefit greatly by having all their labor imported from economically deprived countries.

After our midmorning day at the spa, we grab a bite for lunch and do some shopping. We spend the evening enjoying happy hour at a hotel overlooking the Dubai Mall. We're enamored with its magical water fountains, the hustle and bustle of people everywhere, the towering Burj Khalifa, the incredible skyline of lights, and the balmy air under the setting sun.

The next morning, the air temperature is perfect and there's not a cloud in the sky. It's a gorgeous day for a ride, so we head to the local Harley Davidson shop to pick up our rented bikes and meet a few other riders. We ride to Jebel Hafeet, known for its stark black asphalt road against arid, sepia land with miles and miles of curves to the summit.

After our quick layover in Dubai, Greg and I head to Kathmandu. The city is full of commotion and activity that is sometimes confusing. We learn our way around the city center and start to shop for hiking gear in the Thamel shopping district known for mountaineering shops. We have backpacks, camel packs, and a few layers of hiking gear that we brought with us. Being from a warm climate, we need sleeping bags, hiking pants, down jackets, gloves, hats, and a few other necessities for our 10-day mountain journey in the Himalayas. There are a lot of knockoff shops with the branding and look of The North Face, Kelty, Patagonia, and more. Knowing this, we purchase a few of those items anyway hoping that they at least last the 10-day trip. Next we stop at the local pharmacy and get pills for altitude mountain sickness. We will hike over a pass and will reach a summit of 17,000 feet.

There are plenty of porters and guides willing to help us for our journey, but we decide to do it alone. As much as I'd like to help the local workforce and economy, I just don't care to have a third or fourth wheel tagging along with us. We have detailed maps and the first half of the trek is well traveled up to the Mount Everest base camp, so there'll be plenty of people on that section of the trail.

We fly to Lukla to begin our journey. Lukla is known as the most dangerous airport in the world. It has a steep incline up and over the mountain and a quick descent to the airport landing. Topping off the madness is a short runway and a 90-degree turn. I didn't prepare Greg for this ahead of time, so he's in for the flight of his life! I, on the other hand, want to be in the front-row seat directly behind the pilots of this propjet!

The pilots look like a couple of kamikaze fighter pilots in their leather flight jackets and aviator sunglasses. The jet is small and holds about a dozen passengers. Two other guys beat me to the front seats, but I get a second-row seat. I check out the flight panel and it looks like something from the 1940s. There's nothing modern about it and some of it looks pieced together, but as long as the pilots know what they're doing, I'm fine with that.

The flight from Kathmandu to Lukla is about a 45-minute trip. As we approach Lukla, we know we're in the Himalayas. The white mountains tower below us, far and wide. The scenery from a bird's-eye view is stunning, with high rigid peaks and the snow caps glistening from the sun. As we make our descent into Lukla, we first make a steep ascent up and over a mountain pass. Everyone is leaned back in their seats, gazing out the windows. After we clear the mountain peak, we make a quick downward plunge like a steep drop on a roller coaster ride. From the cockpit window, I see the tiny runway strip with a 90-degree turn coming into view. Before I know it, the airplane tires are screeching on the runway asphalt and as the pilot makes the quick 90-degree turn, I get a glimpse of a solid rock wall in front of us before we turn and essentially swerve to the terminal. We're stopped in front of the terminal and everyone on the plane starts clapping and cheering. We've survived the ordeal.

There is no baggage service, so we get in line to grab our backpacks as we see them. We walk through the small airport terminal that looks like a bombed-out cement building. It's cold and dark. As we exit the terminal, there's a line of porters and guides offering their services. We decline and continue to walk like we know where we're going. Lukla is a small village with one main pedestrian street lined with hostels, backpacking stores, cafes, and shops for last-minute provisions. We continue to walk through the town and when the pedestrian street ends, the Everest trailhead begins, marking the beginning of our 10-day journey.

The first day of hiking, the trail is lined with nonstop shops and teahouses. It feels like an extension of the village with no kind of building or property ordinances. Since this is Greg's first major hike, I've booked our first and only night's accommodation at a hotel with the highest rating. The exterior of the hotel is made of stone and natural woods and beautiful gardens. The interior looks like a mountain lodge that one might find in Colorado. It's very well crafted of all-natural materials.

A young Nepalese woman greets us with a bow and a *namaste*. She has us take a seat on a colorful cushioned bench and returns minutes later with a tray of piping-hot tea and some cookies. This is a typical Nepalese greeting. As we sip our tea, she goes over our reservation and shows us to our room. Again, the room is nicely furnished and has a cabin aesthetic. There's a private bath and hot running water. We're not sure if we'll have hot water at other teahouses on this trip.

The next morning, we rise early to start our full day of hiking. Though the distance we plan to cover is about nine miles, we hear the climb is the most difficult of the journey. At one point, an old local man stops and asks us where we are going. We tell him, *"Namche Bazaar."* His face lights up and he chuckles. I'm sure he's seen many foreigners suffer through this leg of the journey.

And what a thigh buster it is. We make it to Namche Bazaar and the sun is quickly setting. We check out the streets and hillside for teahouses. We find one we like and spend two nights here to acclimate to the altitude. We spend the second day checking out the local markets and shops.

I receive text messages from my bank to confirm charges from a store in NYC for over $1,000. They obviously can't be mine, so I make a call to the credit agency. My card has been hacked. While I'm on the phone, the credit card company advises me to cancel all my credit cards because of the size of transactions made to my account and the possibility that my personal information is being hacked. All of them! I'm in the middle of the Himalayas and my credit cards are the primary tool I use to purchase items. I have some cash, but not that much. The credit card company tells me they can send out new cards, but I don't know where we'll end up retrieving them. Fortunately Greg has his business credit card and we have some cash that we can use for the remainder of the trip, but what a bummer.

Our journey continues as we branch off from the usual Everest trail and head through some of the most beautiful terrain I've ever seen: rigid cliffs and peaks, clear-blue skies, turquoise glacier-fed lakes, snowbanks at higher altitudes, and colorful Himalayan prayer flags strewn from building to building as we pass through small mountain villages.

Each day is more frigid as we ascend. When we reach our teahouse for the night, we usually shower quickly with a little hot water and dry in the chilled air before we jump into our synthetic sleeping bags. After the second night, most of the teahouse interiors are made of rough cement with few windows in the sleeping areas. They are dark, dank, and bitterly cold.

While hiking to the summit, I spot an elderly couple midway sitting on a rock, having a snack, and taking in the incredible view of the Gokyo turquoise lakes below us and Everest off in the distance. Greg and I sit quietly nearby and join the couple in the peace and quiet, crisp mountain air, and all the natural beauty. As we get ready to move on to the summit, I ask the couple a few questions. I find out they're in their seventies and doing this amazing trek. What an inspiration! I want to be like them when I reach that age.

It takes five days to reach our destination, and on the sixth day we climb to the Gokyo Ri summit of 17,000 feet. If we ascended any higher, we'd need oxygen masks. It wears us out to take a few steps and we're gasping for air. There are about 20 others who make it to the top with us. Everyone is smiling and taking pictures of this memorable moment. There's not a cloud in the sky. The luminous sun is reflecting off the snow, and the gray-and-black snow-covered mountains are stark against the deep-azure sky. What a beautiful day!

We descend from the summit and head back to the little mountain village. We spend the evening wining and dining and cherishing such a momentous day. We rest peacefully into the night.

The following morning, we take on the first major challenge of the day. We must cross up and over the Gokyo Ri mountain pass to get to the other side, where it's not as touristy or populated. I ask some of the fellow trekkers and guides about the conditions, and they all say it's snowy but well marked. We soon find that getting up to the pass is no problem, but going down is slick and slippery in the snow. We really need to have crampons on our hiking boots, but the guides told us not to bother. Of course, some of the local guides and porters are hiking in flip-flops. They're used to this white world and its conditions.

Greg and I end up scooting down a portion of the mountain on our butts to avoid a tragic slip, slide, and fall. We don't see a single other hiker the whole day. We make it down to the next base, but the weather is starting to turn bad. The dense, vigorous mix of snowfall, low clouds, and fog obscures my vision. I don't know if I'm looking down or to the side. We use caution as we continue, but our slower pace eventually gets us to our next destination after dark.

When we finally find our next teahouse to camp for the night, it's still exceptionally frigid. We enter the teahouse, get a room, and unload our packs. When we enter the dining hall, the caretaker is sparking up the wood-burning stove with dried yak dung. She adds one yak pie at a time with her bare hands. When the fire is toasty warm, she makes her way over to our table, takes our order, and heads back to the kitchen to prepare our meal without washing her heifer-dusted hands. I'm so hungry that I eat my rice dish anyway. I figure the cooking temperature of the food will have killed any germs she may have otherwise passed on from handling the shit. Greg has lost his appetite and doesn't eat anything, but he hits his Snickers stash in his backpack a little later.

The next two days of hiking are downward and easy. Before we know it, we're back in Kathmandu and it's time to say goodbye. Back to the grind. We go our separate ways. I reflect on what a wonderful trip it was and how wonderful it was to spend it with Greg. However, we didn't have sex on this trip and there was very little touching or embracing. Is it because we spent so much of it outside and in the wilderness? Is our emotional bond to one another dissipating?

The Last Bagram Christmas

The Christmas elf is here and I'm his first visit! He's a handsome fella. The big flirt that he is, he takes off his shirt for me to expose his rippled six-pack and bulging chest and arms, and then gives me a big bear hug. I bet if there were a pole in my office, he'd do a pole dance for me too.

The elf, Chip, is quite a character and we work together on various work assignments. I see him at the gym quite a bit. I've always thought that he was gay, but he claims to be straight. I think given the right opportunity, he'd jump the fence. I've hinted and offered a few times, but he hasn't taken the bait.

He's a Texas rancher in his late thirties or early forties. He has one major downfall: He dips! He's always got a wad of the crap in his mouth and he's always spitting. The first time we met at my office, I told him he had to spit it out and rinse his mouth when he's coming to talk to me. He obeyed and hasn't forgotten that. Damn, for such an attractive man, he's extremely unattractive to me with that habit. Oddly, he has a stunning smile with dazzling-white teeth. This surprises me considering his nasty habit.

He's dancing around the office and flirting, and we take a few pictures together. Once he gets my elf-rating approval, he darts out the door to make his next visit spreading the Christmas joy. What a great way to start the day!

But it's not always like this. The novelty of being in Afghanistan has worn off. My first Christmas here, I received two or three dozen Christmas cards. The number dwindled over the years, and this year I didn't receive even one. No cookies. No rum balls. No gifts. Maybe the "Christian" in my family and friends is deteriorating. The big hoopla in the States is that Christians are waging war (how Christian of them) about whether people should say to one another "Happy Holidays" or "Merry Christmas." The media and Christian leaders really wind it up.

I feel like this nonsense is not worth engaging in at all, but of course I still have an opinion. Working for an international company, we celebrate all walks of life, not just Christian. If Christians haven't noticed, there's a huge demographic change in the United States of America. There are several holidays and celebrations in December: Christmas, Hanukkah, Kwanza, Winter Solstice, HumanLight—sure, Christianity is the largest religion in the U.S., but that doesn't mean we need to adhere to their religious beliefs or a specific holiday greeting. I wish Christians would put the word *Christ* back into *Christian* and practice what they preach. Can't people just be nice to one another? Be thankful people are acknowledging your beliefs and spirituality. Americans are such drama queens and I know the media has a factor in making us that way.

I don't care that I didn't receive anything acknowledging Christmas. I'm not a fan of Christmas. I don't label myself a Christian, nor do I believe in their theology or practices. I cringe at the holiday and how commercial, superficial, and pretentious it's become. It's nothing but a marketing ploy for businesses and consumers to buy, buy, buy—even if they can't afford it.

The whole idea of gift giving is zany. If you buy a gift for so-and-so, then you need to get one for the other. And another. And it's usually gifts that people receive but don't necessarily want or care about. I've been on that receiving end. Greg even told me one Christmas that he was upset and didn't like the gift I gave him. Well you know what? I'm not playing the guessing game. If you want something, go take the money and buy it yourself.

I stopped the gift giving years ago. For nieces and nephews, we set up savings accounts and deposit money into them for holidays. Hopefully they'll appreciate that in the long run when they go off to college. I stopped sending cards. Now I don't even acknowledge the holiday. I'd rather cover my ears and save myself from listening to the same Christmas music over and over for a month or two straight, year and after. It's like being in a time warp.

So what is Christmas? I don't need a special marked holiday to meet with family or give gifts. I gather and give when I can. I certainly don't need a holiday to rejoice and celebrate the cruel and traumatic death of Jesus Christ by pounding stakes through his wrists and hanging him on a cross for onlookers to gawk. A god commits the ultimate sin of a brutal death to his only son for your sins. It sounds more like the work of the devil than a deity. If God is so great, couldn't he create a nonviolent means to end sin or prove his point? And this is what Christians pray to and worship? The rationale is fucked up. That's why I am not a Christian. That's not my god. In fact, I don't believe in God.

So when someone says Merry Christmas to me, I smile, acknowledge it, and return the greeting. Being nice and happy is what it's all about. There's a saying among the Christians, "Love the sinner, hate the sin." Well I say, "Love the believer, hate the belief."

2014:
Leaving Bagram

Bagram Star Wars

I'm awakened from a deep sleep by what sounds like large hydraulic machinery quickly rotating and moving drive gears. Following the movement is a resonance of power-tool shrill mixed with imposing and intermittent puffs of air. Loud sonic poofs one after another— poof, poof, poof—and then an earshot of fireworks that snap, crackle, and pop before fading into the midnight sky. It sounds like something from a Star Wars movie and I wait for The Big Voice to echo across base, *"Incoming, Incoming, Incoming!"* It doesn't. There's silence in the still air. I doze off.

As I walk to the office the next morning, I wonder if I dreamt of all the commotion last night. Where did the noise come from? What was it? I wasn't the only one awakened. I hear people talking about it in side conversations at the office and the DFAC. I run into Trigger and ask him about it. He informs me that Bagram has the new full-fledged defense weapons system called C-RAM (or Counter-RAM). It's a set of systems used to detect and destroy incoming artillery, rockets, and mortar rounds in the air before they hit their ground targets, or to simply provide early warning. We walk over to the C-RAM system displayed on what looks like a transportable flatbed truck. I wonder how they got the C-RAM system up and in place so quickly without me noticing. It's because it's transportable. Trigger tells me, *"What's cool is that the rounds that miss will automatically explode in the air before hitting the ground."* That *is* cool. I don't know how that's done and I don't bother to ask Trigger. It's something way over my head.

We are now living the Star Wars reality.

Speaking of Star Wars, I read an article by a news reporter about the this war. She sketches out the conflict in which an out-numbered and out-gunned Afghanistan insurgency uses guerilla warfare and hit-and-run tactics to undermine a global superpower armed with weapons of mass destruction. Afghanistan fighters are portrayed as the rebel force to protect their own land from the invasion of the outside world. As this war lingers on, we—the Imperial forces—are "stretched thin" trying to hunt down the rebels, leaving key targets vulnerable to concentrated attacks. Welcome to the dark side.

Last Visit Home

The thing I miss most about home is the peace. On base or while traveling, there's an endless stream of noise: the hustle and bustle of a city or the endless cacophony of air traffic, combat missions, and movement on base. Sometimes it's deafening. I've become so numb to the tumult that sometimes walking on base is like being underwater.

Home is my sanctuary. I've created pockets of gardens around the house intertwined and connected by pathways: gardens of colorful roses, thorny cacti, leathery palms, flowering succulents, feathery grasses, aromatic herbs, and fruitful vegetables. I take pride in the landscapes that I've developed and spend hours in the garden watching it grow and bloom. I love watering, nourishing, pruning, picking, digging, smelling, touching, and enjoying it. It's truly my space of spirit and magic. It's here that I find the greatest peace and hear the sweet and subtle sounds of the dog panting alongside me and birds chirping in the trees. There's the buzz of the bees, a breeze rustling through the grasses and trees, water trickling from the rocks and falling into the pool, and my soles crunching the decomposed granite pathway beneath me.

This is my last stint home before I'll be here for good in May. It's great to be here. Home Sweet Home.

The February Storm

There's a storm brewing. I can see it swirling in Greg's eyes. His buddy Devon is stirring up some very strong drinks and handing them to Greg. I set a glass of ice water in front of him, but he's not taking the bait.

We went out for dinner with a couple of friends and now we're back at the house. It's getting late and our friend Troy decides to head home. There's just Devon, Greg, and me here. Devon keeps pouring more stiff drinks. I watch, observe, engage in a little conversation, and plot the outcome of different scenarios of how this evening may end. Devon eventually leaves. Greg heads to the bedroom. I start to clean up.

The storm hits. From the middle of nowhere, I'm in a chokehold and being dragged from behind by the neck like I'm caught up in a typhoon. I'm gasping for air. I feel like I'm being pulled down into deep waters and about to drown. But I fight back. I know exactly what's going on and it's not the first storm that I've weathered. I'm enraged now and I'm out to pulverize the bastard. I'm able to maintain my footing and put an elbow to his head and then his gut. I start stomping on his bare feet with my boots. He thought his broken ankle was a problem before; try a shattered fucking foot.

My defenses are enough to break the hold of the typhoon, and in my moment of breaking free, I escape to the garage door. I have my car keys in my pocket, credit card and cash in my wallet, and a house key pre-hidden in the yard. I punch the automatic garage door opener on the wall of the garage as I'm making a dash to the car. The garage door opens. I lock the car doors and start the car. As I back out of the garage, I look up at the entry door and he's standing in the doorway, glaring at me like Michael Myers in *Halloween*.

One thing that the marriage officiate didn't tell us is that I would be experiencing an earthquake, a volcano eruption, a tsunami, and a typhoon all at the same time.

I spend most of the night lying awake in a hotel.

The Next Day

Today I'm registered to attend a seminar hosted by the U.S. State Department in Dallas. My contract ends in 90 days and I'm seeking my next opportunity and plotting my next move. I would love to work for the U.S. State Department.

I drive by Greg's work to make sure he's there. His motorcycle is in the parking lot. That gives me a window of opportunity to stop by the house.

Our sweet chocolate lab greets me at the door. She's happy to see me, and I give her a hug and a kiss. She follows me to the bedroom and watches me pack a bag. I'm not at the house more than 10 minutes before I'm back out the door and hitting the road to Dallas.

During my drive, I receive several phone calls from Greg. When I see his name appear on caller ID, I let it go to voicemail. He leaves just one message: *"What's going on?"* I don't bother to call him back or take another call. I'm thinking through what I want to do next. Do I stay or go?

After 16 years of being together in a committed relationship, it's really a tough question. I focus on the great times we've shared with our families, hosting holidays and attending weddings, funerals, and special occasions. And the family history—some of our nieces and nephews have known us as a couple since they were born. We've built a fortune together through our careers and flipping houses. We've traveled the world to many exotic and exciting places. I remember our first trip together to San Francisco. There was the Sawtooth Mountains, many national parks, New York, Fort Lauderdale, Paris, Rome, Venice, Thailand, Costa Rica, Mexico, Morocco, safaris in South Africa, scuba diving in Australia, hiking in the Himalayas, our wedding in Canada, and countless camping trips and motorcycle journeys and many other places. I love Greg for all these things. We have a great life.

But then there are the bad times. I see this beautiful, colorful man who has so many wonderful qualities and attributes like that of a rose: love, passion, confidence, devotion and a vibrant history. Beautiful on his own accord. But then there's the thorns . . . the thorns that will take you by surprise and puncture and rip your skin, leaving you to bleed, to hurt, to scab over. It doesn't last a day; it lingers for days, sometimes weeks or longer. It's maybe three or four times a year that I am torn by the thorn, and I always think, *"Is this the last time?"* I can forgive, but I can't forget. He was the first to stray in our relationship. I can never and will never forget the nights locked in a guest bedroom as he pounded on the door for hours. I can't wish away the memories of being locked out of the house or how he'd park his car behind mine so I couldn't leave. I'll never let go of him pushing me into a nightstand and gashing my head open during a cruise vacation. And after the damage was done, I never recall hearing a *"I'm sorry."* In recent years, the many travels abroad and the number of times I heard him say, *"I don't feel the love."* After spending thousands of dollars on trips so we could be together and he doesn't feel the love. Perhaps I should've listened more closely or followed my heart then. The thorns are stuck in my heart and I cannot pull them out. They are deeply rooted in me.

After calling 9-1-1 a couple of times, the calls stopped because the local legislature passed an ordinance that an arrest had to be made. Right, that's all I needed: to have him spend a night in jail and have a criminal record. I'm sure there's a price to pay for that by victims of domestic violence. And more recently he's been talking about getting a gun—the Texas thing to do and have. I believe that if there had been a gun in the house last night, our relationship could've ended in a murder-suicide.

I love him for who he is 99 percent of the time, but the 1 percent of the time—with his alcohol-induced demons—is draining and disintegrating to our relationship, our lives, our marriage, and me.

I must be honest with myself. My heart is telling me to end it. Stop it. I can't love him naturally or effortlessly like I once did. It takes too much work. He was the first to stray in the relationship. Then came other sex partners and then the open relationship. We've both become philanderers. I can't get aroused being with him but have no problem with other men. We no longer have that much to talk about. We've grown apart. Perhaps I've known this for a while. Maybe my tour in Afghanistan became my way of running from an unhappy relationship. Like so many others there, I can join their club now.

Living behind a façade is exhausting. There are so many unhappy marriages out there. We all know those couples who emulate the perfectly married life. They look good together and compliment one another in public. But what really happens behind closed doors is another story. And as one of our friends would say when he socializes with his partner, *"It's show time."* Divorce isn't such a tragedy. The tragedy is staying in an unhappy marriage. I think both of us have been unhappy for a while.

The U.S. State Department seminar is a total blur. No matter how much I try to stay focused on the lectures and briefs and conversations, my mind analyzes and probes for the right thing to do with the current situation. And this is how it is. Every time there's a storm, it takes forever to feel the calm. The storm never passes; it's always lingering or brewing elsewhere. I lose three days to a week or more of my life because it takes that long for me to get over it and to move on. The emotions gust within me and never cease to settle down to the placid water, the setting sun, the still air, or the dying amber. Yes, it's time to move on.

Valentine's Day

I'm at the house when Greg gets home from work. He enters, sees me standing in the kitchen, sifting through some mail, and asks, *"What's going on?"* Then the words of truth leave my lips, *"Greg, there's no more love left in this relationship."* After the unanswered calls, I don't have to expound on that. He says, *"Okay, that's all I need to hear."* He knew before he walked through the door and he probably felt relieved when I just said it. He packs a bag and out the door he departs. It's my last weekend at home before I head back to Afghanistan to finish off my contract; he's giving me the courtesy to spend it here, alone with the dog.

Greg meets his pretty boy Devon downtown. I'm not sure if the two of them were going to celebrate our breakup or if he contacted Devon to seek counsel. Whatever the motive, they've planned to wine and dine on my credit card. I get the phone call. Reluctant to pick it up, I let it go to voicemail. All I hear is Greg saying, *"I see how you are. You're so vindictive."* Who's the victim here? When it comes time to pay, he discovers our financial ties have been severed and the credit cards he tries to use are all declined. I'm the primary credit card holder. To protect myself, I canceled our joint cards earlier in the day. He's yet to discover that our household account has also been closed. However, I ensure all our joint bills are paid from the account. Even after all that's happened, I won't be leaving him hanging.

The Bedouin and the Egyptian

The end is in sight. Agim and Regala have both found new positions on base and will stay on the project longer. I'm happy for them. I've been given a high-priority project, but I'm waiting for legal approval before I can implement it. While I wait for the approval, I have two weeks of vacation that I must use or lose before I depart the project for good at the end of the month. I've been very fortunate in my life to have traveled to five continents, all 50 states, and over 60 countries. While on this project and on this side of the world, I've traveled to about 35 countries in the past five years. I'm about to add two more to my list. I plan a trip to Petra, Jordan, and the pyramids of Egypt. I'm used to traveling with Greg, but now the eagle flies alone.

I fly to the capital of Jordan, Amman. I explore some of the historical and amazing sites of the Citadel, the Roman amphitheater, and the King Abdullah Mosque. After a few days in the capital city, people-watching, taking in sites, and enjoying the aromas and flavors, I head off to Petra—Jordan's wonder of the world. Petra is a famous archaeological site in Jordan's southwestern desert. Dating to around 300 BC, it was the capital of the Nabataean Kingdom. Accessed via a narrow canyon called Al Siq, it contains tombs and temples carved into pink sandstone cliffs, earning its nickname the "Rose City." Perhaps its most famous structure, however, is 45-meter-high Al-Khazneh, a temple with an ornate, Greek-style facade known as "The Treasury."

As I enter the Petra site, there's a line of men offering rides into the park by horseback. A young Bedouin man approaches and I greet him in Arabic, "Salem walaikum." He smiles lightly and replies, "Walaikum Salem." His head is covered with a black-and-white checkered Palestinian scarf. He has a three-day shadow of a beard and spider-line wrinkles on the temples by his eyes, likely from exposure to the sun in the baking summer temperatures. His espresso-colored eyes are looking deeply into my sea-blue eyes as he offers to take us into the park on an unpopulated back trail. We jump on his horse and start our back-trail journey into the park.

The trail is narrow with beaten-down earth. There are patches of green, but it's mostly earth-toned sandstone. We ascend on switchbacks into some cliffs for about 30 minutes. We stop for a break at an opening. The Bedouin leads me into a cave that is dimly lit from the shimmer of light that enters through the opening. I'm looking at the cave walls that jut out with angular black formations. I'm expecting to see hieroglyphs or a ceiling of bats, but there's nothing but the shining black stone that reflects and gleams from the subdued sunlight. I look over at the Bedouin standing in a dark corner of the cave. Our eyes lock and I can see where his hand is. He has other intentions on his mind.

I walk over and put my hand on his crotch. He moves his hand and places it on top of mine, guiding it to rub the fabric of the front of his pants. I can feel the bulge beneath the fabric. I lower his zipper, and his pants open to expose his manhood. He has a thick slab of meat and I hold it and stroke it a few times as I gaze into his eyes. He puts a hand on my shoulder with pressure to signal me to go down on him. I do. I give him what he wants.

We continue our journey along the trail, up and along the summit of red sandstone cliffs. The trail narrows and ends. We get off the horse and continue our journey on foot for a short distance to a large, flat rock that is jutting out and slightly upward from the mountaintop. The Bedouin lies stomach down on the rock and props his head over the ledge. I follow his lead and when I prop my head over the ledge, there it is, the most elaborate temple in the ancient city of Petra: Al-Khazneh, the Treasury Building. It's an intricately carved building hewn in a sandstone cliff. It's breathtaking. The Bedouin and I lie shoulder to shoulder on the ledge of the rock, taking in the breathtaking temple and surroundings without a word for 10 to 15 minutes. I'm in total awe.

We get back on the horse to work our way down to the ancient town. We ride through a narrow gorge of red cliffs that tower a couple hundred feet above us. After we enter the main square, I want to explore this amazing place on foot, alone. The Bedouin and I depart on our separate ways.

I spend the day at Petra and then the night at a Bedouin camp with a band of gypsy travelers. We are fed tidbits and tastes of local dishes and drinks as belly dancers move, twist, and shimmy their hips in undulation around the crackling and glowing campfire under the Nabataean stars.

After leaving Petra in the morning, I head to the Dead Sea to bake in the sun, buoy in a warm mud pack, and float in the hyper-mineral water. The high mineral content of the sea and the mud works magic on the skin. I feel refreshed and rejuvenated. My skin is smooth as silk with a slight gleam. I sleep peacefully through the night.

The time in Jordan goes by quickly. I'm soon Cairo-bound, where the main draw is the Great Pyramid of Giza. The pyramid complex is the oldest of the Seven Wonders of the World, and I plan to spend most of the day there.

There's a line of local people with camels at the entry gate. It's quite a walk to the pyramids, so what better way to get there than on a camel? A young guy offers to take me for a ride to the pyramids on his camel for a small price. As part of the deal, he offers to take a bunch of snapshots of me. I'm sure he's learned, from his experience as a tourist guide, how to pose me in positions that make me look like I'm holding the Great Pyramid in my hand or by my fingertips. We have fun snapping all sorts of photos with goofy poses.

We get back on his camel, and not more than 100 yards into our ride, another man comes galloping on a horse alongside us. He's rattling off something in Arabic to my guide and we stop. I ask what's going on and he tells me that's his brother. They sound like they're arguing, but Arabic always sounds like arguing.

The new guy explains to me that he'll be taking me to the pyramids. As he speaks to me, I notice his stature. He has a beefy, muscular build and broad shoulders. He's wearing long pants, a baseball cap, sandals, and a loose shirt that's unbuttoned to mid-chest, exposing a lush patch of black chest hair. Under the baseball cap are his glimmering dark-chocolate eyes, wooly black eyebrows, and a thick beard of several days pressed on his copper-toned skin. As he speaks, I think he's older than I originally thought, maybe in his mid-thirties. He tells me his name is Amasis and that it means "child of the moon." The other young man doesn't look happy and jumps on the horse to gallop off across the desert floor, leaving a trail of dust in the air. I'm not sure why the other brother insisted on taking over. Just as in Petra, as a single male traveler, I wonder if this Egyptian has other intentions.

As the camel is lying on the ground, Amasis jumps on to take the lead. I follow him quickly and place myself on the camel, directly behind him. He tells me to hang on to his waist as he commands the camel to rise. The camel slowly rises to full stance and I adjust my body tightly behind Amasis, with a full grip around his waist. I move and press my hands on his lats. As I rest my chin on his shoulder, I see a line of sweat between his hairline and his collar. My nose captures a whiff of his earthy, masculine sweat. I slant my mouth toward his ear and tell him that he has a nice, strong body. I can see a squint of a smile from the corner of his lip and he replies, *"Thank you. You too."* That's an affirmation that he's noticed my body. Or is he just being polite and nice?

As we trot across the plateau to the three massive structures, my thoughts are on Amasis's lush chest. I test his internal quests by lifting my right hand from his waist to his chest, sliding it under his shirt and running my fingers through his black forest of dense hairs and up over his left chest. I rub his chest and say in Arabic, *"Bahi barsha!"* Very nice. He replies, *"Shokran."* Thank you. I see a big smile on his face and pound his chest hard just once with the palm of my hand. I shift my hand back down around his waist to his thigh and give it a squeeze. He's still smiling as we stride closer to our destination. I squeeze his waist with my left arm as my right hand fondles his crotch without any indication of resistance. I pocket my hand farther down under his crotch and rest it there until we reach our destination.

Amasis pulls back on the camel reins to stop and then orders it to crouch down so we can get off. Amasis stays behind with the camel as I explore the tomb complex. Amasis points me to the entrance through a dimly lit ascending passage that takes me to the Grand Gallery and into the Queen's Chamber. It's a maze of dark tunnels and passages, ascending and descending, made of limestone casings that take me about an hour to go through. I end in the King's Chamber. I try to imagine what it was like during the time frame that the pyramids were built and wonder how they were built without modern machinery or technology. I guess that's why it's one of the Seven Wonders of the World.

When I exit the final tomb, we get back on the camel once more and exit the park. Amasis is taking me through the back roads of Cairo to a nearby restaurant. We have lunch. I pay for our meal.

He takes me through the crowded streets in the heat of the day, trashed with litter, animals wandering astray, and people everywhere. We stop on a less crowded side street to a hard-surfaced cement building. Amasis secures his camel to a post and we walk up two levels of stairs to a room full of cushions and pillows. He kicks off his sandals when he enters the room and lands on the soft cushioned landing. He pats the cushion and gestures for me to sit next to him. I kick off my running shoes and follow suit. He tells me that we will rest for a bit and then return to the park. I'm up for the siesta. I lie down next to him. He pushes me to my side, puts his arm around me, and we cuddle.

We lie down for an hour or so, and before I know it, we're back on the camel and galloping through the labyrinth of Cairo. I'm laughing much of the way because it's so chaotic and bizarre what we're doing compared to what I'm accustomed to. We're riding a camel down a busy street with pedestrians, horse-drawn carts, and cars and trucks spewing smoke. We stop at a liquor store and Amasis asks me for some money to buy some beer. I give him some Egyptian pounds and he comes out of the store and hands me a sack with four big beers in it. We continue our ride back to the park.

At the park entrance, Amasis has a chat with the gatekeepers. Again, it sounds more like they're arguing than having a casual chat, but eventually they wave us through. With the pyramids in the distance and just a couple hours of sunlight left, Amasis rides us through some dunes to a small oasis of greenery and palm trees. We drink our beers, he fans me with palm leaves, we kiss, and he feeds me his *Barhi* date palm sherbet.

I realize there are many souls in the world wanting to be nurtured and loved when the opportunity avails. I'm living in the moment and if I enter someone's life for the moment, day, week, or longer, I want to give them something to remember. I want to touch hearts.

The park is closing as we exit. Amasis drops me by camel near my hotel, and a few days later, I'm back on a plane to Afghanistan to prepare to demobilize this hellhole once and for all.

Leaving Bagram

Many people refer to this land as "Assghanistan"—a shithole. I have 1,647 days in this shithole, but I had a great journey. Today is April 29, 2014. It's the day I'm demobilizing alongside my good Balkan friend, Arian. Both of us put in our time here and completed our sentences. We sit back in our airline chairs, prepare for takeoff, and hear our last *"Wheels Up"* leaving Bagram. We're finally escaping this place, for good.

The inside of the plane is super quiet, but it always is when leaving Bagram. All I can hear is the air circulating. All the window covers are shut to block the bright sun. As Arian dozes off in the chair next to me, I rest my head and close my eyes and think of returning to

America. I have very mixed emotions about heading home. The thought of returning there is more cold and dreary than I can imagine. It's like going from one war zone to another. Our political parties are so polarized that it's almost embarrassing to me that our once-great country was a leader and idolized in so many ways by other countries and citizens. It's just caught in a downward tailspin now.

The actor Jeff Daniels, who plays a newsroom anchor in the HBO series *The Newsroom*, pops into my head. It's probably the best three minutes of primetime TV that has been aired this century, and the opening scene has gone viral on the internet. His script plays through my head. When asked by a sorority girl what makes the United States the greatest country in the world, he just can't take the bullshit anymore. He goes on a rant about all the ways in which it's not, and he's damn right.

As I listen to *The Newsroom* monologue play through my head, I see flashes of the mass shootings of Sandy Hook Elementary, the Aurora movie theater in Colorado, and the Fort Hood military base killings. They're all major massacres that occurred during my service, and all our politicians who are running the House and Senate can only offer thoughts and prayers as a solution. We allow our politicians to be bought by special-interest groups. We spend more money on war and the military than education and health. We allow pharmaceutical and insurance companies to profit greatly on the ill and injured. A number of politicians would rather kick the poor and needy to the side than give them help or hope to better themselves and become healthy members of society. The Americans who think our country is the greatest surely haven't traveled. They're oblivious to other cultures, nations, and humanity.

The idea of returning to the United States, the vision, appears more dismal and desolate than I can bear. As though walking in the shadow of a dream, so great the vicissitude in my life, I try to put my mind at rest. I reflect on the past four and a half years in the brown, dusty, arid land. I still have never held a gun, let alone shot one. Nor do I ever intend to . . . I'm a lover, not a fighter. I never even rode in a military Hummer. It's time to close this chapter of my life and start anew.

I close my eyes and dream of going someplace better. Someplace green, wet, and lush. A place without mass shootings and news drama and major disagreements. A place surrounded by water, beauty, and ease. Ireland pops into my mind. Yes, I think I'll start my next journey in Ireland.

Beyond Bagram: 2017

After leaving Bagram Airfield in April 2014, I had a quilt made with all of the running T-shirts I collected during my four and a half years at BAF. I've stayed in contact with many people I met on the assignment. I scouted the remainder of the year, traveling through Europe and the Balkans, meeting up with old friends, and making many new ones.

I spent the first month hitchhiking around Ireland. People were friendly and it was easy to catch a ride from point A to point B. At the tail end of most of my rides, the driver would ask, *"Hey, mate, you want to stop at the pub for a pint?"* It seemed to be the Irish thing to do and I loved it. After nearly five years in a war zone, the friendliness of the Irish gave me a whole new perception and reality of humanity.

I flew to Italy to see Rafik, who is living and working there now. Because of his knack for languages, he was able to pick up Italian and speak it fluently in about three months. Besides, with his olive-colored skin and dark features, most Italians think he's a native. It's always a good time with Rafik, and this time I was a passenger on his Italian Vespa, zipping through the streets of Milan. We met again in Venice a few months later and we ate our way through the delicious cuisines and savory wines of the country.

I spent eight weeks hiking in the Alps to get reacquainted with nature and myself. I started my journey in Northern Italy and hiked through

Austria where *The Sound of Music* was filmed. I hiked up and over the Matterhorn of Switzerland, where people were still skiing at the top of the mountain in July. I explored the ancestry of my great grandparents in the Tyrol region of Austria and the Black Forest region of Germany. I saw Hitler's mountain retreat: the Kehlsteinhaus—Hitler's Eagles Nest high up in the Bavarian Mountains. I walked in the footsteps of Germans crossing Checkpoint Charlie and touched the remains of the Berlin Wall. I toured dozens of castles and even a brewery with my mother's maiden name. I sorrowed and heartached through Auschwitz. I explored most major cities in Europe.

I spent a week with Arian and his family in Kosovo. I also got to see Dr. K and several others I worked with at Bagram. I swear I knew half the town, from all the familiar faces I knew from that region. I traversed through Eastern Europe, through Croatia, Albania, Kosovo, Macedonia, Serbia, and Bosnia. I spent my final month in Greece, mostly on the islands of Mykonos and Santorini.

The end of 2014 and the first six months of 2015 were spent traveling through South America. I spent three months in Ecuador enhancing my Spanish at a language academy. I hiked the stunning Cajas and Andes Mountains; traveled to Machu Picchu, Salar de Uyuni in Bolivia, the Mendoza and Santiago wine countries, and the Patagonia region; and took a cruise around the cape and tip of South America from Santiago to Buenos Aires. I roamed through Brazil and the Amazon.

I extended my stay in Rio de Janeiro, as it's one of my favorite cities in South America. The people are beautiful. They live a healthy lifestyle, they have terrific beaches, and the landscapes are incredible. I drifted through the Amazon rainforest and into Colombia. I jumped aboard a sailboat through the San Blas Islands between Cartagena to Panama. From Panama, I returned to the United States and back to work.

I remain friends with Greg and we've had several visits and many conversations since we ended our relationship. I still love him, but only as a friend. We share a lot of experiences and family history. I will be there for him if he needs me.

I met up with Kamal the day before departing to Dublin. I asked him if he was surprised by my breakup with Greg. He replied in a heartbeat, *"No, not really."* I didn't pry for more. I just left it at that and wondered what secrets the two of them kept from me while they were together. Kamal continues to struggle with his sexuality. He dates women now and again to hold up his façade with his family and the Persian community, but those relationships never last.

I managed to stay in contact with many people from Bagram and continue to do so. Agim was caught with a smartphone at Bagram and terminated about a year after I left. He took some time off and is back in Afghanistan, working for another contract in Kandahar. I miss the nightly departures from the office when I would hear him say, *"Shimi plako."*

Jet is working as an HSE specialist on a nearby military base close to his hometown in Kosovo.

Regala left Bagram two years after me. I inspired her by my travels and she spent a lengthy amount of time in South America—mainly Buenos Aires—and Europe. She continues to travel and is engaged to get married to a young American man she met on base.

I've seen my running team from Texas a couple of times. I've been back to Austin and San Antonio, and always make it a point to see Randy, Stella, and Erin. After Stella's father passed, she returned to Bagram and worked there for another two years. She recently married an Air Force pilot, and I saw Regala and quite a few others from the project at her wedding in New Orleans. Team Texas had a few running reunions in Austin, but we stick with the shorter distances nowadays. No marathons, just 5Ks. That's my choice.

I did a road trip to the Midwest and the East Coast. I paid a visit to Trigger and Munera on their organic farm in West Virginia. It was great to see them, and in their new element of living compared to Bagram.

I paid at least three visits to Mona Lee Cartwright on her ranchette in East Texas. She's as feisty as ever and is enjoying retirement life in her small country town on the ranch. She's always fun to visit and that lady knows how to talk to the ranch hands and pour a good glass of wine.

Juliet Alpha cried the day I departed Bagram. I figured she would be there until the project shut down or she died, but she left about six months after me. Her dream was to bicycle across the United States from East Coast to West Coast, and she did. I only heard this through others, as I've not kept in contact with her since I left Afghanistan. That's her choice.

I heard from Motormouth after he left. I tried to reach out to him a couple of times afterward, but I've never heard back from him.

LaWanda worked another few years on the project. Between working in Iraq and Afghanistan, she put in about 10 years as a military contractor after her retirement from the armed forces. She left in 2016 to retire for good. I heard through the grapevine that she claimed to suffer from PTSD. Maybe it's a fraudulent claim, or maybe she's more of a mess on the inside than she ever revealed from her exterior.

Huggy McPherson was reassigned to another project after LOGCAP. I got wind that the company let him go. I cannot confirm, but resources and speculation say his inappropriate behavior as an HR manager finally caught up with him.

Louie Risotto was terminated shortly before I left the project. His Japanese wife handled all their finances and wouldn't give him money to buy a winter coat for the cold weather on base. He was caught taking and using visa cards for an employee reward program.

Max partnered up with another American guy while on base. They got married in 2015 and reside in the United States.

Sam left the project to work for one of our subcontractors. He was based in Turkey for a year. Later, he accepted another project with Barron in Argentina for about a year. He currently works for a major telecommunications company in the U.S. as a senior project manager.

In November 2016, we lost two of our own to a suicide bomber during a Veteran's Day 5K on base. Their loss was greatly felt among our running group and in the company. I especially felt the loss, as I have many pictures of me standing with those two fine men on race days. We ran many of them together. They are greatly missed.

Also in November 2016, our Afghan worker Muhammad finally received his green card to come to the United States. I sent him a Christmas and care package upon his arrival. His family followed a year later and they reside in Texas. I paid him a visit in December 2017.

As far as the many sexual encounters I had on base, I stay in contact with a handful of them, but just as friends. I wasn't looking to pursue a relationship with any of them. It was just a good time while it lasted.

Because, you know, what happens in Afghanistan stays in Afghanistan.

The End

Made in the USA
Monee, IL
02 September 2022

13090386R00238